A theory of property

Cambridge Studies in Philosophy and Law

GENERAL EDITOR: JULES COLEMAN (YALE LAW SCHOOL)

ADVISORY BOARD

David Gauthier (University of Pittsburgh)
David Lyons (Cornell University)
Richard Posner (Judge in the Seventh Circuit Court of
  Appeals, Chicago)
Martin Shapiro (University of California, Berkeley)

This exciting new series will reflect and foster the most original research currently taking place in the study of law and legal theory by publishing the most adventurous monographs in the field as well as rigorously edited collections of essays. It will be a specific aim of the series to traverse the boundaries between disciplines and to form bridges between traditional studies of law and many other areas of the human sciences. Books in the series will be of interest not only to philosophers and legal theorists but also to political scientists, sociologists, economists, psychologists, and criminologists.

Other books in the series

Jeffrie G. Murphy and Jean Hampton: *Forgiveness and mercy*

A theory of property

STEPHEN R. MUNZER

SCHOOL OF LAW
UNIVERSITY OF CALIFORNIA, LOS ANGELES

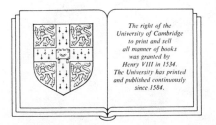

The right of the
University of Cambridge
to print and sell
all manner of books
was granted by
Henry VIII in 1534.
The University has printed
and published continuously
since 1584.

CAMBRIDGE UNIVERSITY PRESS

Cambridge
New York   Port Chester   Melbourne   Sydney

Published by the Press Syndicate of the University of Cambridge
The Pitt Building, Trumpington Street, Cambridge CB2 1RP
40 West 20th Street, New York, NY 10011, USA
10 Stamford Road, Oakleigh, Melbourne 3166, Australia

First published 1990

Printed in the United States of America

Library of Congress Cataloging-in-Publication Data

Munzer, Stephen R.
  A theory of property / Stephen R. Munzer.
  p.   cm. – (Cambridge studies in philosophy and law)
  ISBN 0-521-37284-4. – ISBN 0-521-37886-9 (pbk.)
  1. Property.   2. Right of property.   I. Title.   II. Series.
K720.M84   1990
346.04 – dc20
[342.64]   89–33159
                                                      CIP

British Library Cataloguing in Publication Data

Munzer, Stephen R.
  A theory of property. – (Cambridge studies in
  philosophy and law)
  1. Property
  I. Title
330.17

ISBN 0 521 37284 4 hard covers
  ISBN 0 521 37886 9 paperback

Contents

Preface and acknowledgments   *page* ix

1 Property, justification, and evaluation   1
   1.1 Problems of justification and evaluation   1
   1.2 A solution   3
   1.3 Foundations   9

        Part I: Property rights and personal rights
2 Understanding property   15
   2.1 Popular and sophisticated conceptions of
       property   15
   2.2 Hohfeld's vocabulary and its limitations   17
   2.3 The idea of property   22
   2.4 Expectations   28
   2.5 A misguided enterprise?   31
3 Persons and their bodies   37
   3.1 Body rights   37
   3.2 Body rights as limited property rights   41
   3.3 Personal rights and property rights   44
   3.4 From self-ownership to world-ownership?   56

        Part II: From individuals to social context
4 Incorporation and projection   61
   4.1 Nature of the inquiry   61
   4.2 Extension by incorporation   63
   4.3 Embodiment by projection   67

Contents

4.4	Two transcendental features	71
4.5	Intention and convention	75
4.6	Agency, stability, and expectations	79
4.7	Property and personality	81
5	**Control, privacy, and individuality**	**88**
5.1	Private property and excludability	88
5.2	Control, privacy, and individuality	90
5.3	Problems of distribution	98
5.4	Charity and welfare	110
5.5	An impasse?	117
6	**Property and moral character**	**120**
6.1	Four claims	120
6.2	Virtues, vices, and moral character	121
6.3	From moral to political theory	125
6.4	Republicanism, virtue, and commercial society	138
6.5	Moral character and economic systems	142
6.6	Property and moral ideals	145
7	**Alienation, exploitation, and power**	**148**
7.1	The program	148
7.2	Property as an attribute of societies and persons	149
7.3	Marx on alienation	157
7.4	Alienation and exploitation	169
7.5	Problems of production	174
7.6	Property and power	178
7.7	Social life, economic options, and theory	181

Part III: Justification and distributive equity

8	**Utility and efficiency**	**191**
8.1	Distributive equity	191
8.2	The utilitarian tradition	193
8.3	A principle of utility	196
8.4	Efficiency	198
8.5	A combined principle of utility and efficiency	202
8.6	Utility, efficiency, and property	206
8.7	Preferences and expectations	221

Contents

8.8 Can utility and efficiency account for *rights* of private property? ' 224

9 Justice and equality 227
  9.1 The principle 227
  9.2 Strict equality 230
  9.3 A Rawlsian conception of equal property 233
  9.4 The floor thesis 241
  9.5 The gap thesis 247

10 Labor and desert 254
  10.1 Overview 254
  10.2 The initial labor theory 256
  10.3 The revised labor theory 266
  10.4 Understanding the revised labor theory 285
  10.5 Assessing the significance of the revised labor theory 289

11 Conflict and resolution 292
  11.1 Pluralism and conflict 292
  11.2 The frequency and varieties of conflicts 297
  11.3 Logical consistency, moral realism, and theory acceptance 304
  11.4 Guidelines for application 310

Part IV: Applications

12 Business corporations 317
  12.1 The itinerary 317
  12.2 Efficiency, utility, and the separation of ownership and control 320
  12.3 Toward a comprehensive view of ownership and control 346
  12.4 Standards of corporate behavior 357
  12.5 Ownership, control, and corporate standards in a regime of public ownership 368
  12.6 Coda 378

13 Gratuitous transfers 380
  13.1 Taxation and redistribution 380
  13.2 Wealth inequality and its causes 383
  13.3 Justifying the reduction of inequalities of wealth 395

CONTENTS

13.4 A plan for reducing inequalities of wealth 403
13.5 More charges of adverse impact 411
14 A moral and political theory of takings 419
14.1 Takings and taxings 419
14.2 An approach to the moral and political problem 422
14.3 Utility, efficiency, and takings 425
14.4 The impact of labor-desert and justice and equality 435
15 Takings and the constitution 442
15.1 Some traditional judicial tests 442
15.2 Some other academic approaches 448
15.3 Toward a new constitutional perspective 456
15.4 Applications 460
15.5 Reprise 468

Table of cases 471
Index of names 473
Index of subjects 481

Preface and acknowledgments

I hope that this book will aid our theoretical understanding of property, taken as a topic in moral, political, and legal philosophy, though it is hardly the ultimate truth on this matter. I also hope that, to the extent that the views argued for here are sound, they will serve as a basis for action to make institutions of property better than they now are. At a time when, in most of the countries of the world, a few have great material wealth and others are struggling for the scantiest material resources, making the case for better property institutions is not an optional intellectual endeavor but a practical imperative.

The book is intended for those whose interests lie in philosophy, law, political theory, the social sciences, and corporate organization. The text has been written to be accessible to students in these disciplines. The notes – which are extensive by philosophical standards – enable the reader not only to find support for assertions and arguments in the text but also to identify literature that develops or in some cases disagrees with my own views. Unfortunately, Jeremy Waldron's *The Right to Private Property* (Oxford: Clarendon Press, 1988) came into my hands only as this book was going to press, and I have not been able to take his study into account.

Almost anyone who writes a book of this kind incurs many debts. First and foremost I am indebted to my students. In classes and seminars over the last decade, they debated classical and contemporary writings on property, and commented carefully on successive drafts of this material. I also owe much to my colleagues at UCLA, who sat through more faculty colloquia on my fledgling ideas than they, or I, care to contemplate. Here I am grateful in particular to Alison Grey Anderson, Kenneth L. Karst, and Daniel H. Lowenstein for detailed written comments on many chapters. I have bene-fited, too, from presentations of portions of this work to various conferences and university audiences and, in Los Angeles, to the Law and Philosophy Discussion Group and the Saturday Discussion Group. In the former group, Peter Arenella, Carl Cranor, David Dolinko, and Jean Hampton especially have over the years firmly, but with patience and charity, pointed out shortcomings and encouraged me to repair them. There are also circumscribed debts; many per-sons supplied acute written criticisms of and suggestions regarding particular chapters or parts of chapters; I identify these obligations, when possible after the passage of years, in the notes.

It is a pleasure to acknowledge debts of a higher order of magnitude. Several persons took the time to comment on the entire book at one stage or another. Special thanks go here to Kent Greenawalt, Alan Ryan, M. B. E. Smith, Stephen C. Yeazell, and several anonymous readers. Jules Coleman not only commented incisively but also, in his editorial capacity, gave me much useful general advice on the book. Above all I thank James W. Nickel, who went through two versions of this study and each time gave suggestions for revision that contributed immeasurably to improving the final product.

I have also had a good deal of tangible help. For financial support I am grateful to the Academic Senate at UCLA and the Dean's Fund in the School of Law. Michele D. Titus assisted ably in production and indexing. I wish particularly to thank my secretary, Margaret Kiever, for her efficiency, accuracy, and cheerfulness in preparing the typescript.

I dedicate this book to my parents, Donald and Bernadette Munzer, and to my wife, Cynthia Trangsrud. It saddens me that my mother did not live to see its publication. Yet I like to think that she would have found in it some of the moral earnestness that she displayed so abundantly in her own life and would have seen her own hand in its optimism about humanity.

STEPHEN R. MUNZER
Los Angeles, California

Chapter 1

Property, justification, and evaluation

1.1 PROBLEMS OF JUSTIFICATION AND EVALUATION

Property is a well-known feature of our world. If asked to do so, many people could describe the property institutions of their own country, and some of them could even contrast their own institutions with those of foreign countries. In the United States, for example, many adults could explain that a great deal of land is owned by the federal government for national parks and military bases, that much land is held privately, and that private property of all sorts is not distributed equally. Well-informed persons, moreover, could explain that property institutions in the United States are more similar to those of the United Kingdom than they are to those of the Soviet Union or the People's Republic of China. They would be likely to guess that the distribution of property in "communist" countries is more equal than in the United States, though the standard of living is lower.

Yet many educated people would not stop at cool description or explanation, for they would recognize that property rights can incite passion and be the stuff of revolutions. Just as some people would extol the virtues of a modified capitalism that allows some to amass enormous wealth, even if others are poor, so other people would contend ardently for a more nearly equal distribution of wealth, even if they would resist prevailing forms of communism. Some people, at least, would know that dissatisfaction with then-existing institutions of property played a role in the French Revolution of 1789 and the Russian Revolution of 1917 – though, of

1

course, they might not know the details and might be unaware of the historical controversies surrounding these events. But no need exists to transport people to another time. Many people would be aware that much political unrest in Latin America has something to do with grossly unequal distributions of wealth. Neither is there a need to leave the country. Anyone in a major city of the United States who sees a homeless couple in rumpled clothes, with a sign proclaiming "We will work for food," will be conscious of disparities in income and wealth here and now.

If different property institutions exist, and if they sometimes inspire passion and revolution, there is a need to inquire what property rights are justifiable and to evaluate critically existing property institutions. That is the subject of this book. It is a work of legal, political, and moral theory. Although such a work could grapple with many problems, the two most important here are justification and evaluation.

As to justification, the inquiry, if conducted well, must take seriously the issue of *whether* property can be justified. It may not suppose that it is justified and that the trick is just to figure out what the justification is. Nor may it suppose that only private property needs justifying. Justification is an issue for public property, too. Furthermore, the justificatory inquiry must attend to many particular issues. Some relate to which things, if any, should be open to ownership. Others concern who, if anyone, may own them. Still others deal with the distribution of property. In all of these issues justification – including the limits on justification – is central.

The other main goal is to evaluate critically existing institutions of property. These institutions, plainly, vary so much from one country to another and indeed are so complicated in any given country that a comprehensive investigation is out of the question. Still, it is important to see how an abstract justificatory theory applies in practice. To that end, the book uses the theory developed here to evaluate three features of property institutions in the United States: ownership and control of business corporations, gifts and bequests, and government taking and regulation of private property. The evaluative inquiry is a reminder that, although any philosophical theory requires some abstract arguments, the only actual phenomenon for investigation is property in concrete social situations.

1.2 A SOLUTION

This book will argue that if justification and evaluation are the central problems of the theory of property, their solution lies in a pluralist theory that consists of three main principles and an account of how those principles are related. The theory is "pluralist" in that it contains several irreducible principles that sometimes conflict; when conflicts occur, priority rules can resolve some, but not all, conflicts.[1] The principles are a principle of utility and efficiency, a principle of justice and equality, and a principle of desert based on labor. Although these principles may not be the only principles that make up a satisfactory moral, political, and legal theory of property, they are by far the most important. The theory proposed here justifies some private property and some public property. When the principles are fully specified, and when sufficient empirical evidence is gathered about the situations in which one is to apply them, the theory illuminates many practical problems and thus serves to evaluate property institutions.

Although the content of the three principles will not be fully clear until the arguments for them are given, it will be useful to sketch them here and indicate how each rests on a particular conception of persons. A satisfactory theory of property, this book argues, should include some principle that recognizes the moral import of actions that affect persons' happiness, welfare, preference-satisfaction, or the like.

---

1 This variety of pluralism, sometimes called "intuitionism," is defended in Stephen R. Munzer, "Intuition and Security in Moral Philosophy," *Michigan Law Review*, 82 (1984): 740–54; J. O. Urmson, "A Defence of Intuitionism," *Proceedings of the Aristotelian Society*, 75 (1974–75): 111–19. See also Thomas Nagel, "The Fragmentation of Value," in his *Mortal Questions* (Cambridge: Cambridge University Press, 1979), pp. 128–41.

Suppose that, in order to have a particular candidate for discussion, one selects preference-satisfaction. Then such a principle would rest on one conception of the equal moral worth of persons – namely, that assuming equal strength, the preferences of each person count equally with the preferences of others. This formulation helps to clarify some relations between "utility" and "efficiency." Both of these words, as used here, involve the satisfaction of the preferences of individuals, but only utility assumes that one can make interpersonal comparisons of preference–satisfaction.

The combined principle of utility and efficiency is as follows: Property rights should be allocated so as (1) to maximize utility regarding the use, possession, transfer, and so on of things, and (2) to maximize efficiency regarding the use, possession, transfer, and so on of things. In this principle, the first clause has priority over the second in the following sense: If it is possible to rank alternatives in terms of both utility and efficiency, then one should use the ranking supplied by utility. If, however, it is possible to rank alternatives in terms of either utility or efficiency but not both, then one should use whichever ranking is available. This combined principle is possible because utility and efficiency have in common the concept of individual preference-satisfaction. The principle is not redundant because utility, but not efficiency, presupposes that interpersonal comparisons of preference-satisfaction are possible. As a result, utility supplies both ordinal and interpersonally comparable rankings of alternatives, whereas efficiency supplies only ordinal rankings.

A satisfactory theory should, moreover, include some principle that recognizes the rights of persons. Such a principle would also rest on a conception of the equal moral worth of persons. The conception would differ, however, from the utilitarian conception of equal worth as equal counting, for the latter upholds sacrificing the individual utility of some in order to promote overall utility. Any such sacrifice ignores or undervalues the separateness of persons – that is, the idea that persons have rights not to have certain of their interests traded for overall utility.

4

One can formulate the principle of justice and equality in this way: Unequal property holdings are justifiable if (1) everyone has a minimum amount of property and (2) the inequalities do not undermine a fully human life in society. It recognizes, where feasible, rights to minimal property and to a fully human life in society. This principle is a standard of justice in that it regulates morally how benefits and burdens are to be shared among persons. Its minimum involves the things needed by almost everyone for a decent life. The principle is also a standard of equality in that it requires showing, in the event that persons have different property holdings, why the difference is morally and politically proper. In this principle, the first clause is concerned with the provision of a minimum and the second clause with the narrowing of inequalities even if a minimum is satisfied.

Finally, a satisfactory theory should include some principle of desert or entitlement. Such a principle rests on a conception of persons as agents who, by their actions in the world, are responsible for changes in the world and deserve or are entitled to something as a result. Whereas the first two principles emphasize, in different ways, the equal worth of persons, this final principle emphasizes their differences in merit.

A labor theory of property is the obvious source of such a principle, but at present no agreement exists on how such a principle should be formulated. This book argues that a qualified desert version is the best candidate. A labor-desert principle would maintain that there is a qualified justification for private-property rights because of a person's work. This justification of property rights for the laborer is qualified by the rights of others, limitations on the process of acquisition, post-acquisition changes in situation, restrictions on transfer, general scarcity, and the nature of work as a social activity. The principle sums up how labor and desert, with their traditional emphasis on the individual, can be transferred into a modern social context.

So much for a brief statement of the three principles that make up the theory of property advocated in this book. As

5

§ 1.1 intimates,[2] it is not enough to present only abstract arguments for these principles. Rather, it is essential to be keenly aware of the psychological, social, and economic context to which the arguments apply. And to develop that awareness it is vital to understand how persons and their bodies relate to the world of things. Only if the groundwork is laid well will arguments for the theory itself be convincing.

As a result, this book has the following structure. Part I, on "Property Rights and Personal Rights," explains the concept of property and investigates some of the rights that persons have in their bodies. It argues that some body rights are property rights and others are personal rights. It also identifies the problem of moving from body rights to rights to other things in the world. Part II, entitled "From Individuals to Social Context," shows how property rights in external things begin with individual persons and their actions in the world and eventually affect everyone in society. It elaborates an account of property, personality, and virtue; and, though it rejects Marx's critique of property and alienation, it replaces it with a better understanding of alienation and exploitation as they relate to property. This phase of the book, taken as a whole, forms a psychological, social, and partly normative background theory of property in a contemporary society. Part III, on "Justification and Distributive Equity," argues for the three principles sketched above. It uses the background theory to shed light on the nature of work in a modern economy and on the notions of a minimum of property and a fully human life in society. It also discusses relations and conflicts among the three principles and shows how they form an integrated theory. Finally, Part IV, called "Applications," develops the practical consequences of the theory. It examines three problems in detail: business enterprise in capitalist and socialist economies, the justifiability and taxation of gifts and bequests, and government takings of private property.

---

2 Cross-references are given by numbers for chapter and section separated by a period. Thus, "§ 1.1" refers to Chapter 1, Section 1.

The picture of property rights that emerges, then, locates their justification in a carefully constructed pluralist scheme that knits together utilitarian considerations, considerations of justice of a roughly Kantian or Rawlsian kind, and considerations of desert of a thoroughly un-Rawlsian kind. This scheme is informed by a broad-ranging discussion that distinguishes property rights from other rights, relates property to character and independence, and takes up Hegelian and Marxian anxieties about alienation under capitalism, with limited enthusiasm for their philosophical idiom but with great sympathy for the light they shed on work and welfare in a capitalist economy. This pluralist scheme justifies some public property but not unfettered private ownership. It does uphold a constrained system of private property – whether under a modified capitalism or some form of socialism. At a practical level, the scheme emphasizes workers' rights within business corporations, favors substantial transfer taxes on large gifts and bequests, and supports sensible government regulation of private property.

Why should anyone be interested in this theory? There are two reasons. First, it is, as an intellectual construction, the soundest and most nearly satisfactory theory of property available. Too many theorists attempt to reduce too much to a single perspective. Thus, Locke appeals to labor; Bentham rests his case on utility; Marx protests the evils of alienation. Each of these thinkers, through the intensity of his partial vision, contributes much to thinking about property, but at the same time obscures the validity of other perspectives. The theory proposed here, in contrast, shows how to accommodate competing points of view. And, more successfully than other pluralist accounts, it shows how to combine these perspectives into a coherent framework, not on an ad hoc basis or as a tedious compromise, but on a principled basis.

Second, the theory helps, as a practical guide, to reform and improve existing institutions of property. "By their fruits you shall know them" is an important test. Thus, although this study has the scholarly paraphernalia of an academic book and has a low temperature of argument, at bottom it springs from the desire to make our institutions of property better than they now are. The desire is not enough. Action should follow, or else the desire and the theory are lifeless.[3]

The theory also has limitations, two of which are sufficiently broad and important to mention now. One is that the theory, at least as elaborated here, applies to the property institutions of individual nations rather than to the international system or the global economy. The reason is simply that it is a tall enough order to say something helpful about property rights in particular countries. To limit the theory in this way is by no means to imply that wealthy countries are without obligation to help poor countries or that international justice is unimportant. On the contrary, it is very important, but it is also beyond what this book can treat satisfactorily.[4]

The other limitation pertains to the cross-cultural application of the theory. The three principles themselves, though directed to property, are otherwise fairly broad. Still, reasons exist to stop short of any grandiose claim that the theory is a talisman for all societies – whatever their histories, economies, and cultures may be. Such a claim raises philosophical problems of "relativism" that are too complicated to treat here.[5] Furthermore, some elements of the background theory in Part II of the book – for instance, the importance of control, privacy, and individuality, and the discussion of "localized" virtues – pose hazards for cross-cultural application. Last, and not least, are limits to my knowledge of other societies and their property institutions. So this book will

---

3   This thought, if you like, is a secular version of James 2:15–17.
4   Recent works that grapple with these issues include Charles R. Beitz, *Political Theory and International Relations* (Princeton: Princeton University Press, 1979); Henry Shue, *Basic Rights: Subsistence, Affluence, and U.S. Foreign Policy* (Princeton: Princeton University Press, 1980).
5   See, for example, Jack W. Meiland and Michael Krausz, eds., *Relativism: Cognitive and Moral* (Notre Dame: University of Notre Dame Press, 1982).

rest with the claim, not grandiose but hardly immodest, that its theory of property applies at least to mature Western societies and in particular to the United States.

1.3 FOUNDATIONS

This study might be attacked in various ways. Though repelling specialized criticisms can wait for later chapters, at least one general attack merits consideration here, for it questions the very foundations of the enterprise. The pluralism of the theory sketched in § 1.2 will be unsatisfying to those who crave theories that rest on a single principle or at least on one supreme principle. Some philosophers may see in the trio of principles only the academic lawyer's penchant for ransacking every available cupboard for a multi-course banquet of arguments, with little thought given to the integrity of the meal.

This is not a work of meta-ethics, but it does subscribe to a mixed-value, or pluralist, theory of morality. It holds, further, that consequences are relevant, but not decisive, in justifying principles and in limiting their scope and resolving conflicts among them. Any such position provokes thorny questions. How does one constrain the force of consequences once their relevance is admitted? How does one rank principles if consequences are not decisive? It is part of the human condition and the current state of moral theory that these questions lack unimpeachable answers.

It may be objected that to rest a theory of property on such foundations as these is to place it on sand. It is to fall into "intuitionism." This word has several meanings. Its meaning in the objection is that ultimate reliance is placed on "intuitions" – which different thinkers variously call moral opinions, feelings, or considered judgments. Such intuitions vary from one person to the next, and no hope exists of getting agreement. Thus a work of moral and political theory founded on them can be no more than the personal recommenda-

9

tion of its author. It can carry no weight for anyone whose intuitions are different.

This book does indeed accept a version of intuitionism, but to do so is not objectionable. It does not suppose that there is some psychological faculty that intuits moral truths, or even that there necessarily is something that people can correctly regard as objective moral truth. Nor does it rely straightway on "intuitions" in the sense of mere moral opinions or feelings. Rather, it accepts intuitions only after they have been subjected to some procedure for eliminating those that are apt to depend on bias, prejudice, class associations, or poor empirical information. John Rawls's technique of reflective equilibrium is one, but not the only, such procedure.[6] In the strategy of this book, Parts I and II lay the groundwork for a partial account of property, human nature, and society that frees some judgments about property from distortion. Part III makes use of this groundwork in constructing arguments of justification. The principles arrived at and the resolution of conflicts among them are best appreciated in contexts of application, which is the business of Part IV. Thus, the way in which the work as a whole hangs together is a start on eliminating unreliable intuitions.

It may be retorted that, even if moral and political philosophy can be done in this way, it is better to do it without relying on intuitions of moral substance. R. M. Hare offers a forceful expression of this view.[7] He contends that "substantive" intuitions are appropriate only at what he calls the intuitive level of moral thinking. They are not defensible at the critical level, which relies only on "linguistic" intuitions about moral words and concepts. He argues that critical moral thinking endorses utilitarianism. Specifically, it recommends a form of preference-utilitarianism that is act-utilitarian or highly specific rule-utilitarian at the critical

6 See John Rawls, *A Theory of Justice* (Cambridge, Mass.: Harvard University Press, 1971), pp. 20–21, 48–51, 120, 432, 434, 579. For further discussion, see § 11.3 below.
7 R. M. Hare, *Moral Thinking: Its Levels, Method, and Point* (Oxford: Clarendon Press, 1981).

level, and supports prima facie principles for use, in a general rule-utlitarian fashion, at the intuitive level.

This retort is unsuccessful for two reasons that will be given briefly here.[8] One is that even utilitarianism in the spare version advocated by Hare relies on a substantive intuition of its own – namely, that probable effects on preference-satisfaction are relevant features of actions. Such effects are certainly relevant. But it does not follow that only such effects are relevant. In any event, their relevance does not rest on linguistic intuitions and logico-linguistic methods alone. In general, it seems impossible to construct a moral theory with any content that is free from intuitions of moral substance.

The other reason is that considered moral judgments or intuitions, cleansed by some suitable procedure, are sounder and securer guides to action than might otherwise be thought. Indeed, sometimes people will justifiably have greater confidence in such moral intuitions than in the capacity of, say, Hare's utilitarianism to handle a given case properly. His utilitarianism must, at the critical level, count equally all preferences of equal strength, no matter what their content. To argue critically that a preference should be changed can be a risky business. Such an argument must rely on complicated human reasoning, which, as all know, often proves faulty. It must sometimes embrace the hazards of trying to understand people very different from oneself. And it can require laborious empirical investigations. The investigations would be needed to ascertain existing preferences and their strengths, the satisfaction that would result from a new set of preferences, and the cost of moving from one to the other.

The upshot is that the most adequate foundations for a theory of property are pluralist. They include, as Chapter 11

---

8 For a detailed examination, see Munzer, "Intuition and Security in Moral Philosophy." See also Stephen R. Munzer, "Persons and Consequences: Observations on Fried's *Right and Wrong*," *Michigan Law Review*, 77 (1979): 421–45.

makes clear, a number of considered moral judgments or intuitions that, for all that can be told, are irreducible and can conflict. This is not to say that all moral and political reasoning is a matter of making intuitions consistent. Nor does it show by itself that the three justificatory principles advanced here are the right ones, or the only right ones. The book invites those who disagree to improve on it.

Part I

Property rights and personal rights

Chapter 2

Understanding property

2.1 POPULAR AND SOPHISTICATED CONCEPTIONS OF PROPERTY

Consider how different the world would be if it contained no property. It is logically possible that it could contain all the artifacts that it now does. It could have houses and automobiles, factories and tools. Yet if it did, no one would stand in relation to those artifacts as people do to property. Persons might possess artifacts in the sense of having physical contact with or control over them. But they would have no right to exclude others and no normative power to transfer artifacts to others. Persons would also lack any such right or normative power over things that are not artifacts. They would have no property in land or plants or minerals. Furthermore, no other entity would stand in relation to things as people now do to property. States, cities, tribes, corporations, and partnerships would have no property.

If one turns from what is logically possible to what is causally and socially plausible, the no-property world seems even more different from the world as it is. Perhaps people would make simple artifacts such as knives and huts. But it seems unlikely that they would create such things as automobiles and factories, for these things require great capital investment and cooperative activity. People would probably

Thomas C. Grey, Steven Shiffrin, and Jonathan D. Varat provided helpful comments on various portions of Part I.

15

not make the necessary sacrifices unless they could be confident of substantial control over the use and disposition of these things – which would require property rights. Nor would people be likely to engage in some kinds of farming, mining, and animal husbandry unless they had property rights in the fruits of their activities. Again, business corporations and partnerships are economic arrangements, and without property their existence is improbable.

These contrasts between the no-property world and the actual world suggest two different ways of understanding property. One is the popular conception of property. It views property as *things*. For the most part, property is tangible things – land, houses, automobiles, tools, factories. But it also includes intangible things – copyrights, patents, and trademarks. Many of these things would not exist in a no-property world. The other way of understanding property is the sophisticated conception. One might almost call it the legal conception, for it is very common among lawyers. It understands property as *relations*. More precisely, property consists in certain relations, usually legal relations, among persons or other entities with respect to things. A metaphorical way of stating the sophisticated conception is that property is a bundle of "sticks." It is often added that one should be clear about which "stick" in the bundle one is talking about. One should distinguish the normative power to exclude, for example, from the normative power to transfer. These relations, or "sticks," would not exist in a no-property world.

The first order of business is to sharpen the understanding of property, for otherwise the arguments of this book will be less precise than they can be. It is sometimes asserted that only the sophisticated conception of property is useful in any serious analysis. The assertion is overstated, for § 4.4 shows that it is sometimes justifiable and important to think of property as things. Yet this claim does not make the sophisticated conception unimportant. The next two sections elaborate that conception. Though they are not very original, they are useful in clarifying one's ideas at the outset. Readers with little interest in conceptual analysis will find that most of this book is fully intelligible without elaborate conceptual preparation; they may wish to skim this chapter now and return to it later as the need arises.

One can state the payoff of the chapter as follows. Earlier thinkers confronting the question, What is property?, answer it in different ways. Some hold that property is things; others maintain that it is relations between persons and things, or relations among persons with respect to things; yet others claim that it is a basis of expectations with respect to things; and a few believe that "property" has so many fragmented uses that any overarching normative theory of property is impossible. The position defended here differs from each of these but also retains some elements from all of them except the last. It is perfectly sound to think of property both as things (the popular conception) and as relations among persons or other entities with respect to things (the sophisticated conception) – provided that the context makes clear which conception is meant. Moreover, one can think of property in this way and preserve a role for expectations. Finally, understanding property in this complex way enables one to rebut the claim that "property" has "disintegrated" and so to keep alive the possibility of a general moral, political, and legal theory of property.

2.2 HOHFELD'S VOCABULARY AND ITS LIMITATIONS

If the law views property as relations among persons with respect to things, which relations are involved? A start on an answer lies in Hohfeld's *Fundamental Legal Conceptions.*[1] Writers sometimes refer to the Hohfeldian analysis of property. The reference is misleading. For a reason that will be given at the end of this section, it is more accurate to think of

1 Wesley Newcomb Hohfeld, *Fundamental Legal Conceptions as Applied in Judicial Reasoning,* ed. Walter W. Cook and foreword Arthur L. Corbin (Westport, Conn.: Greenwood Press, 1978 [1919]). The ideas were present in Wesley Newcomb Hohfeld, "Some Fundamental Legal Conceptions as Applied in Judicial Reasoning," *Yale Law Journal,* 23 (1913): 16–59, and in some of Hohfeld's earlier articles.

Hohfeld's theory as an analytical vocabulary. The vocabulary treats certain legal concepts as basic and explains their interrelations. Though Hohfeld intended his theory as a guide to legal analysis, it can also shed light on moral relations among individuals, as later chapters will show.

To understand the key features of Hohfeld's theory, consider Table 1. The "fundamental legal conceptions" are the eight items in the elements and correlatives columns. Hohfeld's notion of a correlative involves two-way entailment.[2] The statement that A has a claim-right to $100 from B entails, and is entailed by, the statement that B has a duty to pay $100 to A. Very different from a claim-right – or, as Hohfeld usually says, simply a right or claim – is a privilege. A privilege is a legal liberty or freedom. It involves not a correlative duty but the absence of a right on someone else's part to interfere. A claim-right is also quite different from a power. A person has a legal power when, by some act, he can alter his legal position or that of someone else. The correlative of a power is a liability. Hohfeld's term "liability" is not equivalent to tort or criminal liability. Nor need a liability be disadvantageous. Rather, a liability is a susceptibility to having one's legal position altered. If A can transfer a farm to B by signing certain documents, A has a power of transfer and B a correlative liability to receive. Finally, a claim-right differs from an immunity. An immunity is a lack of susceptibility to having one's legal position altered by someone else. Its correlative is not a duty on someone else to refrain from altering one's legal position but rather the absence of a power in someone else to alter one's legal position in the way protected by the immunity. If B cannot legally compel A to sell his farm, A has an immunity with respect to B's forcing a sale of the farm. Correlatively, B has no power to force a sale.

Hohfeld's notion of an opposite involves external rather than internal negation. Consider the second row of Table 1,

---

2 This explanation of Hohfeld's notions of correlatives and opposites owes much to lectures on "Legal Rights" by H. L. A. Hart at Oxford University in the late 1960s.

TABLE 1. *Hohfeld's Fundamental Legal Conceptions*

Elements	Correlatives	Opposites
Claim-Right	Duty	No-Right
Privilege (Liberty)	No-Right	Duty
Power	Liability	Disability (No-Power)
Immunity	Disability	Liability

where privilege and duty appear as opposites. Suppose that A has a duty to pay $100 to B. The opposite is not the internal negation: "A has a duty not to pay $100 to B." It is the external negation: "It is not the case that A has a duty to pay $100 to B." Since an absence of a duty of opposite tenor is a privilege, the external negation is equivalent to "A has a privilege to pay $100 to B."

Hohfeld's vocabulary has no serious rival of its kind in intellectual clarity, rigor, and power. It does, however, have limitations. One limitation is that there are reservations about Hohfeld's claim that the eight conceptions are the "lowest common denominators of the law."[3] Some reservations relate to interdefinability, distinctness, completeness, and irreducibility. (1) If conceptions in the first two rows are interdefinable, and if the same holds of conceptions in the next two rows, then conceptions within these respective groupings do not seem distinct in any potent sense. Perhaps the only potent claim is that there are two distinct groupings of not wholly distinct conceptions. (2) As to completeness, Hohfeld presents no argument that the eight conceptions are all the fundamental legal conceptions there are. (3) Even if the conceptions are distinct and complete, they may not be irreducible. One can argue, for example, that Hohfeld's eight conceptions can be reduced to two more primitive and slightly different conceptions of "duty" and "power."[4] Neverthe-

---

3 Hohfeld, *Fundamental Legal Conceptions,* p. 64.
4 See Carl Wellman, *A Theory of Rights: Persons Under Laws, Institutions, and Morals* (Totowa, N.J.: Rowman & Allanheld, 1985), pp. 53–54.

less, these reservations are essentially technical doubts. They do not impair the usefulness of Hohfeld's terminology for most legal and philosophical purposes.[5]

Another limitation is that Hohfeld's theory does not manage to clarify the sense in which disparate legal relations can all be considered rights. In fact, Hohfeld insists that the only proper sense of the word "right" is that in which it involves a correlative duty on the part of someone else,[6] and that to use the word also to cover a privilege, power, or immunity is "looseness of usage."[7] But this insistence ignores, or underemphasizes, a unifying feature of the conceptions in the elements column. They are all rights in the broad sense of being individual advantages secured by law – where advantages include both choices and benefits.[8] It is just that the advantage is sometimes secured by something other than a correlative duty on another person.

A different limitation is that Hohfeld's vocabulary cannot be mechanically applied. The point is not that people can find the vocabulary hard to master – although many law students will testify that it is not easy. Rather, the point is that people cannot employ it accurately without a grasp of the relevant law. A good illustration is the case of *Quinn v.*

---

5 The influence of Hohfeld on academic lawyers is especially evident in the American Law Institute, *Restatement of the Law of Property* (St. Paul, Minn.: American Law Institute Publishers, 1944). Among philosophers, perhaps Carl Wellman has done most to elaborate Hohfeld's theory critically and to apply it carefully to moral problems. See Carl Wellman , *Welfare Rights* (Totowa, N.J.: Rowman and Littlefield, 1982); and, especially, Wellman, *A Theory of Rights.* For an interpretation of Hohfeld's significance in legal and political theory, see Joseph William Singer, "The Legal Rights Debate in Analytical Jurisprudence from Bentham to Hohfeld," *Wisconsin Law Review* (1982): 975–1059.

6 Hohfeld, *Fundamental Legal Conceptions*, pp. 35–41.

7 Ibid., p. 36.

8 No need exists now or later to choose between "will" (choice) and "interest" (benefit) accounts of rights; Chapter 3 in fact advances a combined will and interest theory. See also James W. Nickel, *Making Sense of Human Rights: Philosophical Reflections on the Universal Declaration of Human Rights* (Berkeley: University of California Press, 1987), pp. 19, 21–23.

Leathem, discussed by Hohfeld and other writers.[9] Quinn
tried to get Leathem, a butcher, to substitute union members
for his nonunion employees. When Leathem refused, Quinn
threatened to strike at the shop of one of Leathem's customers unless he stopped doing business with Leathem. After
the customer ceased to buy meat from him, Leathem sought
damages for unfair competition. The key issue here is
whether Leathem had only a *privilege*, or also had a *claim-
right*, to carry on a lawful business. The latter would involve
a correlative duty on Quinn not to interfere, whereas the
former would not. A mastery of Hohfeld's vocabulary is not
enough to resolve the issue. One also needs to know the law
and to make sound policy decisions about it. The beginnings
of a resolution might go like this. The then-existing English
law of unfair competition recognized certain specific duties
stemming from the torts of intimidation, conspiracy, and
inducement of breach of contract. Yet Leathem's asserted
claim-right was not, under then-existing English law, correlative with any of these specific duties. Hence, to make out
Leathem's case it was vital to establish some further duty
on Quinn not to interfere. Hohfeld's system enables one
to distinguish a privilege from a claim-right. It also enables
one to see that if a claim-right is recognized, some new
duty of noninterference must be imposed. An analytical vocabulary does not dictate an answer, but it does clarify the
choice a judge must make in imposing, or refusing to impose, a new duty.

---

9 In Quinn v. Leathem, [1901] A.C. 495, the House of Lords upheld a
   verdict for Leathem. Hohfeld (pp. 42–43) thought that Lord Lindley's
   opinion – see especially [1901] A.C. at 534 – muddled the difference
   between privilege and claim-right. The usefulness of Hohfeld to lawyers and judges is discussed in Thomas D. Perry, "A Paradigm of
   Philosophy: Hohfeld on Legal Rights," *American Philosophical Quarterly*,
   14 (1977): 41–50; Stephen D. Hudson and Douglas N. Husak, "Legal
   Rights: How Useful is Hohfeldian Analysis?," *Philosophical Studies*, 37
   (1980): 45–53; Thomas D. Perry, "Reply in Defense of Hohfeld," *Philosophical Studies*, 37 (1980): 203–09; Perry's position is much the sounder
   of the two.

For immediate purposes, however, the chief limitation is that Hohfeld's system does not say which conceptions are involved in the idea of property. His vocabulary is as applicable to tort and contract and civil procedure as it is to property. What is needed is some way of identifying which conceptions, perhaps specified more fully, might be peculiar to property.

2.3 THE IDEA OF PROPERTY

If one is to use Hohfeld's vocabulary to elaborate the sophisticated conception of property, it will help to conjoin it with an analysis of ownership suggested by Honoré.[10] He sought to specify the standard "incidents" of ownership common to Western legal systems. These incidents are jointly sufficient, though not individually necessary, for ownership. Honoré's list of incidents, slightly modified, includes the claim-rights to possess, use, manage, and receive income; the powers to transfer, waive, exclude, and abandon; the liberties to consume or destroy; immunity from expropriation; the duty not to use harmfully; and liability for execution to satisfy a court judgment. If a person has all of these incidents, or most of them, with respect to a certain thing, then he or she owns it.[11] Honoré's incidents are inspired by, but not identical with, Hohfeld's conceptions. The former are more specific than

10 A. M. Honoré, "Ownership," in A. G. Guest, ed., *Oxford Essays in Jurisprudence (First Series)* (Oxford: Clarendon Press, 1961), pp. 107–47. A lucid integration of Hohfeld and Honoré, different in particulars from that given here, is in Lawrence C. Becker, *Property Rights: Philosophic Foundations* (London, Henley and Boston: Routledge & Kegan Paul, 1977), ch. 2. See also Andrew Reeve, *Property* (Atlantic Highlands, N.J.: Humanities Press International, 1986), ch. 2.

11 Honoré, "Ownership," pp. 108–12. The qualification "or most of them" is necessary because ordinary usage allows ownership to be qualified. For example, people commonly say that they "own" their houses, even though the houses are subject to mortgages, easements, or zoning restrictions.

Even if one makes this qualification, one must acknowledge that "ownership" and its cognates are often used in a still less demanding way. For instance, lawyers sometimes say that a person "owns" rather than merely "has" an easement, even though the text below

the latter since they indicate particular actions or events – to use, to exclude, to be expropriated – with respect to things.

For the purposes of this book it is useful to extend Hohfeld and Honoré as follows. The idea of *property* – or, if you prefer, the sophisticated or legal conception of property – involves a constellation of Hohfeldian elements, correlatives, and opposites; a specification of standard incidents of ownership and other related but less powerful interests; and a catalog of "things" (tangible and intangible) that are the subjects of these incidents. Hohfeld's conceptions are normative modalities. In the more specific form of Honoré's incidents, these are the relations that constitute property. Metaphorically, they are the "sticks" in the bundle called property. Notice, however, that property also includes less powerful collections of incidents that do not rise to the level of ownership. For example, an easement involves primarily a claim-right and a privilege to use the land of another and secondarily a power to compel enforcement of that claim-right and privilege. It would be usual to classify an easement as property or a property interest, even though it does not amount to ownership. Easements, bailments, franchises, and some licenses are examples of *limited property*. Notice, too, that the idea of property will remain open-ended until one lists the kinds of "things" open to ownership. In a legal system, it will be mainly a descriptive task to compile the list. In political theory, it will be a normative problem to show what things should be open to ownership. The reference to

argues that easements involve "limited property rights" rather than "ownership." Again, writers on corporate law usually say that the shareholders "own" the corporation even if its managers "control" it, despite the fact that shareholders' rights amount to rather less than "ownership" as Honoré describes it. Later discussion of the separation of ownership and control follows the usual terminology for the sake of familiarity only (§ 12.2).

At any rate, the key point is to ascertain which legal incidents various persons have. It breeds error to assume that some one person has to be *the* owner, then to launch a search for *that* person, and finally to announce the consequences of his or her *ownership*. See Joseph William Singer, "The Reliance Interest in Property," *Stanford Law Review*, 40 (1988): 611–751, at 637–41.

ownable things is a link between the sophisticated and popular conceptions of property. Notice, finally, that even with a list of ownable things, the idea of property is indeterminate at the margin. No litmus test can separate rights of property from, say, those of contract in all cases. Nor do lawyers' language and reasoning manifest, or require, such a line. It suffices to be able to describe a person's legal position.

The idea of *property rights* is narrower than that of property. Property rights involve only advantageous incidents. Property involves disadvantageous incidents as well. Meant here is advantage or disadvantage to the right-holder or owner. Although property obviously involves disadvantages to persons other than the right-holder, it is important to see that there can be disadvantages to the right-holder as well. Suppose that someone owns a single-family home in a suburban area. Then she has a duty not to use it in ways prohibited by the law of nuisance or by zoning regulations. She may be disabled from transferring it to others with burdensome restrictions – for example, that no one may use it save for unduly limited purposes. If someone wins a court judgment for damages against her, then, subject perhaps to homestead laws, she has a liability that the home be sold to pay the judgment. The duty, disability, and liability are disadvantageous to her. It would be odd to say that they are part of her property rights in the home. But they are part of what is involved in saying that the home is her property. Similarly, easements, bailments, franchises, and some licenses involve *limited property rights.*

This book does not follow Hohfeld by restricting the terms "rights," "property rights," or "rights of property" to claim-rights. So to restrict them ignores a unifying feature of all legal rights – namely, that they are individual advantages secured by law. Any given right is apt to consist of distinguishable advantages. Among them a claim-right, with a correlative duty, need not be the most important. To take a prominent example, the "right" of free speech in the United States is only peripherally protected by duties not to interfere with speaking. The primary protection stems from a disability, imposed on the government by the First Amendment, of making laws that abridge freedom of speech. In the case of property rights, the normative modalities in Hohfeld's elements column are almost always advantageous. And often their correlatives – duty, no-right, liability, and disability – are disadvantageous. But the latter need not be so. Consider the property interest that a beneficiary has in a support trust. The trustee in its discretion has a power to disburse sums for living expenses. The correlative liability of the beneficiary to have her legal position altered by receiving these sums would normally be considered advantageous. Thus, while claim-rights are important, they are not the sole, and need not be the most important, component of property rights. Indeed, it will emerge that the power to exclude and the power to transfer are often the weightiest components of property rights.

The identification of the owners or right-holders facilitates additional terminology. If the owners are identifiable entities distinguishable from some larger group, there is *private property*. The most common example is individual private property, where an individual person is the owner – in severalty, as lawyers say. Other sorts of private property exist when the owners or right-holders are persons considered together, such as partnerships and cotenancies, or are artificial entities that represent the financial interests of persons, such as corporations.[12] Contrasted with private property are various sorts of *public property*. Here the owners are the state, city, community, or tribe. Some forms of ownership involve a mixture of private and public property rights.

Understanding property along the lines suggested by Hohfeld and Honoré has the salient advantage of cross-cultural application – that is, the idea of property, though perhaps not a moral and political theory of property (§ 1.2),

12 Later chapters of this book elaborate as needed more specific conceptions of private property and associated economic structures. For additional detailed discussions from philosophical and historical standpoints, respectively, see James O. Grunebaum, *Private Ownership* (London and New York: Routledge & Kegan Paul, 1987); Richard Schlatter, *Private Property: The History of an Idea* (London: George Allen & Unwin, 1951).

applies to all or almost all societies. If, instead, the idea of property were cast in terms of particular economic or cultural data, it would not illuminate very well property in societies different from those which gave rise to the original data and idea. Granted, if property is conceived along the lines advocated here, variation can still occur in who may own property, which incidents comprise ownership or other property interests, and which things can be owned. But the Hohfeld-Honoré analysis starts from the central truth that property involves relations among persons and with respect to things. It enables one to clarify these relations in widely different social settings. Though the analysis is especially well suited to complicated legal systems in developed societies, it also assists social scientists in analyzing much simpler situations.

A well-known article by the anthropologist Hoebel brings out the point.[13] Hoebel argues, first, that Hohfeld's vocabulary sharpens perception of undeveloped legal and social systems. Hoebel's illustration is Yurok Indian society in northern California prior to the impact of Western civilization. The Yurok had no formal government but did have an informal arrangement for enforcing legal standards by damages. Yurok law permitted something resembling ownership of fishing sites but with qualifications that Hohfeld's conceptions illuminate. The title holder of a fishing site has an exclusive liberty to fish there. He also has a power to grant a temporary liberty to another person to fish in that spot. Should he exercise the power, however, he comes under a duty to prevent his guest from being injured. Thus, if his guest were to slip and hurt herself while fishing, she would have a claim-right against her host for damages.

Second, Hoebel suggests that Hohfeld's vocabulary can avoid some unnecessary wrangles among anthropologists

13 E. Adamson Hoebel, "Fundamental Legal Concepts as Applied in the Study of Primitive Law," *Yale Law Journal*, 51 (1942): 951–66. For the claim that Hohfeld's system is generally useful to empirical social scientists, see A. Irving Hallowell, "The Nature and Function of Property as a Social Institution," in his *Culture and Experience* (Philadelphia: University of Pennsylvania Press, 1955), pp. 236–49.

stemming from the use of overly broad or inapplicable labels. An example is the controversy over the type of ownership of canoes in Melanesia. Some anthropologists held that canoes were "private property." Others maintained that they involved "communal ownership." Hohfeld's conceptions, Hoebel points out, enable observers to describe accurately what is going on without getting embroiled in a larger dispute over private property and communism. The observers might find that the "owner" of a canoe has a claim-right that others not damage it, a liberty superior to that of others to use it, a power to sell or give it away, and an immunity from being forced to sell. They might also find that the "owner" is under a duty to ferry certain travelers, and that failure to discharge the duty would give a traveler a claim-right for damages. Such findings involve a mixture of "private" and "communal" elements. They would not be accurately described by prefixing either label, without qualification, to canoe ownership in that society.[14]

14 The Hohfeld–Honoré analysis is common among philosophers. See, for example, Becker, *Property Rights*, ch. 2. By using it here, one can take easier advantage of the philosophical literature. This choice in no way repudiates the usefulness, as an alternative mode of analysis, of Guido Calabresi and A. Douglas Melamed, "Property Rules, Liability Rules, and Inalienability: One View of the Cathedral," *Harvard Law Review*, 85 (1972): 1089–1128, which is usually understood as identifying tools for protecting "entitlements." Statements in Calabresi and Melamed's terminology can be paraphrased in Hohfeld's language. If A's entitlement is protected by a property rule, then others have a disability (a no-power) in regard to obtaining the entitlement except at a price agreed to by A. If A's entitlement is protected by a liability rule, then others have a disability in regard to obtaining or reducing the value of the entitlement unless they discharge a duty to compensate A *ex post* by a collectively determined amount. If A's entitlement is protected by a rule of inalienability, A has a disability in regard to transferring the entitlement to others.

For philosophical discussion of the work of Calabresi and Melamed, see Jules L. Coleman and Jody Kraus, "Rethinking the Theory of Legal Rights," *Yale Law Journal*, 95 (1986): 1335–71, at 1340–47, which reinterprets their structure to supply the "content" of legal rights. In the language of Coleman and Kraus, Hohfeldian conceptions constitute the "logical form" rather than the "content" of rights. Their content, as developed in this book, is supplied by a combined "interest" and "will" theory whose beginnings are sketched in Chapter 3.

2.4 EXPECTATIONS

There is much that the foregoing elaboration of the idea of property, whatever its advantages, does not reveal about property. In particular, it tells little about the psychological and social dimensions of property. Chapters 4 through 7 explore them in detail. It will, however, be convenient to explain one such dimension here, because it will play an important role at various subsequent stages.[15] This dimension is a connection between property and expectations. In order to make the connection clear, it is first necessary to analyze expectations.[16]

An expectation is a disposition to predict that a certain event will occur together with (characteristically) an attitude of desiring and feeling entitled to count on its occurrence. To clarify this definition it will help to distinguish expectations from predictions, hopes, and simply expecting. Expectations involve predictions but for two reasons cannot be identified with them. One reason is that to have an expectation, though not to predict, is "dispositional" (like knowing or aspiring) rather than "occurrent" (like concentrating or listening). It is possible to say that persons have expectations (but not usually to say that they predict) even when they are asleep or, though awake, are not thinking of the event predicted. The other reason is that different vocabularies apply to predictions and expectations. Predictions have a truth-value, and people speak of them as being verified or falsified. Expectations do not have a truth-value. People speak of them as being protected, sheltered, and secured, or shattered, disrupted, and disappointed, rather than being verified or falsified.

Expectations also differ in attitude from hopes. Persons who hope may have some confidence in the predicted event, but the attitude is typically one of simply desiring or wishing

---

15 See, especially, §§ 4.6, 8.7, 14.3, and 15.4.
16 This section repeats part of the account of expectations in Stephen R. Munzer, "A Theory of Retroactive Legislation," *Texas Law Review*, 61 (1982): 425–80, at 427–35.

for it rather than feeling entitled to count on it. Persons who have expectations, it is true, usually desire the expected event. Yet they typically also feel entitled, to a greater or lesser extent, to count on its occurrence.

The accompanying attitude is such that the phrase "has expectations" is not quite equivalent to the verb "expects." Having expectations differs slightly from simply expecting. People may "expect" to lose a game or to lose money in the stock market, even though the predicted event is undesired. But the noun "expectations," certainly in the legal and philosophical literature, usually is confined to cases in which the predicted event is desired. Sometimes, of course, it is desired *because* it is counted on. Reliance and rearrangement of persons' affairs may bring them to desire an event to which they would otherwise have been indifferent. A little room exists, but not much, for unfavorable expectations. As a matter of intellectual history, confining the noun "expectations" mainly to desired events is perhaps due to the strong association in Hume and Bentham of expectations with the stability needed for personal and social well-being (§ 8.2).

The relevant connection between property and expectations is that property, conceived as a legal structure of Hohfeldian normative modalities, makes possible legal expectations with respect to things. This structure is a ground for the disposition to predict, *inter alia,* the future use and enjoyment of things together with the attitude of feeling entitled to count on them. Moreover, only an attenuated form of property would fail to ground expectations. For it would have to occasion no desire for, no disposition to predict, or no attitude of feeling entitled to count on the future use and enjoyment of things. Such a form of property, if it merits the name at all, would be unstable or bizarre or both. It will emerge later that property-related expectations have deep roots in human agency and the interactions between persons and the world (§ 4.6).

These remarks connect, but do not identify, property and expectations. To identify them would be to subscribe to this sort of analysis: "Property is a set of expectations such that. . . ." One would then have to fill in the ellipsis by specifying those expectations that are property as distinct from those that are something else. Such an analysis would be a mistake. If property is a normative structure, if expectations are dispositions to predict together with a certain attitude, and if the existence of a normative structure requires more than these dispositions-cum-attitudes, then property is not identical with expectations. So Bentham was right, *pro tanto*, to say that "[p]roperty is nothing but a *basis of expectation*"[17] with respect to things. The sophisticated or legal conception of property forms the basis. Part of the psychological dimension of property is the set of legal expectations that individuals have. Part of its social dimension is the concordance of most such expectations in efficacious legal systems. Later portions of this book qualify and develop these partial descriptions.

As an illustration of these remarks, consider again the homeowner introduced in § 2.3. Among her many legal incidents it is possible to reckon claim-rights to occupy and use the premises; privileges and powers to exclude others, to mortgage or lease the property, and to transfer it to others; immunity from expropriation of the house by the government without compensation; liability for property taxes; a duty not to use the premises for industrial purposes; and so on. In the United States most owners of residential property would be aware of these various legal advantages and disadvantages – and many more besides. In consequence, they would, if the distinction drawn earlier is adopted, *have expectations* regarding the advantageous items and would *expect* certain things regarding the disadvantageous items. Most neighbors would be aware of the owner's legal position and her expectations. Accordingly, they would have certain expectations of their own. No doubt additional elements must be introduced to explain, say, whatever social status attaches to being a homeowner. All the same, to supplement the

17 Jeremy Bentham, *The Theory of Legislation*, ed. C. K. Ogden (London: Routledge & Kegan Paul, 1931), p. 111 (emphasis added).

30

Hohfeld–Honoré analysis with an account of property-related expectations helps illuminate the psychological and social dimensions of property.

2.5 A MISGUIDED ENTERPRISE?

Some might claim that it is misguided to analyze property and property rights in the way suggested here because the notion of property is too fragmented to allow for a general theory. A provocative article by Grey seems to make this claim. He contends that the "disintegration" of property ultimately means that property "ceases to be an important category in legal and political theory."[18] Since Grey's contention stands directly in the path of the argument of this book, it is essential to consider what he means and whether his argument is sound.

For Grey, "disintegration" seems to cover two kinds of development. One is the transition from a conception of property as material "things that are owned by persons"[19] to a conception of property as a "bundle of rights" and as including "intangibles."[20] Persons in the eighteenth century and the ordinary layperson today are said to use the former conception, and modern capitalist economies are said to employ the latter. The other development is the proliferation of specialized conceptions.[21] Grey believes that specialists now use the word "property" in different, sometimes conflicting ways. Law teachers see the "law of property" as dealing primarily with land. Some lawyers and some economists think of property rights as being *in rem* rather than *in personam*. Other lawyers conceive of property as whatever is protected from being taken by the government for public use without just compensation. Other economists view property

---

18 Thomas C. Grey, "The Disintegration of Property," in J. Roland Pennock and John W. Chapman, eds., *NOMOS XXII: Property* (New York: New York University Press, 1980), pp. 69–85, at p. 81.
19 Ibid., p. 69 (emphasis omitted).
20 Ibid., pp. 69, 70.
21 Ibid., pp. 71–73.

as an entitlement whose purpose is to advance allocative efficiency. Some legal theorists conceive of property as including not only private-law rights but also public-law entitlements such as welfare assistance. In short, when various specialists today separate property rights from other rights, they use the word "property" in widely divergent senses. Grey maintains that the disintegration of property stems neither from the socialist "attack on capitalism" nor from the advent of a "mixed economy."[22] "Rather," he says, "it is intrinsic to the development of a free-market economy into an industrial phase."[23] The creation of new forms of enterprise requires the splitting or fractioning of the ordinary conception of property.

How does Grey get from this account of disintegration to the result that property is an unimportant category in legal and political theory? Stripped to essentials, the argument seems to involve a quartet of premises and a trio of conclusions:

P1. The eighteenth-century conception of property, which is also the ordinary conception, views property as the ownership of material things.
P2. Traditional capitalism supported property understood according to that conception.
P3. Traditional Marxism attacked property understood according to that conception.
P4. Because of disintegration, property today is not identical with the ownership of material things.

Therefore:

C1. Traditional capitalism is undermined.
C2. Traditional Marxism is undermined.
C3. Property is no longer an important category in legal and political theory.

22   Ibid., p. 74.
23   Ibid.

This argument is thought-provoking but unsound. Consider the premises. P1 is overdrawn. Eighteenth-century thinkers, such as Blackstone, already recognized various forms of intangible property. Examples are such future interests as reversions and remainders and such incorporeal hereditaments as peerages, tithes, and advowsons. Many laypersons today consider copyrights, patents, and trademarks to be property. Thus, what Grey calls the "eighteenth-century," or "ordinary," conception is narrower than the "popular" conception of property described in § 2.1. Its narrowness indicates that it fails to capture adequately how these people think of property.

The accuracy of P2 and P3 turns largely on how much weight is put on the word "traditional" in characterizing the early history of capitalism and Marxism. Perhaps it is natural to see capitalism, at the beginning of the industrial revolution, in terms of tangible items: money (for wages), factories and mines, the goods produced. This picture is accurate to a degree, but it underplays the intangible elements in early capitalism, such as arrangements for commercial credit and the rise of the joint stock company. As for Marxism, at best only the early statements call upon a conception of property as the ownership of material things. In Marx's *Economic and Philosophic Manuscripts of 1844*, the criticism of capitalism invokes the relations between alienation and private property. Even there it is a difficult question how far Marx saw property as tangible things. Yet his three-volume work *Capital* (1867) contains very little discussion of property. It certainly does not make private property the centerpiece of the critique of capitalism. Thus, P2 and P3 hold only if the very heavy weight rests on the most "traditional" versions of capitalism and Marxism. And in that case they fail to capture a significant part of the social and intellectual history of capitalism and Marxism.

P4 is both overdrawn and confused. It is true that intangible property is increasingly important. It is also true that, with the rise of the trust and the publicly held corporation, conceiving of property as a bundle of rights is especially useful. But if the criticism of P1 is sound, intangibles have long been considered property. And seeing property as a bundle of rights is helpful even for simple situations, as the use of Hohfeld's vocabulary in § 2.3 to analyze undeveloped societies illustrates. Moreover, thinking of property as the ownership of material things is central to property even today. Land and houses are premier examples. So, too, are the material necessities of human life – especially food and clothing. And the criminal law in defining theft offenses still conceives of property chiefly as material things. A confusion at the base of P4 is the tendency to believe that what § 2.1 calls the popular and sophisticated conceptions of property are somehow incompatible. That is not so if each is kept to its respective quarters.

Consider now Grey's conclusions. C1 and C2 hold only if early capitalism and early Marxism are seen in an excessively traditional, almost stylized, way. In that sense they are not very arresting propositions. Both capitalism and Marxism can be reformulated so they they do not depend on identifying property with the ownership of material things. The reformulations can be complicated, particularly the Marxian treatment of property and alienation (§§ 7.3–7.4), but they are possible.

Even if Grey's premises were true, his principal conclusion, C3, would not follow. That conclusion is in fact ambiguous. If the word "property" as used in C3 means ownership of material things, C3 is a non sequitur. There may be other perspectives in political theory besides traditional capitalism and traditional Marxism that conceive of property in the same way. For example, arguments for a more nearly equal distribution of tangible items, such as food, clothes, houses, and land, stress the adverse consequences, in the forms of resentment and social unrest, that flow from perceived inequalities. But suppose that "property" as used in C3 means something other than ownership of material things. Then C3 is still a non sequitur. Indeed, it involves the fallacy of equivocation, since the word "property" is used in one sense in P1–P3 and in a different sense in C3. Nor can P4 rescue the argument. Even if P4 were true, it would not follow that, for whatever property is today besides the ownership of material things, property is unimportant in legal and political theory. In fact, three specialized senses of property discussed by Grey make it important in exactly that way. To conceive of property, for example, as whatever is immune from government taking without compensation raises fundamental constitutional and political questions about the balance of power and right between individuals and the state. Again, to view property as an entitlement that should promote efficiency provokes questions about the role of efficiency and justice in a general theory of property. Yet again, to see property as including public-law entitlements – say, to a minimum level of income – raises deep issues of equality and the significance of property to personal development.

The root question is whether C3, even though it does not follow, might nevertheless be true. To answer this question one should distinguish two positions, only the first of which can be vindicated at this point. One is that "property" can be used in several senses, at least one of which makes property an important category in political theory. If the previous paragraph is right, there are at least three senses in which "property" is manifestly an important category. The other position is that "property" can be used in some overarching way such that it is an important category in political theory. This position also claims that though contemporary economic conditions differ from those of one or two centuries ago, thinking in terms of property assists theoretical analysis and clarifies practical inquiry regarding economic organization. Section 2.3 in effect holds that the sophisticated conception of property is overarching, though one must wait for later discussion (§ 4.4) to see whether it can be linked intelligibly to the popular conception of property. Again, the discussion of business corporations maintains that one can best think about corporate enterprise by including economic concepts within a broader perspective that views corporations as a topic in the theory of property rights (§ 12.1). Likewise, the overarching sophisticated conception serves well, this book argues, for the treatments of gratuitous transfers and government takings of private property. Only at the end of the book can the reader judge whether this broad understanding of property is both coherent and important in political theory.

Chapter 3

Persons and their bodies

3.1 BODY RIGHTS

This chapter addresses two main issues. One is the status of
the body and of body rights. It is easy to suppose that, if one
had a theory of property that adequately covered rights in
land, chattels, and intangibles, then one would have a complete theory of property. Yet this supposition is too hasty, for
it fails to consider whether there are property rights in the
human body. The other issue is the relation between body
rights and rights to other things in the world. If body rights
turned out to be property rights, they might then be a
springboard for justifying property rights as usually understood.

Here is how to resolve these issues. As to the former, some
hold that the body should be thought of as property, and
emphasize that each person owns or has title to himself or
herself. Others maintain that the body ought not to be
thought of as property at all, and indeed that it demeans
human beings to think of them or their bodies as property. In
contrast, the position advocated here suggests that, insofar
as one takes an overall view, people do not own, but have
some limited property rights in, their bodies (§ 3.2). One
should, however, combine this broad view with a finer-
grained classification, and recognize a division of body rights
into personal rights and property rights and, in the case of
the latter, a further division into weak and strong property
rights (§ 3.3). This taxonomy offers an intuitively appealing

and theoretically sound way to think about body rights, and it has some potentially fruitful moral and constitutional implications.

In regard to the latter issue, some argue that I own myself and my labor and therefore own whatever my labor produces. Others dismiss this argument as utterly simplistic in the modern world. This chapter offers a more sensitive and balanced perspective on the move from "self-ownership" to "world-ownership" (§ 3.4), and so is a bridge to the topics at the center of this book. The idea of self-*ownership* is questionable. For, as will be argued, body rights as a whole amount to limited property rights rather than ownership, and only some body rights qualify as property rights. Furthermore, even if self-ownership were beyond question, it would be a debatable basis for world-*ownership* – where that includes powerful property rights in external things. One should have little confidence in claims for robust property rights to things in the world – for instance, to land, factories, houses, and automobiles – until the ramifications of such rights are understood. Thus, one needs a psychological, social, and partly normative background theory of property – which is the business of Chapters 4 to 7 – before validating *any* move from body rights to property rights in the world of things. As Chapter 10 shows, a cogent labor theory of property forms one principle of justification for property rights. This principle is, however, only one among several in a pluralist theory, and in any case is quite different from Locke's or Nozick's versions of the labor theory.[1] One cannot argue for or grasp satisfactorily this different version of the labor theory until one has escaped from the clutches of overly simple views of self-ownership and taken to heart the impact of property rights. The new principle therefore requires and follows, not precedes, the background theory.

Some comments on the nature of the argument in this

1 John Locke, *Second Treatise of Government* [1690] §§ 25–51, in *Two Treatises of Government*, ed. Peter Laslett 2d ed. (Cambridge: Cambridge University Press, 1967); Robert Nozick, *Anarchy, State, and Utopia* (New York: Basic Books, 1974), pp. 150–82.

chapter are in order. First, it understands property in a complex and partly novel way. It endorses in one respect and departs in another from the standard legal analysis of property. The lawyer usually views property as a bundle of rights. Section 3.2 builds on the previous chapter and endorses this view. Yet it is also possible to concentrate on particular sticks in the bundle and to identify only some of them as property rights. Section 3.3 does exactly that. The conceptual innovation here lies in the idea that it is useful for purposes of analysis to approach property in this complex way.

Second, it is important to see how the notion of property rights functions in the argument of the next two sections. The argument is not that "property" is a helpful way of *deciding* what to say about various substantive topics. It does not start with the understanding of property in Chapter 2, and then claim, for example, that one could not reach certain conclusions about these topics unless one thought of them in terms of property. Rather, the argument is that "property" is both a possible and an appropriate way of *expressing* some conclusions about these topics that one draws through independent moral reflection. What point or interest attaches to so expressing them? The answer is that the conclusions indicate collectively how much people's bodies are like the things that are generally regarded as fit objects of property rights. This answer will disquiet some. They may regard the human body as highly different from land, houses, automobiles, and furniture – so different that it should not be thought of as property. Yet, if the argument advanced here is sound, this answer, even if disquieting, should be accepted. Indeed, it is in those respects that persons are most different from other things in the world that the concept of property has least application. Among these respects is autonomy, that is, the psychological capacity to be self-governing, which is part of the foundation for a moral right to be treated as self-governing.

Third, it is important to be clear on whether, in any given context, moral property rights or legal property rights are being discussed. Moral property rights are justifiable under moral principles. Legal property rights are property rights that are recognized under a particular legal system, such as that of the United States.

In the initial phase of the chapter (§§ 3.2–3.3), the aim is to arrive at an *analysis* of moral property rights. The analysis is, though, in some measure legally inspired. For § 3.2, like Chapter 2, uses Hohfeld's fundamental legal conceptions as a provisional model for moral property rights. And § 3.3 uses legal examples to illustrate some distinctions. All the same, the moral classification does not derive entirely from Hohfeld and legal materials, for some key distinctions do not always reflect lawyers' linguistic intuitions regarding "property."

The case for this classification does not convert "normative" issues into "descriptive" issues. It does, however, indulge in the following simplifying assumption: *If* the body rights recognized under United States law are morally justifiable, *then* they should be classified in the way suggested. This simplifying assumption is defensible because, given the potential number and complexity of body rights, it would be foolhardy in this brief space to attempt a moral justification for each of them. In light of this defense, the argument does not substitute legal description for normative inquiry. Rather, it leaves open, as topics for a larger investigation, whether, and if so how, each putative body right can be morally justified. Leaving this matter open does not impair the usefulness of the *classification* into personal rights and weak and strong property rights. It only postpones determining *which pigeonholes* in the classification various moral body rights occupy.

The last phase of the chapter (§ 3.4) is concerned with the *moral justification* of body rights whose exercise can result in the acquisition of morally justified property rights in external things. Aside from occasional legal illustrations, the discussion, insofar as it involves body rights that are property rights, deals only with moral property rights. The discussion does not endorse legal positivism. Still, it is assumed that some actual legal property rights have no moral justification and that some moral property rights go unrecognized in some actual legal systems.

3.2 BODY RIGHTS AS LIMITED PROPERTY RIGHTS

Does each person own, or at least have limited property rights in, his or her own body?[2] This section suggests, provisionally, that persons do not own their bodies but that they do have limited property rights in them. For this provisional answer to be clear, it must first say something about persons and their bodies.

This chapter understands persons to be entities to which both physical and mental predicates apply. Thus, one can say of a particular person that she is five feet seven inches tall and is seated in the living room, and that she feels sad, is thinking, or is planning a trip to Europe. This conception of

---

2 St. Paul and Hobbes apparently thought not but Locke and the Levellers may have thought so. St. Paul writes: "You are not your own property; you have been bought and paid for" (1 Cor. 6:19–20, Jerusalem Bible). Hobbes says that, in the state of nature, "every man has a Right to every thing; even to one anothers body." Thomas Hobbes, *Leviathan*, ed. W. G. Pogson Smith (Oxford: Clarendon Press, 1909), ch. 14, p. 99. This passage seems to use "Right" in the sense of Hohfeldian liberty.

 In contrast, the Levellers, especially Richard Overton, thought that human beings had a property interest in their own persons. See C. B. Macpherson, *The Political Theory of Possessive Individualism: Hobbes to Locke* (Oxford: Oxford University Press, 1962), pp. 137–42. Overton writes that everyone has a "selfe propriety, else could he not be himselfe." Ibid., p. 140. This statement seems to confuse self-ownership with self-identity. As for Locke, he says that "every Man has a *Property* in his own *Person*." Locke, *Second Treatise of Government* § 27 (emphasis in original). Earlier, though, Locke writes: "All the Servants of one Sovereign Master, sent into the World by his order and about his business, they are his Property, whose Workmanship they are, made to last during his, not one anothers Pleasure." Ibid., § 6. Perhaps the lawyer's notion of relativity of title can harmonize the Lockean passages. Relative to all other human persons, each person has title to himself or herself. But relative to God, no person has title to himself or herself; rather, God has title to each.

41

persons is not dualistic. It does not hold that persons consist of a nonmaterial soul or mind, to which only mental predicates apply, and a material body, to which only physical predicates apply, and that the soul or mind is somehow joined to the body. Rather, a person is a single complex entity to which both sorts of predicates apply.[3] This conception does not exclude the possibility of nonhuman persons. But for present purposes one may assume that all persons are human beings. More precisely, persons are living human beings.[4] A corpse is not a peculiarly inert person; it is not a person at all; it is only the dead body of a former person.

Persons are, moreover, entities that can have rights because they have interests and make choices. Persons have interests, for example, in being free from pain and in continuing to live. Having interests is a necessary, but not sufficient, condition of having rights. If persons have a right not to be tortured, the reason is partly that they have an interest in being free from pain. Persons also choose. If persons have a right to speak freely or to participate in politics, the reason is partly that they have a capacity to choose whether, and if so how, they will speak or participate. It is not claimed here that only persons have rights. Some may argue that animals have rights because they have some interests and perhaps even some limited capacity for choice. The present claim is

---

3 See P. F. Strawson, *Individuals: An Essay in Descriptive Metaphysics* (London: Methuen, 1959), pp. 87–116. This chapter takes this double-aspect view of persons, as the subtitle of Strawson's book suggests, to be an accurate description of the ontological commitments of human language, but it takes no position on the "true" metaphysical nature of persons. It therefore leaves open issues of dualism, functionalism, and the like as nondescriptive metaphysical theories of the nature of persons.

4 This conception of persons rightly makes it hard to formulate the so-called problem of other minds. Ibid., pp. 94–103. But cf. A. J. Ayer, "The Concept of a Person," in *The Concept of a Person and Other Essays* (London: Macmillan, 1963), p. 82. A difficulty with Ayer's view, however, is that it fails to give criteria for picking out living human bodies that may or may not be the bodies of persons. See Douglas C. Long, "The Philosophical Concept of a Human Body," *Philosophical Review*, 73 (1964): 321–37.

only that persons do have interests and make choices and are potential bearers of rights.

If one understands property in the way proposed in Chapter 2, then the question posed at the beginning of this section may now seem answerable in two quick steps. The first step is to list the rights that persons have with respect to their bodies. The second is to decide whether these rights amount to ownership, limited property rights, or something else.

The two-step solution might go like this. First, the United States legal system limits what people can do with their bodies. It disables persons from selling themselves into slavery and from transferring *inter vivos* any organ that is essential to life. Although suicide and self-mutilation are not crimes, the state will try to prevent persons from killing or mutilating themselves. The law does not allow persons to consent to murder or criminal assault. It also prohibits prostitution. Nevertheless, persons have a power to exclude others, as reflected in prohibitions of rape and battery. They have an immunity against imprisonment for debt and against appropriation of part or all of their bodies. Persons have a right to use their bodies as they wish so long as they do not harm others. They may sell or donate some parts of their bodies while alive, and by will or contract may convey their bodies to medical institutions upon death.

Second, laying this list alongside the analysis of property suggests that persons have limited property rights in their bodies. Too many incidents are lacking to say that persons own their bodies. Restrictions on transfer and the absence of a liberty to consume or destroy, for example, indicate that persons do not own their bodies in the way that they own automobiles or desks. Still, since the catalog lists a great many things that the law permits or enables people to do with their bodies, it would be a mistake to say that they have no property rights in them at all. Hence one draws the intermediate conclusion that they have limited property rights in their bodies.

This answer is agreeably brief, but, though in the end it

will be seen to be on the right track, each of its steps is too superficial and mechanical to be convincing. The first step simply catalogs legal rights that people in the United States have in their bodies. Yet the catalog is incomplete and ignores many qualifications. Besides, other countries might well recognize different packages of legal rights. For instance, some legal systems make it a crime to commit, or attempt to commit, suicide. In any case, one cannot avoid the underlying moral issue of what body rights persons should have. As § 3.1 points out, to resolve this issue one must provide moral argument rather than appeal to what a given legal system recognizes.

The second step takes the mechanical view that one can juxtapose a list of body rights with analysis of property and obtain an answer. This step is doubly unsatisfactory. It ignores the fact that the concept of ownership is compatible with significant restrictions. For example, private servitudes or historic district regulations may bar razing a Victorian house or altering its facade, and yet one would still say that the person who holds title to it owns it. In addition, the second step assumes that the same analysis of property should apply to living human bodies and other material objects in the world. Doubtless it would be strange to have two entirely different analyses, for then "property" would have a different sense in each analysis. Even so, there are many differences between persons and other material objects. As a result, the issue of whether body rights are property rights should only begin with the analysis used for property rights in standard material objects.

3.3 PERSONAL RIGHTS AND PROPERTY RIGHTS

There is an important shift from the last section to this one. Both concern body rights. In both cases body rights are rights to use, manage, dispose of, transfer, exclude others from, and so on, a body.[5] But § 3.2 focuses on the collection or bundle of rights as a whole. It maintains that body rights, taken as a whole, should be seen as limited property rights rather than ownership. In contrast, this section focuses on elements in the collection – on particular sticks in the bundle. It maintains that it is analytically useful to draw attention to the different elements in the collection called body rights and to regard only some of these elements as property rights.[6] In order to maintain this position, one must reject the extreme views that either no body rights or all body rights are property rights, and provide a criterion for determining which body rights should be regarded as property rights.

The extreme views should be rejected. It is unhelpful to say that *no* body rights are property rights. For that would at least make curious the claim, for which § 3.2 gives good prima facie reasons, that persons have limited property rights in their bodies. At least this claim is plausible if one makes the simplifying assumption described at the end of § 3.1. Also, the incidents involved in body rights – namely, to use, manage, and so on – are parallel to the incidents involved in garden-variety property rights. And even if some sticks in the bundle of body rights seem quite different from what one might think of as property rights, it hardly follows that they all are.

It is also unhelpful to say that *all* body rights are property rights. This view might be called the imperial view of prop-

---

5 It would risk begging a substantive ethical question to say "one's own body" rather than "a body." For then the definition of "body rights" would exclude the possible case of rights held by someone else in one's body. In fact, however, almost all body rights are rights that persons have in their own bodies. The formulation in the text also leaves open whether animals and fetuses, though not persons, can have body rights.

6 One could, of course, make a parallel move in regard to property rights in things. But there would be little point in doing so, for transferability will emerge as the key, and it would be generally accepted that, unlike body rights, almost all property rights in things are transferable.

erty, since it holds that all body rights belong to the empire of property. Yet the imperial view is highly counterintuitive. Although compatibility with linguistic intuitions should not be the sole criterion of the soundness of an account of body rights, the imperial view often counts as "property rights" things that such intuitions, influenced by the simplifying assumption that United States law is sound, do not. Consider the constitutional right of free speech. This right is centrally a privilege and an immunity, protected chiefly by a disability on the government, regarding the use of one's mind and vocal chords to express one's opinions. This right is partly a body right under the analysis given earlier. But virtually no one thinks of free speech as a property right.[7] Nor do people think of the criminal law prohibition against murder as involving a property right. Yet since it protects the continued life of human beings, one might argue that it creates a body right. Again, there are constitutional provisions, in the United States and many other countries, restricting personal searches and barring compelled self-incrimination. Because these provisions relate to bodily integrity and the capacity for speech, they seem to create rights that are, in part, body rights. But though the United States Supreme Court once thought of these constitutional protections in terms of property, it now thinks of them mainly in terms of privacy rather than property.[8] Lastly, if rights to reputation are partly body rights, then tort law protections against libel and slander qualify to some extent as body rights. Still, few would see them as property rights.[9]

---

7 But see Wesley J. Liebeler, "A Property Rights Approach to Judicial Decision Making," *Cato Journal*, 4 (1985): 783–804, at 797–804 (property-rights analysis of free speech).
8 See U.S. Const. amends. IV and V. Compare Boyd v. United States, 116 U.S. 616 (1886) (property rationale), with Katz v. United States, 389 U.S. 347 (1967) (privacy rationale). For reservations, see Robert S. Gerstein, "The Demise of *Boyd*: Self-Incrimination and Private Papers in the Burger Court," *UCLA Law Review*, 27 (1979): 343–97.
9 In Anglo-American law, reputation is more likely to be seen in terms of liberty than property. See, for example, Paul v. Davis, 424 U.S. 693, 722–27 (1976) (Brennan, J., dissenting); Henry Paul Monaghan, "Of

The counterintuitiveness of the imperial view may be seen more generally in this way. All moral body rights are rights in the following general sense: They are all morally justified normative advantages with respect to the body that support some moral claim against those who withhold or usurp them. Similarly, legal rights with respect to the body are all normative advantages that support a cause of action against those who withhold or usurp them. If *all* body rights in this general sense were property rights in some *extremely* weak sense, then there would be a substantial element of truth in the imperial view. But this identification has little to recommend it. It conflates body rights and property rights only by understanding the latter so broadly that prefixing "property" to a body right fails to distinguish it from any other kind of body right. And it suggests that the human body is no different from land and automobiles in regard to property; the suggestion is incorrect because human beings are autonomous whereas land and automobiles are not. There is, in fact, an element of truth in the imperial view, but it is less substantial. It is that *some* body rights are property rights. An appropriate classification should preserve this element of truth and bring out some points that the imperial view obscures.

Since both extreme views should be rejected, one must provide a criterion for classifying some, but not all, body rights as property rights. The most useful criterion is *transferability*. One can best understand the usefulness of this criterion by explaining it in connection with the discussion of persons in § 3.2. That discussion saw persons as, *inter alia*, entities that can have rights because they have interests and make choices. This perspective on persons links up with the

'Liberty' and 'Property'," *Cornell Law Review*, 62 (1977): 405–44, at 412 & n.42. Cf. William Van Alstyne, "Cracks in 'The New Property': Adjudicative Due Process in the Administrative State," *Cornell Law Review*, 62 (1977): 445–93, at 479 n.97 (interests in reputation, traditionally described as interests in liberty, are at least as well described as property interests). Perhaps Kant views rights to reputation as property rights. See Immanuel Kant, *The Philosophy of Law*, trans. W. Hastie (Edinburgh: T. & T. Clark, 1887), pp. 138–40.

contrast between "interest" and "will" theories of rights. The former theory holds that the central function of rights is to protect individual interests. The latter theory holds that the central function of rights is to protect individual choices. By a "function" is meant something that a given thing is designed or specially fitted to do. Hohfeld's fundamental legal conceptions straddle traditional interest and will theories of rights. They suggest the need for a combined theory with interest and will components.[10] Very roughly speaking, the main function of claim-rights and immunities is linked to the interest component, and that of privileges and powers is linked to the will component. In elaborating the will component, one must pay particular attention to the nature of the choice that the right protects. In this context, an especially important group consists of choices to transfer. One can exercise different sorts of privileges and powers to transfer. Gratuitous transfers are one sort. Transfers for value received in return are another.

With these observations in hand, one can divide all body rights into *personal rights* and *property rights*. Personal rights are body rights that protect interests or choices other than the choice to transfer.[11] Property rights are body rights that

---

10 Examples of interest theories include Jeremy Bentham, "A General View of a Complete Code of Laws" and "Pannomial Fragments," in *The Works of Jeremy Bentham*, ed. John Bowring (Edinburgh: William Tait, 1843), vol. 3, pp. 155–230; David Lyons, "Rights, Claimants, and Beneficiaries," *American Philosophical Quarterly*, 6 (1969): 173–85; J. Raz, "On the Nature of Rights," *Mind*, 93 (1984): 194–214. For a will theory, see H. L. A. Hart, "Bentham on Legal Rights," in A. W. B. Simpson, ed., *Oxford Essays in Jurisprudence (Second Series)* (Oxford: Clarendon Press, 1973), pp. 171–201. A combined theory using Hohfeld's terminology, to which this section owes a debt, is Carl Wellman, *Welfare Rights* (Totowa, N.J.: Rowman and Littlefield, 1982); Carl Wellman, *A Theory of Rights: Persons Under Laws, Institutions, and Morals* (Totowa, N.J.: Rowman & Allanheld, 1985). See also Chapter 2, notes 8 and 14.

11 Under this definition, it is possible that an entity that is not a person could have "personal rights." Since personal rights are a species of body rights, since an entity perhaps need not be a person to have body rights (see note 5 above), and since entities other than persons might have interests, the possibility exists that some such entity might have "personal rights" as defined here.

protect the choice to transfer. One can array personal rights on two different but related spectra. The first spectrum ranges from rights that protect only interests, through rights that protect both interests and choices, to rights that protect only choices. The second spectrum ranges from rights that are nonwaivable, through rights that are waivable with qualifications, to rights that are waivable at the option of the right-holder. It is tempting to suppose that position on the second spectrum is a straightforward result of position on the first spectrum. That is, rights involving interests would be nonwaivable and rights involving choices would be waivable. In fact, however, no such straightforward relation holds, as some examples will shortly make clear. The reason is that as what a right protects increases in importance, its relative waivability decreases. Thus, one must assess the importance of an interest or a choice; not all interests are more important than all choices, or vice versa. One can subdivide property rights in the body into weak and strong varieties. A *weak property right* involves only a choice to transfer gratuitously. A *strong property right* involves a choice to transfer for value.

This classification is both theory-driven and intuition-driven. It is theory-driven because part of the motivation for introducing it is to aid in the conceptual analysis of body rights and property rights and, eventually, in the moral and constitutional examination of these rights. It is intuition-driven because it is designed in part to handle examples more nearly in accordance with common linguistic intuitions than either of the extreme views rejected earlier. Nevertheless, the classification admittedly engages in some streamlining of these intuitions, for while property rights under legal systems are generally transferable, they are not invariably so. The rights of beneficiaries of spendthrift trusts, for example, are not transferable but are regarded as property rights.[12] Still, transferability is a highly important feature of

12 See, for example, Broadway Nat'l Bank v. Adams, 133 Mass. 170 (1882) (income from spendthrift trust is not alienable or attachable).

property as usually understood. And transferability is even more important in the special case of body rights because of their close connection with autonomy.[13] Furthermore, this analysis is on the right track in making transferability for value the line between weak and strong property rights. Support lies in the thought that property is preeminently something that can be bought and sold in a market.

The new classification regards all of the cases that the imperial view handles counterintuitively as examples of personal rights. The examples are, however, located at different points on the two spectra mentioned earlier. To simplify discussion, assume that treatment under current United States law is morally justifiable. The right not to be murdered is a legally protected interest. It is centrally a claim-right with a correlative duty on others. No one may waive it. The right of free speech is more complicated as regards both the distinction between interests and choices and the matter of waivability. Insofar as it is an immunity against government regulation, free speech is a legally protected interest. This interest can be described as, say, an individual interest in self-development or a social interest in the general benefits of a marketplace of ideas. Yet this interest can also be characterized as an "interest" in autonomy – which links free speech to the will component. Furthermore, insofar as the right of free speech is a privilege, a person may choose to speak or not. Hence, this complex right seems to protect both interests and choices. As regards waivability, one might venture that these interests and choices are so important that the right is nonwaivable. In fact, however, the situation is more qualified. The government may not, for example, pass a law requiring a person to give up the liberty to speak as a condition of receiving welfare benefits. Yet it may, for example, limit the free speech of its own employees.[14] The right of free

13 One need not take a position on the general converse proposition that all transferable rights are property rights, but, again, because of the close connection with autonomy, this analysis will regard all transferable *body* rights as property rights.
14 See, for example, Snepp v. United States, 444 U.S. 507 (1980) (no publication by CIA employees without prior government approval);

speech is not a property right in the body, for one cannot transfer the right to others. Yet it is a right that, with qualifications, can be waived.

Likewise, the privileges against warrantless searches of one's person and compelled self-incrimination are personal rights. The former privilege protects mainly an interest in personal integrity. One can waive the privilege by voluntarily allowing the police to search one's person. The latter privilege protects chiefly the choice of persons to decide whether voluntarily to incriminate themselves. One might conclude that deciding to do so is to waive the privilege. But this conclusion is not quite accurate; for, since the privilege is against *compelled* self-incrimination, speaking out voluntarily does not waive *that* privilege. It would be more accurate to say that speaking out voluntarily takes persons outside the scope of the privilege, even if doing so, misleadingly expressed, is seen as akin to waiver.[15] Lastly, the tort law protections against libel and slander involve both interests and choices. Insofar as they are claim-rights with correlative duties on others, they guard an interest in reputation. Yet insofar as they are backed up by a privilege and a power to bring suit for breach of duty, they are in part legally protected choices to sue for defamation. These protections are waivable.[16] One can choose not to sue and indeed can

United States Civil Serv. Comm'n v. Nat'l Ass'n of Letter Carriers, 413 U.S. 548 (1973) (upholding Hatch Act restraints on political management and campaigning by postal employees).

15 Even this statement is not perfectly accurate. It does not cover one situation in which by speaking out voluntarily one can genuinely waive the privilege. Under Rogers v. United States, 340 U.S. 367, 372–75 (1951), a witness who freely answers self-incriminating questions about a particular subject may not refuse to answer further questions dealing with the same subject if answering them would not expose her to a real danger of further incrimination.

16 More precisely, one can waive the right to sue for civil libel, but cannot stop the grand jury from initiating proceedings for criminal libel. Such proceedings are, however, both infrequent and subject to constitutional limitations. See Garrison v. Louisiana, 379 U.S. 64 (1964) (limiting state power to impose criminal sanctions for criticism of the official conduct of public officials).

enter into a contract not to do so. But such protections, like the privileges against warrantless searches of persons and compelled self-incrimination, are not property rights in the body because they cannot be given or sold to others.

So much for personal rights. Weak property rights are exemplified by the various transfers recognized by the Uniform Anatomical Gift Act.[17] This model statute does not prohibit sales, but it explicitly addresses only gifts made during life or upon death. During life people may donate certain parts of their bodies. Upon death they may, by will or other appropriate document, donate either parts or the entire corpse. Strong property rights are illustrated by the power to sell bodily fluids, such as blood and semen, and in some states to contract for the future delivery of one's body after death in return for present medical care or present or future monetary payment. Another illustration involves the right of publicity – that is, the right to exploit commercially certain interests in one's body, including one's name, voice, and appearance. Consider Elvis Presley. His right of publicity included the exclusive privilege to market such items as Elvis dolls. The right was transferable. During his life Presley could have given or sold that privilege to others. He could also have transferred such a privilege by will. If he had made no will, in some states the privilege would have passed by intestate succession to his heirs.[18] The right of publicity thus includes both weak and strong property rights in the body.

If this new classification has merit, notice that it undercuts some overly simple conceptions of what could count as a property right in the body. First, it undercuts the supposed

---

17 Uniform Anatomical Gift Act, *Uniform Laws Annotated* (St. Paul, Minn.: West, 1983), vol. 8A, pp. 15–67.
18 Judicially, the right of publicity stems from Haelan Laboratories, Inc. v. Topps Chewing Gum, Inc., 202 F.2d 866 (2d Cir.), *cert. denied*, 346 U.S. 816 (1953). On the inheritability of the right of publicity, see, for example, Cal. Civ. Code § 990 (Deering Supp. 1989); Okla. Stat. Ann. tit. 21, §§ 839.1–.3 (West 1983); Tenn. Code Ann. § 47–25–1103 (Michie 1988). See generally Timothy P. Terrell and Jane S. Smith, "Publicity, Liberty, and Intellectual Property: A Conceptual and Economic Analysis of the Inheritability Issue," *Emory Law Journal*, 34 (1985): 1–64.

contrast that property rights in the body must be original rather than acquired, while property rights in other material objects must be acquired rather than original. If "original" means "present at birth," this contrast fails. For if men have a right to give or sell their semen, or if persons have a right to exploit commercially certain interests in their voices and appearance, these rights will rarely be original.[19] Conversely, if at birth someone inherits municipal bonds or a farm, the rights will be original – though, of course, they must previously have been acquired by others. Second, the new classification undercuts the idea that the more intimate something is the less suited it is to be the subject of a property right. This simple idea does square with some examples. For instance, the privilege against compelled self-incrimination, which might be viewed as protecting individuals in the most intimate reaches of their consciences,[20] is a personal rather than a property right. But this idea does not tally with other examples. To illustrate, parts of one's body seem very intimate, and yet the power to transfer them is a property right. Again, the right of publicity sometimes covers aspects of a person that are intimately tied to his or her conception of self, but it is nevertheless a property right.

In addition, the new classification has some potentially illuminating applications to many moral and constitutional problems involving body rights. Space hardly permits a satisfactory discussion here, but it is possible to give some examples. In moral philosophy, thinkers have long wrestled with problems of suicide, slavery, self-enslavement, and

---

19 Persons sometimes have present rights to future performance, including rights with respect to things that do not yet exist, such as a contractual right to occupy a building upon completion even though construction has yet to begin. This qualification is unlikely to apply to the body rights mentioned in the text.

20 See Robert S. Gerstein, "Punishment and Self-Incrimination," *American Journal of Jurisprudence*, 16 (1971): 84–94; Robert S. Gerstein, "Privacy and Self-Incrimination," *Ethics*, 80 (1970): 87–101. For criticism of this position, see David Dolinko, "Is There a Rationale for the Privilege Against Self-Incrimination?," *UCLA Law Review*, 33 (1986): 1063–1148, at 1122–37.

abortion. Some of the "solutions" proposed from time to time have either embraced, or repudiated, the idea of owning or having title to or property rights in oneself as morally relevant.[21] A finer-grained taxonomy, like that advanced here, may help to draw morally pertinent distinctions more clearly than saying, or denying, that persons own their bodies. Again, in American constitutional law, scholars have grappled with the distinction between "liberty" and "property" under the due process clause.[22] The classification of

21 To take just one example, consider suicide. Some invoke property to show that suicide is morally permissible. Thus, a person may commit suicide because "there is nothing in the world to which every man has a more unassailable title than to his own life and person." Arthur Schopenhauer, "On Suicide," from his "Studies in Pessimism," in *The Complete Essays of Schopenhauer*, trans. T. Bailey Saunders (New York: Crown Publishers, 1942), p. 25. Similarly, to argue for a right to commit suicide is "akin to saying that the man who is a decider, a chooser who has a will of his own, possesses himself, is his own 'property', and as such, has property rights in and to his person. His autonomy is his most precious possession, and gives him his property right in and to himself." H. J. McCloskey, "The Right to Life," *Mind*, 84 (1975): 403–25, at 416–17. In contrast, it has been held that "the analogy on which the private ownership argument for suicide is based is an unsound one, at least assuming a no-afterlife metaphysics: in ordinary property-destruction cases the owner of the property continues to exist (and be benefitted or harmed) after he destroys his property, whereas in suicide the owner *is* his destroyed property. . . . [I]t is not at all clear that the underlying notion of one's life as one's private property is philosophically coherent. 'It's *my* life' may express an important sentiment, but not necessarily that one's life is an item among one's belongings." Margaret Pabst Battin, *Ethical Issues in Suicide* (Englewood Cliffs, N.J.: Prentice-Hall, 1982), p. 180 (emphasis in original). A related view contends: "What we own – in any full-blooded sense of that term – we can disown, give away, sell, or otherwise dispose of so that it becomes the property of someone else. We cannot do this with our lives. Therefore whatever the unique relationship this bears to us, it cannot be one of ownership." Eike-Henner W. Kluge, *The Practice of Death* (New Haven: Yale University Press, 1975), p. 119.
22 U.S. Const. amend. V ("No person shall be . . . deprived of life, liberty, or property, without due process of law"); amend. XIV, § 1 ("nor shall any State deprive any person of life, liberty, or property, without due process of law"). Prior to Board of Regents v. Roth, 408 U.S. 564 (1972), the expression "life, liberty, or property" was taken in umbrella fashion so that the individual words often were not given

body rights into personal rights and weak and strong property rights may help with these intellectual struggles. The suggestion is *not* that this classification draws *all* the relevant distinctions or that independent moral and constitutional argument is beside the point, but that applying the classification sheds light on these knotty topics.

Some readers may resist this classification. Perhaps they will regard it as too parasitic on United States law. Perhaps they will contend that the arguments show only that it is possible, not that is is appropriate, to speak of property rights in the body. Or, more interestingly, perhaps they will claim that to speak in this way treats persons as "things" or "commodities."

Several considerations should diminish, if not eliminate, the resistance. First, if "parasitism" amounts only to the simplifying assumption that the treatment of body rights under United States law is morally justifiable (§ 3.1), then it affects not the usefulness of the classification but only which body rights, and how many, belong in each category. The classification itself would lose interest only in the unlikely event that moral argument could show one of the categories to be empty.

Second, to concede the possibility, but not the appropriateness, of the classification is an unpersuasive move unless there is a genuine argument against appropriateness. For the case made in this section is a strong case for the cogency and

distinct meanings. See John Hart Ely, *Democracy and Distrust: A Theory of Judicial Review* (Cambridge, Mass.: Harvard University Press, 1980), p. 19; Monaghan, "Of 'Liberty' and 'Property'," p. 409. However, these words may shelter somewhat different interests after *Roth* and subsequent cases. See, for example, Vitek v. Jones, 445 U.S. 480, 488–91 (1980); Bishop v. Wood, 426 U.S. 341 (1976); Arnett v. Kennedy, 416 U.S. 134 (1974). (Cleveland Bd. of Educ. v. Loudermill, 470 U.S. 532, 540–41 (1985), undermines the force of the *Arnett* plurality opinion.) To notice this feature of the present constitutional landscape is not to endorse the actual understandings of, say, "liberty" and "property" in these cases. All the same, the distinction between personal rights and property rights makes congenial *some* appropriate distinction between "life" and "liberty" on the one hand and "property" on the other under the due process clause.

usefulness of the scheme. To rebut that case one needs an opposing argument, not just a vague resistance to the scheme.

Third, the claim that property-talk depicts people as things or commodities does not ground an argument that will survive examination. This claim may overlook the fact that persons do have physical bodies, and may overemphasize the popular conception that property is things. The sophisticated conception of property, as a bundle of normative incidents, allows for powers to give and to sell – powers that may apply, say, to blood as well as automobiles. If that is correct, then the most likely argument for the claim would be that property-talk somehow demeans people by undercutting their autonomy. This argument is unconvincing. If autonomy is the psychological capacity to govern oneself, and if this capacity underlies a moral right to be treated as self-governing (§ 3.1), then to make the claim stick it would be necessary to show that a *morally justifiable* property right in the body undercuts autonomy. It is hard to see that, for example, a power to give or sell blood does so – save in circumstances where poverty forces people to sell their blood to survive, and in those circumstances a strong property right in one's blood seems morally unjustifiable. In contrast, a power to give or sell oneself into slavery would impair autonomy, but these pages hardly countenance self-enslavement.

3.4 FROM SELF-OWNERSHIP TO WORLD-OWNERSHIP?

The foregoing discussion deals with the first of two main issues confronted in this chapter: the status of the body and body rights. In the process, it fractions body rights into personal rights and weak and strong property rights. The second issue has to do with the relation between body rights and rights to other things in the world. To adapt G. A. Cohen,[23] can one move from "self-ownership" to "world-ownership"?

23 G. A. Cohen, "Self-Ownership, World-Ownership, and Equality," in Frank S. Lucash, ed., *Justice and Equality Here and Now* (Ithaca, N.Y.,

One cannot do so, in any simple way, for at least two reasons. First, it is a mistake to characterize body rights, jointly or individually, as self-*ownership*. Taken jointly, the body rights of each person amount not to ownership but only to a weaker package of limited property rights (§ 3.2). Considered individually, the body rights of each person are not all in the same boat (§ 3.3). Most body rights are personal rather than property rights; examples are rights not to be murdered, not to be searched without a warrant or just cause, not to be compelled to testify against oneself, not to be libeled or slandered, to speak freely, and to exclude others from sexual or other physical contact. Some body rights are property rights – whether weak, such as the right to donate an organ upon death, or strong, such as the right of publicity or the right to sell blood or semen; but these weak and strong property rights are neither so numerous nor so central as to establish that persons "own" themselves. Hence, if self-ownership is a premise on the road to world-ownership, it is a dubious premise.

Second, the idea of world-*ownership* represents such a robust claim that much evidence and argument are needed to establish it. The claim is not, indeed, so powerful as to hold that anyone could own the entire world. Yet it surely holds that persons, by exercising their body rights, such as a right to work, could come to hold quite powerful property rights in particular things, including rights that persist indefinitely and are transferable by gift, sale, and bequest. These rights amount to "ownership" as Honoré uses that term (§ 2.3). But the very power of these property rights is a warning signal. Before allowing such rights, one should consider carefully their impact on persons and societies over

and London: Cornell University Press, 1986), pp. 108–35; G. A. Cohen, "Self-Ownership, World Ownership, and Equality: Part II," *Social Philosophy & Policy*, 3, no. 2 (1986): 77–96. The text is sympathetic to Cohen's perspective but does not purport to reproduce Cohen's actual views or to use "self-ownership" and "world-ownership" exactly as he does. For a brief comment on one feature of the first article, see Chapter 10, note 20. See also § 7.6.

generations. So, even if the premise relating to self-owner-ship were true, one would need to ask many questions before endorsing such arguments, akin to those of Locke and Nozick, as "I own myself and my labor, and therefore I own whatever my labor produces." What body rights are being exercised in laboring? What interactions between persons and the world could generate property rights even in princi-ple? What impact do property rights have on their holders in terms of personality, control, privacy, individuality, moral character, and power? What impact, in these respects, do they have on others? Can persons sell to others their ability to work? What happens if they do so? Do the property rights of one generation affect the situation of subsequent genera-tions so as no longer to leave a level playing field? Till one gets answers to these and kindred questions, it is irresponsi-ble to move from self-ownership to world-ownership.

This conclusion confirms the strategy of this book. One should not proceed from an account of the concept of prop-erty directly to principles of justification. One needs an inter-vening discussion of the psychological, social, and norma-tive dimensions of property to respond to the questions just listed. That is the aim of the background theory to be de-veloped in Part II.

Part II

From individuals to social context

Chapter 4

Incorporation and projection

4.1 NATURE OF THE INQUIRY

Thus far this book has explained the concept of property and shown that some body rights should be considered property rights. It is now time to address the chief subject of this book – property rights in external things of the world. This chapter concerns mainly the analytical foundations of such rights. It is the point of departure for placing, over the succeeding three chapters, persons and property in the context of a full social world. Only within this full context can one later grapple adequately with the justification of public and private property.

In this chapter, the central question is: If persons can acquire property rights in unowned things, how are these rights acquired? One answer – the incorporation theory – holds that external things become property by being brought into the body. Another answer – the projection theory – maintains that they become property by embodying the person in external things.

Richard E. Anderson, Craig Ihara, Andreas Koch, Kurt Nutting, David Polinsky, Warren Quinn, Steven Shiffrin, Abe Socher, David Steinberg, and Katrina P. Ten commented helpfully on various portions of Part II. I am especially grateful to Virginia Held and Samuel C. Wheeler III, who served as commentators on an early version of most of Chapter 4 at a session of the Society for Philosophy and Public Affairs at the American Philosophical Association, Eastern Division Meeting, Washington, D.C., in December 1985.

61

The discussion of these two possible answers takes this course.[1] Section 4.2 rejects the incorporation theory for all but a few cases. Section 4.3 then sets out briefly Hegel's somewhat murky version of the projection theory. The balance of the chapter restates the projection theory in clearer language. Section 4.4 argues for two "transcendental" features of property rights in external things. One is the essential intentionality and causality of owners of property. The other is the essential materiality of property. Section 4.5 discusses the interplay of intention and convention under the projection theory. Section 4.6 argues that the restated projection theory sheds light on the relations among agency, stability, and expectations. Finally, § 4.7 suggests that the restated theory clarifies some connections between property and personality. It is not intended to be a faithful restatement of Hegel. Its philosophical idiom, at least, is quite different from his. The historical discussion, here and in succeeding chapters, not only assists the formulation of a background theory of property institutions but also places the views of this book in the context of earlier speculation about property.

Since this chapter concentrates on interactions between persons and things in the world, it is important to recall the difference between the two conceptions of property first distinguished in § 2.1. One is the popular conception of property as things, and the other is the sophisticated conception of property as a bundle of relations among persons with respect to things. This chapter uses both. The context will suffice to determine how the word "property" is used in any given occurrence.

The immediate inquiry is restricted in three ways. First, this chapter does not attempt to justify any property rights. Such justification requires extended separate discussion,

1 This chapter for the most part follows Stephen R. Munzer, "Property, Incorporation, and Projection," *Noûs*, 23 (1989): 291–306, which is reprinted by permission of the editor of *Noûs*. Section 4.7, however, is new.

but, as § 4.6 points out, part of such a discussion can build on the projection theory. Second, the chapter is an analytical reconstruction that seeks to lay bare what is fundamental to any property rights in external things. To do that it disengages property from many of its usual surrounding social institutions. And it prescinds relations among human beings, for the most part, from any social group to which they may belong. No claim is made that the property rights discussed here are exactly like any actual property rights. Yet understanding the former is indispensable to a full understanding of the latter. Third, this chapter deals almost entirely with individual private property rights. This limitation begs no normative questions, for the underlying concern here is with whatever interactions between persons and the world can generate property rights. Whether the rights be individual or institutional, private or public, they depend on these interactions. It is just simpler to concentrate at first on individual private property rights. As a strategy of composition, one could start with social relations as basic to property and show how one must narrow this perspective in certain ways to take proper account of individuals. Part II of this book instead starts with individuals as basic and shows how one must enlarge this perspective to take proper account of social relations. In principle, either strategy is satisfactory so long as a balanced picture comes out in the end.

4.2 EXTENSION BY INCORPORATION

One putative way of acquiring property is by incorporation. This way need not depend on a claim about property rights in the body. If persons have property rights in their bodies, then it may seem attractive to reason as follows. "When I bring this thing into my body, it becomes part of me. What is part of my body is my property. Thus the thing becomes my property." Nevertheless, even if people had no property rights in their bodies, they might still claim property by incorporation. "At least I have personal rights in my body. These rights give my body a special status. Incorporated things become property because of this special status."

In a fascinating article, Wheeler elaborates this mode of acquisition.[2] Writing in the tradition that stretches from Locke to Nozick, Wheeler attempts to derive property rights from body rights. The operative image of the argument is that property rights are *extensions* of the body that result from *incorporating* external things into the body. It is not quite clear that the attempted derivation is meant to be a sober demonstration rather than a diverting spoof, or to apply to all rather than just a great many property rights. All the same, his argument repays attention.

One can summarize the argument in this way. (1) Persons have a right to exist as independent agents. Hence (2) they have a right not to have their agenthood terminated, as by someone else's destroying their brains. From this it follows that (3a) persons have a right to move and use their bodies as they please so long as they do not violate others' rights, and others have an obligation not to move, use, or transform their bodies against their will. In other words, (3b) persons have an *exclusive* right to move and use their bodies so long as they do not violate others' rights. Hence (4) they have an exclusive right to use anything that is open to acquisition and "incorporated" into their bodies, such as food converted into protein. (5) This right of exclusive use is a property right.

There are several gaps in the argument. One is that proposition (2) does not entail proposition (3a) or (3b). It does entail that others may not, apart from special situations like self-defense, kill a person or destroy his capacity for thought and action. Yet this entailment does not illuminate what

---

2 Samuel C. Wheeler III, "Natural Property Rights as Body Rights," *Noûs*, 14 (1980): 171–93. See also David Braybrooke, "Our Natural Bodies, Our Social Rights: Comments on Wheeler," *Noûs*, 14 (1980): 195–202; John Christman, "Can Ownership be Justified by Natural Rights?," *Philosophy & Public Affairs*, 15 (1986): 156–77, at 168–71.

other duties persons have with respect to the basic rights of others. It does not follow from proposition (2) that other people must refrain from interfering with him in lesser ways than killing him or destroying his capacity for thought and action. To hold that it does follow requires the questionable principle that no effective separation exists between terminating and diminishing agenthood. But in fact the standard cases of termination and diminution differ. This difference exists even if, because of vagueness in the concept of terminating agenthood, there is some marginal indeterminacy and so no sharp boundary separates one from the other. Hence the argument establishes no *exclusive* right for a person to move and use his body as he pleases so long as he does not violate others' rights.

Another gap is that proposition (4) does not follow from proposition (3a) or (3b) in the way that the argument contemplates. The step may hold for the case of food converted into protein. But Wheeler intends that the argument apply to a much wider range of "incorporation." It applies also to the addition of natural or artificial body parts, of clothing and houses, and, given a right of transfer, of money and things that others have an exclusive right to use. The wide scope given to "incorporation" appears connected with his notion that a person's right to move and use his body is independent of, *inter alia*, the fact that body parts are attached, have sensation, and can be controlled by the agent. But this notion and the implicit range of "incorporation" are misguided. The concept of incorporation presupposes that the item incorporated is within or on the normal contours of the human body. Wheeler's likening of clothes to feathers on birds and of houses to shells on turtles is unsound. That *some* species have body parts that can function as raiment or shelter does not show that *all* species, including human beings, can have them. This limitation precludes the "incorporation" of clothes and houses, automobiles and factories. Whatever rights, if any, exist over them do not derive from their "incorporation" into the body.

Still another gap is that proposition (4) does not entail proposition (5). Undoubtedly the "right" to exclusive use of protein in a person's own body is a specially intimate right. But the concept of a specially intimate right with respect to the body is not identical with the concept of a property right. A person may have a property right in a steak or an apple in its original form as food purchased from a grocery store. It would, though, normally be odd to say that he has a property right in the protein or waste products into which his body has metabolized these foods. This final gap may appear to be minor. Yet it illustrates how the attempted derivation conflates typical body parts and typical items of property, and then goes on to conflate typical rights with respect to the body and typical property rights. As § 3.3 shows, some body rights should be thought of as personal rights rather than property rights.

These gaps do not destroy the incorporation theory, but they do make it implausible. For incorporation usually has little bearing on property rights. An exception may lie in introducing things that become body parts. If food becomes tissue or a bit of metal becomes a dental filling, and if there are property rights in body parts, then perhaps these things become property by incorporation.[3] But the vast majority of things in which people claim property rights remain outside the body. They are too large, toxic, or inconvenient to incorporate. Thus very little acquisition involves incorporation in a literal sense.

It might be replied that the incorporation theory is better understood as a nonliteral interpretation of property rights – as involving symbolic, figurative, or metaphorical incorporation. The thought might be that if persons have a right to

---

3 Thus, Locke writes that the "Fruit, or Venison, which nourishes the wild *Indian*, . . . must be his, and so his, *i.e.* a part of him, that another can no longer have any right to it, before it can do him any good for the support of his Life." See John Locke, *Second Treatise of Government* [1690] § 26, in *Two Treatises of Government*, ed. Peter Laslett 2d ed. (Cambridge: Cambridge University Press, 1967) (emphasis in original).

exclusive control of their own bodies, then they can have a right to exclusive control of all things that do not differ in ethical significance from persons' bodies. But for this reply to be persuasive it must not only clarify in what nonliteral sense things are "incorporated." It must also defend the sorites argument on which this nonliteral incorporation rests. In particular, it must explain why the gaps identified earlier fail to show that there is a significant ethical difference between converting food into tissue and, say, putting on clothes or taking possession of a house. Faced with these difficulties, the incorporation theory is unpromising. A different theory is needed.

4.3 EMBODIMENT BY PROJECTION

An alternative way of understanding property rights in external things is projection. This way reverses the incorporation theory. Here the operative image is that property rights are *projections* of the body that result from *embodying* the person into external things. The projection theory can be variously elaborated. One method is Locke's metaphor of "mixing" one's labor with unowned things and so converting them into property.[4] A more detailed and sophisticated method is found in Hegel. This section summarizes Hegel's somewhat obscure account.

To understand Hegel's views it must be kept in mind that his discussion of property in the *Philosophy of Right* occurs in separate dialectical phases of the book under the headings of abstract right, the family, civil society, and the state. The idea that property is an embodiment or projection of personality belongs to the first phase of "abstract right."[5] There he writes: "Since property is the *embodiment* of personality, my inward idea and will that something is to be mine is not

4 Ibid., § 27.
5 G. W. F. Hegel, *Philosophy of Right* [1821], trans. T. M. Knox (Oxford: Clarendon Press, 1965 [1952]), §§ 41–71.

enough to make it my property; to secure this end occupancy is requisite. The embodiment which my willing thereby attains involves its recognizability by others."[6] This passage calls for an explanation of what Hegel means by personality, by its embodiment in external things, and by its recognizability by others.

For Hegel "personality" means roughly the self-actualization of the individual through acts of will. In willing freely individuals define themselves as separate entities and as bearers of moral and political rights. Thus the term "personality" in Hegel's writings does not mean anything like the popular notion of individual flair or panache. Rather, personality involves the initial stage in which persons by willing set themselves off from and assert rights against other persons.[7] Here property is extremely important. For Hegel thinks that the relations that individuals have, in terms of their moral and political personhood, to other individuals stem initially from their respective rights of property.[8] In order to understand these thoughts it may help to look at them from the standpoint of intellectual history. Hegel views personality as the kind of formal moral and political personhood discussed by philosophers of the Enlightenment, especially Kant.[9] They often thought of persons as entities having moral and political rights, in particular rights of property. So it is no surprise that Hegel says: "Personality essentially involves the capacity for rights and constitutes the concept and the basis (itself abstract) of the system of abstract and therefore formal right. Hence the imperative of right is: 'Be a person and respect others as persons'."[10] Later

---

6 Ibid., § 51 (emphasis in original).
7 "Personality is the first, still wholly abstract, determination of the absolute and infinite will. . . ." Ibid., § 41.
8 "Right is in the first place the immediate embodiment which freedom gives itself in an immediate way, i.e. *(a)* possession, which is *property-ownership*." Ibid., § 40 (emphasis in original).
9 Immanuel Kant, *The Philosophy of Law*, trans. W. Hastie (Edinburgh: T. & T. Clark, 1887). Some of Kant's views on property are examined later (§ 6.3).
10 Hegel, *Philosophy of Right*, § 36.

he adds that "it is only as owners that . . . two persons really exist for each other."[11]

If this is personality, how does it embody itself in external things and so make them into private property? It does so by *occupancy,* which covers both taking possession of a thing and using it. Hegel's discussion of taking possession may seem at first only a turgid treatment of first possession borrowed from Roman law. He says that persons can take possession of something by grasping it physically, by "forming" it (which includes tilling the soil, cultivating plants, and taming and feeding animals), and by marking it as theirs. Physical grasping may appear to be the paradigmatic mode of taking possession, but it is temporary and restricted in scope. Forming something and, even more, marking it as one's own are less restricted and more sophisticated ways of taking possession. Use of things, especially their persistent use, is the more developed mode of occupancy. The contemporary reader will rightly be intolerant of obscurities in Hegel's discussion and skeptical of the sharp separation of taking possession and use. Still, the analysis articulates the idea that persons, bodies, and property are intimately connected. Persons by using their bodies cause changes in external things and thereby assert claims to them. They project or embody their personality in them. That is how unowned things can become property.

To grasp the importance of causing physical changes in external things it is necessary to see why Hegel requires that the embodiment of a person's will be recognizable by others. The root idea, which the next section recasts more precisely, is that property is an intersubjective concept. Property could not exist, Hegel seems to think, if there were only one human being in the world. For a person to have something as *his or her property* there must be other persons who (1) do not have it as their property and (2) can recognize that the thing belongs to someone else. The first condition requires

11 Ibid., § 40.

the existence of other people so that the contrast between "his" or "hers" and "theirs," and between "his" or "hers" and "not his" or "not hers," makes sense. The second condition shows why Hegel requires some physical transformation – grasping, forming, marking, using – to convert non-property into property. Without such transformation other persons could not tell that someone had already projected his will into the thing.

Although the immediate purpose is expository rather than critical, to forestall misunderstanding, let several objections be clear. In contrast to Hegel's view,[12] it is not only, or even mainly, as owners that persons exist for one another. Furthermore, Hegel errors in thinking that if persons embody their will in an unowned object, they necessarily acquire a right to *own* rather than merely a right to *use*. Indeed, they may not even get the latter if the unowned object is closed to ownership and use. Hegel writes: "A person has as his substantive end the right of putting his will into any and every thing and thereby making it his, because it has no such end in itself and derives its destiny and soul from his will. This is the absolute right of appropriation which man has over all 'things'."[13] To ascribe to persons such an unlimited right over nature is, however, to assume a particular outcome of some controversial issues in environmental ethics. The putative justification offered by Hegel – that external things have no will – is inadequate. This shows that unowned things differ from human beings. It does not show that human beings have a right to own them; still less does it prove that they have an "absolute" right of appropriation. Moreover, even if unowned things have no will or right to object, other persons do. As Chapter 10 shows, a person's liberty and power of acquisition are curtailed by various factors, including the impact of the acquisition on others.

12 Ibid., § 40.
13 Ibid., § 44.

4.4 TWO TRANSCENDENTAL FEATURES

In order to restate the projection theory more precisely, it is important to isolate some transcendental features of property. A "transcendental" feature of property is a condition on the possibility of property as it can exist for human beings. Two such features are latent in Hegel's account. One is the essential intentionality and causality of owners of property. The other is the essential materiality of property. Although transcendentality is stronger than universality, neither feature is "transcendental" in the sense that something lacking either or both features would be unintelligible to human beings, or even unintelligible to them as the property of a very different species. The word "transcendental" as used here differs, of course, from the term "transcendent" as used of something that exists apart from the material world. Whereas "transcendent" in this sense is opposed to "immanent," "transcendental" is opposed (roughly) to "derived from experience."

The first transcendental feature means that property must, at some point, involve the intentions of entities that can cause physical changes in the world. The qualification "at some point" is important. This transcendental feature does not require that *all* acquisition of property involve intentions by the acquirer. For example, one may inherit property unawares. Nor does it require that *all* acquirers of property be capable of having intentions, as a corporation that purchases a factory demonstrates. Nevertheless, the first transcendental feature does imply that at least all initial acquisition – that is, acquiring a thing for the first time – is intentional. It also suggests that the standard case of other acquisition is intentional, and that corporate owners ultimately must be owned by entities capable of having intentions.

The case for calling this feature transcendental is as follows. If either intentionality or causality were missing, intersubjective recognizability would be impossible. Such recognizability does not require acquiescence or actual

71

recognition, or even the existence of more than one person in the world.[14] But it does require that it be possible for other human beings, if there are any, to recognize that a person is claiming property rights. Given the way that human beings can acquire knowledge of matters of fact about the external world, there must be intentionally caused changes to recognize. Thus if persons were like stones, there would be no normative claim to recognize. For stones cause physical changes not through intentional acts but only through being propelled against other material objects by extraneous physical forces. Or if persons were telepathic (but not telekinetic), unembodied entities with neither spatial location nor physical causality ("ghosts"), they could cause no physical changes in the world. Hence there would be nothing to recognize. Therefore, in neither case would there be any way for anyone to recognize anything as belonging to anyone else. Since the idea of property presupposes intersubjective recognizability, there would be no property rights in external things. It is, then, essential to such rights as they can exist for human beings that property involve, at some point, the intentions of entities that can cause physical changes in the world.

The second transcendental feature is the essential materiality of property. It means that property must, at some point, involve material objects. Once again the qualification "at some point" is important. This transcendental feature does not mandate either that all property be material or that all property rights be rights in material objects. Intangible property, such as copyrights and patents, is a counterexample to these putative requirements.

To clarify and establish this feature requires resolution of two issues. One is how embodied entities such as human persons can have property in nonmaterial things. The answer is: only through some physical manifestation. Intang-

---

14 This chapter takes no position on whether, if there were only one human being in the world, that individual could form the concept of a person.

ible property is not property in abstract things or ideas *tout court*. Copyrights and patents, for example, traditionally require some writing or drawing or model through which rights are claimed. Nor would the power to exclude be effectual unless there could be rules pertaining to physical manifestations of intangible property. An example would be a legal rule forbidding people to produce a patented machine without a license from the patent owner.

The other issue is how far certain unembodied entities (ghosts as defined above) could have property in material things. The answer is: only to a limited extent. Suppose that there are ghosts. Given telepathy, they can communicate intentions to one another regarding material things. They might invent their own spectral system of titles. They might even, as does human society, regard their system of property as an indicator of status. But ghosts could not occupy or physically use or physically transfer material things, since ghosts are not telekinetic and have no spatial location. Nor could they exclude one another from material things. Thus most of the point of human property would be lacking.

It is, therefore, essential to property as it can exist for human beings that it involve, at some point, material objects. Without a physical manifestation people cannot have rights in nonmaterial things. And without the embodied nature of persons most of the point of human property would be absent. These reflections suggest that the two transcendental features of property are connected. For unless property owners are entities that can have intentions and cause physical changes in the world, they cannot have property rights in a significant way. These transcendental features amount to a creative way of elaborating on Hegel's remark above that "my inward idea and will that something is to be mine is not enough to make it my property; to secure this end occupancy is requisite."[15]

To conclude this section, notice a conceptual and a normative point about the restated projection theory. The con-

15 Hegel, *Philosophy of Right*, § 51.

ceptual point is that, if property has these transcendental features, it is possible to grasp more clearly a connection between the popular and sophisticated conceptions of property. The present discussion shows that the popular conception, which views property as things, is not, as some philosophers and lawyers might think, wholly misguided. Given the essential materiality of property, material things must be involved, at some point, even in the case of intangible property. And, given the essential intentionality and causality of owners, property must, at some point, involve intentionally caused changes in material things. In these qualified respects, material "thinghood" plays an important role in property. The present discussion also shows that, in claiming property rights, one must claim certain relations that, at some point, involve intentionally caused changes in material things. The sophisticated conception of property, which views property as relations among persons with respect to things, is still the more serviceable conception for most analytical purposes. Nevertheless, the popular conception has a depth which might be overlooked.

The normative point is that recognizing a right to the necessities of life is compatible with the projection theory. Someone might object: All persons have, by being born, a right to life and therefore a right to the necessities of life; but then property rights to these necessities do not derive from either projection or incorporation. The reply is: Even if such a right exists, it amounts only to a *general* claim on the world's resources. To convert that claim into a property right to *particular* things requires projection (as in gathering food, putting on clothes, or constructing shelter) or, in a few cases, incorporation (as in eating food that becomes tissue).[16]

16 In rare cases the distinction between projection and incorporation is indeterminate. If in one motion someone scoops berries from a bush into his or her mouth and swallows them, there is just such a borderline case. Yet it does not follow from the existence of borderline cases that standard cases fail to present a clear distinction. But cf. Locke, *Second Treatise of Government*, § 28; Thomas Mautner, "Locke on Original Appropriation," *American Philosophical Quarterly*, 19 (1982): 259–70, at 262, 264. A standard case would be one in which, say, grain is

4.5 INTENTION AND CONVENTION

The role of intention under the restated projection theory needs amplification. If property has the transcendental features described, then it is possible to interpret the projection theory in a nonmetaphorical way. The theory does not require that personality be injected into things much as coloring might be put into liquid or a dye into cloth. Rather, to say that persons project or embody themselves into things just requires that they interact with the world in a manner that manifests the two transcendental features. This interpretation avoids some difficulties with Locke's metaphor of mixing one's labor with unowned things in order to gain property rights in them. Nozick punctures this metaphor. "[W]hy isn't mixing what I own with what I don't own a way of losing what I own rather than a way of gaining what I don't? If I own a can of tomato juice and spill it in the sea . . . , do I thereby come to own the sea, or have I foolishly dissipated my tomato juice?"[17] The restated projection theory stresses that the person's intention in interacting with the world is to gain property rights rather than to expand effort to some other purpose or to no purpose at all. If Alexei inscribes "Alexei + Anna" inside a heart that he has gouged into a tree, he would rarely be claiming property rights in the tree or even in his drawing. He would be proclaiming his love for Anna.

No way exists to fix precisely the minimum content of an intention to gain property rights. Persons need not intend to obtain rights that are indefinite in duration and transferable *inter vivos* and at death. But they must intend to claim some

---

planted, some weeks later harvested, then milled, then stored on a shelf, after a while made into bread, and finally eaten in a day or two. *Pace* Mautner, this case does not involve a "continuous process," for there are interruptions; it is not "arbitrary" to distinguish among these various activities; and there is a lot of difference between "grabbing" and "gobbling."

17 Robert Nozick, *Anarchy, State, and Utopia* (New York: Basic Books, 1974), pp. 174–75. For Locke's reference to mixing one's labor, see Locke, *Second Treatise of Government*, § 27.

Hohfeld–Honoré normative modalities or incidents regarding the things with which they interact. They seem almost certain to insist on the claim-rights to possess and use and the power to exclude. They are likely also to insist, for example, on a claim-right to damages from someone who later destroys the thing, or a power to transfer it to a family member, or an immunity against forced transfer without compensation. If it is not clear what intentions, if any, persons have, one may need to impute intentions based on behavior. Such imputation is apt to be questionable if interpretations of behavior are biased or based on insufficient knowledge. For instance, the United States Supreme Court has usually given little weight to aboriginal Indian possession.[18] This outcome may turn partly on the claim that such possession reveals no intention to have property rights in the full sense of Anglo-American property law. This claim is questionable. Even if it were accurate, it would not follow that the United States legal system has treated Indian interests fairly.

A vexed issue remains. What is the interplay, if any, between intention and convention in property rights? Someone might contend that the restated projection theory places too much weight on intentions and fails to recognize an indispensable role for conventions. Social or legal conventions must prescribe *which* intentional acts suffice for property. Hegel's scattered references to occupancy doctrines from Roman law tacitly recognize this need.[19] But the need, it may be said, merits explicit, not tacit, recognition.

In order to assess this view, it is necessary to say something about conventions. For present purposes, a convention is a standing solution to a problem of coordinating behavior, which solution, over time, assumes a normative character. Driving on the right side of the road is, in the United States, a convention in this sense. Now since there are many vari-

---

18 See, for example, Johnson v. M'Intosh, 21 U.S. (8 Wheat.) 543 (1823); Tee-Hit-Ton Indians v. United States, 348 U.S. 272 (1955).
19 Hegel, *Philosophy of Right*, §§ 54–64 passim.

eties of human behavior, there are many species of conventions. One species is linguistic conventions. Here semantic and grammatical rules enable people to communicate. Of the many species of extralinguistic conventions, especially relevant here are the various social and legal conventions dealing with the acquisition of property. Social and legal rules often embody conventions. The rule of first capture for wild animals is one such legal convention.[20]

If these brief remarks on conventions are sound, then one must distinguish as follows. For property rights there must, at some point, at least be (1) an embodiment of (2) a person in (3) external things through (4) an action done with an intention to claim property rights that (5) has effects recognizable by others. Some conventions may be necessary to do all this. If all this requires communication, and if communication requires linguistic conventions, then at least conventions of that sort are in play.

Yet it does not follow that social or legal conventions, or social or legal rules, are required. If the preceding arguments are sound, a rudimentary form of property is possible without them. In this form, the word "property," as understood in the popular conception, refers to things in the world that stand in certain relations to persons – namely, those relations that derive from the two transcendental features. These features are logically antecedent to, and must be reflected by, any social or legal conventions or rules. The features do not, of course, settle many details regarding such conventions or rules. But one cannot, on conceptual grounds alone, rule out the intelligibility of natural property rights—that is, moral property rights in a state of nature.

The upshot is that for property rights there is at most a necessary interplay only between intention and linguistic conventions. This conclusion is, however, subject to some serious qualifications. First, the intelligibility of natural property rights is not the same as their justifiability. Second, the

---

20 See, for example, Pierson v. Post, 3 Cai. R. 175, 2 Am. Dec. 264 (N.Y. 1805).

conclusion presupposes that one can separate linguistic from extralinguistic conventions. This presupposition might be false. It can be argued that some social or legal commitments can be built into the language that people use. [21] Third, even if property rights in external things do not *necessarily* involve social or legal conventions, plainly actual property institutions *in fact* involve them.

It is useful to illustrate this last qualification with a legal example. Consider the essential materiality of property. Earlier it was argued that only through some physical manifestation is property possible in nonmaterial things. Thus, copyrights and patents traditionally require some writing or drawing or model through which rights are claimed. However, legislatures or courts can institute legal conventions that allow for more transitory "physical manifestations." A recent California statue confers property rights in "any original work of authorship that is not fixed in any tangible medium of expression."[22] Under this statue, a group of musicians who are improvising might claim property rights in their performance even if they do not record it or transcribe musical notes onto paper. Here there is a physical manifestation, but it is a fleeting one. It is the sound waves propagated by the musicians that strike the eardrums of listeners. One might make an analogous observation about, say, the performance of a mime, even if it is not filmed or reduced to written instructions or descriptions. One can debate whether allowing such property rights as these is sound policy. But even these rights require some physical manifestation.

---

21 The argument might parallel Quine's claim that one cannot separate analytic statements, whose truth supposedly hinges on the meanings of words used to make them, from synthetic statements, whose truth depends on empirical facts. See Willard Van Orman Quine, "Two Dogmas of Empiricism," in his *From a Logical Point of View*, 2d rev. ed. (Cambridge, Mass.: Harvard University Press, 1961), pp. 20–46. But see H. P. Grice and P. F. Strawson, "In Defense of a Dogma," *Philosophical Review*, 65 (1956): 141–58.
22 Cal. Civ. Code § 980(a)(1) (Deering Supp. 1989) (amended 1982).

4.6 AGENCY, STABILITY, AND EXPECTATIONS

A salient aspect of the projection theory is its concern with agency. Agency, in its philosophical rather than legal sense, involves actions done from needs, wants, desires, motives, dispositions, inclinations, ends, purposes, plans, projects, and so on. Suppose that the word "ends" is used to apply to all of the above. Then willing and intending both involve ends. The role of willing in Hegel's version of the projection theory displays a concern with agency. So, too, does the role of intentionally caused changes in the world under the re-stated projection theory. A closer look at agency reveals a link between the Hegelian and utilitarian perspectives on property.

Agency sometimes requires stability. For though some ends are transitory, others are abiding. Of the latter, some, like maintaining a friendship, do not involve material things – at least not in any direct way. But other abiding ends do involve material things. Examples include growing crops, writing books, and developing a business. In such cases, the ends will be frustrated if the material things needed to achieve them are unavailable. It is no good trying to grow wheat if next week someone else can plow the field over for corn. Thus, stable possession and use are necessary to achieve some abiding ends.[23]

If, however, agency sometimes requires stability, then stability in turn sometimes requires property rights that generate expectations. It may not necessitate the freely transmissible property rights of indefinite duration common in Western legal systems. Yet at a minimum there must be secure access to possess and use material things so long as the end in question requires them. For persons would never pursue many ends unless such access could be guaranteed. It does not follow that these are good ends, nor is it clear what form the guarantees will or should take. Still, if such

---

23 Something resembling this line of thought may be found in Dudley Knowles, "Hegel on Property and Personality," *Philosophical Quarterly*, 33 (1983): 45–62.

stable property rights exist, and if expectations are dispositions to predict coupled with an attitude of desiring and
feeling entitled to count on the occurrence of the predicted
event (§ 2.4), then the rights will ground expectations about
the continued possession and use of material things.

These connections among agency, stability, and expectations link two intellectual traditions. One is the utilitarian tradition deriving from Hume and Bentham.[24] It insists
that all property worth the name grounds expectations. The
other tradition derives from Hegel.[25] It suggests that expectations relating to property stem from human agency. If
property-based expectations were absent from human experience, persons and their interactions with the world would
differ markedly from the way they in fact are. The intellectual linkage may surprise those who do not speak of
Hume, Bentham, and Hegel in the same breath, for traditional utilitarianism does not concern itself much with agency. The Hegelian tradition seems to supply a more penetrating analysis of expectations about property because it ties
them to an underlying account of human agency in the
world of things. Perhaps part of a justification of property
rights could build on this account. It is an open question
whether a sophisticated utilitarian could provide an account
of agency that yields an equally penetrating analysis of expectations and so diminishes the surprise.[26]

24 See David Hume, *A Treatise of Human Nature*, ed. L. A. Selby-Bigge
(Oxford: Clarendon Press, 1960 [1888]), bk. III, pt. II, §§ II–IV, pp.
484–516; Jeremy Bentham, *The Theory of Legislation*, ed. C. K. Ogden
(London: Routledge & Kegan Paul, 1931), pp. 109–23, 148–98.

25 Hegelian agency in turn has its roots in Kantian autonomy. Whereas
autonomy as understood in § 3.1 involves only a psychological capacity for self-government, Kant's conception of autonomy, among other
things, places much greater weight on rationality – in particular on
governing one's conduct by principles that square with the moral law
rationally understood. What seems common to Kant's and Hegel's
view is some idea that private property is indispensable to expressing
one's will and freedom and thereby creating oneself. For more on
Kant, see § 6.3.

26 The rudimentary sort of property argued for in § 4.5 does not require
expectations any more than it requires rules. Consequently, it differs
from the understanding of property advanced by George E. Panichas,

4.7 PROPERTY AND PERSONALITY

It remains to explore a prominent feature of Hegel's theory – the significance of personality. This preliminary discussion distinguishes connections of different sorts and strengths between property and personality, criticizes an uncautious psychological view of the connections, and suggests how succeeding chapters must enlarge the investigation.

In order to specify relations between property and personality, one must be clear on both. In fact, "personality" has different meanings, and failure to distinguish them only spawns confusion. If property presupposes that persons initiate changes in the world, then the changes are apt to have effects on their initiators. The effects correspond to three senses of the word "personality." These effects often resist cross-cultural generalization. They point to empirical, not necessary or transcendental, connections between property and personality.

Sometimes "personality" means moral and political personhood. This is Hegel's notion of personality. Is property *necessary* for personality in this sense? It does not seem so. It is true that, if property rights can be justified, they are one sort of moral and political right. But other sorts exist – for example, the right to vote or to be free from arbitrary arrest. If people succeed in claiming these other moral and political rights, then they have achieved moral and political personhood, even if they lack property rights.

Is property, however, at least *conducive* to personality in Hegel's sense? In two respects it seems to be. First, property rights are, other things being equal, an independent com-

"Prolegomenon to a Political Theory of Ownership," *Archiv für Rechts- und Sozialphilosophie*, 64/3 (1978): 333–56. Although actual systems of property involve both rules and expectations, the present account disagrees with Panichas to the extent that he supposes that the most fundamental sort of property must involve them. Also, Panichas's account oscillates between "reasonable" and "legitimate" expectations as if there were no difference between them (pp. 336, 339, 341), whereas in fact it is important to distinguish between them (see Stephen R. Munzer, "A Theory of Retroactive Legislation," *Texas Law Review*, 61 (1982): 425–80, at 429–35).

ponent of moral and political personhood. To cause changes in the world (for example, grasping, marking, using) in order to claim something as one's own is to claim a right over it. To do that presupposes that the claimant is an entity that can have rights. And that sort of entity is a moral and political agent. Second, property rights can, other things being equal, protect other rights. A common argument maintains that only property rights can make secure other moral and political rights. Even if the argument fails in this strong form, a weaker version is likely to show that property can play some protective role. If so, then property rights promote personality by sheltering other moral and political rights.

Nevertheless, the cautionary phrase "other things being equal," used for both points, signals that matters may not be so simple. If property rights have an adverse impact on other rights, whether rights of the property holder or of others, then the net effect of property rights may be to retard moral and political personhood. Also, Hegel's conception of personality, in the section on "abstract right," seems to presuppose an individualistic moral and political personhood. Yet perhaps there are other, communitarian views of moral and political personhood. If so, private-property rights might diminish personhood in the event that they foster the isolation of persons from one another.[27]

A different sense of "personality" is awareness of individuating characteristics. Property is not indispensable to the *existence* of the awareness. To consider it indispensable would be to hold that unless persons could stake intersubjectively recognizable claims to external things, they would be unaware of themselves as separate individuals. And to hold that is false. As soon in human prehistory as persons began to ascribe states of awareness – such as feeling pain or being tired – to themselves but not simultaneously to

27 Margaret Jane Radin, "Property and Personhood," *Stanford Law Review*, 34 (1982): 957–1015, at 971–78, 991–1013, draws on Hegel in developing and applying a communitarian theory.

all others, they possessed an awareness of themselves as individuals, even if there was no private property.

All the same, property might bear on the *degree* of self-awareness. Here some might claim that, for each person, self-awareness would increase in direct proportion to property, on the ground that to own more property is to have more individuating characteristics. They might also claim that, for societies, the rise of self-awareness would correspond to the rise of institutions of private property. These are bold empirical claims, and no way exists to test them here. Still, reflection casts some doubt on them. On the one hand, it is possible to imagine a society in which there is private property, but all houses, cars, clothes, and so on are the same. Here it is not obvious that private property heightens awareness of individuating characteristics. Here more property does not seem to lead to more self-awareness. On the other hand, it is also possible to imagine a society that lacks private property, or at least has very little of it, but supports persons' efforts to develop their talents, accentuate differences in personal appearance, and the like. Here less property may not lead to less self-awareness.[28] In assessing empirical claims, one cannot put much weight on a fanciful contrast. Yet if the contrast could be borne out, it would favor only a weaker claim: Private property has a bearing on degree of self-awareness, but it is only one factor among many.

Finally, there are many psychological conceptions of personality[29] and, in fact, a sizable psychological literature on

---

28 Compare the static examples in the text with a dynamic example in which a sect with mostly communal property and much uniformity in dress and behavior gradually allows its members more individual and familial private property. Some members may dress and furnish their homes differently from other members and so, perhaps, become more aware of individuating characteristics and express their own individuality. See Karl Peter and Ian Whitaker, "The Acquisition of Personal Property Among Hutterites and Its Social Dimensions," *Anthropologica*, 23 (1981): 145–55.

29 See, for example, Jess Feist, *Theories of Personality* (New York: Holt, Rinehart and Winston, 1985), pp. 8–9; Ronald Forgus and Bernard H. Shulman, *Personality: A Cognitive View* (Englewood Cliffs, N.J.: Prentice-Hall, 1979), pp. 9–11.

property.[30] Although these pages can do justice to neither, it will help to contrast two rather different psychological conceptions of personality. One understands personality broadly as a structure that determines the individual's thought and action in relation to the world. For example, Allport writes that "personality is the dynamic organization within the individual of those psychological systems that determine his characteristic behavior and thought."[31] Plainly, this definition is broad enough to allow for a great deal of empirical investigation of the relation of property of various sorts to different persons' beliefs, desires, attitudes, values, traits, and so on. Equally plainly, its breadth makes silly or out of place an inquiry into whether property is "necessary for" or "conducive to" personality in this sense. Yet though that inquiry is inappropriate, one can expect that specialized empirical studies might reveal much about the connections between property and one feature or another of personality so understood.

A different psychological conception understands personality as the desirable integration of the self's thoughts and attitudes. In the psychological literature on property, Beaglehole, writing over a half century ago, exemplifies this view of personality.[32] This view is not only less broad than the previous conception; it is also more explicitly evaluative. Beaglehole's account centers on the development of personality over time by *(inter alia)* both cooperation with and aggression toward others regarding property. He holds that property is necessary for, or at least conducive to, personality in this sense. Here, however, the concern is not with the details of Beaglehole's rather dated treatment but with some observations and distinctions that are pertinent to assessing any account of this general type.

30   See Floyd Rudmin, "Psychology of Ownership, Possession, and Property: A Selected Bibliography Since 1890," *Psychological Reports*, 58 (1986): 859–69.
31   Gordon W. Allport, *Pattern and Growth in Personality* (New York: Holt, Rinehart and Winston, 1961), p. 28.
32   Ernest Beaglehole, *Property: A Study in Social Psychology* (London: George Allen & Unwin, 1931), especially pp. 283–87, 295–312.

First, one must understand how much and what kind of property is meant. Suppose the claim is that property is *necessary* for self-integration. The claim is implausible if "property" here means substantial assets for both personal consumption and productive use. But if property means a few personal articles over which one has exclusive control, then the claim is less farfetched. Similarly, if the claim is weakened, so that property is only said to be *conducive* to personality, it becomes relatively more plausible – subject to what is said below.

Second, developing personality is not the same as retaining it. Even if people need property to develop self-integration, it does not follow that they must continue to own property in order to retain it. Some might question whether people could renounce forever the right to acquire property. Still, they could renounce the property that they currently own and in fact not acquire more later. Perhaps some monks and nuns, in taking and keeping a vow of poverty, do so.[33] It is implausible to say that they lose their personality.

Third, one should not exaggerate the role of property in self-integration. Suppose that the child's property plays some role. Even so, it is nonproperty in the form of other persons (parents, siblings, playmates) that is most important to development. Furthermore, much that is property and plays a significant role in personality development is not the *child's* property – for example, the home in which he lives, his neighborhood, the trees outside his window.[34]

33 John Tettemer, *I Was a Monk* (New York: Knopf, 1951), writes that, under the Passionist vow of poverty, the monk "renounces any possessions he may have and all right forever to possess or own any material thing" (p. 76). To express possession or belonging the monks generally used the first-person plural possessive, sometimes with amusing results – as when a novice asked "out of sheer habit permission of the novice master 'to wash *our* feet' " (ibid., emphasis in original). Tettemer had no power to revoke his vow, but his order eventually released him from it and other vows (p. 279).

34 Much of Beaglehole's discussion rests on the child psychology of his day and needs revision in light of current research. See the relevant entries in Rudmin's bibliography in note 30.

Fourth, quantifiers are important. Is an account of this type supposed to apply to all, most, or some persons, and to all, most, or some societies? The strongest claim – that it applies to all persons and all societies – is implausible. People vary enormously. Hence it is risky to maintain that all persons, in any society, need property to develop or retain personality. Societies also vary enormously. Hence one must tailor the claim to the society. In societies that place great importance on wealth and commodities, people who lack property may, perhaps, have stunted personalities. Yet in societies where there is little private property, or where little importance attaches to it, people who own little may suffer no dimunition of personality.

Finally, one must clarify the status of personality as self-integration. This is not a value-neutral concept. For it is implicitly contrasted with some other condition of the self – say, disassociated thought and behavior. Since this sense of "personality" is to some extent evaluative, one must explain and justify the respects in which it is so. It seems, in part, to involve a functional evaluation. It claims that people do better in society if they are self-integrated than if they are not. This claim seems correct. But notice that since societies vary, what is a functionally valuable form of self-integration is apt to vary. If so, "personality" does not cover some unique cross-cultural attribute of persons.[35]

This brief discussion points up how much remains to be done in order to provide a full background theory of property institutions. Stepping back, one can say that the projection theory is better than the incorporation theory at analytically reconstructing property rights. The best version of

35 The evaluation can also be partly moral or political. A close reading of Beaglehole's account suggests that he harbors an ideal personality. This personality fits very well a particular form of economic organization – namely, one variety of capitalism. But his methodology is suspect. He does not show that capitalism is a splendid economic system given the necessity of property for personality development. Instead, he tends to work back from a capitalist economy to construct a model of human personality which lends itself to that sort of economy.

the projection theory involves the two transcendental features described in § 4.4. This version illuminates some connections between property and personality. With qualifications, private property is conducive to personality as moral and political personhood. It also has a bearing on personality in the sense of self-awareness, but only as one factor out of many. And its connections with different psychological conceptions of personality appear difficult to ascertain.

In fact, the short treatment of personality, and especially of psychological understandings of personality, suggests at least three ways in which succeeding chapters must enlarge the inquiry. First, to the extent that property has a bearing on self-integration, it will help to explore other conditions and expressions of self-integration. This exploration in some measure looks back to Kantian and Hegelian themes of self-creation through the exercise of one's freedom. Yet it also looks forward to more concrete connections of private property with control, privacy, and individuality. Second, insofar as personality is a structure that determines a person's traits, attitudes, and values, it is necessary to appraise the effects of property on these features of personality. The appraisal should, of course, acknowledge Hegelian concerns about property and personhood. Yet it must not stop with the concept of a person but rather press on to the concept of a *good* person, and therefore should pay special attention to the bearing of property on moral character. Third, if property relates to one or more psychological conceptions of personality, it may be that some property institutions will have pathological effects on personality. Here the inquiry echoes Hegelian concerns about the stunting or deformation of personhood by poverty. But even more it has to address Marx's worries about private property and alienation. The next three chapters, then, take up these matters in turn. They aim not to develop a psychology of property rights but to complete the background theory of property institutions.

Chapter 5

Control, privacy, and individuality

5.1 PRIVATE PROPERTY AND EXCLUDABILITY

The preceding discussion of property and personality leaves at least two loose ends regarding personal characteristics and situations. It does not pursue things besides personality that property might affect. Nor does it relate property to economic organization. This chapter tries to rectify these shortcomings.

The discussion steers between two extremes and establishes an intermediate position. It rejects, on the one hand, the extreme view that private property is necessary to achieve the personal goods of control, privacy, and individuality, and that achieving them offers a powerful justification for private property. The discussion also rejects, on the other hand, the extreme view that private property has but a tenuous relation to these "goods," which, because they reflect either weird or "bourgeois" values, can hardly provide much of an argument for private property anyway. The chapter secures instead an intermediate position: Important connections exist between private property and control, privacy, and individuality. These connections hardly demonstrate that strong private-property rights are essential to a satisfactory society. But they do indicate that private property does some good things – though exactly which things, and how much good, varies from one economic system to another. The argument for this intermediate position is not a boring compromise. For it casts doubt on laissez-faire capitalism, repels the suggestion that charitable donations or welfare benefits can cure the evils of economic inequality, links property rights in certain economies to self-respect and self-esteem, and introduces the concepts of minimal and appropriately equal property holdings that will play key roles in Chapter 9. The present chapter, like its predecessor, formulates no explicit principle for justifying either public or private property, but it has implications for justification.

One can frame the investigation in this way. In the case of "private property," as defined in § 2.3, the owners are identifiable entities distinguishable from some larger group such as the state or community. Here are two further definitions. A "private-property system" is an arrangement in which most or at least a great deal of property is owned by individuals, by individuals considered together as with partnerships and cotenancies, or by artificial individuals such as corporations. A "private-property economy" is an arrangement in which the means of production are mostly privately owned and the market performs distributive, not just allocative, functions.[1] All private property economies are private property systems, but not vice versa.

The starting point of the investigation is *excludability*. An incident of ownership, listed in § 2.3, is the power to exclude (excludability). This incident means that the owner can legally exclude others from his property. In all legal systems the power to do so is limited rather than absolute. Excludability is not the same as *exclusion*, for owners might not exercise the power to exclude. In fact, however, owners often do exercise this power. Furthermore, excludability is not *exclusiveness*. Often several persons have legal interests in the same thing. Hence no one person necessarily has an exclusive interest. Familiar examples are joint ownership, as with partnerships

---

1 Distribution concerns the assignment of income and wealth to individuals. Allocation concerns the assignment of resources to various uses in order to promote economic efficiency. The distinction follows John Rawls, *A Theory of Justice* (Cambridge, Mass.: Harvard University Press, 1971), p. 273.

and cotenancies; the relations between mortgagor and mortgagee and between landlord and tenant; and the present interest of a life estate holder and the future interest of a reversioner or remainderman. Some interests, such as easements, are inherently nonexclusive.[2] Nevertheless, the various interest holders acting together, and sometimes each acting singly, can exclude others.

5.2 CONTROL, PRIVACY, AND INDIVIDUALITY

If owners have a power to exclude in a private-property system and economy, then they can establish and protect various personal goods. Among them are such overlapping items as autonomy, personality, self-respect, self-esteem, liberty, control, privacy, and individuality. These items are "goods" in the sense that they are often valued either in themselves or as means to other things that are valued or both. It does not follow that they are the only or the most important goods, or are incapable of misuse or perversion. It would take too much space and be somewhat repetitive to discuss all of these goods. Chapter 3 touches on autonomy and Chapter 4 on personality; the end of § 5.4 briefly discusses self-respect and self-esteem, which play a role in Chapter 9; liberty is rather broad, and receives some attention in Chapters 8 through 10. Here it will be most useful to concentrate on control, privacy, and individuality and their connections with excludability. The investigation will reveal a good deal about property and liberty as well. Cultures vary in the ways that property relates to control, privacy, and

2 See, for example, Thomas F. Bergin and Paul G. Haskell, *Preface to Estates in Land and Future Interests,* 2d ed. (Mineola, N.Y.: Foundation Press, 1984), chs. 2–4 (life estate holder and future interest holder); Cornelius J. Moynihan, *Introduction to the Law of Real Property,* 2d ed. (St. Paul, Minn.: West, 1988), chs. 3 and 10 (cotenancies and landlord and tenant); George E. Osborne, Grant S. Nelson, and Dale A. Whitman, *Real Estate Finance Law* (St. Paul, Minn.: West, 1979), chs. 1, 4–5 (mortgagor and mortgagee). For easements, see American Law Institute, *Restatement of the Law of Property* (St. Paul, Minn.: American Law Institute Publishers, 1944), §§ 450 et seq.

individuality. The illustrations to follow seem accurate at least for a developed late twentieth-century society with a capitalist or a mixed economy. For other societies, different connections may exist between property and these personal goods, and different illustrations may be required.

Control is the power to act, command, and restrain. Private property confers various forms of control. Consider a person who owns some personal property (money, clothes, books, furniture, a car, a boat), a single-family home, and a small factory that makes clothing. Since the owner has a power to exclude others, he has, first of all, substantial control over what *he* does with his property. Within broad limits he can spend his money as he wishes, wear and read what he likes, and travel where he wants. In his house and factory, he is not, of course, legally free to commit an assault or to create a nuisance. But save for actions that the law prohibits, restricts, or requires, he can legally do as he wishes. He can eat or smoke or rearrange the furniture in his house. He can stride the halls and inspect the records in his factory. Next, the owner has control over *others* because he can decide, within broad limits, who may read his books or use his car, and who may enter his home or business. This control stems directly from the power to exclude.

Another form of control, also directly related to excludability, is the owner's power to keep the *state* from interfering. Rarely may the state take his money or commandeer his car or boat without compensating him. The United States Constitution bars the government from quartering soldiers in private homes except in time of war. In many countries, the police may ordinarily conduct a criminal search and seize papers or other effects only with a warrant, and they must justify a proposed search before a magistrate will issue a warrant. The government may also be able to make civil health and safety inspections, particularly of the factory. Yet here, too, the owner's control over entry is substantial.

Still another sort of control is the owner's dominion over the *behavior* of others whom he allows in. He is, so to speak, a mini-sovereign over his personal effects and in his home and

91

factory. The legal extent of his sovereignty is apt to be greater in his home. In the workplace, his rights may be limited by wage and safety legislation or by union contracts. A final variety of control rests on protection from *misfortune*. Owning a significant amount of property can, of course, make one vulnerable to some misfortunes, such as large thefts, because one has more to lose. But large property holdings also provide some insulation from the financial and psychological impact of inflation, economic downturns, joblessness, and natural disasters. This protection is especially important in private-property economies with few social welfare programs.

In each of these five areas (except the last) legal, not actual, control is meant. If burglaries are rampant, the owner's actual ability to exclude others may fall well short of his legal power to exclude them. Actual control can also be affected by economic conditions. If many garment workers are unemployed, the factory owner may be able to set wages and working conditions more effectively than he could otherwise.[3]

It is no accident that the phrase is *"private* property." If a legal system is efficacious, so that legal and actual control substantially overlap, property ownership will also foster privacy. For present purposes, privacy is a condition in which the government and other individuals are not intruding into or gathering information about a person's acts, decisions, affairs, or intimate qualities.[4] Once again, excludability is central. Just as actual control may be thought of as the outward aspect of an efficacious power to exclude, so is

---

3 On property and control, see Morris R. Cohen, "Property and Sovereignty," *Cornell Law Quarterly*, 13 (1927): 8–30, and § 7.6 on property and power.

4 Academic discussions of the concept of privacy are in disarray. The rough definition in the text is intended only to fix ideas for the limited purposes of this chapter; it covers both what one might call intrusional privacy and informational privacy. For other approaches, see, for example, Ruth Gavison, "Privacy and the Limits of Law," *Yale Law Journal*, 89 (1980): 421–71; Tom Gerety, "Redefining Privacy," *Harvard Civil Rights–Civil Liberties Law Review*, 12 (1977): 233–96; W. A. Parent, "Recent Work on the Concept of Privacy," *American Philosophical Quarterly*, 20 (1983): 341–55.

privacy its inward aspect. Property functions more as a shield than a sword in the case of privacy. Privacy differs markedly from autonomy; the latter involves a psychological capacity for self-government and, unlike privacy, may be thought of as an aspect of liberty; still, excludability protects autonomy as well as privacy. Privacy is closely related to and overlaps, but is not identical with, solitude, seclusion, and secrecy; the power to exclude can be used to protect all of them. Privacy is important because it contributes, perhaps even is indispensable, to a sense of personhood, self-directed thought and action, and the capacity for love and friendship.[5]

As with control, it is helpful to isolate different ways in which privacy is sheltered by property ownership. To begin, the owners' power to exclude reduces the information about them which is available to other individuals and to the government. Next, it protects owners in the recesses of their homes and workplaces. They can do things that they regard as intimate, shameful, embarrassing, or just silly. Furthermore, the power to exclude hinders government regulation of intimate acts or relations with others, such as sexual practices. Lastly, it allows owners to keep out things that in-

The text defines privacy as a *condition* rather than as *control over a condition*. It is only a definition of *privacy*, not of a *right to privacy*. In regard to the latter, one should distinguish philosophical and legal, and within legal, constitutional and nonconstitutional, analyses. In a vast literature, see, for example, Kenneth L. Karst, "Right of Privacy," in Leonard W. Levy, Kenneth L. Karst, and Dennis J. Mahoney, *Encyclopedia of the American Constitution* (New York: Macmillan/Free Press, 1986), vol. 3, pp. 1577–81; William L. Prosser, "Privacy," *California Law Review*, 48 (1960): 383–423; Judith J. Thomson, "The Right to Privacy," *Philosophy and Public Affairs*, 4 (1975): 295–314; Samuel D. Warren and Louis D. Brandeis, "The Right to Privacy," *Harvard Law Review*, 4 (1890): 193–220.

5 See, for example, Stanley I. Benn, "Privacy, Freedom, and Respect for Persons," in J. Roland Pennock and John W. Chapman, eds., *NOMOS XIII: Privacy* (New York: Atherton, 1971), pp. 1–26; Charles Fried, "Privacy," *Yale Law Journal*, 77 (1968): 475–93; Joseph Kupfer, "Privacy, Autonomy, and Self-Concept," *American Philosophical Quarterly*, 24 (1987): 81–89; James Rachels, "Why Privacy is Important," *Philosophy & Public Affairs*, 4 (1975): 323–33.

terfere with their leisure, solitude, and thought processes. The law of nuisance, for instance, circumscribes the liberty of others to disturb owners by loud sounds, bright lights, noxious smells, or particles of dust or smoke. Here the protection of privacy afforded owners is indirect. It pertains, in any case, to security from intrusion rather than preventing information about them from flowing to others.[6]

In order to appreciate the manifold connections between property and privacy, it helps to distinguish between necessary and sufficient conditions, between popular and sophisticated conceptions of property, and between property however conceived and the physical condition of the world. Focus first on whether property suffices for privacy. Suppose that you like to sunbathe nude. The physical condition of the world is such that you must do so during daylight hours and that trees or roofs must not block the sunlight. Will property assure you privacy for nude sunbathing? If "property" here means "private property," and if, under the popular conception, this in turn means things, then owning private property need not yield privacy. For example, owning a large ranch will not ensure your privacy if the government or ordinary citizens can fly over your land in helicopters to watch you. The sophisticated conception views property as relations among persons with respect to things. If private property so conceived embraces a power to exclude, and if that power enables you to bar helicopters from flying over, then you can have more privacy for nude sunbathing than you would apart from that power. In short, although there need be no tight connection between property conceived as

6 On connections between privacy and the material conditions of life, see Fernand Braudel, *Civilization and Capitalism – 15th–18th Century*, vol. 1, *The Structures of Everyday Life: The Limits of the Possible*, trans. Siân Reynolds (New York: Harper & Row, 1981), chs. 3 and 4, especially pp. 203–09, 274–85, 304–11, 329–30. If people wash in communal bathhouses, sleep in dwellings that give everyone access to all places at all times, and lack eating utensils or closets and cupboards for storing personal items, then privacy will be greatly inhibited. Braudel exaggerates, however, in stating that "[p]rivacy was an eighteenth-century innovation" (p. 308).

things and privacy, there is a closer connection between the power to exclude, viewed as one stick in the bundle of property rights under the sophisticated conception, and privacy.

Now focus on whether property is necessary for privacy. Could you have privacy without property? Once again, the physical condition of the world is relevant. For example, suppose that apartments have thin walls and that they are crowded, that is, have a small amount of floor space per occupant. As a result, neighboring tenants may hear what is going on inside and thereby reduce informational privacy, and overcrowding within may interfere with intrusional privacy. Private property, understood as things, may not help. A privately owned apartment in Hong Kong could have thinner walls and be more crowded than a state-owned apartment in Prague. Certain private-property rights, understood in accordance with the sophisticated conception, may assist privacy if they embrace a power to exclude, but they are not pertinent, since the issue here is whether private property is necessary for privacy rather than whether it is sufficient. In fact, it is not necessary, because a society could have other legal rules that promote privacy. For example, it could have rules setting work and other schedules in order to hold to a minimum the number of persons in apartment buildings and in individual apartments at any given time. As an analogy, think of the rotation of sailors' bunks on a submarine. Such examples do not show that other legal rules can advance privacy as easily or as well as a power to exclude, but they do establish that this power and private property are not necessary for privacy.

Private property is also connected with individuality. Consider once more the person who owns some personal property, a single-family home, and a factory. The control and privacy afforded by these items of property enable him to develop his individuality – that is, his separate and special attributes as a reflective human being. Individuality is not ignorant self-fulfillment; it requires some self-awareness. But it should not be confused with narcissism. Nor is it the same as selfish or single-minded preoccupation with a person's own interests and aims. The development of individuality can take many different paths. A person can express his personality and taste in his clothes or his car. He can use the boat to fish and perhaps to proclaim that he loves the outdoors. In his home he can paint, write poetry, entertain friends, tell jokes, make love, raise children, do calisthenics. In his factory he can design dresses, purchase fabric, test the market, create a reputation, counsel workers, make money, enjoy power.

There is, though, no close fit between property and individuality. Those without property can also cultivate their special attributes. Monks and nuns can deepen their practice of prayer or contemplation; thinkers, poets, and baseball pitchers can practice their crafts. Again, those with property may do little that suggests the development of individuality; a person might watch game shows on television incessantly or sleep fourteen hours a day out of boredom. Moreover, a person with property might exploit qualities which seem undesirable and which therefore do not fit well under the honorific phrase "development of individuality." Examples are a person who decorates the house with a collection of beer cans to annoy his spouse and a ruthless entrepreneur who exploits employees. At this stage, the point is merely that private property, as a result of the control and privacy it affords, facilitates the development of some attributes that are generally regarded as desirable.

There are further qualifications as to how closely property relates to the goods of control, privacy, and individuality. (1) The relations can vary with type of property. Without modest amounts of personal property, many people would feel bereft of these goods. To own real property in the form of a modest home, though not essential, is also conducive to these goods. Both types of property ordinarily pose few risks to others' obtaining the same goods. But to own productive property, such as a factory, may not yield much privacy to the owners. And if factory owners wield their power oppressively, that may diminish employees' control over their lives and impair their individuality. With small farms and small businesses, the problems may be fewer and the personal benefits greater. The figure of Wang Lung in Buck's novel *The Good Earth*[7] attests to the importance of farmers' land to their control and individuality.

(2) For owners, property imposes burdens as well as confers benefits. Burdens such as liability to taxation and responsibility for management and proper use can adversely affect control, privacy, and individuality. For instance, wealthy persons who have their needs tended to by servants may find their privacy lessened. Again, great wealth can sometimes hinder control and individuality. Widely different writers have observed that often in landed aristocracies the property owns the person, not the other way round. Thus, even though as a general matter property enhances choice, sometimes it fetters its owners.[8]

(3) Income as well as property can promote control, privacy, and individuality. Income enables the recipient to rent property. In many ways, renting property is a good substitute for owning it. This is especially so if the income used for rent comes from secure, meaningful employment. Yet in any legal system in which the state may not take property without paying for it, income and property are not completely fungible. Property often provides more security and more economic, social, and political power than income. Income can disappear more easily than property – for instance, when there is widespread unemployment or the income derives from politically vulnerable welfare programs.

7 Pearl S. Buck, *The Good Earth* (London: Methuen, 1931).
8 Statements of the idea that aristocratic landed wealth owns and controls the person include Karl Marx, *Critique of Hegel's "Philosophy of Right,"* ed. Joseph O'Malley (Cambridge: Cambridge University Press, 1970), pp. 94–113; Sophy Burnham, *The Landed Gentry* (New York: G. P. Putnam's Sons, 1968), pp. 197–212. "Middle class" persons can also feel hemmed in by possessions. A few might even feel emancipated by an economic downturn that dictates lower consumption. See Cynthia Hollander, "Thanks for the Recession," *Newsweek*, July 25, 1983, at 11. There may be backsliding. See Anthony Brandt, "The Thrill of Owning," *Esquire*, May 1984, at 17–18.

Some types of income, as from an annuity or a trust fund, may be more stable. But they are unavailable to most people because they depend on prior accumulations. Moreover, such types of income may not promote individuality as well as income from meaningful work. One of the reasons property is important is that income and property are not wholly equivalent.

5.3 PROBLEMS OF DISTRIBUTION

If excludability is connected in these ways with the personal goods of control, privacy, and individuality, some may be tempted to make a pair of bold claims. One holds that these goods are an important part of the justification of private property. The other maintains that the best system of property is a particular type of private-property economy. That type is a laissez-faire capitalist economy. Here this means an arrangement in which almost all means of production are privately owned and operated for profit under competitive conditions with very little government regulation. A possible reason for making both claims as a package stems from a certain picture of human motivation. It shows individuals as moved by a desire to maximize satisfaction of their preferences and persons collectively as best able to achieve this end in a laissez-faire capitalist economy. Those attracted by this view of human motivation may concede that, in this economy, property will be distributed unequally. Yet they will insist that, all things considered, it is still the best type of economy.

This section attacks both claims and the associated picture of human motivation. The attack has only a limited purpose. It would get ahead of the story to offer any principles for justifying property. That is the business of Part III. Here the aim is to make a case for questioning an overly simple putative justification of a flawed economic system. The arguments that follow may seem a heavy hammer to use on the (to many) rather unattractive nut of laissez-faire capitalism. But, for those who find this form of capitalism attractive, it is to be stressed that the present arguments are not intended or claimed to be decisive against that economic system.

The guiding thought is that although laissez-faire capitalist economies do not necessarily create unequal distributions of property, as a matter of fact they do create inequalities that spawn serious problems. Assume *arguendo* that if property is distributed equally, then no problems arise because everyone will have equal amounts of control and privacy and an equal opportunity to develop individuality. Some might challenge this assumption in the alternative. Either equality will create problems of its own, or equality will be unmaintainable because of differences among human beings. This challenge may prove correct. It is put aside here in order to concentrate on a pair of problems stemming from unequal distributions. One is that some persons may not have enough property to develop *minimal* control, privacy, and individuality. The other is that some persons may not have enough property to develop *appropriately equal* amounts of these goods.[9]

The minimal level. The first problem arises in this way. Those who make both claims do not value property for its own sake. They prize it because it leads *(inter alia)* to control, privacy, and individuality, which are valuable either in themselves or for other ends or both. If these goods are thus valued, it is almost certain that those who make these claims suppose that there is some minimal amount of them which is desirable. They may, of course, differ over what that amount is and find it hard to quantify. Now persons can have greater or lesser amounts of property. Evidently they

9 In equating poverty with lack of property, the following discussion simplifies, since persons with high incomes are not poor even if, because they consume all of their incomes, they have less property than some with small incomes. "Wealth" is ambiguous. If it means property, then it is the opposite of poverty in the simplified sense just explained. If it means anything of economic value, then it includes income as well as property and so is not the opposite of poverty in the simplified sense.

can also have greater or lesser amounts of control, privacy, and individuality. If property is conducive to these goods, then the amounts are apt to be related. To put the matter cautiously: At low to moderate levels of wealth if other things are equal, the more property persons have, the more of these goods they are likely to have. It therefore appears that if persons have no or sufficiently little property, they may not be able to develop even minimal control, privacy, and individuality. The connections hold weakly if "property" refers to things but strongly if it refers to relations among persons with respect to things, and numbers a power to exclude among those relations (§ 5.2).

This argument involves two minimums – a minimal amount of property and a minimal amount of control, privacy, and individuality. The latter minimum is a partial function of the former. A definition of the minimal amount of property should include both objective and relative elements. This minimum cannot be set solely by an objective yardstick. Assets of $10,000 or annual income of $10,000 in 1990 dollars will be too high or too low depending on the society in question. Again, ownership of certain commodities, like so many articles of clothing and a home with so many rooms, will be too high for some societies and too low for others. But the minimal amount of property cannot be identified with the average amount of property. For, if it were, and if strict equality were lacking, then some would necessarily fall below any minimum set. Thus, the standard for the minimum of property would not be a useful criterion – unless, implausibly, strict equality were sought and the minimum defined as strict equality. These reasons suggest that a workable definition of the minimum must include both objective elements (say, the amount needed for subsistence) and relative elements (say, some largest permissible shortfall from the average level of property). For analogous reasons the minimal level of control, privacy, and individuality must also involve a mix of objective and relative components.

It is useful to make concrete the abstract possibility that less than a minimal amount of property may lead to inadequate control, privacy, and individuality. Imagine a person living in circumstances that are very common in many cities of the United States. She rents, under a written month-to-month lease, a run-down thin-walled apartment with two bedrooms in a deteriorating neighborhood. The apartment has running water and a toilet but inadequate heat and no air conditioning. She is without a husband but has six children ranging from three to twelve years. She works sporadically as a cleaner of offices and homes. Her private property consists of clothes, dilapidated furniture, some food, and several hundred dollars in cash.

Now consider the effects of this situation. As to control, she has the same legal rights as others to be free from unreasonable search and seizure, quartering of soldiers in peacetime, and unwelcome guests. However, the apartment lease probably grants the landlord the legal right to inspect the premises at reasonable times, and limits her legal rights to modify the apartment or accept additional permanent residents. She thus has less legal authority over the premises than a homeowner would have. Her actual control in any event is likely to fall well short of this. In a crime-ridden area she may suffer from burglaries and even assaults in her home. More pronounced are the effects on her privacy. Thin walls, common hallways, and other circumstances of apartment living make it hard to keep activities from the ears and eyes of neighbors and even, perhaps, from police surveillance. With so many children in a small home, she may find it difficult to keep personal effects and intimate acts from the attention of her family. This may interfere with her leisure and solitude, as may noise and smells from other apartments in the building. In many cities, the lack of air conditioning presents the choice in summer of sweltering in the home or forgoing privacy by going out to the street. For the development of individuality the consequences are substantial. The home environment and the financial inability to go elsewhere reduce the opportunities to cultivate her special attributes as a human being. The impact on control, privacy, and individuality comes partly from the physical condition of her immediate world (for example, a crowded apartment with thin walls) and partly from lacking certain incidents of property (for example, a power to bar inspections by her landlord). Even in light of all these effects, it follows only that she will have a harder time developing and maintaining minimal control, privacy and individuality, not that she will necessarily be without them. Still, the risk is great that she will lack minimal amounts of these goods.

It may be objected that although every person needs *some* minimal amount of these goods, it does not follow that all persons need *the same* minimal amount. The logical point is valid. Yet it would be a mistake to draw from it the conclusion that the low amount possessed by this urban apartment dweller exceeds her minimum. Even if people differ natively in regard to basic need for control, privacy, and individuality, socialization is likely to reduce those differences. Hence within any given society the minimal need may not vary so much. In the United States, which is the setting of the illustration, the minimum is apt to be elevated because of the high standard of living. Furthermore, the objection fails in any case to show that if there are pronounced differences in minimal need, those with more than the lowest minimum will invariably fall into economic classes of society where the minimum can be met. The apartment dweller in the example might have a high minimum that the circumstances of her life make it impossible to satisfy.

Appropriate equality. The reasoning that points up the problem of lack of appropriately equal control, privacy, and individuality is somewhat similar. It requires, however, several assumptions that were not needed earlier. One is that although no one has so little property that minimal amounts of these personal goods are not available to all, there are wide differences in property holdings. A second assumption is that across a broad range of levels of wealth, with other things being equal, the more property persons have, the more control, privacy, and individuality they are likely to have. This assumption is stronger than that used to discuss the minimal level of these personal goods, which applied only at low to moderate levels of wealth. It is, however, weaker than the proposition that at *all* levels of wealth, more property brings with it a probable increase in these goods. That proposition seems false. The burdens imposed by very large amounts of property can actually decrease these goods. A final assumption is that some normative principle of permissible inequality is available for evaluating distributions of both property itself and the goods of control, privacy, and individuality. As before, a mix of objective and relative components is needed to define when levels of property and of these goods are appropriately equal.

For purposes of the argument, it matters little what principle of equality is used, so long as some principle is admitted. Chapter 9 advocates a combined principle of justice and equality. It is premature to introduce that principle now, however, because an accurate grasp of its content presupposes the arguments of this chapter and Chapters 6 and 7. Accordingly, this section relies, for illustration, on two other possible principles of equality. One is utilitarian: Unequal distributions are permissible just if, and to the extent that, they lead to a larger amount of total satisfaction. Another, analogous to Rawls's difference principle, is: Unequal distributions are permissible just if, and to the extent that, they lead to the greatest amount of satisfaction for the least well off.[10] Once these assumptions are made, the rest of the abstract argument is similar. If at many levels of wealth more property likely means more control, privacy, and individuality, and if persons lack an appropriately equal amount of property, then they are likely to lack an appropriately equal amount of these goods. As before, these connections hold weakly if one understands "property" as things and hold strongly if one understands it as relations among persons with respect to things and counts a power to exclude among those relations.

10 The difference principle states that social and economic inequalities should be to the greatest benefit of the least advantaged. See Rawls, *A Theory of Justice*, pp. 60–65, 78–83, 302–03.

This abstract possibility can also be rendered concrete. Imagine a society with substantial natural resources and a population of fifty million. Exploitation of these resources together with international market conditions has created great wealth. Even though many products, especially auto-mobiles and luxury items, are imported, the balance of pay-ments remains favorable. Out of the total population, about five million people are quite wealthy. They enjoy large homes, have expensive cars and furniture, travel ex-tensively, and educate their children in academically super-ior schools. At the other end of the scale, about five million people live quite modestly. Their standard of living exceeds that of the apartment dweller described earlier. Yet they rent small homes or apartments, drive old cars or take public transportation, work for low wages, and send their children to mediocre schools. No law bars change of employment or residence, but little realistic prospect exists for social or eco-nomic advancement. If wealth were distributed more equal-ly, not only would the property holdings of the least well off rise, so also would the total amount of satisfaction in society. The distribution of property, then, is not appropriately equal under either the utilitarian or the quasi-Rawlsian principles given earlier.

Now consider the effects of this situation. The very wealthy have great legal and actual control over their lives, substantial opportunity for privacy, and enormous scope for developing their own special attributes. The five million who are least well off may have a dull existence in which actual control and privacy are modest and the opportunities for creative expression and free development are limited. Unlike the urban apartment dweller, the least well off possess a minimal amount of control, privacy, and individuality. But they have significantly lower amounts of these goods than those who are quite wealthy. The difference is significant because of the way the least well off are apt to view them-selves and their social world. They will likely see their eco-nomic and social opportunities as limited, decry the mediocre education available to their children, and resent the wealthy. These reflections, in turn, may undermine their sense of worth and endow their social perceptions with resignation or bitterness or both. It seems reasonable to conclude that the five million least well off probably lack appropriately equal amounts of control, privacy, and individuality.

It may be objected that "appropriate equality" can vary from one person to another and that, though every person will find *some* degree of inequality intolerable, it does not follow that all persons will find *the same* degree of inequality intolerable. As before, the logical point is valid. Still, it would be wrong to draw from it the conclusion that the inequality described above is appropriate. First, socialization may reduce any pronounced variation in native tolerance for inequality. Second, no guarantee exists that those with the greatest tolerance for inequality will number themselves among the least well off. Third, the objection in any case misses the mark. The issue is not what the least advantaged can psychologically put up with or fail to notice. It is what amount of inequality can be justified as a matter of moral and political principle.

Human motivation. It is useful to step back for a moment and look at some psychological and political presuppositions that commonly, though not necessarily, underlie the two claims considered in this section. The psychological presupposition is that persons act to maximize preference-satisfaction, and that important among their preferences is a desire for property. If persons' actions in satisfying their preferences benefit others, it is coincidental that they do so. Since property is limited, persons pursuing their own preferences are thrown into competition with one another. A second presupposition, political in nature, is that it is useful to allow persons to keep whatever they produce by their own labor and ingenuity. Allowing them to do so in an atmosphere of competition will increase the total social product to the greatest extent possible. It will not, of course, generate a limitless supply of property. The best economic structure, then, is a system of inducements, resting on the desire for property, to create more and more wealth. Since these inducements reside in a decentralized market system, the private-property economy par excellence is laissez-faire capitalism. A final presupposition, likewise political, is that the interests of society are in the end nothing more than the sum of the interests of all individuals. For each person to pursue his or her private interest, especially the desire for ever more property, simply is to pursue the public interest.[11]

Each of these presuppositions is partly incorrect. To begin, individuals' preferences are not so self-interested and necessarily antagonistic as portrayed. It is a psychological fact that human nature is so constituted that sometimes persons desire the good or happiness of others. Consequently, sometimes only the good or happiness of others can satisfy that desire. It may be protested that, even so, it is still *their* satisfaction that results. The protest is dubious. For if they desire the happiness of others, the object of their actions is still others' happiness rather than the satisfaction of their desire for it. But even if the protest is allowed, the point remains that persons are so constituted as sometimes to

11 The presuppositions can be seen as a reformulation of the view advanced in Adam Smith, *An Inquiry into the Nature and Causes of the Wealth of Nations* [1776], ed. Edwin Cannan and pref. George J. Stigler (Chicago: University of Chicago Press, 1976), vol. 1, bks. I and III, pp. 5–97, 399–445. There Smith relies on the division of labor and persons' endeavoring to "better their own condition" to yield, by an invisible hand, a "progress of opulence" in which society as a whole is better off. Though Smith has a favorable view of the division of labor in Book I (vol. 1, pp. 5–97), he criticizes it in Book V (vol. 2, pp. 213–486) because of its effects on workers. In *The Wealth of Nations* generally, Smith tends to take a narrowly economic view of self-interest. In *The Theory of Moral Sentiments* [1759], ed. Dugald Stewart (London: George Bell & Sons, 1892), however, Smith takes a more expansive view that is akin to the Butler-Hume position on human motivation sketched in the next paragraph of the text. Whether, and if so how, the two views are consistent is the "Adam Smith Problem." Albert O. Hirschman, *The Passions and the Interests: Political Arguments for Capitalism before Its Triumph* (Princeton: Princeton University Press, 1977), pp. 109–13, describes the problem, but despite his intimations to the contrary, it is difficult to see that he solves it. For related discussion, see §§ 6.3 and 6.4.

want to help others. In Hume's words, "there is some benevolence, however small, infused into our bosom; some spark of friendship for human kind; some particle of the dove kneaded into our frame, along with the elements of the wolf and the serpent."[12] It is, therefore, by no means coincidental that persons in satisfying their own preferences may benefit others. It is not, of course, necessarily intentional either. It results from the way people are psychologically structured. To use Butler's terminology, self-love and benevolence, though distinct affections, are not necessarily opposed to each other. Accordingly, the desire for property need not always throw persons into competition with one another. Both social conditioning and natural sentiments such as sympathy can lead to a structure of desires that relies less on competition and more on cooperation.[13]

The political underpinnings of laissez-faire capitalism are likewise vulnerable. If the account of human motivation is defective in the ways just argued, then it may not always be useful to allow persons to keep whatever they produce. Labor in an atmosphere of competition need not maximize

---

12 David Hume, *Enquiries Concerning the Human Understanding and Concerning the Principles of Morals,* ed. L. A. Selby-Bigge, 2d ed. (Oxford: Clarendon Press, 1966), p. 271.

13 The psychological assumption, to the extent that it is a variant of psychological egoism, is examined under the heading of "self-love" by Joseph Butler, *Fifteen Sermons Preached at the Rolls Chapel* [1726], ed. W. R. Matthews (London: G. Bell & Sons, 1964 [1914]), especially Sermon XI, "Upon the Love of Our Neighbour." At the end of Sermon XI, Butler observes that imagining there to be opposition between self-love and benevolence probably lies in a misleading analogy with property (pp. 180–81). He seems to argue that if happiness were like property, then there would be only a certain amount of it, and so if one person were to be happier, his or her neighbor must be less happy. Butler is right that there is no fixed quantity of happiness. But he is wrong about property if he means that there is a fixed amount of it and one person's gain must be another's loss. Not all versions of a market economy rely on the idea that persons are self-centered or selfish. See F. A. Hayek, *Law, Legislation and Liberty,* vol. 2, *The Mirage of Social Justice* (Chicago: University of Chicago Press, 1976), pp. 107–32, especially p. 110. However, Hayek's account still seems vulnerable to the argument in the penultimate paragraph of § 5.3.

the total social product. The largest product may spring from a system of inducements that stresses both competition and cooperation. Indeed, the course of history casts doubt on the proposition that utility is best advanced by laissez-faire capitalism. Among the notorious consequences of early modern industrial capitalist economies were enormous inequalities, the exploitation of one class by another, the dehumanization of both the exploiter and the exploited, inordinate political power for the propertied and little political power for the propertyless, and the undermining of the civil and political rights of those with little or no property, including the civil right of acquiring property.[14]

Furthermore, the relation between public and private interest is much more complicated than is assumed. If the criticism of the psychological assumption is correct, then the public interest will reflect the partly cooperative, or at any rate not necessarily antagonistic, character of many private interests. And should the objections to the political basis of laissez-faire be well-founded, then the public interest may require the restraint of private interests that, if pursued unfettered, would involve insufficient cooperation and produce many harmful consequences. Thus the interests of the community need not be so mundane as the interests of individuals, especially the desire for ever more property. In particular, the community is not bound to take individuals' desires and interests as it finds them. It may be appropriate to modify the existing motivational and economic structure in order to produce a more cohesive and egalitarian society.

These presuppositions commonly (albeit not necessarily) underlie the justifications of property that are in question. It should not be thought, however, that the presuppositions

14 Nineteenth-century accounts include, of course, Karl Marx, *The Economic and Philosophic Manuscripts of 1844*, ed. Dirk J. Struik (New York: International Publishers, 1964), and Émile Zola's novel *Germinal* (1885), trans. L. W. Tancock (Harmondsworth, Middlesex: Penguin, 1954). For academic histories, see, for example, E. P. Thompson, *The Making of the English Working Class* (New York: Vintage, 1966), and, for the preindustrial phase, Braudel's three-volume work, *Civilization and Capitalism*.

can be adjusted at will and the case for laissez-faire capitalism survive intact. The key difficulty is to show how adjusted presuppositions can generate the result that laissez-faire capitalism meshes optimally with human motivation. To illustrate, consider an attempt to substitute something close to, but slightly different from, a Butler-Hume view of human motivation. It is agreed that people do not act solely from self-interest. It is also agreed that people seek more than individual or joint economic goods. They have, say, desires for love or friendship or companionship. Thus, the idea is that people are structured psychologically so that happiness consists in satisfying a wide range of desires. The desires are for economic and noneconomic goods, both individual and joint.

But why should this revised view of human motivation comport better with laissez-faire capitalism than with some other economic arrangement? Given this view, it is appropriate to aim for that output of all goods which best satisfies human preferences. Even if laissez-faire capitalism produces the most economic goods, it may distort or retard the production of noneconomic goods. Some other economic system might do better. Moreover, no need exists to concede the idea that laissez-faire capitalism even produces the most economic goods. Since it aims at the maximization of economic output, it is a strange bedfellow for a theory of human motivation that encompasses both economic and noneconomic goods. It would thus be mysterious, and not a little wondrous, that laissez-faire capitalism should best unleash the economic productive capacities of human beings so structured psychologically. It is more likely that some other economic arrangement would respond better to their preferences even with respect to the output of economic goods.

Conclusions. If the foregoing examination is sound, one may draw some provisional conclusions. First, there are strong reasons for doubting that laissez-faire capitalism is the best type of economy. In fact, it appears to be highly objectionable. Second, one should be skeptical of the claim that the personal goods of control, privacy, and individuality are an important part of the justification of private property. At least in a private-property economy, problems of distribution can cause many to lack an appropriately equal, or even minimal, amount of these goods. Whether these goods can play some more limited justificatory role is unclear. Third, a common argument for laissez-faire capitalism relies on a dubious picture of human motivation. It is an open question what type of economy would be supported by a more accurate picture. Fourth, any account of the distribution of property should grapple with two distinct issues: whether everyone has at least minimal property and whether everyone has appropriately equal property. One issue deals with a threshold and the other with the narrowing of inequalities. At this point, it is not clear how to answer fully the question, "Minimum property for what?" "For at least minimal control, privacy, and individuality" is only part of the answer. It is even less clear how to specify the permissible width of inequalities of wealth. Clarity will result only when the full background theory of Part II is in hand, and will take the form of the Floor Thesis and the Gap Thesis defended in Chapter 9.

5.4 CHARITY AND WELFARE

Before these provisional conclusions can be confirmed and developed, two arguments should be examined. These may be called the argument from charity and the argument from welfare. If either is cogent, much of the sting of the previous section would be avoided. In fact, both arguments fail.[15]

---

15 An early but far-seeing analysis of property, poverty, and the limits of charity and welfare is offered by G. W. F. Hegel, *Philosophy of Right* [1821], trans. T. M. Knox (Oxford: Clarendon Press, 1965 [1952]), §§ 195, 241–48. These passages are illuminatingly discussed in Shlomo Avineri, *Hegel's Theory of the Modern State* (Cambridge: Cambridge University Press, 1972), pp. 147–54. See also § 7.2 below and Richard Teichgraeber, "Hegel on Property and Poverty," *Journal of the History of Ideas*, 38 (1977): 47–64. For suggestive discussion of the transformation of medieval Catholic forms of charity into Reformation and

The argument from charity runs as follows. A private-property economy would indeed lead to grave difficulties were no corrective action taken. Yet corrective action in the form of charity would actually result. Those having much property would be moved by sympathy and self-interest to share some of their wealth with the less fortunate. Such charity would repair the damage to the least well off. It would also produce another good – namely, beneficent action by the well-to-do with accompanying feelings on their part of having done what is morally right or even praiseworthy.

This argument is unsatisfactory. (1) Private charity does not redistribute property effectively. Insofar as identifiable misfortune spurs the wealthy to give, the donations may prove inadequate if the wealthy consciously or unconsciously avoid the poor, or if the poor do not come to their attention. There are many other motivations for giving – reputation, personal ties, business connections, tax deductions, and so on. Even so, the well-to-do may not give enough, or may give too much to some and too little to others.

(2) Charity can have an undesirable impact on the beneficiaries. Although receipt of monetary and other donations gives beneficiaries more opportunity for control and individuality in some ways, there are risks in receiving charity, in particular risks of dependence and fawning displays of gratitude, which can impair control and individuality. Establishing themselves as candidates for charity, and especially allowing themselves to be monitored for future dispensations, can diminish beneficiaries' privacy. In addition, they can experience some loss of dignity and autonomy.

Counter-Reformation forms and then into early modern charitable institutions, see John Bossy, *Christianity in the West, 1400–1700* (Oxford: Oxford University Press, 1985), pp. 140–52. At one point Bossy remarks: "Value for money, the decay of reciprocity, a sense that God had somehow transferred his favour from the poor to the rich, were dark shadows thrown by the erection of the edifice of professional charity" (p. 148).

111

(3) Charity can also have an undesirable impact on donors. It can create smugness, self-deception, or a false sense of nobility and generosity on their part. Donors may give idiosyncratically and hence respond more to their own biases and prejudices than the needs of others. They may give inadequately and still regard their duty as done or even see themselves as noble and generous. Most important, their acts of charity and concomitant feelings may blind donors to the causes of poverty and inequality, disable them from identifying their own possible responsibility for these misfortunes, and so leave the root causes of these ills untouched. Thus, while donors should have positive feelings about their charity, there is a risk that giving can have some undesirable effects on their character and self-knowledge.

These objections are not objections to charity as such. Charity is important in the public life of the community to supplement other funds. And works of charity, in their private aspect, may still be the performance, as the case may be, either of what persons ought to do or of what it is supererogatory to do. Nevertheless, the objections do establish that private charity does not eliminate poverty and inequality and carries substantial costs of its own.

The argument from welfare merits more extensive discussion. It holds that harmful distributions of property can be rectified by payments from the state that are viewed not as a gratuity or "handout" but as an entitlement. That is, if persons satisfy certain conditions – say, those specified in a statute or administrative regulation – then they are entitled to receive the welfare benefit specified. The most important such benefits would be poverty assistance, old-age benefits, and unemployment compensation. Their purpose is to give everyone a minimal amount of property and, to a lesser extent, to even out distributions of income and wealth. They should, therefore, provide for all at least a minimal amount of control, privacy, and individuality, and perhaps also an appropriately equal amount of these goods. Since the various welfare benefits are viewed as entitlements, these ends can be accomplished without loss of autonomy by recipients.

Indeed, it is vital that these entitlements be seen not only as claim-rights to certain benefits, which bring in the interest component of a theory of rights, but also as liberties to spend welfare payments as the recipient desires and as powers to invoke a hearing process if benefits are denied, which introduce the will component.[16]

This argument is also unsatisfactory. For a start, it appears essential to a sense of worth to think of welfare benefits as entitlements, yet it is often difficult to do so. They are at best entitlements only in the conditional sense that if persons meet the conditions in the statute or regulation, then they have a right to the benefits. Aside from the statute or regulation they have nothing. Hence their "entitlement" can be diminished or eliminated if the statute or regulation is modified or repealed. And not only are claim-rights to benefits vulnerable; liberties to spend benefits as desired and powers to compel a hearing are on even thinner ice; the net result is to retard autonomy and to increase dependency.

Moreover, government benefits differ. Only some of them are plausible candidates for being called entitlements. The case is fairly strong for, say, old-age benefits that are provided in a scheme of social insurance. Here contributions are required of all workers, benefits are proportional to contributions, and the entire arrangement functions as a substitute for a private annuity or a private pension plan. The case is less strong for unemployment benefits. And it is weak for most forms of poverty assistance. Often these are more like a gratuity, even though, unlike private charity, they do not rest on the unfettered discretion of a donor but on legal requirements.

As a matter of social psychology, many welfare benefits are not conceived as entitlements – by recipients, by other citizens, or both. Other citizens especially are apt to view poverty assistance as state charity or, pejoratively, as a

---

16 On this last point, see Carl Wellman, *Welfare Rights* (Totowa, N.J.: Rowman and Littlefield, 1982). On "will" and "interest" theories, see in the present book Chapter 2, notes 8 and 14, and Chapter 3, note 9.

"handout." If an argument could show that people have a moral right to subsistence, the case for regarding some welfare benefits as entitlements might seem won. But such an argument, even if sound, will fail to convince many people. If the unconvinced are the majority, and if they view welfare benefits as a handout, then the current climate of opinion will be such as to lower welfare recipients' sense of worth.

At all events, most welfare programs do little to erode inequalities in income and property. Perhaps Sweden is a leading exception. But in the common run of welfare systems the main object is to provide subsistence when unemployment, illness, or old age threatens the ability to survive. As a result, most systems endow persons with only a *minimal* amount of property and thus provide, at best, only minimal control, privacy, and individuality. Left untouched, then, is the problem of providing *appropriately equal* amounts of property and these personal goods.

In fact, there are reasons for doubting whether most welfare programs provide even *minimal* control, privacy, and individuality. One reason is that the operation of such programs often undermines these goods. The problem arises in this way. If a welfare system does not monitor initial and continuing eligibility for benefits, then its costs rise enormously through laxity, oversight, fraud, and other causes. But if the system monitors effectively, then though costs may be held in check, the aims of the system suffer. Consider poverty assistance. Initial eligibility will require proof of income level and other requirements of the statute that provides for welfare benefits to the poor. To gather this information is often to intrude on applicants' lives. Later assessment of continuing eligibility and proper use of benefits may be even more intrusive. It can involve, for example, home visits by government caseworkers.[17] Consider also that monitoring may respond to the political passions of the time. A striking example concerns social security old-age benefits in the United States. In the McCarthy period, the Supreme

17 See Wyman v. James, 400 U.S. 309 (1971).

Court upheld a statute making deportation for membership in the Communist Party a ground for terminating benefits.[18] It did so even though membership was neither illegal nor a ground for deportation when the person later deported was a member, and even though the system required contributions of all workers. The Court's decision impaired the deported person's control and opportunity for individual development in his last years.

Another reason for doubt is that, over the long run, persons may exhibit an objectionable dependence on a system of welfare. The dependency and its effects take various forms. In the United States, evidence is growing that second and third generations of some families receive poverty assistance for years. More precisely, whereas white families often cease to be poor and their poverty generally does not persist across generations, most persons who remain poor and whose children are apt to remain poor belong to racial or ethnic minorities.[19] Thus arises a permanent "underclass" marked by chronic joblessness, widespread illegitimacy and single-parent homes, and inadequate skills and education. If, instead, a country were to adopt a much more thoroughgoing welfare system, designed to erode differences in income and property and to provide lifelong security, there is a risk that the system could spawn an enormous and officious bureaucracy. The results could include diminished incentives to work, great intrusion into personal affairs, and a dullness or listlessness on the part of many people. It may be that the more enveloping a system of benefits is, the greater is the risk of stagnation.

These objections are not objections to public welfare programs as such. Few societies can do without them. They are vital in giving needy persons at least some assistance. All the

18 Flemming v. Nestor, 363 U.S. 603 (1960).
19 See, for example, Kenneth L. Karst, *Belonging to America: Equal Citizenship and the Constitution* (New Haven: Yale University Press, 1989), p. 125; William Julius Wilson, *The Truly Disadvantaged: The Inner City, the Underclass, and Public Policy* (Chicago: University of Chicago Press, 1987), pp. 26–29, 63–92, 174–77.

same, the objections show that welfare systems, at least in their current forms,[20] offer no adequate solution to problems of unequal distributions of income and wealth. They do little to ensure appropriately equal control, privacy, and individuality unless they depress these goods for many. Nor do they provide very well a minimum level of these goods. To some extent, welfare programs even retard attainment of the minimum.[21]

A final note: Private charity and public welfare also have an effect on the personal goods of self-respect and self-esteem. These words are often used interchangeably, but one can see them as standing for separate but related concepts.[22] Self-respect is a state of regarding oneself as having inner moral worth. Self-esteem is a sense of one's worth deriving from one's characteristics, advantages, and attainments. A person's self-respect can be too low, but it is problematic to say that it can be too high. Ordinarily, people are aware of their level of self-respect, but room for misapprehension exists. For example, if slaves or members of a low caste fail to display resentment or indignation at violations of their moral rights, or if they feel no degradation after

20 Little reliable evidence is available on so-called "workfare" programs, which have been tried in a few cities. "Workfare," strictly speaking, is an obligation to perform unpaid work in return for welfare benefits. More broadly, some job-search or skills-training requirement may be imposed. See Judith M. Gueron, *Work Initiatives for Welfare Recipients: Lessons from a Multi-State Experiment* (New York: Manpower Demonstration Research Corp., 1986). After three years of a five-year study, the interim findings challenge some claims made by both defenders and critics of workfare.

21 For concern in the United States about "government largess" (which is broader than, but includes, welfare programs), see Charles Reich, "The New Property," *Yale Law Journal*, 73 (1964): 733–87. Reich's work is criticized from different angles in, for example, William H. Simon, "Rights and Redistribution in the Welfare System," *Stanford Law Review*, 38 (1986): 1431–1516; Stephen F. Williams, "Liberty and Property: The Problem of Government Benefits," *Journal of Legal Studies*, 12 (1983): 3–40.

22 The text draws heavily on, but does not entirely follow, David Sachs, "How to Distinguish Self-Respect from Self-Esteem," *Philosophy & Public Affairs*, 10 (1981): 346–60.

abusive treatment, they have low self-respect, even were they to claim that they have adequate self-respect. In contrast, a person's self-esteem can be too high as well as too low. Thus, an arrogant person may have excessive or unwarranted self-esteem. People are generally aware of their level of self-esteem, but room for misassessment exists here, too. Loss of self-respect can, but need not, be a ground for lowered self-esteem, and retaining self-respect in the face of difficult circumstances is a ground for keeping up self-esteem. A lowering of self-esteem often does not reduce self-respect.

If substantial inequality in income and wealth exists, and if charity or welfare is enlisted to reduce it, the consequences are apt to be graver for self-esteem than for self-respect. Self-respect, as a regard for inner moral worth, is compatible with great material inequality. Recipients can view charity and welfare as acknowledgments of that moral worth, and providers of help need not fear developing too much self-respect. Although low self-esteem can sometimes produce low self-respect, often only extreme differences in social status, as in slave or caste societies, will generate low self-respect. Yet redressing economic inequality, by either charity or welfare, can have a serious impact on self-esteem. Recipients can feel dependent, powerless, cheapened; their low self-esteem is undesirable. Providers, especially donors, can feel haughty and unwarrantedly noble or generous; their high self-esteem is inappropriate. These brief remarks on self-respect and self-esteem thus identify some further difficulties with charity and welfare, and lay part of the groundwork for a more satisfactory discussion of justice and equality in Chapter 9.

5.5 AN IMPASSE?

The argument thus far seems to lead to an impasse. In a private-property system and economy, property is highly conducive to control, privacy, and individuality. Laissez-faire capitalism is one form of private-property economy.

Under it there tend to be extremes of wealth and poverty. But if the distribution of property is thus unequal, it deprives some persons of appropriately equal, and even minimal, amounts of control, privacy, and individuality. Neither private charity nor public welfare can adequately restore these goods. At least in a private-property system or economy, it is unclear that anything secures them quite so well as private property. Yet if there is private property, how is one to avoid problems of unequal distribution?

This is a serious question. It compels one to rethink the place of property in society. But it would be rash to conclude that the question identifies an impasse from which there is no escape. In fact, at least three possible ways out exist. A keener awareness of their strengths and weaknesses must await the next two chapters. Even then it would be a mistake to suppose that only one, if any, of the options is worth pursuing. This book does not decide among these options – which are, after all, points on a continuum – but uses them as a prism to reflect the characteristics of different institutions of property (§ 12.6). At any rate, the aim here is simply to describe the choices.

One option is to have a private-property economy that differs from laissez-faire capitalism. As these concepts are defined in § 5.1 and § 5.3, respectively, such an economy would have at least one, but for simplicity will be understood to have all, of the following characteristics. Most productive resources are privately owned, but the public owns some significant portion of them. There are restrictions on competition or profit maximization. And there is significant government regulation of property or the economy in other ways. The thought behind this option is that an economy with these characteristics will not have great inequalities in property holdings. It will therefore ensure not only minimal, but also appropriately equal, amounts of control, privacy, and individuality.

A second option is to have a private-property system that is not a private-property economy. From the definitions of these concepts in § 5.1, such a system would have these features. At least a great deal of consumptive property is privately owned. Some, but not most, productive resources are privately owned. And the market performs only allocative functions. Here the thought also is that a system with these features will not have great inequalities in property holdings. It will ensure appropriately equal, as well as minimal, control, privacy, and individuality.

A third option is to have an arrangement that is not a private-property system at all. It has virtually no private ownership of productive resources and comparatively little privately owned consumptive property. The thought here is twofold. First, the arrangement will engender little disparity in property holdings. As a result, there is likely to be little disparity in control, privacy, and individuality. Second, this arrangement will deemphasize these "goods." They may be desirable in a private-property system, but it does not follow that they are desirable in all economic arrangements. In fact, they are sometimes undesirable. Though control over one's own life is generally defensible, control over others' lives often is not. Privacy and individuality are desirable at least in a private-property economy, but may be undesirable in an economy that is not even a private-property system if they thwart communal values such as solidarity. Thus, the final option equalizes levels of control, privacy, and individuality insofar as these "goods" are thought defensible, and reduces their importance in human life insofar as they are not. It encourages sharing and community and fosters what one might almost call a power to include.

Chapter 6

Property and moral character

6.1 FOUR CLAIMS

To illuminate property on the path from individuals to social context, it is necessary to expand the inquiry. Chapter 4 concluded with a provisional discussion of personality. Chapter 5 then related property to the personal goods of control, privacy, and individuality. These were not, however, specifically moral goods and revealed little about moral character. If one is to appreciate the connections between property and moral character, one must say something about virtues and vices and about the links between property and character traits in different kinds of societies.

This chapter examines some connections between property and moral character. It does not deal with virtue as a possible justifying argument for private property,[1] and it does not contend that private property is either a necessary or a defeating condition for having a good moral character. Rather, the chapter makes four main claims. First, even the briefest consideration of Plato, Aristotle, Kant, and Adam Smith yields some key points regarding property and moral character. Second, the republican tradition in political theory helpfully supplements, but should not replace, these key points. Third, different sorts of economic systems promote, and inhibit, somewhat different sorts of property-related

---

1 Lawrence C. Becker, *Property Rights: Philosophic Foundations* (London, Henley and Boston: Routledge & Kegan Paul, 1977), pp. 81–87, correctly finds such arguments wanting.

virtues and vices. Fourth, the ideal of a person who has exactly the right character traits in relation to property is a highly problematic ideal. Before one can argue for these claims, though, it is necessary for the sake of clarity to say something about virtues, vices, and moral character.

6.2 VIRTUES, VICES, AND MORAL CHARACTER

A virtue is a more or less abiding character trait that disposes a person to think or act in ways that are generally beneficial both for the person having the trait and for others, and that either enhances some positive feature or corrects or modifies some shortcoming of human beings. The trait need not be permanent but must be fairly constant; indeed, one would probably not call it a "trait" if it were momentary or spasmodic. Virtues are connected with doing something, whether thinking or acting, and rely on some disposition to think or act in a certain way. What is done must, moreover, confer benefits and perform either some enhancing or some corrective function. One would not call a character trait a virtue if it is harmful or neutral, or if, like a propensity to pursue self-interest or sexual desires, it reflects the way human beings are prone to act anyway. Whether a virtue enhances or corrects depends on one's view of human nature. For example, if one believes that people take a modest interest in the interests of others, benevolence will be a virtue that enhances this positive feature by developing it to a noteworthy degree. If one believes that people are basically self-centered, benevolence will be a virtue that corrects a shortcoming of human beings.

This characterization of virtue is oriented toward moral virtues, such as honesty and benevolence, but not only them. It also allows for intellectual virtues, such as wisdom and intellectual integrity, and for virtues that are neither moral nor intellectual, such as cheerfulness. It does not suppose that there is a sharp line between moral and nonmoral nonintellectual virtues. Nor does it, unlike some theories, define virtue as a mean, deal explicitly with the use of virtues to bad ends, make a connection between virtues and either habits or the will, or take a position on "theological" virtues such as faith, hope, and charity. As a whole, this understanding of virtue by and large follows Aristotle, Aquinas, and Foot.[2]

This view of virtue yields a contrasting picture of vice: A vice is a more or less abiding character trait that disposes a person to think or act in ways that are generally harmful both for the person having the trait and for others, and that either detracts from some positive feature or succumbs to some undesirable proclivity of human beings. Dishonesty, foolishness, and crankiness are, respectively, examples of moral, intellectual, and nonmoral nonintellectual vices.

Virtues and vices, taken together, are the main components of a person's *character* but they do not exhaust it. A normal propensity to pursue sexual activity or one's self-interest is part of one's character but is neither a virtue nor a vice. Differently, a propensity to tell jokes can be part of a person's character, but it is neither a virtue nor a vice. In fact, *many* personal qualities do not seem to be virtues or vices – think of a person who is described as serious, dignified, enigmatic, and imperturbable; yet these qualities seem part of his or her character. Readers who are suspicious of the category of nonmoral nonintellectual virtues have an additional reason for seeing a person's character as broader than

---

2 See Aristotle, *Nicomachean Ethics* 1103ª11–1109ᵇ29, in Richard McKeon, ed., *The Basic Works of Aristotle* (New York: Random House, 1941) (trans. W. D. Ross); St. Thomas Aquinas, *Summa Theologiae* Ia 2ae QQ. 55–67, in *Summa Theologiae* (London: Blackfriars, 1964), vol. 23 (trans. W. D. Hughes); Philippa Foot, "Virtues and Vices," in her *Virtues and Vices* (Berkeley: University of California Press, 1978), pp. 1–18. The text diverges from these writers in the following ways: Aristotle emphasizes the role of habit (1103ª11–18), and partly defines virtue as lying in a mean (1106ᵇ36–1107ª3). Aquinas also emphasizes the role of habit (Ia 2ae Q. 55), and discusses theological as well as moral and intellectual virtues (Ia 2ae QQ. 57–62). Foot connects virtues with the will (pp. 4–8), considers whether one might display a virtue in acting wrongly or badly (pp. 14–18), and identifies the corrective, but not the enhancing, function of virtues. Overall, the terminology in the text is closest to that of Foot.

his or her virtues and vices. They may contend that such traits as cheerfulness, affability, and tactfulness, or crankiness, cantankerousness, and petulance, which some might see as nonmoral nonintellectual virtues or vices, are part of a person's character but are actually neither virtues nor vices. It is not important to rebut this contention here. It is important to insist that a person's moral virtues and moral vices are the main, if not the only, components of his or her *moral character*.

One can classify virtues in many ways, but for present purposes it helps to differentiate among what will be called general virtues, variable instantiations of general virtues, localized virtues, and differentiated virtues. General virtues are character traits that are virtues in all, or almost all, societies. Any list of general virtues is bound to be controversial, but plausible candidates include honesty, benevolence, kindness, justice, and common sense (practical rationality). Even if these are general virtues, one should notice that they can be variably instantiated. That is, what counts as displaying the virtue varies from one society to another. For example, consider two societies that have different conceptions of kindness toward the elderly when they become terminally and painfully ill. One society performs euthanasia on them, and the other allows their lives to run a natural course while treating them gently and respectfully.

Next, localized virtues are character traits that are virtues only in some societies. Industriousness is an example of a localized virtue. In a small, isolated society where needed food, clothing, and shelter are readily obtainable with little effort, the trait called industriousness is not really a virtue because it is not the case that it generally benefits those having it and others. It is a virtue in a society with a large population and scanty resources where much effort is necessary to build a satisfactory way of life.

Finally, differentiated virtues are character traits that, for a given society, are virtues for persons who occupy certain roles or positions but need not be virtues for persons who occupy different roles or positions. Differentiated virtues can

123

be general but are more likely to be localized virtues. Some might contend that in a feudal society, obedience and docility are virtues for serfs and not for nobles, whereas boldness is a virtue for nobles but not for serfs, or that, in a capitalist society, cooperativeness is a virtue for assembly-line workers and not for entrepreneurs, while competitiveness and aggressiveness are virtues for entrepreneurs but not for assembly-line workers. Much argument and evidence are needed to make such a contention stick. For a danger exists that some societies will encourage certain persons, such as women or unskilled workers, to acquire character traits like servility or obsequiousness that are not virtues at all.

At this stage, it is important to note that all virtues – whether general, variably instantiated, localized, or differentiated – must satisfy the definition of a virtue given at the beginning of this section. This requirement precludes calling servility a virtue, for servility does not benefit the servile person and in fact probably does not benefit others either. Still, the requirement is not so stringent as to rule out localized or differentiated virtues. Correspondingly, there are general vices such as dishonesty, variable instantiations of general vices (imagine manifestations of maliciousness), localized vices (think of wastefulness), and differentiated vices (consider lack of competitiveness in a capitalist entrepreneur).

The relevance of this classification is as follows. Though space permits no discussion of relativism, one may contrast briefly two views on the objectivity of virtue and moral character. An "unconditionally objective" view, such as that of Aristotle and Aquinas, holds that all human beings have an essential nature, and that this essential human nature enables one to identify character traits that promote the good of all beings sharing that nature.[3] In contrast, a "con-

---

3   See Aristotle, *Nicomachean Ethics* 1106^{a}22–24; St. Thomas Aquinas, *Summa Theologiae* Ia 2ae Q. 63. For a similar contemporary view, see J. Budziszewski, *The Resurrection of Nature: Political Theory and the Human Character* (Ithaca and London: Cornell University Press, 1986), chs. 1–3 and Mezzalogue.

ditionally objective" view, such as that of Wallace,[4] maintains, in effect, that if people are to live in communities, and if both people and communities are to flourish, then people must possess certain character traits. Such traits, when developed in individuals to a noteworthy degree, are virtues. In order to make out the claims of this chapter, one need not accept the unconditionally objective view. A conditionally objective view, and indeed a view less strong than that, will suffice. It will be enough because, since the project is to display links between property and character traits in different sorts of societies, the chief concern is conditional. That is, if societies and persons are to do well, then certain linkages are apt to exist between property rules and institutions on the one hand and character traits on the other. Actually, the project at hand requires something less strong than Wallace's account, which is rather universalist. The relevance of the division of general, variably instantiated, localized, and differentiated virtues is now apparent. Only if all links between property and character traits were at the level of general virtues and vices would the present project be as universalist as Wallace's position. In fact, as the following sections will bring out, most of the links are not at that level.

6.3 FROM MORAL TO POLITICAL THEORY

One must now extend this account of virtue and moral character to political theory. It will help if the extension has some historicity, if only that of intellectual history. This section discusses four figures – Plato, Aristotle, Kant, and Adam Smith – who saw connections among property, character, and society. The chief variables are which sorts of property they addressed, which character traits they esteemed, what kind of society they favored, and whether they envisioned a key role for labor in the creation of property rights. This survey cannot achieve great depth, but it will

4 James D. Wallace, *Virtues and Vices* (Ithaca and London: Cornell University Press, 1978).

enable one to distill some useful points for an account of property and moral character.

The variables just mentioned are nowhere more evident than in Plato's divergent discussions of property in the *Republic* and the *Laws*.[5] The *Republic* depicts an ideal society. The rulers and auxiliaries have political power but almost no private property. Ordinary citizens have private property within limits but almost no political power. Plato does not, then, hold that private property should be distributed equally. His thought is rather that the ideal is to have each group in society perform its proper function, and that private property would be a distraction for the rulers and auxiliaries. Nevertheless, he wants to bar unduly unequal distributions among ordinary citizens, for he believes that wealth and poverty can cause society to disintegrate. Wealth also leads to "luxury" and "indolence" and poverty to "meanness" and "viciousness."[6]

In contrast, the *Laws* portrays a practical, second-best society. If the ideal is to have common ownership among the rulers and auxiliaries – "Friends have all things in common"[7] – the practically achievable is to have individual private possessory rights for all with an underlying communal ownership.[8] All land is divided into lots and apportioned by lot equally to each citizen. Roughly equal distribution is maintained through population control, inheritance regulations, and restrictions on gold, silver, lending, and moneymaking.[9] If any citizen acquires more than four times as much property as the citizen having the least, the surplus

---

5 Plato, *Republic* 416[d]–423[a], in *The Dialogues of Plato*, trans. B. Jowett 4th ed. (Oxford: Clarendon Press, 1953), vol. 2; Plato, *Laws* 736[c]–745[b], in ibid., vol. 4.

6 Plato, *Republic* 421[d]–422[a]. By "luxury" Plato seems to mean the habitual use of or indulgence in what is choice or costly, rather than whatever is choice or costly and conduces to great enjoyment. See the *Oxford English Dictionary*, 2d ed. (Oxford: Clarendon Press, 1989), s.v. "luxury," sense 3 (rather than sense 5).

7 Plato, *Laws* 739[c].

8 Ibid., 740[a].

9 Ibid., 740[b]–744[a].

goes to the state.[10] Like the *Republic*, the *Laws* also opposes wealth and poverty partly because of their adverse impact on virtue.[11]

Plato's discussions do not take one very far. It is true that wealth and poverty can undermine character. But no uniform connection exists between wealth and luxury or indolence on the one hand or between poverty and meanness or viciousness on the other. Wealthy people are sometimes generous and public-spirited, and poor people are sometimes industrious and noble. Indeed, people with an intermediate amount of property can be lazy or mean. At the level of society, it is true that the sorts of property that a society allows can affect political community. Yet the ideal society of the *Republic* is open to many familiar general objections. One particular objection relevant here is that it is naive to suppose that private property and political power can be severed, as Plato maintains. Even the allegedly practical society of the *Laws* requires an enormous amount of state interference. Both the justifiability and the feasibility of such interference are open to doubt. Although it may be important, for reasons of both moral character and social cohesion, to have some constraints on the distribution of private property, it is far from clear that Plato describes constraints that, even if helpful in his own time, will work well in the present age.

Aristotle is far less visionary. His *Politics* favors private rather than communal ownership on grounds that relate to the smooth functioning of a society and its economy. "Property should be in a certain sense common, but, as a general rule, private; for, when every one has a distinct interest, men will not complain of one another, and they will make more progress, because every one will be attending to his own business."[12] Even private property should to some extent be

10   Ibid., 744^e–745^a.
11   Ibid., 742^e–743^d, 744^e.
12   Aristotle, *Politics* 1263^{a}25–29, in Richard McKeon, ed., *The Basic Works of Aristotle* (trans. Benjamin Jowett). For his criticisms of Plato, see ibid., 1263^{b}23–1266^{a}30.

available for common use, and the legislator should regulate property so as to encourage a "benevolent disposition" in people.[13] Aristotle also says that two virtues require private property: "temperance towards women" and "liberality."[14] He is, moreover, concerned about highly unequal distributions of property, and remarks that "poverty is the parent of revolution and crime."[15]

Aristotle takes one a little further than Plato. Aristotle does mention, though he fails to develop, an important ground – smooth social and economic functioning – for preferring private to communal property. He recognizes nonetheless the destabilizing effects of poverty in societies that have wide inequalities in property holdings. And he connects property to some character traits not mentioned by Plato.

Nevertheless, Aristotle's discussion is marred by some major shortcomings. First, he fails to show how property can be "in a certain sense common, but, as a general rule, private." Still less does he show how smooth functioning justifies the combination.

Second, the idea of "temperance towards women" as a virtue rests on an outmoded and morally indefensible view of women. Aristotle's thought seems to be that, unless private property exists, there could not arise temperance in the form of each man's keeping his hands off the wives of others. One would have thought that women, as morally autonomous persons, should have an equal choice and responsibility in such matters. Apart from that, one can make some qualified sense of private property and temperance, though it would hardly appear to be a major argument for private property. The complex virtue called temperance has at least two aspects – moderation and restraint. Moderation seems as possible with communal as with private property. For example, if people can eat and drink as much communal

13 Ibid., 1263^{a}40.
14 Ibid., 1263^{b}9–14.
15 Ibid., 1265^{b}11–12.

provisions as they want, they can display "temperance" by eating and drinking moderately rather than to excess. However, private property may be specially related to restraint, for if everything is held in common, people cannot display "temperance" by keeping from using or interfering with the things of others. This point does not merely state a logically necessary condition – that people cannot keep away from others' things unless some things are the property of others. It also states a social and psychological precondition – that the requisite sort of disposition of restraint cannot arise unless private property exists. This precondition will, however, need to be stated carefully, for some forms of restraint can be displayed by not interfering in prohibited ways with communal property.

Third, Aristotle's discussion of liberality is suggestive but incomplete. His thought seems to be that, without private property, one cannot be liberal or generous in sharing one's things with others. Once more, private property is not just a logically necessary condition – that one cannot share what is not one's own.[16] It appears also to be a social and psychological precondition – that one cannot have the disposition that grounds the character trait of liberality without things of one's own. Nevertheless, having private property is hardly a sufficient condition of liberality. Some people who own property are stingy.

Fourth, like Plato, Aristotle lacks an account of the interrelations of property, virtue, and labor. This deficiency may be due to the fact that in Greek society much work was done by slaves, who were not citizens and not full members of society. Aristotle's acceptance of slavery[17] is one of the least attractive features of his political philosophy.

16 Becker, *Property Rights*, p. 86, slightly overstates his case in rejecting the idea that private ownership is "a necessary condition for the development of any possible element of virtue."
17 See Aristotle, *Politics*, 1252^a1–1255^b40. An older but still useful examination of Plato and Aristotle on property is Richard Schlatter, *Private Property: The History of an Idea* (London: George Allen & Unwin, 1951), ch. 1.

Passing over later classical and medieval speculation,[18] one encounters a quite different theory in Kant[19] – though here it is possible to address only those features of it that are relevant to the inquiry at hand. Kant makes willing and possession (occupancy) central to the theory of property. In the spirit of his critical philosophy, one might ask, How is private property possible? Kant's answer, in effect, is that it is possible only because of the willing and acting of persons. Persons are equal moral agents. They can make unowned things in the world theirs by intending to have them and then following up on that intention by "occupying" them.[20]

Like Hegel, Kant borrows his elaboration of occupancy from Roman law.[21] But there are differences. Hegel sees willing and occupancy as fragments of a detailed social context.[22] Kant, however, sees them more as the grounding elements of a sort of social-contract theory in which rational and equal persons reciprocally bind themselves under an authoritative will to respect one another's property rights. Kant seems to hold not only that willing and possession are

---

18 For a survey, see Schlatter, *Private Property*, chs. 2–4. High points, from the perspective of the present inquiry, include Seneca's view that although ideally there would be no private property, "avarice" came about and private property arose (p. 26); the views of Gratian and Rufinus that possession has its origin in "avarice" (p. 43), and of Alexander of Hales that the law of nature prescribes ownership in common before the Fall (when humankind was sinless) and private property after it (p. 44); Aquinas's position that although private property is "natural and good" (p. 50) and therefore not necessitated by corruption or sin, the most perfect condition, as in monasticism, is to have communal property or no property at all (p. 54); Wycliffe's contention, *pace* Aristotle, that even if people would take better care of private property, that does not invalidate the principle that sinful humankind should opt for communal property (p. 69); and the formulation of a labor theory of property by Sir John Fortescue (pp. 72–76).

19 Immanuel Kant, *The Philosophy of Law*, trans. W. Hastie (Edinburgh: T. & T. Clark, 1887).

20 Ibid., pp. 81–84.

21 Ibid., pp. 81–84, 87–99. Cf. G. W. F. Hegel, *Philosophy of Right* [1821], trans. T. M. Knox (Oxford: Clarendon Press, 1965 [1952]), §§ 41–71 (abstract right), and the critical discussion in § 4.3 above.

22 See Hegel, *Philosophy of Right*, §§ 182–256 (civil society) and 257–360 (the state).

necessary for private property but also that private property is necessary for a complete and autonomous will as postulated by practical reason.[23] He says, moreover, that only a "provisory" mine and thine exist in the state of nature; a constitution and civil society – the authoritative will de-psychologized – are needed to back them up and certify them.[24]

Kant does not subscribe to the Lockean view that there are full private-property rights in the state of nature and that society merely makes those rights secure. Rather, society also, and more importantly, certifies private-property rights by giving them a moral claim. Thus, for Kant, private property in the state of nature involves factual possession that lacks full normative significance. A constitution and civil society not only back up this sort of private property by force but also endow it with a fuller normative significance. In the main, Kant envisions a narrow role for the state as a protector and certifier of rights of private property and contract. Yet he also suggests that the sovereign – the authoritative will now repsychologized – has the power, as "supreme proprietor" but not private owner of the soil, to assess taxes, provide for the police, and run the economy.[25]

Kant's theory is a step forward in some respects and a step back in others. To his credit, Kant calls for a political community made up of equal persons and thus repudiates the slavery (though not the sexism)[26] that weakened Greek and other theories. In addition, he constructs an ideal society that interprets the social-contract tradition in new ways and offers a distinctively modern legal account of private property.

23 Kant, *Philosophy of Law*, pp. 62–64. See also Chapter 4, notes 9 and 25.
24 Ibid., pp. 76–80, 90–94, 155–58.
25 Ibid., pp. 182–88. Mary Gregor, "Kant on Welfare Legislation," *LOGOS: Philosophic Issues in Christian Perspective*, 6 (1985): 49–59, argues convincingly that Kant's theory supports only minimal welfare legislation designed to make people independent.
26 Kant recognizes a category of "household possessions" – that is, a man's wife and their children and servants – as property. Kant, *The Philosophy of Law*, p. 109. See Howard Williams, "Kant's Concept of Property," *Philosophical Quarterly*, 27 (1977): 32–40, at 33.

All the same, some features of Kant's theory are troubling. First, the entire production has an exceedingly formalistic and abstract air. Whereas in Aristotle one finds a clear-headed sense of how property functions at least in an ancient Greek city state, in Kant one gains little sense of what property means to people in any actual society. Of course, Kant's project differs from the project of this chapter. His project is to connect an abstract notion of private property with a formal conception of an autonomous will. The present project attempts, more mundanely, to display connections between actual private property and moral character. In fairness to Kant, one should not criticize him for failing at something he was not trying to do. But it is important to see that his project, however well executed, would fail to illuminate many connections between property and moral character.

Second, even in the formal elaboration of Kant's theory, a tension exists between the agreement of free individuals to constitute and respect rights of private property and the use of coercion to enforce those rights against recalcitrant individuals. One cannot solve this hoary problem here. Still, it is important to see that this type of problem does not, as some critics claim, afflict Kant only as an apologist for "bourgeois" private property.[27] An analogous tension besets any theory in which free individuals agree upon communal ownership or public ownership of the means of production and then use force to quell recalcitrants.

Third, the free and equal moral agents of Kant's theory may have widely unequal amounts of property in fact. Even though all are equal before the law, Kant accepts extreme economic inequality.[28] As both Plato and Aristotle point out, wealth and poverty can lead to undesirable character traits.

Fourth, Kant's theory contains an unacceptable division

27 See Howard Williams, "Kant's Concept of Property," at 39–40, who cites and partly agrees with Lucien Goldmann and Herbert Marcuse.
28 See Alan Ryan, *Property and Political Theory* (Oxford: Basil Blackwell, 1984), p. 74.

between persons as rational moral agents and persons as flesh-and-blood individuals each with a distinct character. The former construct society and private property in terms of rational rules rationally derived. The latter must live within that society, but their character traits and affective regard for one another are private matters beyond the reach of the law.[29] The division is unacceptable because, if at all feasible, one should try to build an institution of property that reinforces rather than ignores moral character. The root of this bifurcation may lie in Kantian moral philosophy, which has difficulty in making adequate sense of character, personal relations, and moral experience.[30] Of course, some might again observe that Kant's project differs from the present project. Yet the point remains that, given his abstract conception of moral character, his project, even if well done, would not shed much light on connections between private property as it exists and the sorts of moral character persons actually have.

Only with Adam Smith does one step into a world close to one's own. He develops a view of property and labor in an early modern commercial and industrial society. He presents one version of this view in *The Wealth of Nations* and another in *The Theory of Moral Sentiments*.[31] The latter is of primary interest here because it deals more with human character. In it Smith bases morality on sympathy (a capacity to place oneself imaginatively in the shoes of others and consider what one would then feel) rather than empathy (a

29 See ibid., pp. 74–76.
30 See Bernard Williams, "Persons, Character and Morality," in his *Moral Luck: Philosophical Papers 1973–1980* (Cambridge: Cambridge University Press, 1981), pp. 1–19, especially pp. 1–5, 14–19.
31 Adam Smith, *An Inquiry into the Nature and Causes of the Wealth of Nations* [1776], ed. Edwin Cannan and pref. George J. Stigler (Chicago: University of Chicago Press, 1976); Adam Smith, *The Theory of Moral Sentiments* [1759], ed. Dugald Stewart (London: George Bell & Sons, 1892). For comparisons between the two views, see, in a large literature, Albert O. Hirschman, *The Passions and the Interests: Political Arguments for Capitalism before Its Triumph* (Princeton: Princeton University Press, 1977), pp. 100–13.

spontaneous, nonreflective identification with others).[32] In a recent article, Phillipson suggests that Smith is mainly concerned not with moral theory but with the practical morality that could be based on the sentiment of sympathy and applied in daily living, especially living in a commercial society.[33] As far as character is concerned, Smith does not confine his attention to "virtue," which he understands as qualities deserving of admiration and celebration. He also addresses "propriety," which he views as qualities deserving of approval only.[34] Smith believes that an uncritical reverence for wealth and power corrupts moral sentiments. He has low regard for the nobility, whom he considers overcome by indolence and luxury, and for unskilled laborers, whom he considers "benumbed" and "brutalized" and made "stupid" by poverty and mindless work.[35] He thinks somewhat better of the gentry because of what he sees as their sociability, industriousness, and intelligent husbanding of resources.[36] He approves of servants, journeymen, and skilled laborers – they are "frugal, industrious, God-fearing, and literate."[37] All of these favorable qualities Smith places under the head of propriety. As Phillipson puts it, "the pursuit of propriety had become an alternative to the pursuit of virtue, and the voluntary society and the coffee-house had emerged as an alternative to the *polis* in this world of provincial morality."[38]

---

32 Smith, *The Theory of Moral Sentiments*, pt. I, § I, ch. II, pp. 10–13. See J. Ralph Lindgren, *The Social Philosophy of Adam Smith* (The Hague: Martinus Nijhoff, 1973), pp. 21–25; Nicholas Phillipson, "Adam Smith as Civic Moralist," in Istvan Hont and Michael Ignatieff, *Wealth and Virtue: The Shaping of Political Economy in the Scottish Enlightenment* (Cambridge: Cambridge University Press, 1983), pp. 179–202, at pp. 183–85. It is not clear whether one is to use one's own preferences or others' preferences in deciding what one would then feel; or whether either use yields an impartial spectator (see Phillipson, pp. 185–87).
33 Phillipson, "Adam Smith as Civic Moralist."
34 Ibid., pp. 179–81, 189.
35 Ibid., pp. 190, 192–93.
36 Ibid., p. 192.
37 Ibid.
38 Ibid., p. 199.

Smith's portrayal is acute. He seems to be the first, or one of the first, major thinkers to see clearly that many qualities ignored or insufficiently stressed by classical and abstract writers are important to the functioning of an economy. It is true that not all of these qualities are character traits. Literacy is not a character trait; neither is intelligent husbanding of resources, as distinct from a knack for it. And some qualities, such as being God-fearing, are character traits but have no particular place in a secular political theory. Yet sociability, industriousness, and frugality are character traits. More broadly, Smith's investigation is quite different from that of earlier writers. He has his feet on the ground in a way that Kant does not. And although, like Plato and Aristotle, he views wealth and poverty with reservations and identifies connections between property and character, the differences are marked. Plato and Aristotle ignore labor, concentrate on perfection and undoubted virtues, view property statically (as just there), emphasize theoretical education and universal goals, and see society as an organism composed of functionally related persons having largely common or integrated ends. In contrast, Smith exalts labor, concentrates on traits of propriety, views property dynamically (as the outcome of a process of production), stresses practical education and more limited or particular goals, and sees society as a collection of individuals bound together no doubt by sympathy but mainly pursuing individual ends.

For present purposes, two reservations are in order. One relates to the description of character traits such as sociability, industriousness, and frugality as examples of "propriety" rather than "virtue." *Pace* Smith, there is a case for calling them virtues. If sociability means an easy agreeability in dealing with others, and if people are often, say, somewhat distant, shy, or formal with those who are neither friends nor family, then sociability would seem to be a virtue as understood in § 6.2. For it is a more or less abiding character trait, typically benefits both those having the trait and others, and corrects a shortcoming of human beings. It is, moreover, a general virtue because it would be a virtue in all or almost all societies. Industriousness and frugality are also virtues. At least they are so if human beings as a rule have a propensity to be a bit lazy or wasteful, respectively, for then these traits have a corrective function. Still, to be industrious or frugal is to possess not a general but a localized virtue, since it is easy to imagine societies in which these traits would not be especially beneficial. Although § 6.2 did not *define* virtue as lying in a mean, these traits, if carried to excess, will no longer be virtues. It is not virtuous to be garrulous, excessively devoted to work, or penny-pinching. Furthermore, sociability, industriousness, and frugality hardly rank with honesty or benevolence. Indeed, it is not entirely clear that they are *moral* virtues. As the previous section mentions, a sharp line may not separate moral from nonmoral nonintellectual virtues. Sociability lies somewhere between benevolence and cheerfulness on the scale from moral to nonmoral. Frugality, a wag might suggest, would be a moral virtue only in Scotland. Of the three traits, industriousness probably has the strongest claim to being a moral virtue. Yet, whether moral or not, these traits do seem to be virtues of some sort. In saying this, one may not necessarily be disagreeing with Smith, who may have been applying a more stringent conception of virtue in relegating them to the status of propriety.

A different reservation has to do with the narrowness of Smith's account, in two respects. First, even if property and work in a modern economy are connected with these low-brow virtues, may not property also be connected with more high-minded virtues? Second, even if a commercial society makes these lowbrow traits virtues, may it not also foster character traits that are injurious to those having them and to others – vices in short? The next section takes up these questions by considering the republican tradition in political theory.

Before turning to that tradition, however, one can distill some key points from the figures discussed here. First, wealth and poverty can have an adverse impact on character.

As Plato suggests, wealth can lead to indolence and poverty to meanness. Aristotle and Smith bring out additional reasons for worrying about the effects of extreme economic inequality on character.

Second, many different connections, of various strengths, exist between property and moral character. More precisely, property arrangements and their associated economic systems can, variously, make possible, facilitate, render likely, or generate some character traits, and make impossible, inhibit, render unlikely, or block other character traits. They can, moreover, do so for a few, some, many, or all people in the society. As a rule, it is problematic to identify necessary connections between property and moral character that hold for all persons and societies. Most connections are looser and often hold only for some persons or some societies.

Third, one can, within limits, show how various character traits relate to different kinds of property. The critical discussion of Aristotle indicates, for example, that a person can exhibit temperance or intemperance in different ways in relation to public and private property. Of special interest are the links between character traits and private property. Without private property, there is little if any room for such virtues as liberality or generosity or such vices as stinginess or miserliness. A more complicated illustration is "avarice," which has been the name sometimes for a genuine vice and at other times for a more nearly neutral character trait of pursuing one's financial self-interest.[39]

Fourth, if one thinks of property not statically as something that is just there but dynamically as something that results from work, other character traits come to the fore. This statement is particularly true if one is thinking of private property in a commercial and industrial society. In that case, traits such as industriousness and frugality emerge as vir-

39 See Hirschman, *The Passions and the Interests*, pp. 9–12, 20–21, 41–42, 54–55, 107–08.

tues. Extremes such as laziness and excessive devotion to work, and prodigality and penny-pinchingness, respectively, emerge as vices. In addition, traits such as sociability, stability, self-reliance, and probity in business dealings are apt to be especially useful in that sort of society. Unlike generosity and stinginess, which relate to the use of property once acquired, traits such as industriousness and probity in business dealings relate to productive activity that can result in acquiring property in a modern economy.

6.4 REPUBLICANISM, VIRTUE, AND COMMERCIAL SOCIETY

The republican tradition, which should not be confused with the Republican Party in the United States, is a set of related positions that stress the importance of certain civically oriented character traits for a sound system of government. The tradition embraces such precapitalist thinkers as Machiavelli and Harrington as well as such later writers as Madison. Republicanism, also called civic humanism, has historical, legal, and philosophical implications. Historians have drawn on republicanism to give American history an interpretation different from an unalloyed "liberal" understanding. Academic lawyers have used it to read the United States Constitution as something other than an effort to balance factional interests. Political philosophers have seen it as an alternative to various forms of "liberalism," especially interest-group pluralism. The chief elements in republicanism thus understood include emphasis on "virtues" of independent self-governance, public-spiritedness, and political participation; opposition to "corruption" in government; the role of property as a basis for civic involvement; practical deliberation and dialogue in the political and legal process; interaction between persons and society in developing the character traits needed for sound government; and opposition to many of the character traits associated with a market society. Republicanism is not a tightly knit theory but a group of loosely related positions; many of its distinctive claims cannot be addressed here.[40]

In the present context, the main point of interest has to do with the republican attitude toward property and virtue. The attitude has a critical and a constructive component. On the critical side, republicans object to character traits associated with commercial societies. They do not see them as virtues. They also object to the so-called *doux commerce* thesis, that is, the claim that commerce softens or sweetens unattractive "passions" and replaces them with attractive passions or with "interests." They sometimes even say that commerce corrupts virtue.[41] On the constructive side, republicans elaborate the following alternative position. Property is a basis for civic participation. It may be a condition of voting or office holding. In any case, it gives persons the leisure and educational opportunities for effective participation.[42]

40 For original sources, see, for example, Niccolò Machiavelli, *The Discourses*, in *The Prince and The Discourses*, intro. Max Lerner (New York: Modern Library/Random House, 1950); James Harrington, *The Political Works of James Harrington*, ed. J. G. A. Pocock (Cambridge: Cambridge University Press, 1977); *The Federalist*, intro. Edward Mead Earle (New York: Modern Library/Random House, 1937), nos. 10, 51. Contemporary elaborators include J. G. A. Pocock, *The Machiavellian Moment: Florentine Political Thought and the Atlantic Republican Tradition* (Princeton: Princeton University Press, 1975); Frank I. Michelman, "The Supreme Court, 1985 Term – Foreword: Traces of Self-Government," *Harvard Law Review*, 100 (1986): 4–77; Frank Michelman, "Law's Republic," *Yale Law Journal*, 97 (1988): 1493–1537; Cass R. Sunstein, "Beyond the Republican Revival," *Yale Law Journal*, 97 (1988): 1539–90.

41 See generally John Patrick Diggins, *The Lost Soul of American Politics: Virtue, Self-Interest, and the Foundations of Liberalism* (New York: Basic Books, 1984), pp. 143–46; Hirschman, *The Passions and the Interests*, pp. 9–66; Albert O. Hirschman, "Rival Interpretations of Market Society: Civilizing, Destructive, or Feeble?," *Journal of Economic Literature*, 20 (1982): 1463–84. Cf. Sunstein, "Beyond the Republican Revival," at 1557 and n.93, who contends that some forms of republicanism display a more hospitable attitude to commerce.

42 Republican writing sometimes does not attend as much as it should to the issues of whether, and if so, why, participating in civic and political matters is good. For some judiciously skeptical comments on these issues, see M. B. E. Smith, "The Value of Participation," in J. Roland Pennock and John W. Chapman, eds., *NOMOS XVI: Participation in Politics* (New York: Lieber-Atherton, 1975), pp. 126–35.

The three character traits most useful for participation are independent self-governance, public-spiritedness, and practical wisdom. The first is the trait of freely choosing one's ends and the means of achieving them and can be seen as an abiding exercise of autonomy as understood in § 3.1. The second involves the disposition to take a keen interest in and follow through on civic matters. The last is included within but not coterminous with most philosophical accounts of practical reason, practical reasoning, or practical wisdom, and is directed mainly toward the judgment useful in civic participation. Thus, republicans concentrate not on the character traits needed to produce property but on those needed to use it wisely and effectively in civic affairs.[43]

The republican tradition usefully supplements earlier accounts of property and character. It identifies as virtues character traits – namely, independent self-governance, public-spiritedness, and practical reason in civic affairs – that were overlooked or at least understressed by other writers. And insofar as property is conducive to these virtues, the republicans identify an important feature of private property.

All the same, it would be a mistake to substitute the republican tradition for these other accounts, for at least two reasons. First, republicanism offers a blinkered perspective on property and character. It does indeed spot some connections that other traditions have slighted or ignored, but this fact is only a reason to add republican virtues to the list. It is not by itself a reason to remove from the list the virtues identified in § 6.3. In reply, republicans may point to their criticism of the *doux commerce* thesis. But the force of this criticism, which should not be confused with the Marxian objections considered in the next chapter, is in doubt. As a matter of history or sociology, it is far from clear that com-

---

43 See Diggins, *The Lost Soul of American Politics*, pp. 146–49. Contrast the opposite emphasis in Adam Smith; see Istvan Hont and Michael Ignatieff, "Needs and Justice in the 'Wealth of Nations': An Introductory Essay," in Hont and Ignatieff, *Wealth and Virtue*, pp. 1–44, at pp. 11–12.

merce has always and everywhere had the deleterious effects claimed. As a matter of political theory, it is even less clear that a commercial society must produce such effects. In fact, the latter half of the eighteenth century saw several interesting attempts by American thinkers to show how it could avoid producing them.[44]

Second, republicanism, at least in its traditional forms, is uncritically indulgent of private property and economic inequality.[45] Even if private property is conducive to civic virtues in some societies, it is not logically or causally necessary to them in those societies. For example, property ownership need not and should not be a qualification to vote or hold office, and the state can make available to all the educational opportunity useful for civic participation. To the extent that property is conducive to certain virtues in a given society, that fact is one argument for redistributing wealth in that society. There may well be other, stronger arguments for redistribution, but for the moment one can mark the traditional republican indifference to economic inequality or even hostility to its reduction as a potentially suspect feature.

Some contemporary versions of republicanism seek to avoid this second deficiency. Under traditional versions, property was important because it freed the owner – the landed proprietor or yeoman farmer – from dependence on others, and so enabled him or her to set individual goals and pursue them and to participate in politics. It thus gave the owner a stake in a property-protecting community. These relationships explain in part the traditional republican indifference or hostility to redistribution. Redistributing wealth might destabilize the state and therefore undermine the owner's stake in the continuance of a smoothly operating property-protecting community. Some contemporary ver-

---

44 See Thomas A. Horne, "Bourgeois Virtue: Property and Moral Philosophy in America, 1750–1800," *History of Political Thought*, 4 (1983): 317–40.

45 See, for example, Joyce Appleby, *Capitalism and a New Social Order: The Republican Vision of the 1790s* (New York and London: New York University Press, 1984), pp. 8–19, who stresses the elitism of federalist versions of republicanism.

sions of republicanism, however, are sensitive to distributional issues, whether in reinterpreting older versions or in applying republican values to current problems.[46] Perhaps no contemporary version goes quite far enough. What needs to be said is that if private property is such a good thing, then everyone ought to have some of it. But it need not be quite the same sort of property. Whereas the usual sorts of property should be distributed more equally, secure protection should be afforded such items of the "new property" as welfare rights.[47] This broadening and partial transformation of property rights can also foster independent self-governance and political participation. Yet even the most promising contemporary versions of republicanism do not capture all of the connections between property and virtue. For that one needs to canvass the effect of property arrangements on moral character in a range of economic systems.[48]

6.5 MORAL CHARACTER AND ECONOMIC SYSTEMS

This section argues that different sorts of economic systems promote, and inhibit, somewhat different sorts of property-related virtues and vices. Think back to the three economies identified as options in § 5.5. The options are united in rejecting laissez-faire capitalism. To the grounds for rejection

46 See, for example, Geoffrey R. Stone, Louis M. Seidman, Cass R. Sunstein, and Mark V. Tushnet, *Constitutional Law* (Boston: Little, Brown, 1986), p. 6; Frank I. Michelman, "Possession vs. Distribution in the Constitutional Idea of Property," *Iowa Law Review*, 72 (1987): 1319–50; Sunstein, "Beyond the Republican Revival," at 1551; Cass R. Sunstein, "Interest Groups in American Public Law," *Stanford Law Review*, 38 (1985): 29–87, at 30 n.8, 56–59, 72–73.

47 See, for example, Frank I. Michelman, "Constitutional Welfare Rights and *A Theory of Justice*," in Norman Daniels, ed., *Reading Rawls* (Oxford: Basil Blackwell, 1975), pp. 319–47; Charles Reich, "The New Property," *Yale Law Journal*, 73 (1964): 733–87.

48 Section 6.4 is less sympathetic to republicanism than are such contemporary elaborators as Michelman and Sunstein. For critical reaction to their work, see the comments in "Symposium: The Republican Civic Tradition," *Yale Law Journal*, 97 (1988): 1493–1723.

given in Chapter 5 one can add that laissez-faire capitalism promotes some vices and inhibits some virtues. In fairness, one must acknowledge that it hardly has a monopoly on promoting vice and inhibiting virtue and that it also promotes some virtues, such as business acumen and market boldness, that other economic systems may stifle. Nevertheless, it can spawn ruthless and uncaring treatment of workers by entrepreneurs and managers, generate proud and haughty behavior in the rich, and contribute to obsequiousness and servility in the poor. As a result, the first option – a private-property economy that differs from laissez-faire capitalism – tries to avoid a high incidence of the vices that mark laissez-faire capitalism and to leave some room for the specific virtues that it fosters. The second option – a private-property system that is not a private-property economy – tries to reduce vices characteristic of capitalism to an even greater degree. The third option – an arrangement that is not a private-property system at all – tries to alter the range of virtues that are distinctively property-related virtues and to eradicate vices that have a close tie to private ownership.

Despite their differences, these economic systems can each be interpreted to reveal a concern for justice. For each embraces, in a different way, some mechanism to ensure minimal, and appropriately equal, amounts of both property and personal goods. To embrace some such mechanism is to display a concern for justice. Justice is not only, as Rawls says, "the first virtue of social institutions."[49] It can also be a character trait of persons. As such, it is a disposition to make sure that society, including the institution of property, renders to each person his or her due. A concern for justice undermines the tie between civic virtue and economic inequality that traditional republicanism indulges. Room remains for the republican virtues of independent self-governance, public-spiritedness, and practical reason in civic affairs, but in the main vehicles other than proprietary

49 John Rawls, *A Theory of Justice* (Cambridge, Mass.: Harvard University Press, 1971), p. 3.

independence must secure them. The concern for justice also betokens a desire to stamp out various forms of injustice. As Bernard Williams acutely argues,[50] the many forms of injustice cannot all be traced to a *single* pleonektic motive. Sometimes persons act unjustly because of fear, jealousy or revenge, and *pleonexia* can cover both greed, which is a genuine vice, and competitiveness, whose viciousness is debatable. Nevertheless, the vice of injustice in regard to the distribution of property springs mainly from pleonektic motives – from desires to have more than is one's due or indifference to whether others have what is due them.

Apart from a common concern with justice, the three economic systems are similar in some respects and differ in others so far as moral character is concerned. The first system permits the full range of virtues, such as liberality, and vices, such as stinginess, for which private property is a precondition. It also permits the many virtues and vices often associated with private economic activity. These include such good character traits as industriousness, frugality, self-reliance, and probity in business dealings, and such corresponding bad ones as laziness and excessive devotion to work, prodigality and penny-pinchingness, financial dependency, and dishonesty and sharp practice in business. The various distributional restrictions will inhibit the formation of vices to some degree, but it can hardly eliminate them. These restrictions may allow enough private accumulation to support civic virtues to a slight extent, but the link will be feeble compared with that in an aristocratic society or even in laissez-faire capitalism.

Under the second system, since people can still own property for consumption, they can still be generous and still be stingy. But since people are less able to own productive resources, the situation of other virtues and vices will change. Consider industriousness and frugality. Public business enterprises could still offer incentives to motivate em-

50 Bernard Williams, "Justice as a Virtue," in his *Moral Luck*, pp. 83–93. For Aristotle's views, see *Nicomachean Ethics* 1129^{a}1–1138^{b}15.

ployees to work assiduously. And people could manage family resources carefully to have more funds available for things they prefer. Yet the market would no longer be the chief determinant of industrious and frugal behavior. One can speculate whether such vices as laziness or wastefulness would increase. In any event, the second system is almost certain to eliminate proprietary independence as a foundation for civic virtues in the republican tradition. It is also likely to reduce the opportunity to exhibit such virtues as probity in business dealings or such vices as dishonesty in trade or sharp business practices. Such traits may, however, persist in a weakened or altered form in public economic enterprise – think, for example, of pilferage by employees. Finally, insofar as persons share common aims in production, such traits as reciprocity[51] and cooperativeness may become more common.

To choose the third system may, and generally will, underscore a deep commitment to justice, reciprocity, cooperativeness, solidarity, and community-mindedness as virtues. It will leave little scope not only for virtues related to business but also for other virtues associated with private property. One can, of course, still be generous with one's time or with one's modest personal effects; but works of charity, for example, will be sharply curtailed and indeed may be largely unnecessary. Because this final system has never been implemented in a large Western society, one can only speculate whether it would lead to a loss of industriousness and self-reliance.

6.6 PROPERTY AND MORAL IDEALS

If the previous section is sound, then although the three economic systems share a concern for justice, each advances, and retards or makes inapplicable, the development of somewhat different character traits in relation to property. It seems likely that this conclusion would hold for the many

51 See Lawrence C. Becker, *Reciprocity* (London and New York: Routledge & Kegan Paul, 1986).

other kinds of economic systems that one might describe. In consequence, there is no unique set of virtues and vices that a person can possess or is likely to possess under all economic systems. Hence, to choose an economic system is to limit the range of property-related virtues and vices that persons living under that system can or are likely to have. And to formulate an ideal moral character in relation to property is to limit the range of economic systems in which persons could exemplify that ideal.

The three-part moral is as follows. First, if one has great confidence in a particular view of moral character, one may construct an ideal set of property-related virtues and let the economic chips fall where they may. Even here the construction of an ideal is no simple matter. In a different context, Foot mentions the "thought that so far from forming a unity in the sense that Aristotle and Aquinas believed they did, the virtues actually conflict with each other: which is to say that if someone has one of them he inevitably fails to have some other."[52] If Foot is right, then even for a given economic system the possibility of conflict, or incommensurability of choice, exists in regard to moral character.

Second, if one has great confidence in a moral theory that justifies a particular economic system, one can accept with equanimity the virtues and vices that result. On the whole, political theories of property and economic systems have paid insufficient attention to their impact on moral character.

Third, each sort of confidence is a specimen of over-confidence. A better theory of property and economic systems will make room for both perspectives. That is, one must look to the justifying principles that undergird a system of property and its associated economic institutions in constructing an account of moral character, and one must keep an eye on property-related virtues and vices in building a justification for property and economic arrangements. Furthermore, the best theory is apt to be pluralist, and the most

52 Philippa Foot, "Moral Realism and Moral Dilemma," *Journal of Philosophy*, 80 (1983): 379–98, at 397.

promising pluralist theory is likely to have an independent role for considerations of moral character. Thus, in elaborating the theory and applying it to practical problems, one must not only look at principles of justification but also attend to the character traits that result in economic systems that satisfy those principles, and be prepared to modify those principles if those traits do not, on due consideration, make room for and promote acceptable moral characters. At the same time, general principles defended by moral argument can furnish reasons for modifying one's views about which moral characters are acceptable.[53]

53 Though the text suggests some sympathy for Foot's view that utilitarians cannot appeal unproblematically to the "best state of affairs," it also supports a version of pluralism that she would find uncongenial. See Philippa Foot, "Utilitarianism and the Virtues," *Mind*, 94 (1985): 196–209.

Chapter 7

Alienation, exploitation, and power

7.1 THE PROGRAM

One must reckon with the bad as well as the good. The three previous chapters identify some good things that property, and specifically private property, helps to accomplish: the development of personality; the securing of control, privacy, and individuality; the fostering of some beneficial character traits. Even these chapters point out some undesirable aspects of property institutions. Yet anyone who sees private property as a downright nasty affair will object that the main complaints have yet to be addressed. What about alienation, exploitation, and the misuse of power? Since Marx, at least, must not these possible consequences of private property be taken into account?

Indeed they must. No acceptable background theory of property institutions can ignore them. Therefore, this chapter aims to relate property, alienation, exploitation, and power in a full social context. It suggests that though private property can do some bad things, it need not do them or at least do so many of them as to rule out all arrangements of private property. The chapter supplies, then, the final part of the background theory needed to begin the difficult task of formulating explicit principles to justify, and limit, property.

The discussion follows this path. Just as referring to intellectual history proved helpful in developing an account of property and moral character, so will it also in elaborating the themes of this chapter – though, once again, the survey cannot achieve great depth. One cannot understand Marx's concerns well without grasping his reaction to Hegel. Although Hegel rightly maintains that property is an attribute of societies and persons, he allows property holdings unduly to influence political representation. Marx's discussion of capitalism, alienation, and private property improves on Hegel. Although Marx's own views are flawed, it is possible to build on his insights. The insights prompt a revised account of alienation and exploitation and a more general treatment of problems of economic production. They also underscore some connections between property and power. The chapter concludes by reviewing some characteristics that a satisfactory theory of property should have. These desiderata are a touchstone for the account of justification and distributive equity and for the applications of this account in Parts III and IV of the book.

In what follows, the names "Hegel" and "Marx" refer to philosophers who may not be identical with their historical namesakes. The inquiry is difficult enough without fussing over problems of interpretation. It suffices if the Hegel and Marx of this chapter hold views that strongly resemble, and are at least as either plausible or interesting as, the views of the real Hegel and the real Marx.

7.2 PROPERTY AS AN ATTRIBUTE OF SOCIETIES AND PERSONS

Property discloses much about societies and persons. This sentence expresses a compound thought. First, for all societies, if one describes the institution of property as it exists in a society, the description reveals something important about that society. Second, for each society, if one describes what a person owns, the description reveals something important about that person.[1]

---

1 The compound thought differs from, but owes much to, the exposition in Shlomo Avineri, *Hegel's Theory of the Modern State* (Cambridge: Cambridge University Press, 1972), pp. 88–89, 106–07, 135–37, 171, 213. Avineri's treatment draws on works of Hegel's besides the *Philosophy of Right*.

One can see this compound thought as the core of Hegel's later reflections on property in the *Philosophy of Right*.[2] The reflections, though often obscure, yield several main points. The section on "abstract right," sketched in § 4.3, gives a highly individualistic, natural-rights view of property. Later sections on "civil society" and the "state" modify that view. Civil society is, roughly, the legal and social arrangement that goes best with laissez-faire capitalism. Here property is protected by a legal system that allows persons to pursue their own aims. For Hegel, "state" is a term of art. It does not apply to every political institution having a single independent government within a definite territory. It applies just to those that both incorporate and surpass the individualistic aims of civil society. Property rights are less powerful in the state than in civil society. Thus, property as it exists under abstract right is at once annulled, preserved, and transcended *(aufgehoben)* in civil society and the state.

Consider the transition from abstract right to civil society. To describe the situation of property is to grasp something important about that society. Hegel regards early modern German society – that is to say, up to a fairly brief period before his own time – as a civil society. Here government exists mainly to preserve private property; people are not public-spirited; they concentrate on their own interests. Taxation exists principally to fund the institutions, such as the police and the courts, needed to protect individual interests – including, in particular, property rights.[3] These property rights are, however, no longer the unfettered rights gained by occupancy in the manner discussed in the section on abstract right. Instead property rights exist only insofar as the law recognizes them:

2 See G. W. F. Hegel, *Philosophy of Right* [1821], trans. T. M. Knox (Oxford: Clarendon Press, 1965 [1952]), §§ 41–71 (abstract right), 182–256 (civil society), 257–360 (the state). Omitted is Hegel's intervening treatment of property in the family, §§ 170–80, which requires separate consideration.

3 In §§ 240–45, Hegel discusses the problem of poverty and government welfare programs. In these passages he seems to allow for a broader use of taxation than in other places.

The principle of rightness passes over in civil society into law. My individual right, whose embodiment has hitherto been immediate and abstract, now similarly becomes embodied in the existent will and knowledge of everyone, in the sense that it becomes recognized. Hence property acquisitions and transfers must now be undertaken and concluded only in the form which that embodiment gives to them. In civil society, property rests on contract and on the formalities which make ownership capable of proof and valid in law.

Original, i.e. direct, titles and means of acquisition . . . are simply discarded in civil society and appear only as isolated accidents or as subordinated factors of property transactions.[4]

Thus the relation between private property and personality is transformed: "Since property and personality have legal recognition and validity in civil society, wrongdoing now becomes an infringement, not merely of what is subjectively infinite, but of the universal thing which is existent with inherent stability and strength."[5] To put this into a common-law mode, crimes against property are not merely person-al wrongs but breaches of the king's peace. They pose a danger to society. Hence to protect property is also to protect society.

Within civil society, to describe what people own is to say something important about them. For the type and amount of property they own partly constitutes their social position. If they own a great deal of consumptive and productive property, they occupy a favored position. If they own very little, they occupy a much lower position. In both cases, the position affects how the occupants see themselves and how others see them.

Consider now the transition from civil society to the state. Once again a description of the institution of property re-

4   Ibid., § 217.
5   Ibid., § 218.

veals something important about the society. Hegel sees the Germany of his own day as a state. It protects property rights in many ways. But taxes now support a wider array of public goods. Since taxation has broader purposes than in civil society, property rights are less powerful. Concomitantly, the state can pursue aims that civil society cannot. For instance, the state can seek to develop and reinforce public-spiritedness and solidarity. Still, Hegel does not conceive of the state as abolishing private property. Abolition would be inconsistent with his criticism that "the principle that underlies Plato's ideal state violates the right of personality by forbidding the holding of private property."[6]

It is therefore no surprise that, within the state, describing what persons own discloses something important about them. Even in the state, inequalities of wealth can exist. And even in the state Hegel supposes there to be a connection between property and personality. Of course, welfare programs can soften the impact on a person's social position, but unequal property holdings are bound to affect that position. Since political power is partly a function of social position, inequalities also affect political power. Still, the effects, in Hegel's view, are sometimes desirable.

An illustration of this last remark is Hegel's account of political representation in the state. The guiding idea is to have property-defined classes represented in the legislature. Of the various classes, by far the most important is the landed gentry. He thinks the gentry to be specially suited to govern in the public interest. Since members of the gentry owe their position to birth, and since their property is subject to primogeniture (that is, it must descend to the eldest male child), Hegel believes that they have neither need nor possibility of favoring their own interest. Thus they can further the interests of all.

6 Ibid., § 46. As the translator observes (p. 322 n.23), *Republic* 416–21 precludes only the guardians from holding private property. But cf. *Laws* 739.

This class is more particularly fitted for political position and significance in that its capital is independent alike of the state's capital, the uncertainty of business, the quest for profit, and any sort of fluctuation in possessions. It is likewise independent of favour, whether from the executive or the mob. It is even fortified against its own wilfulness, because those members of this class who are called to political life are not entitled, as other citizens are, either to dispose of their entire property at will, or to the assurance that it will pass to their children, whom they love equally, in similarly equal divisions. Hence their wealth becomes inalienable, entailed, and burdened by primogeniture.[7]

So much for exposition. To appraise Hegel's discussion, one should first acknowledge the insights. The overarching thought – that property discloses much about societies and persons – contributes a great deal to the understanding of property. It is, moreover, an acute move to identify types of arrangements and show how property differs in each. Some will greet skeptically the types that Hegel identifies – abstract right, civil society, and the state. They may be more skeptical of the dialectical progression that he claims from one to the next. Even so, there is some sound sense in his discussion. Any doctrine of acquiring property by occupancy, unaffected by social rules, is highly individualistic. Such acquisition plays a tiny role in contemporary society. For nowadays legal rules specify what counts as occupancy, and there are few unowned things open to ownership left to acquire. Thus Hegel is right to conclude that any theory of property based on "abstract right" is one-sided and incomplete. This conclusion applies, *mutatis mutandis*, to most libertarian theories of acquisition, such as that of Nozick.[8] Similarly, since most legal systems have detailed rules for the transfer and registration of property, Hegel is also right to hold that in civil

7 Hegel, *Philosophy of Right*, § 306.
8 Robert Nozick, *Anarchy, State, and Utopia* (New York: Basic Books, 1974), pp. 150–82. See § 3.4 above and §§ 10.3–10.4 below.

society property rests on legal "formalities." Yet again, in economically complex welfare states, property rights are far from sacrosanct. In them taxation supports more than the minimal government functions needed to protect property rights. Thus Hegel's insistence that in the state property has a more curtailed function also seems correct.

Nevertheless, some major shortcomings render Hegel's discussion ultimately unsatisfactory. First, he still forces the connection between property and personality. Section 4.7 argued that, in the domain of abstract right, property is at best somewhat conducive to, not necessary for, moral and political personhood. Moving to civil society does not avoid this argument. Even in civil society one can develop and retain such personhood by claiming and having other political and civil rights. A transition to the state is likewise unavailing, for there ownership is less protected and less important to personhood than in civil society. Furthermore, if one switches to a psychological sense of "personality" as self-integration, the argument of § 4.7 remains unaffected.

Second, Hegel has no way out of the seeming impasse described in § 5.5. He is, to his credit, the first to spot the problem. In civil society, there are extremes of wealth and poverty; charity and welfare erode dignity; the market is unable to handle goods produced by government-created jobs. Poverty is endemic to civil society and ineliminable from it.[9] But even a dialectical solution eludes Hegel. He fails to show that the state can avoid poverty and its effects. As Avineri writes, "Though [Hegel's] theory of the state is aimed at integrating the contending interests of civil society under a common bond, on the problem of poverty he ultimately has nothing more to say than that it is one of 'the most disturbing problems which agitate modern society'. On no other occasion does Hegel leave a problem at that."[10]

9 See Hegel, *Philosophy of Right*, §§ 195, 241–45.
10 Avineri, *Hegel's Theory of the Modern State*, p. 154. See Hegel, *Philosophy of Right*, addition to § 244. Teichgraeber criticizes Avineri, but it is difficult to find points in his article that both diverge from Avineri's position accurately understood and supply sound argument for a

Notice that poverty is a more vexing problem for Hegel than it would be, say, for a utilitarian. A utilitarian can justify poverty if, by summing and balancing over all individuals in society, there must be some who are poor in return for higher average or total utility. Of course, the disutilities to the poor stemming from their poverty, including the disutilities of inadequate personality development, must be taken into account in calculating social utility. But lacking is any reason in principle why the calculation could not result in the poverty of some being justified for the good of all. Hegel rejects utilitarianism and trade-offs of this sort between the rich and the poor. Hence poverty is more troubling for him precisely because he cannot allow that some – namely, the poor – may be sacrificed for the good of all.

Third, Hegel's account of the state endorses an undue influence by property on other areas of society, especially on politics. The problem relates to political representation and to the role of a landed gentry. The basic criticism, first formulated by Marx, is that even with land burdened by primogeniture, the gentry will promote its own interests rather than the interest of all. It is therefore not specially fitted for action in the public interest.[11]

different position. See Richard Teichgraeber, "Hegel on Property and Poverty," *Journal of the History of Ideas*, 38 (1977): 47–64, at 59–60, 63–64.

11 See Karl Marx, *Critique of Hegel's "Philosophy of Right,"* ed. Joseph O'Malley (Cambridge: Cambridge University Press, 1970), pp. 94–113. Marx elaborates the criticism with some forbidding terminology of his own. The following summary makes use of O'Malley's introduction, pp. xxvii–xl; Shlomo Avineri, *The Social and Political Thought of Karl Marx* (Cambridge: Cambridge University Press, 1968), pp. 27–31.

If one were to take a straightforward, realistic view of society, Marx suggests, one would conclude that persons are the "subjects" and that the things which they possess or own (property) are "predicates." The terms "subject" and "predicate" here are used not in their grammatical senses, but as the "determining" and "determined" members, respectively, of a two-place relation. Hegel's discussion of landed property, however, "inverts" the relation of subject and predicate. For Hegel, landed property under a burden of primogeniture becomes the subject. And individual members of the landed gentry over generations become predicates of that landed property. To correct the situa-

Hegel lacks a convincing response to Marx's criticism. One possible response is the empirical gambit. Hegel could say that it is just an empirical question whether the landed gentry will act in its own class interest. Marx cannot settle the issue by an abstract argument. This response is dubious in part because it would be unlike Hegel to convert the issue into an empirical question. Worse, the answer is almost certain to go against Hegel. Landed aristocracies in almost all countries have acted in their class interest, not in the public interest.

A different response is the dialectical gambit. Hegel could say that his theory just describes the current state of world history and progress. There are bound to be "contradictions." World history must, and will, go forward. In the process, the "contradictions" that Marx identifies will be resolved. The difficulty with this response is that it conflicts with Hegel's approving attitude toward the Prussian state and its gentry. So, even though this response may square with Hegel's philosophy of history, it would require him to renounce the sympathy with the Prussian state that per-

tion it is necessary to "invert the inversion." Here Marx applies the so-called transformative method that he adapted from Ludwig Feuerbach. Marx argues that it is necessary once again to see persons as central and property as appendages or modifications of persons, not vice versa.

The criticism is deeper than just saying that Hegel incorrectly has the tail wagging the dog. Marx's point is that Hegel's treatment of property in the state is misleading and distorts political representation. Hegel is committed to regarding political representation and state-service as the subject and the political qualities of individual members of the landed gentry over generations as the predicates. Here, too, it is necessary to "invert the inversion" to gain an accurate view. Once the transformative method is applied, it becomes clear that the actual political qualities of individual landowners are determining (subjects), and that the political representation and state-service, or lack of them, that landowners provide are functions of the political nature of landowners (predicates). And once this is done, it becomes clearer why the landed gentry will represent their own interests rather than serve the public interest. Thus Hegel has a muddled theory of political representation. The broader point that Marx seems to make is that in general property relations determine class interests and class relations.

156

meates his political philosophy. Except for the Hegelian defender who wishes to preserve Hegel's philosophy of history while parting with some salient features of the *Philosophy of Right*, the dialectical gambit offers little hope. Even then it concedes that the account of the political representativeness and fitness for public service of the landed gentry is replete with "contradiction."

7.3 MARX ON ALIENATION

Marx in effect rectifies some of Hegel's shortcomings, but his independent views have difficulties of their own. Marx's treatment of alienation, capitalism, and private property in the *Economic and Philosophic Manuscripts of 1844* is hard to interpret. It is hoped that the text at least strongly supports the following interpretation. Alienation is separation. Specifically, it is the separation of persons from nature, from the products of their labor, from themselves, and from other human beings.[12] Under alienation persons encounter as "other" the world of material objects and human beings and even themselves.

12 The *Economic and Philosophic Manuscripts of 1844*, ed. Dirk J. Struik (New York: International Publishers, 1964), speaks of both alienation *(Entäusserung)* and estrangement *(Entfremdung)*. Marx often uses the terms interchangeably. If the terms have different meanings, it is hard to say what they are. One possibility is that estrangement refers to the loss of the object produced (p. 109) and alienation to the way the objects produced become alien and dominate human beings in a hostile way (pp. 108, 131). This section uses the term "alienation" to do double duty, if that be necessary, for the terms "alienation" and "estrangement" as they occur in Marx's text.

   The domination exercised by material products is related to Marx's later idea of the "fetishism of commodities." See Karl Marx, *Capital* [1867], ed. Frederick Engels and trans. Samuel Moore and Edward Aveling (New York: International Publishers, 1967), vol. 1, pp. 71–83. According to this idea, "commodities" (material products of labor in a capitalist society) are viewed by people in that society as having human qualities (for example, needs), whereas human beings (workers and capitalists alike) are viewed as lacking human qualities. Viewing matters in this way reverses the proper direction of control. People see, for example, machines as needing workers rather than workers as needing machines.

Alienation arises from work carried out under certain conditions. All labor involves "objectification" *(Vergegenständlichung)* – that is, the creation or transformation of material objects. But not all objectification involves alienation. Labor in communal societies and artisan labor in a feudal economy involve no, or at least very little, alienation. But labor under capitalism necessarily involves alienation. There the worker owns neither the tools nor the raw materials used in production. The capitalist owns them and receives the product of labor. He pays the worker only a subsistence wage. The word "capitalism," as used in the *Manuscripts,* applies to many of the same arrangements as "laissez-faire capitalism," as defined in § 5.3. But Marx often uses "capitalism" pejoratively and requires substantial exploitation of workers. In contrast, § 5.3 tries to employ "laissez-faire capitalism" dispassionately and does not build exploitation into its definition.

Chief among the leading features of alienation are these. (1) Alienation involves a set of objective relations of separation stemming from production. It is not a set of feelings of anger, unhappiness, or depression. Yet while such feelings are not the essence of alienation, they usually accompany it. The worker "does not affirm himself but denies himself, does not feel content but unhappy, does not develop freely his physical and mental energy but mortifies his body and ruins his mind."[13] (2) Both workers and capitalists suffer from alienation, albeit in different ways.[14] The capitalist mode of production deforms the humanity of both, even though the capitalist may lack unpleasant feelings. (3) Alienation ultimately reflects persons' separation from their "species-being" *(Gattungswesen)* – that is, their essence as objectifying social beings. Marx's concept of species-being is fuzzy. Apparently it is a concept of philosophical anthropology. It performs both critical and constructive functions. The

13 Marx, *Manuscripts*, p. 110.
14 "[E]verything which appears in the worker as an *activity of alienation, of estrangement*, appears in the non-worker as a *state of alienation, of estrangement*." Ibid., p. 119 (emphasis in original).

concept of species-being is a critical vehicle for exposing the gravity of the mutilation by capitalism of persons' nature as social beings. Labor "produces beauty – but for the worker, deformity. It replaces labor by machines, but it throws a section of the workers back to a barbarous type of labor, and it turns other workers into machines. It produces intelligence – but for the worker stupidity, cretinism."[15] The concept of species-being is also a constructive tool for depicting the future communist society. In that society, bourgeois private property will be abolished,[16] objectification will express human qualities, and material objects will no longer dominate humankind. Marx's picture of this society is hazy. It appears to involve two stages, in the first of which, sometimes called "crude communism,"[17] some alienation may remain.[18] In the second stage, or mature communism,[19] human beings are realigned with their species-being and alienation will cease.[20] Alienation stems, then, from production rather than from a maldistribution of property. Marx does not argue that alienation will cease if property distributions are made fairer or more nearly equal. The correction lies in a new social system involving a different mode of production.

Marx's account at least addresses, even if it does not re-

15 Ibid., p. 110.
16 In *The Communist Manifesto* (1848), Marx and Engels direct their attention to this sort of private property. "[M]odern bourgeois private property is the final and most complete expression of the system of producing and appropriating products, that is based on class antagonisms, on the exploitation of the many by the few." Karl Marx and Friedrich Engels, *The Communist Manifesto*, in Arthur P. Mendel, ed., *Essential Works of Marxism* (New York: Bantam, 1961), p. 26. This work advocates the abolition, not of private property in the humdrum sense of consumer goods acquired by labor, but "modern bourgeois private property," that is, property in the form of capital that exploits wage labor. The acknowledged consequence is the abolition of "bourgeois" freedom, individuality, and independence. Ibid., p. 27.
17 Marx, *Manuscripts*, p. 133.
18 Ibid., pp. 133–34.
19 Ibid., pp. 135–46.
20 Ibid., pp. 138–39, 140. The division into two stages follows Avineri, *The Social and Political Thought of Karl Marx*, pp. 220–39.

move, the deficiencies of Hegel's discussion. Hegel forces an allegedly desirable connection between property and personality. Marx, on the other hand, contends that private property under capitalism has effects, most of them undesirable, on both those who have and those who lack property. Again, Hegel does not solve the problem of poverty. Marx, in contrast, insists that it is a mistake to see the problem chiefly as a matter of distribution. It is mainly a matter of production. Finally, Hegel allows property ownership unduly to influence other areas of society – particularly politics. Yet Marx claims that one must restructure production and society to eradicate such undue influence.

To see whether Marx has a satisfactory account of property, alienation, and society, one must answer at least three questions. What is the relation between alienation and private property? Is alienation a necessary feature of capitalism? Will alienation be absent from the mature communist society? The balance of this section argues that the answers Marx can provide to these questions are unsatisfactory.

A tempting response to the first question is that private property causes alienation. Unless the capitalist has a certain amount of private property in the form of money, he cannot pay laborers. And it is only when laborers are paid a subsistence wage and the capitalist wrests away the remaining value produced ("surplus value") that alienation arises. Nevertheless, one passage suggests just the opposite – namely, that alienation causes private property. "[O]n analysis of this concept [of alienated labor] it becomes clear that though private property appears to be the source, the cause of alienated labor, it is rather its consequence."[21] Yet it is hard to see how this can be so. Alienated labor is supposed to be characteristic of capitalism. It is unclear how the capitalist mode of production can get under way unless there is first a certain amount of private property.

The most plausible move is to hold that the causal connec-

21 Marx, *Manuscripts*, p. 117.

tion is in some sense chain-linked. Marx himself, after the sentence just quoted, goes on to say:

> Later this relationship becomes reciprocal.
> Only at the last culmination of the development of private property does this, its secret, appear again, namely, that on the one hand it is the *product* of alienated labor, and that on the other hand it is the *means* by which labor alienates itself, the *realization of this alienation.*[22]

The meaning of this passage is far from clear. Here is a reconstruction that distinguishes two senses of "private property."[23] Private property in the first sense means privately held wealth in the initial stages of being put to use as capital. In this sense, private property is a cause of alienation or alienated labor. The analysis in the *Grundrisse* suggests that the capitalist mode of production cannot arise until there is an accumulation of potential capital in the form of money from trade or lending.[24] This money is the initial form of

22 Ibid. (emphasis in original).
23 These senses are technical meanings employed only in this section. They do not modify the way that "private property" is defined in § 2.3 and used elsewhere in this book.
24 The suggestion, in more detail, goes like this. In both the *German Ideology* (1846) and, especially, the *Grundrisse* (1858) Marx examines property and historical periodization. (Relevant portions of the *Grundrisse* are also available in English under the title *Pre-Capitalist Economic Formations*, ed. E. J. Hobsbawm (New York: International Publishers, 1964); the editor's introduction, to which this sketch is indebted, is valuable. Cf. also Marx, *Capital*, vol. 1, pp. 713–16.) In the *Grundrisse*, Marx divides precapitalist economic systems into three main types – the "oriental" (or "Asiatic"), "ancient classical" (Greco-Roman), and "Germanic" (or feudal). Despite enormous differences, these three modes of economic organization have in common the aim of producing in order to sustain human beings as members of the community. In all these forms, to use Marx's language, the economic object is the production of "use values." Marx, *Pre-Capitalist Economic Formations*, p. 80. "Thus originally *property* means no more than man's attitude to his natural conditions of production as belonging to him, as the *prerequisites of his own existence.*" Ibid., p. 89 (emphasis in

private property as capital in the early modern industrial world. Private property in the second sense means privately held wealth after a capitalist system is fully under way. In this sense, alienation or alienated labor is a cause of private property. The idea is that such private wealth, especially in the form of privately owned means of production, fully expresses the alienated labor that gives rise to it.

So in the end it is not the case that private property both causes and is caused by alienation, if "private property" is always to have the same sense. Such a position involves a difficult, perhaps insoluble, problem of explaining how the

original). Only from the Germanic or feudal form, however, is there an evolutionary transition to capitalism.

Marx's account of the transition is not entirely clear, but three main factors appear to be involved. First, there must be an accumulation of potential capital in the form of money from trade or lending. Second, changes must occur in rural social structure that allow peasants to become day laborers for a wage. Third, urban crafts must develop to a point where they produce nonagricultural commodities for an internal market. By this complex route, aided it may be supposed by technological developments, there arises capital in the strict sense of industrial capital. Workers now sell their labor to the owner of the means of production (the capitalist); the owner pays the worker wages; the owner keeps the excess value produced. Capitalism first appears alongside feudal modes of production and then overwhelms them.

Of special interest in this complex process is that the worker must stand in a relation of nonproperty to the means of production. He must cease to own land and tools. If slavery or serfdom has existed, that property relation too must be dissolved and persons become free laborers. They then "confront all objective conditions of production as *alien property*, as their own *non-property*, but at the same time as something which can be exchanged as *values* and therefore to some extent appropriated by living labour." Ibid., p. 104 (emphasis in original). Hence there must occur also a certain change in attitude. The economic object, in Marx's language, is now the production of "exchange-values" rather than "use-values." Ibid., pp. 105, 111. The capitalist must intend to use private property in the form of capital to produce ever greater amounts of wealth rather than merely to use the excess money for the consumption of luxuries. These, then, are the well-springs of alienation. People see one another in a market way, as exchange values rather than use values. Private property, in Marx's view, means that they no longer relate to one another fully as human beings.

reciprocal causal relation arises. The reconstruction, which distinguishes two senses of "private property," avoids this chicken-and-egg problem, comports with Marx's account of the birth of capitalism in the *Grundrisse,* and restates sympathetically the kind of doctrine that might have appealed to Marx. If one adopts the reconstruction, however, it is not quite accurate to assert reciprocal causation, for there is no single connection that is reciprocal. Rather, there is a short chain of causal connections: private property in the first sense causes alienation, which in turn causes private property in the second sense. Over time, one would expect that both sorts of connections would still occur; in that way the connections, though not exactly reciprocal, are continuing.

Some may object that Marx did not see the connection between alienation and private property as a *causal* connection. He saw it as a *noncausal* connection. But what sort of noncausal connection? One answer is that it is an analytically necessary connection.[25] The necessity is expressible in one or more of the ways common among contemporary Anglo-American philosophers of language – such as logical, conceptual, or semantic necessity; one-way or two-way entailment; analyticity; and so on. This answer is doubtful. The Marx of the *Manuscripts* was a student of Hegel. It is foreign to Hegel's logic, and to other logical doctrines of Marx's time that would have appealed to him, to endorse any view of necessity held by contemporary analytic philosophers.

Another answer suggested by analytic philosophy is supervenience. Some philosophers maintain that the properties that make something good or beautiful are dependent on and necessarily determined by, but not reducible to, other properties, such as the characteristics of a person or the physical properties of a painting.[26] In short, goodness or

25 *"Private property* thus results by analysis from the concept of *alienated labor.* . . ." Marx, *Manuscripts,* p. 117 (emphasis in original).
26 See, for example, R. M. Hare, *The Language of Morals* (Oxford: Clarendon Press, 1952), pp. 80–81, 131, 134, 145, 153–55, 159; Jaegwon Kim, "Supervenience and Nomological Incommensurables," *American Philosophical Quarterly,* 15 (1978): 149–56; Frank Sibley, "Aesthetic Concepts," *Philosophical Review,* 68 (1959): 421–50, at 424.

beauty supervenes on these other properties. In the same vein, one might suggest that for Marx, alienation supervenes on private property created under a capitalist mode of production. More fully, the property of alienation is dependent on and necessarily determined by, but not reducible to, the material properties of private property generated by a capitalist mode of production. Although this suggestion may have some philosophical promise, it is far from clear that Marx would have embraced the contemporary analytic philosopher's concept of supervenience. In addition, this brief sketch does not explain the sense of "necessarily" – such as logical or causal – involved in alienation.[27]

A rather different answer, advanced by Ollman,[28] is that Marx saw a noncausal connection between alienation or alienated labor and private property that involves an "internal relation." The doctrine of internal relations is a doctrine that the young Marx might have adopted, or adapted, from Hegel. An "internal" relation is not conceived to hold between two things – two "relata" – that exist independently and can be thought of independently. It is instead a relation that holds between things that must be thought of together. Thus an internal relation involves a kind of necessary connection, but it does not involve an analytically necessary relation in a contemporary sense. According to the suggested answer, Marx thought of private property and alienated labor as very intimately connected. They are so interdependent that it is impossible to think successfully about one without also thinking about the other.

Ollman's answer has some difficulties. First, the doctrine of internal relations is unclear. Hence, to explain Marx's views on alienation and private property in terms of internal relations is to explain *obscurum per obscurius*.[29] Second, even

27 Cf. Kim, "Supervenience and Nomological Incommensurables," at 152 (appropriate interpretation of "necessarily" varies).
28 Bertell Ollman, *Alienation: Marx's Conception of Man in Capitalist Society*, 2d ed. (Cambridge: Cambridge University Press, 1976).
29 This criticism does not apply if one defines an external relation as a "relation of comparison" and an internal relation as a "relation of (causal) interaction." See Jon Elster, *Making Sense of Marx* (Cambridge:

were the doctrine clear, its correctness as a philosophical account of (even some) relations is debatable. The central difficulty, for any two items claimed to be internally related, is whether they can be given any genuine status as particular, identifiable things.[30]

The upshot is that one might answer in several ways the question of how alienation and private property are related. To hold that the relation is analytically necessary or supervenient is an implausible interpretation of Marx. And it seems unpromising to do political philosophy by constructing analytically necessary connections. In contrast, to hold that alienation and private property are internally related is a plausible interpretation. But it is not philosophically promising. If so, the best overall interpretive and philosophical candidate is that there are linked causal connections. Private property *qua* rudimentary capital causes alienation. And alienation causes private property *qua* fully developed capital. The ultimate merits of this answer cannot, however, be assessed without a closer look at capitalism.

These reflections prompt the second question: Is alienation a necessary feature of capitalism? The answer turns partly on the meanings of "alienation" and "capitalism." If alienation applies to a set of unpleasant feelings, then, although its existence is a matter of concern, it does not necessarily accompany capitalism. Capitalists and workers might, and sometimes do, feel happy or at least contented. If alienation, as suggested earlier, applies to a set of objective relations of separation stemming from a certain mode of production, then other problems arise. Should the word be so understood, the proposition that alienation is a necessary feature of capitalism would have to be true by virtue of the

Cambridge University Press, 1985), pp. 92–95. But then the internal-relations analysis would collapse into the linked-causal-connections analysis given earlier. As Elster points out (p. 92 n.3), his definitions of external and internal relations are quite different from Ollman's.

30 See especially G. E. Moore, "External and Internal Relations," in his *Philosophical Studies* (London: Trench, Trubner & Co., 1922), pp. 276–309.

nature of alienation or alienated labor, of wage labor, and of the capitalist mode of production. To claim that, however, is just to make the proposition necessarily true. Its necessary truth would have to depend, in turn, either on the doctrine of internal relations or, possibly, on the meanings of the terms used to state it by virtue of some philosophical concept of analyticity, conceptual or semantic necessity, entailment, or the like. Nevertheless, the doctrine of internal relations is vague and quite possibly mistaken. And some contemporary philosophical account of necessity seems far from what Marx meant. Hence Marx appears to lack an adequate account of why the proposition should be necessarily true. This lack suggests a pair of deeper problems. If the proposition is necessarily true, perhaps it is so only by virtue of Marx's stipulation, which would make it trivial. Also, the practical import of the proposition now seems in doubt. If workers and capitalists are happy, or at least contented, it is not obvious that the set of objective relations called alienation should matter.

The defender of Marx need hardly be speechless in the face of these problems. To begin, if alienation is a necessary feature of capitalism, the truth need not be trivial. Necessary truths expressed by sentences such as "Bachelors are unmarried" are indeed trivial and boring. So also are necessary truths depending on stipulation. But Marx's view that alienation is a necessary feature of capitalism falls into neither group. What makes his view different is that, if true, it is unobviously and interestingly true. And it is so because it rests on a theory involving concepts of alienation, capitalist production, and species-being.

The defender of Marx can also reply that even though alienation may not manifest itself as unhappiness or malaise, it hardly follows that it is not a matter of concern. Because of the possibility of illusion or self-deception or, as Marx might put it, of false consciousness, the fact that a person has no awareness of a certain feature of reality does not mean that it is absent. A housewife exploited by her husband and children might be mindlessly unaware of her condition and even have a rather cheerful outlook on her station in life. So also might a slave exploited by a seemingly beneficent master. Still, that hardly means that their exploited and servile condition does not exist or that it fails to undermine their humanity. Here, it might be said, Marx's account of species-being is especially relevant. Given persons' nature as objectifying social beings, alienation involves a mutilation of their species-being whether an individual person is aware of the alienation or not.

Although one can offer these defenses in Marx's behalf, they do not overcome the problems. First, if alienation is a necessary feature of capitalism, and if the necessity rests on a theory, then one must elaborate the theory so as to establish the necessity. Marx does not do so. Any attempted elaboration is apt to be problematic. On the one hand, if "capitalism" covers only the highly exploitive arrangement of Marx's day, one might be able to establish the necessity. But then capitalism so understood will be quite different from most contemporary developed mixed economies. On the other hand, if capitalism applies to all private-property economies (§ 5.1), it will be relevant to many contemporary economies. Yet then one will almost certainly not be able to establish the necessity. Even if one could do so, it would not follow that all private-property systems (§ 5.1) must exhibit alienation. Hence at least two, and maybe all three, of the options described in § 5.5 would remain open. As § 12.6 explains, Marx's notion of alienation is problematic in some respects in its application to contemporary modified capitalist economies.

Second, the appeal to false consciousness is inconclusive. Lack of awareness of something touching one's self-respect is a matter for concern,[31] but that is not true of all things of which one is unaware. So more must be said to show why alienation merits concern. If the first point is right, and if

---

31 See Thomas E. Hill, Jr., "Servility and Self-Respect," in Joel Feinberg and Henry West, eds., *Moral Philosophy: Classic Texts and Contemporary Problems* (Encino and Belmont, Calif.: Dickenson, 1977), pp. 484–93.

alienation is supposed also to characterize objective relations stemming from contemporary economies, then one needs an argument for the proposition that feelings of happiness or contentment should be dismissed as false consciousness. The notion of species-being is too vague and slippery to launch such an argument.

There is, finally, a corollary to these two points. If they are both right, then the linked-causal-connections view of private property and alienation is philosophically less attractive. The view is still a plausible interpretation of Marx. And it may even be a plausible position regarding the capitalism of Marx's day. But it does not follow that there are linked causal connections between private property and alienation, if one refers to private property as it is defined in § 2.3 and as it exists in many contemporary economies.

There remains the third question: Will alienation be absent from the mature communist society? Recall that Marx's answer seems to be that a first stage ("crude communism") will still involve some alienation, but that a second stage ("mature communism") will have property only in an unalienated form. It is difficult to assign content to this statement. If one returns to primitive communalism or to the artisan labor of a feudal economy, one might avoid alienation. Yet to counsel such a return is to offer no practical help to the current day. If, as most commentators agree, Marx rejects such a return, one must explain how alienation will vanish. The notion of species-being is too vague for this purpose. Nor can one explain it by excising some feature of contemporary economic organization. The *German Ideology* (1846) and the *Critique of the Gotha Programme* (1875), for example, suggest that mature communism will abolish the division of labor. But if Marx is to avoid objections of utopianism, he must explain how a contemporary society can survive without a division of labor. And if, instead, mature communism has such a division, then one still needs to show how it avoids alienation.

It may be replied, in Marx's behalf, that it is impossible to say in any detail what the mature communist society would be like or what sort of property would exist in it. One argument for this reply reads Marx in a historicist, not determinist, way. It is possible to look back and understand why an earlier historical situation led to the current situation. Yet it is not possible, so the argument goes, to look at the current situation and predict what future society will grow out of it. This may be true. But it does not explain why alienation must be absent from the mature communist society.

In the end, Marx lacks a satisfactory account of property, alienation, and society. He shows neither that all "capitalist" societies must suffer from alienation nor that mature communism can avoid it. His notion of species-being is too vague to have much explanatory or constructive power. Even if alienation were a necessary feature of the capitalism of Marx's time, the situation of private property in most "first world" countries differs markedly. Productive property is now subject to heavy government regulation. As a result, owners of productive property are less able to exploit employees. One must also acknowledge the existence of labor unions, unemployment insurance, welfare programs, and wide investment by persons and institutions (including unions and pension funds) in business enterprise. Their existence does not eliminate the risk of alienation in some broader, non-Marxian sense. Certainly people can feel disaffected and unhappy. But one must try to construct an account oriented to contemporary realities to improve on what Marx has to say.

7.4 ALIENATION AND EXPLOITATION

If the foregoing criticisms of Marx are sound, some may claim that any attempt to relate property to alienation or production is misguided. This claim is false. The present section makes use of some recent writing on alienation and exploitation; philosophical promise, not fidelity to Marx, is the guidepost.[32] The next section elaborates the importance of production to the theory of property. Together the two sections help formulate part of an account of what is required, so far as property is concerned, to have a fully human life in society. This conception of a fully human life in society will play a key role in the principle of justice and equality argued for in Chapter 9.

Persons are alienated if (1) they have extremely negative beliefs and attitudes about their lives and (2) these beliefs and attitudes are caused by a gap between their ideal and their available human potential. The first clause is concerned with such beliefs and attitudes as worthlessness, meaninglessness, and powerlessness rather than, say, mild dissatisfaction or transitory disappointment. In the second clause, human potential is the capacity to develop and flourish as persons. Their ideal potential is their capacity in a society that is historically possible in their time and place. Their available potential is their capacity in the society in which they actually live. This understanding of alienation requires, then, not merely that there be extremely negative psychological states, but that these states be the causal product of a gap between ideal and available human potential. If the gap is narrow, these states are unlikely to result.

Notice several features of this understanding of alienation. First, it places only modest demands on a philosophical anthropology. It avoids the pitfalls of Marx's treatment of species-being. It requires nothing so bold as a general theory of human nature. Still, it does presuppose some account of human beings – how far they can develop and flourish in their actual society and in some different society that is

32 See Allen E. Buchanan, *Marx and Justice: The Radical Critique of Liberalism* (Totowa, N.J.: Rowman & Littlefield, 1982), ch. 3; Elster, *Making Sense of Marx*, ch. 4; John E. Roemer, *A General Theory of Exploitation and Class* (Cambridge, Mass.: Harvard University Press, 1982); Allen W. Wood, *Karl Marx* (London, Boston and Henley: Routledge & Kegan Paul, 1981), chs. 1, 2, and 4. For discussion of recent writings on these topics, see N. Scott Arnold, "Recent Work on Marx: A Critical Survey," *American Philosophical Quarterly*, 24 (1987): 277–93, especially at 283–88.

historically possible for them. Careful work in sociology should give empirically testable content to this account.[33] Second, this understanding of alienation makes it a matter of degree. The degree springs from the severity of the negative beliefs and attitudes and, to the extent that one speaks of alienation in a society, the number of persons who are alienated. Third, this understanding can, if desired, be supplemented by an account of false consciousness. The present definition specifies two conditions that are jointly sufficient for alienation. A more complete definition that gives necessary and sufficient conditions for alienation should add some counterfactual clause. The clause might read: or if (3), in case persons lack such beliefs and attitudes, they lack them only because of some illusion or false consciousness. This section will not try to develop a sound counterfactual analysis. Fourth, this understanding of alienation is quite general. Alienation is not, by definition, tied to private property, capitalism, particular forms of production, or the labor theory of value, or precluded under socialism or communism.[34]

The next step is to show how this understanding of alienation underlies an account of exploitation. Persons are exploited if (1) others secure a benefit by (2) using them as a tool or resource so as (3) to cause them serious harm. This account builds on the fact that "exploit" is a transitive verb and that in sentences of the form "A exploits B," it should be possible to identify both the exploiter (A) and the exploited (B). The first clause of the definition identifies the exploiters as those who secure a benefit – usually for themselves but sometimes also for third parties. The second clause identifies the exploited as, in part, those who are used as a tool or resource – are not treated as essentially persons. Exploiters and exploited can be groups as well as nameable individuals. The final clause points out that the exploited must suffer

---

33 For a survey, see Joachim Israel, *Alienation: From Marx To Modern Sociology* (Boston: Allyn & Bacon, 1971), ch. 7.
34 On alienation in socialist societies, see ibid., ch. 8.

serious harm. Specifically, the harm must either be the same as or must cause the extremely negative beliefs and attitudes, such as worthlessness, meaninglessness, and powerlessness, that are involved in alienation. If one were to supplement the understanding of alienation with an account of false consciousness,[35] then one could say that the requisite harm existed if, in the event that extremely negative beliefs and attitudes were lacking, their absence stemmed from some illusion.

Some features of this account of exploitation merit comment. First, it makes exploitation, like alienation, a matter of degree. This result is sensible because one would ordinarily be inclined to say that persons can be more or less alienated and more or less exploited. At the margin, it will be difficult to say, and will not make much difference, whether someone is the tiniest bit alienated or exploited or is only somewhat dissatisfied or disadvantaged.

Second, this account of exploitation is quite general. It is not, by definition, tied to private property, capitalism, particular forms of production, or the labor theory of value, or precluded under socialism or communism. The generality of the account allows forms of exploitation to which Marx paid little attention. For example, if in a given society men typically use women as a tool for sexual gratification, and if as a result women feel powerless or worthless (or lack these

---

35 Such an account may be easier to formulate if thinkers avoid a rigid Marxism. Thinkers cannot cry "false consciousness" just because others fail to accept their own Marxist political position. Further, if thinkers were to accept the historical materialist strand in Marxist theory, then, given that all states of consciousness are produced by material conditions, they may find it hard to show what distinguishes the "false consciousness" of the deluded from the "true consciousness" of the Marxist intellectual. For additional considerations, see David Miller, "Ideology and the Problem of False Consciousness," *Political Studies*, 20 (1977): 432–47. A more promising account of false consciousness – or less tendentiously, illusion – might use the literature on self-deception and on counterfactuals. See, for example, David Lewis, *Counterfactuals*, rev. ed. (Cambridge, Mass.: Harvard University Press, 1986); David Pears, *Motivated Irrationality* (Oxford: Clarendon Press, 1984), ch. 3.

feelings only because of illusion), one can speak of sexual exploitation and, underlying it, sexual alienation.

Third, this account nevertheless captures the leading case of exploitation for Marx. This case arises in the labor process of capitalism. According to Marx, capitalists use workers as a tool or resource for production, pay them only a portion of the value of their labor, and harm workers by keeping the "surplus value" of their labor. Here capitalists exploit workers, and both workers and capitalists in different ways are alienated. One can describe this case of exploitation without using the labor theory of value as the basic postulate. Instead, one uses equilibrium prices to define the value of labor, and defines exploitation in terms of property relations rather than in terms of surplus value.[36]

Is exploitation unjust? Of late this question has sparked much debate in Marxist theory. Some thinkers claim that Marx rejected all talk of "justice" as so much bourgeois claptrap and that no remotely Marxian account of exploitation should be seen as a matter of justice. Other thinkers hold that Marx made room for a theory of justice and that the topic of exploitation is part of that theory. No need exists to decide this debate here.[37] But it is important to notice how plausible it is to regard the account of exploitation sketched in this section as a matter of justice. Put generally, a standard of justice regulates morally how benefits and burdens are to be shared among persons. Any such standard proceeds from some view of the moral worth of persons. If so, then to exploit people is to treat them unjustly. For one is not then treating them as entities with moral worth but as tools or resources to secure a benefit even though they suffer serious harm. This harm rests, moreover, on an underlying analysis

---

36 See Roemer, *A General Theory of Exploitation and Class*, ch. 5; John E. Roemer, "Property Relations vs. Surplus Value in Marxian Exploitation," *Philosophy & Public Affairs*, 11 (1982): 281–313.

37 Kai Nielsen, "Arguing about Justice: Marxist Immoralism and Marxist Moralism," *Philosophy & Public Affairs*, 17 (1988): 212–34, examines the recent literature.

of alienation. That analysis suggests that to cause people to feel worthless, meaningless, or powerless can hardly be to view them as entities having moral worth. This connection between exploitation and injustice does not mean that the theory of exploitation is coextensive with the theory of justice, but it does show how Marxian concerns with exploitation can be transported to the kind of political theory that regards justice as central.

7.5 PROBLEMS OF PRODUCTION

It remains to tie the work process to this discussion of alienation and exploitation. Even if one rejects Marx's specific views, one can elaborate generally the importance of production to the theory of property. In virtually all economies production involves a "division of labor." This phrase sometimes refers to the partition of work into different tasks – the *technical division of labor,* which can be further divided vertically and horizontally. The vertical division partitions tasks within a given productive process in which some persons have authority – not necessarily legitimate – over others. The persons involved may perform the same or different tasks. Within law firms, partners have authority over associates; within corporations, executives have authority over management trainees and secretaries. The horizontal division of labor partitions tasks that either are not part of the same productive process or, if part of it, do not involve authority. Carpenters, plumbers, and lawyers illustrate this partitioning. Sometimes, however, the "division of labor" refers to the status that attaches to performing a task. In the United States, a surgeon has a higher status than a salesclerk. This partitioning of status in relation to work role is the *social division of labor.*

These distinctions help to illustrate some possible problems of production. (1) Some workers may lack, and be aware that they lack, control over production. This is especially true of lower-echelon workers in a vertical division of labor. It can also occur in a horizontal division of labor.

174

(2) Some workers may feel inferior because of the role they play in production. The feelings of inferiority reflect the social division of labor, which depends partly on the technical division of labor. (3) Production may cause economic dislocations that seriously affect some workers. For example, unemployment can be devastating financially and psychologically. It can also throw the unemployed onto charity or welfare rolls, with the undesirable results described in § 5.4. (4) Production may adversely affect other areas such as family life. If workers must toil long hours, and if all but young children must work, then energy may be lacking for familial caring and intimacy. Or if higher-echelon workers bring home the authoritative attitudes that they display at work, they may stunt the development of children who are unable to handle pressure or intimidation well. (5) Production may lead people to think of themselves so much in terms of their work role that they lose sight of the whole person. As a reality, this danger is evident in the social division of labor of many countries, particularly the United States. As a theoretical shortcoming, it is present in the writing of many socialists, including Marx, who overemphasize work at the expense of reflection and leisure.

These various problems of production need not involve alienation and exploitation as understood in § 7.4, but they can do so. Here is an example that builds on the first illustration in the previous paragraph. Suppose that semiskilled workers assemble components into small appliances in a large factory. Their work is routine and repetitive. They have no voice in the speed or conditions of their work or in the design of the finished product. Supervisors watch them carefully, urge them to work faster when they slow down, and upbraid them for mistakes. Because production managers watch over supervisors, and in turn production executives monitor the managers, assembly workers are unable to better their lot by dealing directly with their supervisors. The workers are alienated. They have so little control over production that they feel powerless in the work process. This feeling stems from a gap between a work regimen that is possible in their time and place and their actual work regimen. The workers are also exploited. They are being used as a tool or resource, and serious harm is done to them. One can fill out the example differently to identify those who benefit. If the beneficiaries are the shareholders and senior executives of a corporation in a private-property economy, the exploitation is but one step removed from the sort that Marx discussed. If the beneficiaries are elite managers, who are rewarded for high production with summer homes and university places for their children, the exploitation is similar to that in more than one "socialist" country in the world today.

The incidence of problems of production varies among economies. One might hazard that, other things being equal, they would occur, in increasing order of likelihood and severity, in nonprivate-property systems, private-property systems, private-property economies, and laissez-faire capitalist economies. Even if this conjecture proves correct, it does not follow that the list is in decreasing order of preference. The phrase "other things being equal" keeps open the possibility that any given economy might take steps to eliminate or reduce problems of production. Anyway, these problems are only one factor of many in choosing among economies.

These problems can, moreover, be connected with problems of distribution. The connections are not necessary but empirical. A given society can have both kinds of problems, neither, or either without the other. In fact, all societies have both kinds of problems in various guises. Here are some possibilities. If workers receive widely different wages, as often happens in vertical and horizontal divisions of labor, then over time substantial inequalities of wealth are apt to arise. With the inequalities come the problems described in § 5.3. Again, even if inequalities of wealth are initially confined to consumptive property, over time they are likely to generate unequal ownership of productive resources. With such unequal ownership there often come the problems of production described in this section. Yet again, these latter problems can have a direct impact on control, privacy, and individuality. Lack of control over production is part of the total amount of control, or lack of it, that workers have over their lives. Impairment of family life and overemphasis on work role can retard the development of individuality. Hence problems of production can independently affect these goods adversely, and can accentuate the adverse effects on them of problems of distribution.

Problems of distribution and production affect everyone. Obviously they affect the least well-off. But they also affect the most fortunate by undermining a sense of common humanity. No sound argument exists for denying that all persons share a common humanity. If it is shared, it should be recognized, for that will help everyone to treat others as persons. Yet the problems described here and in § 5.3 impair that recognition. A common human tendency illustrates the impairment: When things are going well for people, misfortune can seem far away. Consider a group of people who have comfortable homes, secure jobs with high status, and many material possessions to enhance the enjoyment of life. For them such misfortunes as hunger, poor clothing, inadequate shelter, burdensome debts, unemployment, or crushing, ill-respected jobs are distant.[38] As a result, those for whom things are going well feel safe and happy, perhaps even smug and overconfident. Often they overestimate how much they deserve their good fortune and have a distorted sense of self-esteem. These attitudes, in turn, tend to impair a sense of common humanity. And they increase the misfortune of the least well-off, for the latter have reinforced the sense that they are cut off from and inferior to the rest of

---

38 There are many other examples of good fortune – good health, friendship, happy family life. Misfortune can also take other forms – sickness, ostracism, soured family relations. The text prescinds from these other factors and concentrates on the material aspects of good and ill fortune.

society. Thus problems of distribution and production affect all members of society in different ways.[39]

7.6 PROPERTY AND POWER

It is time to extend an aspect of the last two sections – the connections between property and power. Here "power" is used not in Hohfeld's normative sense (§ 2.2) but in the sense of an actual capacity to do or prevent something. If an institution of property leads to alienation and exploitation, it does so in part because those who have great property resources have the power to cause serious harm to those who have few such resources. If serious problems of production exist, they do so in part because those with great property resources have the power to control work regimen – even if the problems are not so grave as to exemplify alienation and exploitation. By the same token, property can involve power even if it engenders neither problems of production nor alienation and exploitation. Many humdrum uses of property for power, at least initially, are subtle and do not create these grave problems.

Why should anyone care about connections between property and power? Part of the answer, surely, is that great differences in property holdings can produce great imbalances of power, which in turn can thrust those who have little into dire straits. This chain of events is most insidious when people try to defend the resulting state of affairs by referring to original acquisition. A biting passage from Marx's *Capital* puts it this way:

> This primitive accumulation plays in Political Economy about the same part as original sin in theology. . . . In times long gone by there were two sorts of people; one, the diligent, intelligent, and, above all, frugal élite; the other, lazy rascals, spending their substance, and more, in riotous living. . . . Thus it came to pass that the former sort

39 Compare Marx's thought that both capitalists and workers suffer from alienation. See note 14 above.

accumulated wealth, and the latter sort had at last nothing to sell except their own skins. And from this original sin dates the poverty of the great majority that, despite all its labour, has up to now nothing to sell but itself, and the wealth of the few that increases constantly although they have long ceased to work. Such insipid childishness is every day preached to us in the defence of property.[40]

Yet Marx's passionate complaint is hardly a complete answer, for it invokes in effect only the extreme conditions that generate alienation, exploitation, and severe problems of production. To round out the picture one should recognize that modest differences in property holdings can produce modest, but perhaps objectionable, differences in power, and that any attempt to justify private property must therefore take account of differences in power that would result. From at least the 1920s American legal and political thinking has stressed this point. For example, Robert L. Hale talks of power in terms of "coercion" and underscores the role of government in protecting property rights. In consequence, Hale says, the distribution of income "depends on the relative power of coercion which the different members of the community can exert against one another."[41] Similarly, Morris R. Cohen speaks of the power associated with property as akin to "sovereignty."[42] He suggests that different sorts of property require different justifications and that, insofar as property confers sovereignty, justifications of property must be analogous to justifications of sovereignty. Some readers may balk at the claim that the power associated with property is identical with "coercion" or "sovereignty," but nonetheless acknowledge that property involves power of some sort.

40 Marx, *Capital*, vol. 1, pp. 713–14.
41 Robert L. Hale, "Coercion and Distribution in a Supposedly Non-Coercive State," *Political Science Quarterly*, 38 (1923): 470–94, at 478.
42 Morris R. Cohen, "Property and Sovereignty," *Cornell Law Quarterly*, 13 (1927): 8–30.

Can one avoid connecting property and power by maintaining that transactions involving money or other forms of property are voluntary transfers between consenting adults? Perhaps the best reason for thinking that this is possible comes from Nozick's delightful example of Wilt Chamberlain, the famous basketball player.[43] Why should anyone object, asks Nozick, if those who wish to see Chamberlain play deposit voluntarily an extra twenty-five cents into a box with his name on it, which leads to the result that Chamberlain has a very high income relative to others in society? G. A. Cohen replies: Widespread contracting of this sort can worsen the lot of future generations. So ticket purchasers not only get the gains they expect "but also unforeseen consequences which render negative the net value . . . of the transaction" – including consequences in which "some come to have unacceptable amounts of power over others."[44]

A sounder reply would acknowledge connections between property and power but stop short of holding that the differences in power *must* be unacceptable. The Chamberlain parable, writ large, *can* have negative consequences. These consequences can include a diminution of the effective liberty of some persons in the future. To this extent, Cohen is correct that some appropriate pattern of distribution may be needed to preserve liberty. Nevertheless, to show that resulting differences in power must be "unacceptable" is a taller order. For one thing, it is necessary to fill in the surrounding institutional details. To worsen the situation of future generations evidently presupposes something about inheritance. But whereas Nozick's private-property rights are transmissible by will or intestate succession, a more qualified arrangement could subject such rights to substantial taxes in order to give each generation something close to a level playing field. Furthermore, one needs much empirical information and moral argument to establish that the "net value" of

43 Nozick, *Anarchy, State, and Utopia*, pp. 160–64.
44 G. A. Cohen, "Robert Nozick and Wilt Chamberlain: How Patterns Preserve Liberty," *Erkenntnis*, 11 (1977): 5–23, at 9, 10.

Chamberlain-type transactions must be "negative" or that the resulting differences in power are "unacceptable." Finally, power is hardly the only feature of private property. Hence, even were the consequences of a given arrangement of private property undesirable if considered in terms of power alone, they could be offset if the arrangement had other effects that were desirable and could not be secured as well under different arrangements.

7.7 SOCIAL LIFE, ECONOMIC OPTIONS, AND THEORY

The discussion of power, in its references to Nozick and G. A. Cohen, returns the reader to the concerns first identified in § 3.4: the difficulties of moving from "self-ownership" to "world-ownership" and the need for a background theory of property institutions. The last four chapters provide the main elements, if not the entirety, of an acceptable background theory. These chapters avoid excessive individualism in their approach to property. They are significant for what they reveal about human life in society, economic options, and the nature of theorizing about property. One may consider each subject in turn.

The chapters of Part II suggest that any account of justice in property distribution should pay attention to both minimal needs and a fully human life in society. Chapter 4 identifies the foundations of the interactions between persons and the world that generate property rights in external things. Chapter 5 carries the inquiry further by showing, in § 5.3, the importance of property to both minimal and appropriately equal control, privacy, and individuality. Chapter 6 explores the interactions between property and moral character and proposes, in § 6.5, that different economies can seek in different ways to secure a just distribution. The present chapter enables one to make the search more precise. It shows how alienation, exploitation, various problems of production, and substantial differences in power can frustrate justice.

This book has yet to propose a criterion of justice. But if

one takes justice broadly as a moral standard that regulates the sharing of benefits and burdens among persons, one can sketch the following twofold intuition concerning justice. On the one hand, justice requires that each person have a minimum amount of property. It is not obvious how to fix the minimum – either theoretically or practically.[45] But it seems plausible to say that, given a suitable specification of the minimum, it will violate justice if some persons have less than that. Or more precisely, a violation will occur if it is feasible to provide a minimum and if persons do not, as ascetics might, reject having the minimum. On the other hand, justice also requires that there not be too large a gap between the property holdings of some and those of others. How large is "too large"? No firm answer is yet available. Section 5.3 gives no criterion of "appropriately equal" distributions. Yet Chapter 6 implies that the gap cannot be so large as to preclude or seriously hinder the development of the property-related virtues possible in a given society. And this chapter implies that it cannot be so large as to alienate or exploit persons, create serious problems of production, or leave some persons with substantially less power than others. Hence, these chapters give part of the content of what it is to have access to a fully human life in society. Intuitively, justice seems to require such access when feasible and not rejected.

Consider once again the three economies presented as options in § 5.5 and examined for their impact on moral character in § 6.5. The present chapter sheds further light on their strengths and vulnerabilities. The first option – a private-property economy other than laissez-faire capitalism – is the most likely to cause alienation and exploitation or to create serious problems of production or substantial differences in power. To avoid such difficulties, substantial taxation, sound redistributive programs, and heavy restric-

---

45 See Amartya Sen et al., *The Standard of Living* (Cambridge: Cambridge University Press, 1987), for many interesting reflections on the difficulties involved here.

tions on owners and managers of productive resources may be necessary. Not surprisingly, the third option – an economic arrangement that is not even a private-property system – seems the least likely to encounter such difficulties. Even so, the third option will require more substantial justifying reasons than are generally given for it; panegyrics about community and solidarity are no substitute for arguments. It is also necessary to show the proposed arrangement to be viable – no easy task, as those familiar with "utopian" socialist thought can attest. One may wonder whether this arrangement avoids the problems of production detailed in § 7.4 only to incur gross inefficiency.

These reflections may seem to favor the second option – a private-property system that is not a private-property economy. Still, one difficulty is to describe the system plausibly and concretely. Another is to show that it is superior to alternative arrangements. Assume, if you like, that it yields more nearly equal property holdings, appropriately equal control, privacy, and individuality, and opportunity to develop moral character and is only moderately at risk for alienation, exploitation, problems of production, and imbalances of power. Yet in doing these things the system may produce lower overall wealth and, other things being equal, lower overall welfare. If it does, then the question is whether the gains in equality make up for the losses in wealth and welfare. It is not suggested that a scale exists on which one can weigh the gains and losses. But somehow one must judge this system against alternatives.

Finally, one comes to the nature of a satisfactory theory of property. Section 1.2 remarks that sound arguments for the justification of property, whether public or private, cannot be wholly abstract. It contends that one must also attend to the psychological, social, and economic context in which the arguments apply. That contention might well have seemed devoid of content at the time, but it is now possible to list some of the chief features of this intricate context.

First, Chapter 4 identifies two transcendental features of property, connections among human agency, stability, and property rights, and empirical relations between property and various senses of personality. As Hegel brings out (§ 7.2), such foundational elements are transmuted in actual property institutions. A key task, then, is to show what the transmutation looks like. One line of inquiry should concentrate on expectations (§§ 2.4 and 4.6). Expectations relating to the possession and use of things bring together two divergent perspectives. One is Hegel's rather metaphysical view. The other is the down-to-earth utilitarian view. A successful treatment should decide when expectations are rational and institutionally legitimate and when, even so, they may be overridden.

Second, a satisfactory theory of property should offer a balanced solution to problems of both distribution and production. The past performance of the most conspicuous political traditions is mixed. Anyone tempted to paint with a very broad brush might complain as follows. Classical liberalism, from Adam Smith to Hayek, relies on the market to organize production efficiently and to distribute income and property. It thereby tends to slight both problems. Modern liberalism, from Mill to Rawls, addresses distribution more successfully than production. But problems of production are troubling in their own right and can create problems of distribution. Socialism, from Marx onward, tends to exalt production and to slight distribution. Yet problems with distribution are independently worrisome and can lead to problems of production. Furthermore, on the side of production, socialist economies in both theory and practice raise grave concerns about efficiency. Of course, it would require much time and erudition to justify this manifold complaint. All the same, it is clear that an agreed balanced solution is lacking.

This book is unlikely to succeed where so many distinguished thinkers have failed, but perhaps attention to the following would help. (1) If one can justify redistributive taxation on both income and gratuitous transfers, that will be part of the story. The taxes should be neither so light as to accomplish little nor so onerous as to extinguish incentives to produce. (2) The revenue should be used partly to assuage immediate hardship – hunger, poor clothing and shelter, and inadequate health care. But to prevent redistribution from being a "handout" that elicits the difficulties of private charity and public welfare programs, revenue should also be used for job training and general education. Only in such changes lies much hope for a changed distribution that can persist. (3) Production should be reorganized to promote meaningful work. Reorganization requires giving employees more control over the work place and the work process. The elements of reorganization might include better working conditions, some job rotation, an employee role in choosing and executing production goals, and giving workers some financial stake in the performance of the enterprise (for example, through profit sharing). To implement such changes may yield somewhat less social wealth. Yet one cannot simply assume that, should this be so, an increase in wealth is more valuable than an increase in meaningful work.[46] (4) The place of production in a full human life needs to be reevaluated. *Homo faber* must make room for *homo cogitans* and *homo ludens*. Reflectiveness is after all a mark of humankind. Ordinarily reflection is mainly personal and "produces" little or nothing in a material sense. Still, to dismiss it as bourgeois or romantic self-indulgence is short-sighted. For reflection is important to personal integration and to being fully human. Again, human beings need leisure. It is tempting to see leisure as instrumental to work: Leisure is good because it dissipates stress and rejuvenates, and so enables people to work harder or better. Yet without argument one should not reject the idea that leisure may also be good in itself, or at least instrumentally good for something besides work.

Third, a satisfactory theory should limit the role of property in the following way. On the one hand, property has a

46 Pope John Paul II, *Laborem Exercens* ("On Human Work") (London: Catholic Truth Society, 1981), offers much of interest even to non-Christians. For a radical secular view, see Adina Schwartz, "Meaningful Work," *Ethics*, 92 (1982): 634–46.

legitimate role in sheltering persons from intrusion by others and the state. Here property functions as a "guard" or "fence." It protects, *inter alia,* such goods as control, privacy, and individuality. On the other hand, property must be kept from having an undue influence on other areas of society. No sound criterion of "undue" influence is currently available. Hegel, despite insights about property as an attribute of societies and persons, allows property to exert great influence on political representation. Marx identifies the problem, but his own theory is unsatisfactory. Among contemporary writers, Walzer's theory of "complex equality" and "spheres of justice" can be seen as an effort to confront this issue.[47] Briefly, the idea is both to ensure appropriate equality within each sphere and to prevent one sphere from unduly affecting another. Unfortunately, Walzer lacks a precise account of the identity and individuation of spheres and of when an effect by one on another is undue.

Fortunately, the present enterprise does not require a general theory of this sort. It will be a respectable start if one can adjust some of the linkages between private property on the one side and political representation and civil and political rights on the other. Some points are obvious. A political system that has property qualifications for office or voting ties ownership to the most basic of political rights. It thereby stifles the voice of the propertyless in political matters and undermines their civil and political rights. Even without such property qualifications, if the well-to-do can spend an unlimited amount on political campaigns and lobbying, they will have a disproportionate impact on the political process. This truth underlies the jocular "golden rule": Those who have the gold make the rules. The reality is no joke. In systems with no limits on political spending, those with much wealth often have a much more important role than others in determining which interests are represented and in specifying which civil and political rights exist and what

47 Michael Walzer, *Spheres of Justice: A Defense of Pluralism and Equality* (New York: Basic Books, 1983).

protections they receive. There are, of course, competing interests in free speech and political participation that should affect the details of legislation in these areas. But ownership should not be a prerequisite for office or voting, and some restrictions should exist on private campaign spending and lobbying.[48]

48 More controversial are the many specific ways in which the property rights of some can clash with the civil and political rights of others. See, for example, PruneYard Shopping Center v. Robins, 447 U.S. 74 (1980) (shopping center); Edwards v. Habib, 397 F.2d 687 (D.C. Cir. 1968) (Wright, J.), *cert. denied*, 393 U.S. 1016 (1969) (rental dwelling); State v. Shack, 58 N.J. 297, 277 A.2d 369 (1971) (labor camp).

Part III

Justification and distributive equity

Chapter 8

Utility and efficiency

8.1 DISTRIBUTIVE EQUITY

Part III of this book investigates the principles that should govern property arrangements. The investigation builds on the previous four chapters; without them, any justificatory arguments would remain abstract and their force uncertain. Part II, then, forms a psychological, social, and partly normative background theory in the light of which Part III now formulates explicit principles to justify and limit property rights. It will be recalled from § 1.2 that this book offers a pluralist theory of justification. The theory contains three principles: utility and efficiency, justice and equality, and desert by labor. The first three chapters of this part present the case for each of these principles in turn; the final chapter considers possible conflicts among the principles and guidelines for applying them.

Although public as well as private property requires justification, one can grasp the intellectual structure of the inquiry by concentrating for a moment on private property. If a society allows private property, it should ask how much inequality, if any, in property holdings is permissible. This

For many helpful criticisms and suggestions regarding Part III, I am indebted to Dawn Aberg, G. A. Cohen, John Martin Fischer, Mitch Gunzler, James Lamoureux, Suzanne K. Metzger, Ann I. Park, Joseph Raz, Lynn Sicade, and Ruth Zacarias. I owe a special debt to Lawrence C. Becker and James W. Nickel for acute comments on a précis of Part III presented to the American Philosophical Association, Central Division Meeting, Cincinnati, Ohio, in April 1988.

is a question about distributive equity. The ethical pluralism of this book creates room for at least two competing perspectives. One is that the test for distributive equity is the moral *merit* of persons. The word "merit," as used here, covers both desert and entitlement[1] deriving from persons' actions in the world. If persons differ in moral merit, unequal property holdings may well be justifiable. The other perspective is that the test for distributive equity is the moral *worth* of persons. If, as many ethical systems hold, persons have equal moral worth (or dignity or status) as moral agents, these systems may well regard unequal property holdings as prima facie unjustifiable. The two perspectives are asymmetrical. Under the latter, equal distributions require no special justification, but unequal distributions do. Under the former, an equal distribution needs a special justification every bit as much as a particular unequal distribution does.

The chapters in Part III relate as follows to the two competing perspectives. Taken together, they reject the skeptical positions that persons have *no* moral worth and *no* moral merit and that they must have *equal* moral merit. This chapter and the next discuss ethical theories of moral worth. Chapter 8 elaborates a principle of utility and efficiency. This principle supposes that persons have equal moral worth because, in assessments of overall utility, each person counts for one and no person counts for more than one. Chapter 9 pursues what can loosely be labeled "Kantian" interpretations of equal moral worth. These interpretations claim that the utilitarian idea of equal counting does not go far enough, for counting persons equally in the utilitarian sense ignores the fact that persons have rights not to have certain of their interests traded for overall utility. Chapter 10 develops a revised labor theory of property as a premier account of how, based partly on differences in moral merit, property holdings might justifiably be unequal. Finally,

---

1 The use of "entitlement" here is similar to that of Nozick's "entitlement" theory of justice. Robert Nozick, *Anarchy, State, and Utopia* (New York: Basic Books, 1974), pp. 150–82. Chapter 10 of the present work uses the word more broadly; see Chapter 10, note 5.

Chapter 11 argues that it is coherent to include these different perspectives in a single, integrated pluralist theory.

8.2 THE UTILITARIAN TRADITION

This chapter defends and applies a combined principle of utility and efficiency. This principle refines the contribution of the utilitarian tradition to the theory of property. The combined principle is not the same as utilitarianism. Utilitarianism is the position that the principle of utility is the sole ultimate standard of right and wrong. It can allow subordinate principles, as in rule utilitarianism, provided that the principle of utility endorses them. The principle of utility holds that right actions are those that maximize utility for all. Different utilitarians understand "utility" differently – for example, as pleasure, happiness, welfare, preference-satisfaction, and so on. The combined principle differs from utilitarianism because it does not accept utility as the *sole* ultimate standard of right and wrong. In this book, utility can sometimes be overridden by desert based on labor and by justice and equality. Hence the combined principle is part of a pluralist moral theory (§ 1.2).[2]

The combination has two parts. The first is a version of the principle of utility. It holds that one should maximize utility regarding the use, possession, transfer, and so on of things. The second is a version of the principle of efficiency. It holds that one should maximize welfare so far as the use, possession, transfer, and so on of things is concerned. The word "efficiency" has at least three meanings. Each is related to, but not identical with, utility. Only in § 8.5 will the sense in which utility and efficiency form a combined principle become clear.

2   The development of this principle draws on Stephen R. Munzer, "A Theory of Retroactive Legislation," *Texas Law Review*, 61 (1982): 425–80; Stephen R. Munzer, "Intuition and Security in Moral Philosophy," *Michigan Law Review*, 82 (1984): 740–54. The former article also discusses Bentham's views on property (at 472–74). Though the latter article criticizes and rejects R. M. Hare's utilitarianism as expounded in his *Moral Thinking: Its Levels, Method, and Point* (Oxford: Clarendon Press, 1981), those acquainted with his book will see that this chapter, particularly §§ 8.3, 8.4, 8.6, and 8.8, owes much to his vigorous defense of that moral theory.

Since this chapter reformulates the utilitarian contribution to thinking about property, a brief statement of the early contributions will help to make the inquiry intelligible. Hume is the initial utilitarian theorist of property.[3] He thinks of property as the stable possession of things. But though people even in a state of nature might possess things, what could make their possession stable? Hume's answer is human conventions. A convention is not a promise but a general sense of common interest. People see that it is in their interest not to disturb others' possession of certain things provided that the others do not disturb their own possession of certain other things; the other persons, *mutatis mutandis*, see matters likewise. By degrees these conventions lead to coordinated behavior, become more specific, and embrace more people. They engender expectations of continued use of one's possessions. Over time, conventions and their concomitant expectations yield both the fact and the psychological sense of stability in possession.

Hume's discussion does not separate explanatory and justificatory functions, but for him utility seems to perform both. Utility in the sense of common interest explains how private property arises. And it justifies both the general institution of private property and specific rules of property law. Upon the first establishment of society, the cardinal rule is that people get to continue to possess whatever they currently possess. Thereafter, utility justifies rules pertaining to occupation, prescription, accession, and succession. Beyond that, people can always transfer property by contract.

Bentham treats property in terms of expectations and utility in much greater detail.[4] "Property," he writes, "is nothing

---

3 David Hume, *A Treatise of Human Nature*, ed. L. A. Selby-Bigge (Oxford: Clarendon Press, 1960 [1888]), bk. III, pt. II, §§ II–IV, pp. 484–516.
4 Jeremy Bentham, *The Theory of Legislation*, ed. C. K. Ogden (London: Routledge & Kegan Paul, 1931), pp. 109–23, 148–98. On the connections between expectations and stability in Bentham's work, see Gerald J. Postema, "Bentham's Early Reflections on Law, Justice and Adjudication," *Revue Internationale de Philosophie*, no. 141 (1982): 219–41, especially at 220–28.

but a basis of expectation; the expectation of deriving certain advantages from a thing which we are said to possess, in consequence of the relation in which we stand towards it."[5] Thus Bentham, unlike Hume, explicitly defines property in terms of expectations. The connection with utility proceeds from the following thought. Even animals can experience pleasure and pain, but human beings, unlike animals (or so Bentham thinks), anticipate the future. Hence they can also experience pleasure when their expectations are fulfilled and pain when they are disappointed. If, as Bentham maintains, utility is the presence of pleasure and the absence of pain, then *ceteris paribus* utility will be promoted by securing persons' expectations with respect to things they possess. Interestingly, Bentham's discussion in *The Theory of Legislation* invokes, not utility directly, but subordinate principles of security, subsistence, abundance, and equality. Of these he stresses security as the most important for utility.

Bentham offers both a theory of property and a reconstruction of the English property law of his day. He discusses ways of acquiring title, provides a theory of contractual exchange, suggests rules for wills and intestate succession, criticizes various forms of common ownership, and allocates risks of loss of property. Whereas Hume complacently endorses property rules deriving from Roman law and eighteenth-century Scottish law, Bentham examines his own legal system closely, even though many contemporary readers will find his proposals mainly cosmetic in character.[6]

Efficiency comes into the picture in this way. A stock objection to utilitarianism is that it has no sound basis for interpersonal comparisons of utility. The principle of utility requires maximizing utility across all individuals. But no way exists, it is claimed, to balance a gain in one person's individual utility against a loss in that of another. To avoid this

5 Bentham, *The Theory of Legislation*, pp. 111–12.
6 For other utilitarian figures, see Alan Ryan, *Property and Political Theory* (Oxford: Blackwell, 1984), ch. 4. Good contemporary presentations include Lawrence C. Becker, *Property Rights: Philosophic Foundations* (London, Henley and Boston: Routledge & Kegan Paul, 1977), pp.

real or alleged difficulty, some thinkers, mainly economists, substitute for utility some notion of welfare. More precisely, they substitute a notion of individual welfare that does not allow interpersonal comparisons of welfare.[7]

8.3 A PRINCIPLE OF UTILITY

The first order of business is to state and defend a principle of utility. The version proposed here requires maximizing preference-satisfaction. A preference is a state or disposition to put one thing before others in one's estimation. Thus, one might prefer apples to strawberries or mountains to the seashore. Actual choices are good evidence of preferences. But "preference" as used here does not suppose that actual choices are identical with, or conclusive evidence of, preferences. The present discussion uses "preference" straightforwardly. It does not presuppose that some particular psychological or other theory of preferences is correct.[8]

Understanding utility as preference-satisfaction calls for comment. First, this understanding is common in the philo-

---

57–67; Alan Ryan, "Utility and Ownership," in R. G. Frey, ed., *Utility and Rights* (Minneapolis: University of Minnesota Press, 1984), pp. 175–95. Later chapters of this book reveal the impact of other thinkers who are either utilitarians or influenced by utilitarianism. See especially Chapter 13 on gratuitous transfers (J. S. Mill and Josiah Wedgwood) and Chapter 14 on takings (Frank I. Michelman). Chapter 12 on corporations examines critically, but still reveals the impact of, economic writing that has intellectual roots in the utilitarian tradition.

7 A good review of the intellectual history among economists is Robert Cooter and Peter Rappaport, "Were the Ordinalists Wrong About Welfare Economics?," *Journal of Economic Literature*, 22 (1984): 507–30. See also Becker, *Property Rights*, pp. 67–74.

8 For simplicity, the text supposes that if a person prefers, say, apples to strawberries, it will maximize that person's satisfaction to have apples rather than strawberries. This is a simplifying supposition because it ignores other determinants of satisfaction besides persons' having what they prefer. For sophisticated discussion of preferences and choices, see Amartya Sen, *Choice, Welfare and Measurement* (Cambridge, Mass.: MIT Press, 1982), pp. 1–106.

sophical literature.[9] Second, an advantage of this understanding is that it avoids some difficulties of other interpretations of utility. For example, to read utility as either pleasure or happiness may be too narrow, and it embroils one in philosophical controversies about the nature of pleasure or happiness. Third, understanding utility as preference-satisfaction also has the advantage of dovetailing with the treatment of efficiency in the next section. If efficiency involves maximizing welfare, and if welfare is understood as preference-satisfaction, then utility and efficiency share the same underlying concept. Fourth, the principle of utility used here counts equally all preferences of equal strength. The preference of a sadist to inflict pain has the same weight as the preference of a hospice worker to ease pain, if the preferences are equally strong. If one were trying to formulate the most promising form of utilitarianism, one might, perhaps, exclude or discount the sadist's preference. However, doing so runs the risk of introducing a nonutility factor into the principle of utility. Accordingly, for the purpose at hand, it seems wiser to understand the principle of utility in a straightforward way.

One defense of this principle of utility rests on the following substantive moral intuition: A morally relevant feature of actions is their capacity to satisfy or dissatisfy preferences. This intuition recognizes that what people prefer matters to them. This recognition in turn rests on one conception of the equal moral worth of persons – namely that, assuming equal strength, the preferences of each person count equally with the preferences of others.[10] From that point, the principle of

9   See, for example, Hare, *Moral Thinking*, especially chs. 5–7. James Griffin, *Well-Being: Its Meaning, Measurement, and Moral Importance* (Oxford: Clarendon Press, 1986), chs. I–IV, canvasses other understandings of "utility," or, to use his term, "well-being."
10 It is not a sound objection that since the psychological makeup of some people endows them *generally* with stronger preferences than others, this conception favors intense people over phlegmatic people. If the amount of satisfaction corresponds to the strength of preferences, then stronger preferences have a greater claim to be satis-

utility commands the highest satisfaction of the preferences of all persons. This defense does not assume that capacity to satisfy preferences is the only morally relevant feature of actions, or that the principle of utility is the only, or the ultimate, principle of morality.

8.4 EFFICIENCY

In order to avoid interpersonal comparisons of utility, some thinkers substitute efficiency as a criterion of social choice. Since efficiency invokes individual welfare, and since individual welfare will be understood here as individual preference-satisfaction, the efficiency criterion relies on the same substantive moral intuition and the same conception of persons as does the principle of utility. The trick is how to get from individual welfare to a criterion of social choice without interpersonal comparisons.

The general difficulty with such comparisons is supposed to be that whereas in deciding upon a course of action, the principle of utility requires maximizing utility across all individuals, no standard exists for comparing the utility of one person with that of another. Actually, this general difficulty breaks down into several distinct problems. Among them are skepticism about the existence of other minds, about meaningful discourse concerning the experiences of others, and about reliable assessments of what someone else is experiencing or would experience if a certain course of action were followed.[11]

Of these problems the first two belong to epistemology and the philosophy of language. It is therefore inappropriate

---

fied; that is the point of the clause "assuming equal strength." However, though this objection is not telling against a principle of utility that forms part of a broader moral vision, it does underscore the attractiveness of a pluralist theory in which factors other than preferences play a role.

11 The following paragraphs draw on the illuminating treatment in Hare, *Moral Thinking*, ch. 7. For an extensive recent discussion, see Griffin, *Well-Being*, chs. V–VIII.

to expect a work of political theory to solve them. But this book must confront the final problem insofar as it involves practical difficulties. In a way the problem does not seem very great. Most people suppose that they have a pretty good idea, based on analogy with their own experiences, of how many things feel to others. Few would believe a person who was twisting another's arm violently behind her back and professed surprise when his victim reported pain. However, a significant practical problem remains. If a person is trying to understand the impact of a course of action on others whose way of life is very different, then it may be hard to grasp what it feels like to them. Suppose that a large group of citizens will benefit from an oil pipeline across an arctic region of their country where it will transform an aboriginal Indian way of life. Even if the citizens are considerate persons who accept the principle of utility, they might underestimate the anguish and malaise that the Indians would experience were the pipeline built. It may be said that the citizens should ask whether *they* would like the pipeline built if they were in the Indians' position with the *Indians'* preferences. This may be the right analytical maneuver.[12] Yet the practical problem remains of having sufficient insight to grasp Indian preferences and the impact on them of the pipeline. It will sometimes be hard not only to obtain precise measurements of utility but even to make the more rough and ready assessments that fall to legislators and administrators.

This practical problem with interpersonal comparisons afflicts moral and political principles besides the principle of utility. It arises for any position that recommends beneficence or uses a concept of harm. The issue here is whether it sidesteps the problem to substitute for the principle of utility a criterion of efficiency as a criterion of social choice. The term "efficiency" has many meanings that re-

---

12 See Hare, *Moral Thinking*, pp. 94–96, 220–28. For a critical examination, see Bernard Williams, *Ethics and the Limits of Philosophy* (Cambridge, Mass.: Harvard University Press, 1985), pp. 82–92, 213.

quire careful discrimination. The most important are Pareto superiority, Pareto optimality, and Kaldor-Hicks efficiency. All are concerned with individual welfare rather than social welfare across individuals. Each involves comparison of states of a system regarding the allocation of resources to produce individual welfare.[13]

Briefly, these notions of efficiency differ as follows. For two states of a system, S_2 is Pareto superior to S_1 if and only if in moving from S_1 to S_2 at least one individual increases in welfare and no one decreases in welfare. A system is Pareto optimal if and only if no one could have an increase in welfare without at least one person's suffering a decrease in welfare. Hence a Pareto optimal system has no Pareto superior. S_2 is Kaldor-Hicks efficient with respect to S_1 if and only if in moving from S_1 to S_2, those whose welfare increases could fully compensate those whose welfare diminishes so that at least one individual has an increase in welfare. Kaldor-Hicks efficiency requires only hypothetical, not actual, compensation. Each of these criteria of efficiency yields only ordinal, not cardinal or interpersonally comparable, rankings. Each has a different relation to utility.

It may appear that none of these criteria of efficiency gets around the practical problem of interpersonal comparison. With the Pareto criteria, it is necessary to tell how the welfare of all individuals is affected. With Kaldor-Hicks efficiency, one must determine how much gainers have gained in order to determine whether losers could be fully compensated and still leave someone better off.

Yet these first appearances are a bit deceiving, at least as regards the Pareto criteria. Properly understood, the Pareto criteria rest only on reports by individuals of whether they are better or worse off. They require no offsetting or balanc-

13 See Jules L. Coleman, "Efficiency, Utility and Wealth-Maximization," *Hofstra Law Review*, 8 (1980): 509–51, at 512–20. On Kaldor-Hicks efficiency, see Nicholas Kaldor, "Welfare Propositions of Economics and Interpersonal Comparisons of Utility," *Economic Journal*, 49 (1939): 549–52; J. R. Hicks, "The Foundations of Welfare Economics," *Economic Journal*, 49 (1939): 696–712.

ing across individuals and hence no interpersonal comparison in the sense in question. The Pareto criteria do not escape the problem of other minds or the problem of the intersubjective meaningfulness of reports of experiences. But those are general philosophical issues appropriately left unresolved here.

Matters are more complicated in the case of Kaldor-Hicks efficiency. A well-known technical problem is that under some conditions each of two states may be Kaldor-Hicks efficient with respect to each other – a result known as the Scitovsky paradox. Although Scitovsky himself has offered a criterion for social improvement that avoids the paradox, his criterion turns out to yield nothing beyond Pareto optimality.[14] An important practical difficulty is that if there are both gainers and losers, it is hard to determine whether there is a net gain without interpersonal comparisons to determine if gainers could amply compensate losers with at least one winner remaining better off. Perhaps the difficulty yields to a trial-and-error method. Suppose that in the move from S_1 to S_2 some individuals report gains and others report losses in welfare. It seems possible, by trial and error, to pose hypothetically a number of rearrangements or trades such that eventually at least one person might report a gain and no one report a loss. If so, then S_2 would be Kaldor-Hicks efficient with respect to S_1. This maneuver is not legerdemain. Yet it has difficulties of its own. Even if no interpersonal comparisons are used in the final-report stage, they will be used in framing a set of hypothetical rearrangements or trades. Also, working with these hypothetical situations will require either a complete list of all possible rearrangements and trades or uncommon shrewdness in making up the list. Otherwise, the final reports might suggest that S_2 is not Kaldor-Hicks efficient with respect to S_1, but the suggestion would be false if there were some over-

14 See Allan Feldman, *Welfare Economics and Social Choice Theory* (Boston: Martinus Nijhoff, 1980), pp. 142–45; T. de Scitovsky, "A Note on Welfare Propositions in Economics," *Review of Economic Studies*, 9 (1941): 77–88.

looked rearrangement or trade that would have satisfied the criterion.

In the end, it is doubtful that any of the criteria of efficiency has a general advantage over utility as a criterion of social choice. The Pareto criteria, unlike the principle of utility, manage to avoid interpersonal comparisons. But both of these criteria will almost always be satisfied in any situation involving many people and complicated alternative courses of action – as will generally be the case in the choice of a system of property – for any change will almost always make *someone* worse off. Yet it seems absurd to rest content with a criterion whose practical implication is that virtually no improvements can be made in existing property institutions. That leaves Kaldor-Hicks efficiency. It is a more realistic guide to social choice. All the same, either it fails altogether to avoid interpersonal comparisons or it ultimately avoids them only through a cumbersome trial-and-error method that almost surely must use interpersonal comparisons at some stage. Hence Kaldor-Hicks efficiency is not in a much different practical boat from utility.

8.5 A COMBINED PRINCIPLE OF UTILITY AND EFFICIENCY

It remains to state utility and efficiency as a combined principle that specifically concerns property and to clarify why the combination is both possible and advantageous. The combined principle maintains that property rights should be allocated so as (1) to maximize utility regarding the use, possession, transfer, and so on of things and (2) to maximize efficiency regarding the use, possession, transfer, and so on of things. In both clauses, "and so on" covers all other Hohfeld–Honoré incidents of property identified in § 2.3. In this principle, clause (1) has priority over clause (2) in the following sense: If it is possible to rank alternatives in terms of both utility and efficiency, then one should use the ranking supplied by utility. Thus efficiency functions as the junior partner in the combination. If, however, it is possible to rank alternatives in terms of either utility or efficiency but not both, then one should use whichever ranking is available.

A combined principle is possible because utility and efficiency both have something in common and differ in a key respect. What they have in common is the concept of individual preference-satisfaction. They differ in that the principle of utility, but not the principle of efficiency, supposes that interpersonal comparisons of individual preference-satisfaction are possible. As a result, they also differ in that utility supplies both ordinal and interpersonally comparable rankings of alternatives, whereas efficiency supplies only ordinal rankings. In ordinal rankings, the measurement of each person's preference-satisfaction can be individually (intrapersonally) cardinal – numerically precise – but usually will not be so. In interpersonally comparable rankings, the measurement of each person's preference-satisfaction can be collectively (interpersonally) cardinal – that is, numerically precise in terms of some common system of units. Almost always, however, the measurement will be collectively non-cardinal – either because the measurement is numerical but specified only as a range or, more likely, because it is non-numerical and rough. Since collectively cardinal measurements are, to put it mildly, rare, interpersonally comparable rankings will typically give only a rough idea of how much better one alternative is than another. An ordinal ranking tells that one alternative is better than another but not how much better.

For at least four reasons, a combined principle is more advantageous than a principle stated in terms of either utility alone or efficiency alone. First, if both interpersonally comparable and ordinal rankings are possible, the former ranking will help in the resolution of conflicts. Since this book offers a pluralist theory of property, the principle of utility and efficiency can conflict with the labor-desert principle and the principle of justice and equality. Suppose, for example, that one is considering a policy for redistributing income. Suppose that a conflict exists because whereas the principle of justice and equality favors the policy, the principle of utility and efficiency finds that it will yield less utility than some alternative policy. One factor in resolving the conflict is *how much* less utility will result. For example, it will be easier to override the principle of justice and equality if following that principle would produce a very large shortfall in utility.

Second, if ordinal rankings constructed out of interpersonally noncomparable preferences are impossible, then certain interpersonally comparable rankings, if available, may order alternatives. The point involves Arrow's Impossibility Theorem. Put briefly, the theorem states that, given some highly attractive assumptions (completeness, transitivity, Pareto consistency, "nondictatorship," and the irrelevance of independent alternatives), it is sometimes not possible to construct a social-welfare function from individual noncomparable preferences that satisfies all of the assumptions. Obviously, many will resist the idea that preferences can be interpersonally comparable. In fact, Arrow himself explicitly rejects this idea. Furthermore, it can be argued that, even given interpersonal comparisons and individual cardinality, a related impossibility theorem holds. Yet at least in the special case where there are interpersonal comparisons with collective as well as individual cardinalities, one may well get an ordering of alternatives.[15]

Third, if in a given case interpersonal comparisons are not available, one can fall back on efficiency. Efficiency involves

15 See Kenneth J. Arrow, *Social Choice and Individual Values*, 2d ed. (New Haven: Yale University Press, 1963). For the theorem and its interpretation, see pp. 46–60 (original formulation), 96–103 (corrected statement). Arrow rejects interpersonal comparisons on pp. 9–11, 111–18. Elsewhere, however, he seems more willing to accept them, and perhaps even intimates the point that, if such comparisons were possible, his theorem (or an analogue of it) might not apply. Kenneth J. Arrow, "Public and Private Values," in Sidney Hook, ed., *Human Values and Economic Policy: A Symposium* (New York: New York University Press, 1967), pp. 3–21, at pp. 18–20. Thomas Schwartz, "On the Possibility of Rational Policy Evaluation," *Theory and Decision*, 1 (1970): 89–106, disputes Arrow on this point and offers a related impossibility theorem, but one may question whether Schwartz distinguishes clearly and unswervingly between individual and collective cardinality. Schwartz's theorem does not seem to hold if there are collectively cardinal interpersonal comparisons.

making at least one person better off without making anyone worse off. Since efficiency supplies an ordinal ranking, it serves as an index of utility in that if an alternative promotes efficiency (at least Pareto superiority), then it promotes utility (even though one cannot tell by how much it does so over another alternative). Of course, if Arrow's Theorem rears its head, one must look to ways of avoiding it. Examples include various nonaggregative methods of social choice such as logrolling and consensus building.[16]

Fourth, the combined principle allows one to draw coherently on two different bodies of literature. The philosophical literature, if it speaks about either, generally speaks of utility rather than efficiency. Some of that literature sheds light on the theory of property. The economic literature, if it speaks about either, generally speaks of efficiency rather than utility. Some of that literature illuminates the theory of property.

The combined principle formulated in this section is one of the three central principles in a satisfactory theory of property. This principle is not, however, a general principle of morality, for it refers only to the various incidents of property, and hence is too specific to be a general moral principle. Still, it presupposes that some more broadly stated principle of utility and efficiency *is* a general principle of morality. As a result, the principle of utility and efficiency formulated here carries an implicit other-things-equal clause. A property arrangement might satisfy that specific principle and yet be part of an overall situation in which preference-satisfaction is lower than it could be were the property arrangement changed. Thus the optimal overall situation might require a

16 See, for example, James M. Buchanan and Gordon Tullock, *The Calculus of Consent: Logical Foundations of Constitutional Democracy* (Ann Arbor: University of Michigan Press, 1962), pp. 331–34 (Appendix 2 by Tullock); Gordon Tullock, "The General Irrelevance of the General Impossibility Theorem," *Quarterly Journal of Economics*, 81 (1967): 256–70. See also William H. Riker, *Liberalism against Populism: A Confrontation Between the Theory of Democracy and the Theory of Social Choice* (San Francisco: W. H. Freeman & Co., 1982); Jules Coleman and John Ferejohn, "Democracy and Social Choice," *Ethics*, 97 (1986): 6–25.

property arrangement that, considered alone, is not the most useful or efficient. Hence, from now on, this book assumes that the contrary hypothetical situation just sketched does not exist and that other things are equal: If a property arrangement satisfies the principle of utility and efficiency formulated here, then it is part of some overall situation that satisfies a broadly stated principle that is a general principle of morality. The intellectual advance thus far is the orchestration of both utility and efficiency into a property-specific principle. It is now time to put that principle to work.

8.6 UTILITY, EFFICIENCY, AND PROPERTY

It is a mistake to think that there is only one question about utility, efficiency, and property. There are many. This section discusses some of them. It deals mainly with private property. Six of the most important questions are these: Does the principle of utility and efficiency justify any public property? Does it justify any private property? Does it say anything about the distribution of private property? Does it play a role in designing an institution of private property? Does it justify particular rules of property law? Can it justify radical changes in existing property institutions?

(1) The principle of utility and efficiency justifies some public property as defined in § 2.3 – namely, where the right-holder is some entity such as the state, city, or community. At least it does so if one makes some plausible empirical assumptions about people's preferences. Among these assumptions are the propositions that people prefer to have a way of life secure from foreign attack; access to education, roads, parks, and other public facilities; protection against fires, crime, natural disasters, and downturns in the economy or in their personal financial situation; and availability to their immediate descendents of similar conditions.

Given these assumptions, utility and efficiency support public property of at least the following sorts. The government should have the materials for national defense. These materials include land for military bases, weapons of various sorts, and stockpiles of strategic supplies such as oil, water, and fuel. The government should also have property for many sorts of public facilities – especially land for roads, parks, schools, and government offices, including structures erected on this land and needed equipment. Similarly, it should have things to protect its citizens from misfortune. It will need fire stations and police departments. It will need both cash and emergency food, clothing, and shelter to help people when such calamities as severe earthquakes and storms, economic depressions, or personal and social upheavals like unemployment and homelessness occur. Chapter 5 on control, privacy, and individuality underscores the importance both of these personal goods and of the need for a welfare system to help supply them in dire circumstances. Finally, to provide for future generations, the government should have the requisite materials, including especially natural resources such as timber and oil and land.

Some qualifications apply to this argument for public property. First, it does not justify a precise amount of public property or show that public property should be a certain fraction of the assets of a society. People's exact preferences and other empirical details really matter here. Second, sometimes persons will prefer a given thing but may not prefer that the government provide it. In fact, if they prefer strongly that the government not intervene, they may be willing to sacrifice the thing otherwise preferred. On occasion, they will have incompatible preferences and will need to give up at least one of them. For example, if someone prefers a balanced budget, a military build-up, increased government spending on the poor, and no new taxes, and if it is impossible to satisfy all of these preferences, then anyone who can add will see that at least one of them has got to go. Third, the argument will differ somewhat depending on whether a particular item of public property is a public good. Demand for a "pure public good" is neither excludable nor rivalrous. National defense is an example of a pure public good, for it is impossible to provide defense for some but to exclude others who do not want it. Because of the free-rider problem, the market cannot register accurately individual preferences for pure public goods. The same largely applies to "mixed public goods," such as roads and parks, which are in some measure excludable or rivalrous. Hence some political choice must determine the amount of public goods. In contrast, for items that are not public goods in the technical sense just specified, such as education or disaster relief, one might use a market-mimicking device or a demand-revealing tax scheme[17] to some extent in ascertaining individual preferences for them. For example, one might look, in part, at the cost of private schooling or earthquake insurance to determine how much property the government should set aside for education or disaster relief.

A possible counterargument is that the government need not own property of these various sorts. It suffices if the government has access to revenue which it can pass through to citizens or use to rent property. Though this counterargument has some weight, it may well not prevail. For one thing, while it is *possible* without government ownership to satisfy some preferences, the counterargument must show more than that. It must show that nonownership is *best promotive* of preference-satisfaction, which is much harder to do. For another, the counterargument is more plausible for some items of possible public property than for others. To illustrate, it will be difficult to rent armaments or military bases, since these things have no legitimate civilian uses, and it would be imprudent for the government to allow such things to pass out of its control. Again, many government buildings, such as prisons and police and fire stations, are not readily adaptable to nonpublic uses, and hence – assuming *arguendo* that private property is justifiable – investors usually will not want to put their capital into structures that have such a narrow market.

Nevertheless, the counterargument does have a point: It is possible for the government to use tax revenues to rent

---

17 On demand-revealing taxes, see Feldman, *Welfare Economics and Social Choice Theory*, pp. 122–29.

facilities for some public purposes, and the principle of utility and efficiency requires that one investigate what no doubt
complex arrangement achieves these purposes at the lowest
cost. This point must, however, be put alongside the government's need to respond flexibly to people's preferences.
Often that flexibility favors either ownership of public property or the legal power to abrogate or modify private rental
contracts between the government and individuals or both.

   (2) Likewise, the principle of utility and efficiency justifies
some private property. At least it does so if one makes some
plausible empirical assumptions about people's preferences.
These assumptions include the propositions that people prefer to have intimate articles as a basis for personality, a range
of personal goods such as control, privacy, and individuality, and an opportunity to develop such beneficial character
traits as are appropriate in their society. At the same time,
they prefer not to have their lives distorted by alienation and
exploitation, disrupted by various problems of distribution
and production, or adversely affected by large differences in
economic power. Part II of this book helps to understand the
depth and intensity of these preferences. Though that portion of this work may not have complete cross-cultural
application, it reveals a great deal at any rate about developed Western societies.

   On the basis of these assumptions, utility and efficiency
support private property of many sorts. People should have
property rights in articles for personal use, such as clothing,
grooming equipment, and some modest furniture. They
should have property rights in things that foster control,
privacy, and individuality. In a private-property system
(§ 5.1) these things will include a wider range of clothing and
furniture, as well as books, cars, money, and probably
homes. In a private-property economy (§ 5.1) they will also
include some equity interest in the means of production. In
an economic arrangement that is neither a private-property
system nor a private-property economy (§ 5.5) many fewer
such things are likely to satisfy preferences. Similarly, the
usefulness of property for the development of certain desir-

able character traits is apt to vary among these different economic options (§ 6.5). In all these cases, to say that people "should have property rights" is to say that utility and efficiency support making them available to people generally through the operation of an appropriate economic system, not that every person must have such rights or that no person may reject them.

The foregoing argument does not, with one exception, justify private ownership of the means of production. The exception is that if one assumes a private-property economy to be justified, then people living under such an economy are apt to have preferences whose satisfaction will result from owning productive resources. But since the principle of utility and efficiency may be the most plausible justification for a private-property economy, until one constructs that justification it seems gratuitous to assume that sort of economy to be justified. As will become evident in Chapter 12 on business corporations, the theory of property advocated in this book permits, but does not require, a private-property economy.

Insofar as one seeks, then, to justify private ownership of the means of production on the basis of utility and efficiency, the argument must go something like this. One can get a little mileage, but not much, from the idea that people derive great preference-satisfaction from owning the means of production. A preference for such ownership is largely the product of an ongoing system in which such ownership is already allowed. Thus, if one is starting from scratch, one cannot plausibly suppose that such a preference is widespread. A more promising strategy is to suggest that an economic system can better satisfy consumer preferences if it allows ownership of productive resources, for such owners will respond more rapidly and at less cost to those preferences. Such a system will produce more goods and tend to direct them to those who want them most and so increase overall preference-satisfaction. Once the system is under way, of course, a preference for an equity interest in the means of production will be among the preferences that the system satisfies. It scarcely needs saying that the argument will be sound only to the extent that the system prevents alienation, exploitation, severe problems of production, and great differences in economic power, as discussed in Chapter 7, because they involve intense preference-dissatisfaction.

These general arguments for justifying some private property on the basis of utility and efficiency should not be confused with a more specific position on efficiency and private property. This is the idea that a regime of strong private-property rights is efficient, or at least is presumptively so. A recent exchange between Michelman and Demsetz confirms that even presumptive efficiency, in their sense, is dubious.[18] Suppose that a regime of strong private-property rights involves at least strong rights over one's body and labor, exclusive ownership of things (especially the products of labor), and freedom of transfer.[19] But it does not follow, even given that individuals are rational maximizers of their own satisfaction, that private property is presumptively more efficient than, say, regulated ownership. The reason, as Michelman shows, is that further premises are needed. The premises relate, for example, to preferences for certain institutions and to the effects of uncertainty, free riding, and forced sharing. These additional premises may be either empirical and in need of evidence or confirmation or nonempirical and in need of further moral and political argument.

Demsetz acknowledges that private property is neither necessarily efficient nor always morally acceptable, but says

18 Michelman understands "efficiency" as a broad maximization criterion that encompasses both utility and at least the Pareto criteria of efficiency. See Frank I. Michelman, "Ethics, Economics, and the Law of Property," in J. Roland Pennock and John W. Chapman, eds., *NOMOS XXIV: Ethics, Economics, and the Law* (New York: New York University Press, 1982), p. 3 n.2. The main burden of his article, though, is against economists and academic lawyers who advocate efficiency rather than against utilitarians.

19 The phrase "regime of strong private-property rights" is a succinct way of referring to the arrangement that Michelman describes. Ibid., pp. 4–5, 8–21. It is not identical with a "private-property system" or "private-property economy" as defined in § 5.1.

that this is "hardly surprising."[20] Perhaps the reader should be pardoned some surprise, given Demsetz's views about private property and the internalization of externalities.[21] Be that as it may, Demsetz errs in claiming that Michelman seeks an "a priori connection of property with rationality and efficiency, a linkage independent of the wants and proclivities of people."[22] Instead, Michelman is trying to sketch the nature of persons to see what sorts of premises would have to be true for private property to be at least presumptively efficient.[23] Efficiency, like utility, supports some private property if one makes some plausible empirical assumptions about people's preferences. It is another matter to show that it supports, in all circumstances, some detailed institutional arrangement of property, private or otherwise.[24]

(3) The principle of utility and efficiency also bears on the distribution of private property. That principle, given some plausible assumptions, favors a moderately equal distribution. It does not favor a strictly equal distribution. Too many advantages, eventually reducible to preference-satisfaction, lie with sensible incentives and wage differentials and with (limited) freedom of contract to make strict egalitarianism cogent.

20 Harold Demsetz, "Professor Michelman's Unnecessary and Futile Search for the Philosopher's Touchstone," in Pennock and Chapman, eds., *NOMOS XXIV*, p. 41.
21 Michelman, "Ethics, Economics, and the Law of Property," p. 32 n.80, refers to Harold Demsetz, "Toward a Theory of Property Rights," *American Economic Review*, 57 (1967) (Papers and Proceedings): 347–59.
22 Demsetz, "Professor Michelman's Unnecessary and Futile Search for the Philosopher's Touchstone," p. 44.
23 This reading accords with Duncan Kennedy and Frank Michelman, "Are Property and Contract Efficient?," *Hofstra Law Review*, 8 (1980): 711–70, at 714.
24 Space permits no adequate treatment of the much-discussed view that society ought to aim at the maximization, under Kaldor-Hicks efficiency, of wealth. See Richard A. Posner, *The Economics of Justice* (Cambridge, Mass.: Harvard University Press, 1981), ch. 4, which advocates this view and refers to some of the opposing literature. Suffice it to say that although the principle of utility and efficiency attaches some value to "wealth" as an instrumental good, it does not make it an intrinsic or a sole good (neither does Posner – see pp. 107–08), and other principles of the pluralist position offered here depart from the view of efficient wealth maximization.

What assumptions, then, are required for moderate egalitarianism? One is the diminishing marginal utility of money and other material goods to satisfy preferences. This assumption means that each extra unit of these goods produces less preference-satisfaction than the previous one. It is an empirical assumption because it rests on psychological evidence concerning the way people actually are. This assumption, in order to be useful, does not require that all material goods exhibit diminishing marginal utility for all persons. It does require that this be true of material goods and persons generally. So understood, the assumption is plausible and indeed underlies the so-called marginalist revolution in economics in the 1870s. As a technical point, it is consistent to reject interpersonal comparisons but to accept diminishing marginal utility. Hence, this assumption comes into play even if only efficiency rankings are available.[25]

A second assumption is that wide differences in wealth produce preference-dissatisfaction in those who are least well-off. Evidence of such dissatisfaction includes resentment, hopelessness, and malaise. The problems of distribution identified in § 5.3 illustrate this assumption.

A third assumption is that if inequalities of wealth involve unequal ownership of productive resources, and if this unequal ownership spawns alienation, exploitation, severe problems of production, or large differences in economic power, then intense preference-dissatisfaction results. This assumption presents the results of §§ 7.4–7.6 in terms of utility and efficiency.

A fourth, and for immediate purposes final, assumption is

---

25 William A. Klein, *Policy Analysis of the Federal Income Tax* (Mineola, N.Y.: Foundation Press, 1976), pp. 14–18, gives a straightforward explanation of diminishing marginal utility. Harold M. Groves, *Tax Philosophers* (Madison: University of Wisconsin Press, 1974), sketches the marginalist revolution of the 1870s. For discussion of whether money exhibits diminishing marginal utility, as do other material goods, see Walter J. Blum and Harry Kalven, Jr., *The Uneasy Case for Progressive Taxation* (Chicago: University of Chicago Press, 1963) (edition with added introduction), pp. 40–42, 45–49, 56–63, 68, 93.

that increased satisfaction would result if certain sorts of existing preferences were rationally changed. So even if existing inequalities of wealth, say, do not make those poorly off highly dissatisfied because they do not currently have preferences to the contrary, one must look to the satisfaction they would have were their preferences changed. More on this last point appears at the end of the section.

If these assumptions hold, then the principle of utility and efficiency favors a moderately equal distribution of private property. As a result, if one is building a theory of property, one should include appropriate mechanisms to institute and maintain a moderately equal distribution, ignoring, for the moment, the impact of the principle of justice and equality and the labor-desert principle. This argument is, however, not sufficiently finely tuned to say what mechanisms utility and efficiency favor. A combination of taxes and redistributive programs may seem to be an obvious answer. But those who are familiar with the literature on tax policy know that these matters are quite complicated.[26]

It is useful to highlight a point of contact between the answers to the second and third questions formulated at the beginning of this section. It is erroneous to think that moderate egalitarianism presupposes that one is dividing up a fixed quantity of material goods. Rather, the quantity is variable. As the answer to the second question brings out, an economy that satisfies the principle of utility and efficiency will, other things being equal, produce more material goods than an economy that does not. The point of contact, then, is that this principle bears *both* on how many and what kinds of goods are produced *and* on how those goods are distributed. In other words, the principle relates to the size of the pie as well as the distribution of the pieces.

(4) The principle of utility and efficiency can also play a role in designing an institution of private property. To show this it would be cumbersome to apply that principle alone in a series of different areas. For that reason, Part IV of this

---

26 See, for example, the works cited in note 25.

book applies it along with other principles to specific problems. Still, it may help at this stage to indicate how utility
and efficiency – still understood as invoking individual preference-satisfaction – can shed light on insitutional design.
Here are some examples.

Utility and efficiency are quite important in assessing the
modern corporation and its relation to public and private
ownership. A case can be made that, as a general guide, it
advances economic productivity to have corporations pursue
profit maximization as a unique goal. If greater productivity
yields a greater capacity to satisfy human preferences, there
is a connection between corporate profit maximization and
the promotion of preference-satisfaction. Still, the connection is a weak one, and the guide is only a rule of thumb.
Many of the qualifications derive from a sensitive application
of the principle of utility and efficiency itself. It is not obvious
that the highest economic productivity for society as a whole
can always be compounded out of the profit-maximizing
activities of individual corporations. More important, several
factors weaken the connection between profit maximization
and preference-satisfaction. One is that how profits are distributed – to shareholders, managers, employees, to some
combination of them, or, more broadly, to the public at large
– affects the calculation. It cannot be assumed that turning
over all profits to the shareholders yields the most satisfaction. But the principle of utility and efficiency, however
sensitively applied, is not the whole story. Justice has claims
of its own; what is most useful for society may not be fair to
everyone. The pursuit of profits also raises questions about
the effect on human character. It may not be sensible to
admonish people, in the economic dimension of their lives,
to seek maximum profits in competitive markets, and then to
exhort them, in other dimensions of their lives, to foster
more cooperative traits. Chapter 12 pursues these matters.

In the area of gifts and bequests and their relation to the
distribution of wealth, the principle of utility and efficiency is
an important instrument of political criticism. Pronounced
wealth inequalities exist in Great Britain and the United

States. Inadequate taxation of gifts and inheritances allows these inequalities to persist. The inequalities are counter to utility and efficiency, for heavy costs flow from current distributions of wealth. Persons at the nether end of the spectrum often lack opportunities to develop their capacities, particularly the capacity for meaningful work. They are also more likely to lack self-esteem and to be resentful and hopeless than those who receive much gratuitous wealth. In the end, the costs fall upon society as a whole. This is especially true of those who, shackled by poverty and lack of opportunity, give up, become ineffective workers, and consume far more in welfare payments and other resources than they produce. Thus overall satisfaction declines. There are reasons, given in Chapter 13, for believing that the inequalities of wealth in Great Britain and the United States are also unjust. As a result, both the principle of utility and efficiency and a principle of justice and equality favor heavier taxes on gratuitous transfers.

Moreover, utility and efficiency shed light on government takings of private property. Since they support at least some private property, there will be preference-dissatisfaction if the government withdraws that property from its owners. The burden should be on the government to show why compensation should not be paid. Furthermore, the relation between takings and distributive justice must be clarified. If property is distributed fairly, and if government actions redirecting social resources have haphazard distributive effects, then no issue of distributive justice is involved. Subject to a few qualifications, preference-satisfaction is an appropriate standard for decision. However, if property is distributed unfairly, and if government actions affecting property have identifiable distributive effects, then distributive justice is involved. A possible example would be land reform programs in countries where wealth is very unjustly distributed. In such a case the aim of the government actions should be to make a corrective redistribution. Here it will be matter of context whether actions affecting property rather than, say, tax schemes, are the best means of redistribution. Chapters 14 and 15 explore these matters systematically.

Finally, the principle of utility and efficiency furnishes a general reason for making liberty a prominent feature of an institution of private property: If people are free to act in certain ways with respect to their property, then they will likely better satisfy their preferences. To illustrate, utility and efficiency support a wide range of transactional powers, such as the powers to buy, sell, rent, give, pledge, mortgage, or bequeath property. As Hume remarks, since the things that people have can "depend very much on chance, they must frequently prove contradictory both to men's wants and desires; and persons and possessions must often be very ill adjusted."[27] He goes on to say that because different parts of the world produce different commodities, and because people pursue different employments, "a mutual exchange and commerce"[28] are required. Transactional powers over one's belongings are also conducive to satisfying preferences that relate, say, to one's occupation, political beliefs, or place of residence. Thus, a person may donate money to a political candidate, or a victim of persecution may want to sell his or her assets in order to have the resources to flee and start a new life in another country. Again, to give a different illustration, utility and efficiency support the rights to possess and use articles that advance one's personality and individuality. Examples include mainly items of personal property such as clothes, utensils, furniture, books, mementos, religious articles, and art objects. As Chapters 4 and 5 make clear, private property plays a significant role in developing personality and individuality, and history testifies to the strength and ubiquity of preferences of human beings to express themselves through personal articles.

At this point, one need not multiply illustrations. It suffices to see that, given common human preferences, the principle of utility and efficiency supports powers and rights

27 Hume, *A Treatise of Human Nature*, bk. III, pt. II, § IV, p. 514.
28 Ibid.

to act freely with respect to one's property in order to satisfy these preferences. This freedom, as will emerge later, is limited. Moreover, liberty is derivative rather than basic in the theory of property proposed here. But it does not derive from utility and efficiency alone; the principle of justice and equality and the labor-desert principle also support some aspects of liberty (§§ 9.4 and 10.4).

(5) The foregoing remarks deal with the role of utility and efficiency in designing institutions that permit private ownership but with significant qualifications. It is another matter to show that utility favors specific rules of property law. Obviously no sharp line divides institutions and specific rules, for rules of all kinds, general and specific, constitute institutions. Yet there is a contrast, which an example may bring out.

In the design of property institutions, one might confront the issue of whether ownership of land for houses by joint tenants is justified by the principle of utility and efficiency. Resolving it would require deciding whether a certain kind of thing – namely, land – is open to private ownership, and whether two or more people considered together as joint tenants should be able to own it. A little thought would suggest how one might bring considerations of utility and efficiency to bear on these decisions. All the same, specific rules regarding severance, right of survivorship, and liability of the joint property to execution for the debts of one joint tenant call for less philosophizing and more empirical information. To decide upon such rules requires filling in the surrounding legal structure and gaining knowledge of the effects of various rules. Utility and efficiency are pertinent to such decisions but as a much-mediated factor rather than as a direct application. Economics can help here. Often it can offer a rigorous way, given certain assumptions, of identifying the likely effects of different rules. Such microeconomic choices can often be analyzed in terms of efficiency.[29] But, whatever the usefulness of economics, the application of any

29 See, for example, Richard A. Posner, *Economic Analysis of Law*, 3d ed. (Boston: Little, Brown, 1986), ch. 3.

fairly abstract principle, including the principle of utility and efficiency, requires information about the world and some intermediate stages of deliberation; § 11.3 pursues these matters.

(6) Some may question whether utility and efficiency can justify radical changes in existing property institutions. The question arises in the following context. So far the discussion has proceeded as if one were designing property institutions on a clean slate. But there is no clean slate. And existing property arrangements may depart dramatically from an ideal design. Yet, since those arrangements will have generated many preferences for those favored by the system, radically to change the arrangements would frustrate those preferences. Hence considerations of utility and efficiency seem to block radical changes.

It is, however, a great mistake to think that in applying the principle of utility and efficiency one must take preferences as one finds them. Bentham may, it is true, have been unduly solicitous of existing expectations and hence the established distribution of wealth. But if Bentham erred, one need not repeat his mistake. It makes sense, from the standpoint of utility and efficiency, to move to a set of preferences that it is possible to satisfy and that, if satisfied, will yield the most satisfaction. Thus there can be an argument of utility and efficiency for disrupting even rational and institutionally legitimate expectations about property. It is plausible to maintain that what is relevant is a rational argument for preference change, not, say, coercive persuasion ("brainwashing") or subliminal, chemical, or surgical transformation of preferences or even specious argument. For abuses, and thus eventual disutilities, would often result from such nonrational modes of changing preferences. Furthermore, even if greater pleasure would come from the judicious use of nonrational ways of changing preferences, a higher-order preference may be in play. Whether people prefer to satisfy a certain preference may depend in part on the genesis of the preference; on the whole, people may well prefer not to have to satisfy preferences produced by nonrational means.

But even though one can deploy arguments of this sort, two factors constrain them. One is existing preferences themselves. Sometimes people obtain a good deal of satisfaction from satisfying preferences that intuitively are highly obnoxious. Consider preferences in medieval times, when great extremes of wealth and power might have been accepted as being in the nature of things. Or consider preferences in a caste society today where similar extremes might be accepted on similar grounds. Such preferences are apt to be highly resistant to rational change because they are supported by a pervasive religious world view and powerful social norms. It may be objected that change can be introduced with an eye to the long run. That is, one can disappoint the tolerance of one generation for the status quo in order to produce a robust preference in succeeding generations for a moderately equal distribution of wealth. The reply is twofold. It is hard to count on the success of any project that must be carried out over a long time. And it is problematic to reduce the satisfaction of a given generation in order to enhance that of future generations.

A second factor is the cost of persuading people that it is rational to have different preferences from those that they currently do. Exchanging existing preferences for new preferences that many people find more acceptable consumes resources – time, energy, money. If one focuses solely on the respective sets of preferences, one may find that more satisfaction would result from the new preferences. But people also have preferences regarding the use of resources. Hence they may prefer that a given quantity of resources be employed in some way other than to move from an existing set to a new set of preferences, even though, if the move consumed no resources, they would derive more satisfaction with the new preferences. In short, the cost of changing preferences will block some exchanges that, if they were costless, otherwise would be made.[30]

30 The argument for this second factor borrows from R. H. Coase, "The Problem of Social Cost," *Journal of Law and Economics*, 3 (1960): 1–44, at 15–19.

If these constraining factors operate in a given case, they limit radical change in an existing institution. They limit it, indeed, even in the case where an ideal design in terms of utility and efficiency alone would depart sharply from existing arrangements. Thus, the proper conclusion is not that the principle of utility and efficiency is unhelpful, but that an appropriate pluralist theory of property must do better. This book endeavors to supply such a theory.

8.7 PREFERENCES AND EXPECTATIONS

With this general account of utility, efficiency, and property in hand, it will be useful to display a linkage between preferences and expectations. Some preferences, owing to their ubiquity or strength or both, are apt to figure prominently in applying the combined principle. Expectations are such a variety of preferences. Expectations, as defined in § 2.4, are dispositions to predict that a certain event will occur together with (characteristically) an attitude of desiring and feeling entitled to count on its occurrence. If the predicted event is the continued use and enjoyment of what one currently possesses, the expectation is likely to involve a strong preference. Thus it would promote utility and efficiency, other things being equal, to satisfy the preference by protecting that use and enjoyment.

Given that the combined principle supports some private property rights, even though expectations accompany those rights (§§ 2.4 and 4.6), it would not follow that all expectations relating to property are equally strong or equally worth protecting. To grasp this point fully, and to formulate some helpful structural criteria, it is necessary to consider how expectations are formed.[31] Some expectations arise from Humean conventions that by degrees give rise to rules of property law. Probably some of the most ancient rules protecting possession were originally conventional rules in

31 These issues are pursued more thoroughly in Munzer, "A Theory of Retroactive Legislation."

this sense. Yet many expectations arise from other ways of creating legal rules – adopting a constitution, enacting legislation, deciding court cases, promulgating administrative regulations, and so on. Such rules are "conventional" in the sense that they might have been otherwise than in fact they are. But they are not "conventional" in Hume's sense. So the expectations that people have about property reduce to matters about how knowledge and beliefs about legal rules arise.

No general attempt to deal with these matters can be made here, but it is possible to say that, due to the complexity of most legal systems, error can creep into the forming of expectations. A person might expect, say, to be able to open a beauty shop in her home and be unaware that a zoning ordinance bars her from doing so. Also, expectations can be circumscribed by constitutional latitude for changes in the law, by legislative expectations, and by shifting social and economic conditions. For instance, the owners of a junkyard near the edge of a city might expect that they will be able to continue their business indefinitely, or that, if the city proposes to make their land use illegal, they will be compensated. In fact, things may be more complicated. So long as the junkyard is not and never becomes a nuisance, it probably cannot constitutionally be "zoned out of existence" at a stroke without compensation. Nevertheless, courts have upheld the phased elimination of nonconforming uses. That is, the junkyard owners may be confronted with a new zoning ordinance that will make their use illegal after five years have elapsed – without compensation.[32] To some it is tempting to view expectations as involving agreements or promises or binding declarations of intent by a legislature or other legal authority. In fact, though, this view of expectations does not do justice to the more complicated and qualified way that expectations are often formed in modern legal systems.

32 See Board of Supervisors of Cerro Gordo County v. Miller, 170 N.W.2d 358 (Iowa 1969).

In light of this brief sketch of the formation of expectations, it is possible to identify two structural criteria – rationality and institutional legitimacy – for deciding which expectations the law should protect. These criteria are not singly necessary and jointly sufficient for protection. But if both are met, some opposing reason would have to be given for not protecting the expectation.

A rational expectation satisfies three conditions. It involves an appropriately accurate and detailed knowledge of the law on the part of those subject to it or their advisers. It evinces some ratiocinative ability to make predictions on the basis of that knowledge. And it reveals some ability to replicate the expectations and reasoning of others, especially officials.[33] To illustrate, a person may rationally expect her estate to be distributed after her death as she directs if she executes a will drawn up for her by a lawyer well-versed in such matters.

A legitimate expectation meets two conditions. It is supported, first, by the underlying justifications of the laws inducing it and, second, by the fundamental principles of the legal system as a whole. Notice that this is expressly a notion of institutional rather than moral legitimacy. Under fugitive slave laws, slaveowners probably had rational and institutionally legitimate expectations regarding the return of runaway slaves. But the expectations were not morally defensible.

If an expectation is both rational and legitimate, it presents a strong though not invincible structural claim for protection. The claim is structural because it rests on the web of ex-

---

33 This account does not suppose that subjective assessments of probability must, in order to be rational, conform precisely to relevant objective probabilities. If one were to insist on so strict a standard, one might find little or no rationality in the world. See generally Amos Tversky and Daniel Kahneman, "Judgment under Uncertainty: Heuristics and Biases," in Daniel Kahneman, Paul Slovic, and Amos Tversky, eds., *Judgment under Uncertainty: Heuristics and Biases* (Cambridge: Cambridge University Press, 1982), pp. 3–20. Many of the essays in this volume illustrate this point.

pectations and the pattern of institutional justification within a given legal system. It is typically a strong claim because it usually leads to the economical use of the resources of the system. For it will be cheaper and easier, other things being equal, to protect expectations that are generally compatible, and rational and legitimate expectations usually will be.[34]

8.8 CAN UTILITY AND EFFICIENCY ACCOUNT FOR *RIGHTS* OF PRIVATE PROPERTY?

This question may interest only philosophers who hold certain views about the concept of rights.[35] Some of them may object to language in § 8.6 about "rights" of private property. The thought behind the objection is that the principle of utility and efficiency can ground only property *interests* subject to the hegemony of preference-satisfaction. It cannot ground property *rights*. It cannot morally support the enforcement of legal property *rights* when not enforcing them in a given case would promote preference-satisfaction. This is because one feature of a right is that it has the power to "trump" competing considerations of utility.

Imagine that Martin, an elderly widower with no children, owns a large single-family home. It would, by virtue of its size, location, and amenities, make a splendid senior citizens

---

34 It is not possible to pursue this subject more deeply here, but Regan's "co-operative utilitarianism" may offer the best utilitarian vehicle for developing these thoughts because it takes account of the interdependence of expectations and other factors in deciding what one ought to do. See Donald Regan, *Utilitarianism and Co-Operation* (Oxford: Clarendon Press, 1980), especially chs. 8–12.

35 The treatment of this question makes use of an exchange between Lyons and Hare. See David Lyons, "Utility and Rights," in J. Roland Pennock and John W. Chapman, eds., *NOMOS XXIV: Ethics, Economics, and the Law* (New York: New York University Press, 1982), pp. 107–38; R. M. Hare, "Utility and Rights: Comment on David Lyons's Essay," in Pennock and Chapman, eds., *NOMOS XXIV*, pp. 148–57. The idea of rights as "trumps," popularized by Dworkin, is adapted by Lyons. Compare Ronald Dworkin, *Taking Rights Seriously* (Cambridge, Mass.: Harvard University Press, 1978) (paperback ed.), pp. 81–130, 184–205, with Lyons, pp. 111–12 and n.6.

center. Suppose it is said that the center is very badly needed, that no other premises would do nearly as well, and that the community cannot afford either to build a center or to pay Martin the fair market value of his home. The objection is that although more preference-satisfaction would flow from the community's taking the home for a center without compensation, Martin in fact has justified legal property rights that the community must respect. The principle of utility and efficiency is therefore at variance with a considered moral judgment that Martin has property rights that ought to be respected. If the principle is the whole story, then Martin has only property interests, not property rights. If the considered judgment is correct, then Martin has property rights for which utility cannot account.

This example is humdrum compared with the dramatic cases that populate the literature – framing an innocent person in the general interest, killing one person to prevent someone else's killing twenty, saving a brilliant surgeon over one's son when only one can be saved, and so on. But even if one were to accept a broadly stated principle of utility and efficiency as the sole ultimate principle of morality, the issue at stake and the line of reply are the same. First it is necessary to ascertain that, in the case given, utility and efficiency really do compel taking Martin's home without compensation. Here it is terribly difficult to fill in the details realistically. Why will only his property do? If the center is so badly needed, why is it not feasible to use tax revenues either to build a new center or to pay Martin for his home? The difficulties go well beyond the immediate case. One can marshal many reasons why government should respect property rights. Among them are the likelihood that official duties generated by sound moral thinking should be upheld and the adverse consequences – resentment, demoralization, insecurity, unrest, retaliation, and so on – that would flow from expropriating Martin's property. Given that Martin's plight can hardly be kept secret, other property owners will feel threatened.

In short, once the consequences of taking Martin's home

without paying for it are identified, it is far from clear that it would really advance utility and efficiency to do so. If this line of reasoning applies, one can show why Martin's property rights should be respected. Suppose, though, that it does not apply. In that case, is there any persuasive argument for sticking with the initial considered moral judgment? If, all things considered, utility and efficiency really *do* require expropriation without compensation (which seems highly doubtful), would it be justified to enforce Martin's property rights? It is hazardous to rest an affirmative answer on the initial judgment. For the case puts in doubt judgments of that sort. It may be said that any property "rights" that the principle of utility and efficiency can support are less powerful than those that other philosophical traditions can support. To this the response is either that this is not so (because other traditions sometimes allow rights of property to be qualified by other considerations in cases of conflict), or that, if it is so, the other traditions are extreme and rest on some inadequately defended moral position (for example, an extreme natural rights or libertarian view).

The foregoing reply to the objection holds even if one were to accept a broadly stated principle of utility and efficiency as the sole ultimate principle of morality. Yet this book can offer a sturdier reply, for it proposes a pluralist theory of property. Hence, even if the principle of utility and efficiency offered here, which is property-specific (§ 8.5), could not account for property rights, other parts of the theory, in particular the labor-desert principle, are able to do so. Consequently, despite the fact that utility and efficiency are part of the theory, the theory as a whole can preserve the considered judgment that there are property rights. There are, more precisely, both moral property rights and legal property rights whose enforcement is morally justified that do not succumb to somewhat weightier considerations of utility and efficiency in a given case. This proposition differs from the stronger, and highly dubious, claim that considerations of utility and efficiency can never be sufficiently weighty to override property rights.

Chapter 9

Justice and equality

9.1 THE PRINCIPLE

This chapter argues for a combined principle of justice and equality. The principle maintains that unequal property holdings are justifiable if (1) everyone has a minimum amount of property and (2) the inequalities do not undermine a fully human life in society. This principle is a standard of justice in that it regulates morally how benefits and burdens are to be shared among persons. It is also a standard of equality in that it requires showing, in the event that persons are treated differently, why different treatment is morally proper.

The combined principle proceeds from an interpretation of the equal moral worth of persons. This interpretation differs from the utilitarian interpretation of equal worth as equal counting. The present interpretation can be loosely labeled "Kantian."[1] It contends that counting persons equally does not go far enough. Equal counting is compatible with sacrificing the individual utility of some in order to promote

1 Here "Kantian" indicates not Kant's specific views on property (on which see §§ 4.3 and 6.3) but the central views of his moral philosophy. See, for example, Immanuel Kant, *Groundwork of the Metaphysic of Morals*, trans. H. J. Paton (New York: Harper & Row, 1964); Immanuel Kant, *Critique of Practical Reason*, trans. Lewis White Beck (Indianapolis and New York: Bobbs-Merrill, 1956). The Kantian interpretation of the equal moral worth of persons is not the same as what Rawls calls the Kantian interpretation of justice as fairness. See John Rawls, *A Theory of Justice* (Cambridge, Mass.: Harvard University Press, 1971), pp. 251–57.

overall utility, and any such sacrifice ignores or undervalues the separateness of persons. Here separateness is not isolation or atomism, for persons live in societies. Separateness also differs from the idea that there are distinct persons who have individual interests. Rather, it involves the idea that persons have rights not to have certain of their interests traded for overall utility. Or, to use the more precise language of §§ 2.2 and 3.3, the rights are not to have certain morally justifiable individual advantages sacrificed for overall utility. These "advantages" involve both minimal property and a fully human life in society and include choices as well as interests in a strict sense. Hence, this chapter develops the combined will and interest theory of rights introduced in § 3.3.

Two differences stand out between the principle of utility and efficiency and the principle of justice and equality. One is a difference between the substantive concepts employed. The principle of utility and efficiency uses preferences. In contrast, the principle of justice and equality uses basic needs and basic capabilities. To explicate these concepts fully would demand a book of its own. For the moment, a basic need is something that is urgently required for some essential end, and a basic capability is some power to act or function that is necessary for self-respect and healthy self-esteem.[2] Later sections try to identify which needs and capabilities are basic in the present context and to relate them to preferences.

The second difference between the two principles is structural. True, each principle has two clauses or components. But in the principle of utility and efficiency each clause states a requirement, and one component (utility) has priority over the other (efficiency) when both can be determined. In the principle of justice and equality, which makes the background assumption that a society can achieve

2   As in § 5.4, the text largely follows David Sachs, "How to Distinguish Self-Respect from Self-Esteem," *Philosophy & Public Affairs*, 10 (1981): 346–60.

a minimum for all, only the first clause states a requirement: Everyone should have the minimum.[3] This is the Floor Thesis. The second clause states a side constraint rather than an independent requirement: Inequalities must not be too great. This is the Gap Thesis. The second clause, then, constrains inequalities of wealth that might be justifiable under the principle of utility and efficiency or the labor-desert principle. It is not called a "ceiling" thesis, for it aims to limit not what the wealthiest may have but the size of the difference between the wealthy and others. Of course, setting a floor and an acceptable gap may in effect imply a ceiling; still, the point is not to set some maximum otherwise identified but to rule out an overly wide gap. Furthermore, neither component of the principle of justice and equality is prior to the other in regard to which can be determined or measured. Although in theory and practice one might well try to ensure minimal property before worrying about inequalities, utility is not "prior" to efficiency in that sense.

The strategy is to discuss possible "Kantian" principles of justice and equality. The chapter entertains and rejects several such principles. It then makes a case for the combined principle stated above. Though Chapter 11 systematically examines conflicts among principles in a pluralist theory of property, the present chapter makes a modest beginning on that examination by suggesting how the principle of justice and equality qualifies the principle of utility and efficiency. The principle of justice and equality, like the principle of utility and efficiency (§ 8.5), is specific to property, presupposes that otherwise defensible property holdings are not affected by other features of the social situation, and relies on the justifiability of some general moral principle. It

3 If the background assumption were not made, the first clause would state a side constraint. Certainly special problems of justice and equality arise when a society is too poor to provide the minimum for all or even for many. In such circumstances, one should insist on a distribution approaching strict equality (§ 9.2) except when departing from it advances the long-range prospects of those who are seriously deprived. This book directs most attention to societies that satisfy the background assumption.

is, however, less clear how best to formulate a broad Kantian principle than to state a broad utilitarian principle.

9.2 STRICT EQUALITY

The first candidate is strict equality: If persons are of equal moral worth in a Kantian sense, then they must all have the same amount of property. Why ought this to be so? One answer understands the principle instrumentally. It mandates strictly equal holdings in order to achieve some goal – usually strictly equal utility for all.

The instrumental version is unsatisfactory. For one thing, the principle is ill adapted to the stated goal. To simplify matters, assume that the goal is equal utility and that utility is preference-satisfaction. Now property is just one factor out of many bearing on a person's level of preference-satisfaction. Other factors include health, friendships, temperament, and so on. Even if one sought to produce equal satisfaction, it might be best to do so with an unequal distribution of property. Persons with excellent health and many friendships may need much less property to experience satisfaction equal to that of persons not similarly blessed. Indeed, if everyone had equal property holdings, then equal utility might be impossible to produce. A way might not exist to raise the utility of persons with wretched health or disastrous personal relationships enough to equal that of those not so afflicted.

To sidestep these difficulties one might abandon the idea of equal property and concentrate on the goal of equal utility. But this goal is unappealing for many reasons. (1) It may be hard to measure utility well enough to apply the principle successfully. This will be especially so if some people try to conceal their level of satisfaction in order to prompt redistributions of property that would raise their level above that of those who are more honest or less adept at dissembling. (2) The goal may be impossible to achieve for some. Probably no number of Mediterranean villas will be enough to raise the utility of someone who has severe endogenous depres-

230

sion to the level experienced by most other people. (3) The aim is especially unattractive when persons have consciously cultivated an expensive taste – say, exotic food or vintage automobiles. For in order to produce equal utility one would have to redistribute property to those with expensive tastes. Doing so will, other things being equal, reduce the utility of those from whom resources are shifted. (4) One must sometimes make an independent moral assessment of preferences. There should be room for a theory of value or human nature that excludes or discounts some preferences because of their content. Otherwise one could be stuck with counting equally (assuming equal strength), for example, the preference of the Marquis de Sade to inflict sexual torture and that of Mother Teresa to help the poor. If one wishes to state a version of utilitarianism that guards against the introduction of nonutility factors, one may defensibly opt to count such preferences equally (§ 8.3). But to develop a more cogent theory, such equal counting is suspect. Here one should exclude or discount some preferences because of their content.[4]

It is not much more plausible to understand the principle of strict equality noninstrumentally. Here the idea is that only equal holdings answer to the equal moral worth of all persons. Assume for the moment that equal moral worth requires equal treatment. Even so, if equal treatment is a standard that applies to the sum of all features or areas of a person's life, it does not follow that property must be distributed equally. It is fallacious to argue that what is true of a whole must be true of each of its parts. If what matters is that overall treatment be equal, property might still be distributed unequally, for unequal holdings could be offset by superior treatment in some other feature or area of a person's life. Unless one makes property an idée fixe or clings to the fallacy of division, equal treatment does not require equal property.

4 See Stephen R. Munzer, "Intuition and Security in Moral Philosophy," *Michigan Law Review*, 82 (1984): 740–54, at 752–53.

There is, moreover, a problem with the assumption that equal moral worth requires equal treatment. The problem is that a gap exists between saying that people are equal in moral worth and saying that they ought always to be treated equally. A familiar way of formulating the gap is to observe, with Ronald Dworkin, that equal moral worth requires not *equal treatment* but that persons be *treated as equals*.[5] Sometimes a right to treatment as an equal generates a right to equal treatment and sometimes it does not. To identify the difficulty is not to endorse Dworkin's specific views on equality. The point is just that any transition from equal moral worth to equal property holdings must be defended – which it is exceedingly difficult to do.

Two further points regarding the principle of strict equality require mention. One is theoretical. The foregoing objections do not refer to *other* principles relevant to a theory of property. This book argues for a principle of utility and efficiency and a principle of desert based on labor. These principles are sometimes incompatible with that of strict equality. Hence, if these arguments are sound, additional grounds exist for rejecting strict equality. These arguments also constrain a more moderate standard of equality. The other point is practical. It would be difficult to achieve an equal distribution of property even once. If people are free to consume or exchange property, it would be even harder to keep the distribution equal. Redistribution is a tricky business for any egalitarian position. It is superlatively tricky for the position of strict equality.

Some readers may agree with all of the above criticisms but feel that they fail to take account of an element of plausibility in strict egalitarianism. Yet what is this element? It may be replied that strict equality supposes that minimizing wealth

---

5   See Ronald Dworkin, *Taking Rights Seriously* (Cambridge, Mass.: Harvard University Press, 1978) (paperback ed.), p. 227. For now one may leave aside the criticism that Dworkin's notion of equal concern and respect (pp. 180–83, 272–78, 368) is too exiguous to provide a good account of the distinction or a satisfactory theory of equality. But see note 24 below.

differences would be a good thing. Or it may be replied that strict equality guarantees equality of bargaining power, which in turn guarantees that persons will not be able to take advantage of one another in other areas of social life – for example, in politics. These answers are unconvincing arguments for strict equality. Equal bargaining power can erode over time if people can transact freely, and in any case can only assist, not guarantee, the absence of advantage taking. More important, neither answer identifies an element that is unique to strict egalitarianism. A position that seeks to narrow inequalities, defended in § 9.5, also captures these elements. This position is a better way to accommodate the attraction that some feel toward strict equality.

9.3 A RAWLSIAN CONCEPTION OF EQUAL PROPERTY

If the rejection of strict equality is well founded, it nevertheless remains to see what nonutilitarian principle of justice and equality, if any, can be justified. The most prominent contemporary philosopher of justice, Rawls, has argued for a nonutilitarian account that is often seen as Kantian. Although his position is unsatisfactory in some important respects, examining it critically points the way to a more successful treatment of justice and equality in property holdings. Rawls's *A Theory of Justice* lacks an explicit theory of property. Yet it is possible to construct an account of the distribution of property that, though unclear on some key points and wanting in detail, fits plausibly with his position on justice.

The correct principles of justice, according to Rawls, are those that would be chosen by rational, self-interested parties in the "original position." In this hypothetical situation, the parties are deprived of knowledge of their own desires and talents, their class or status, and the level of development of their country. Behind this "veil of ignorance" they are, while conversant with the general facts about human society and with the laws of economics and other social sciences, unable to tailor principles to their own advantage because they do not know what their own interests are. Indeed, the veil of ignorance prevents the parties from knowing even their own conception of the good. At this juncture, it may seem that they lack sufficient information to make any significant choices. Rawls tries to eliminate this difficulty by introducing the notion of "primary goods." These are things that it is supposed rational persons want whatever else they want. Among these Rawls lists rights and liberties, powers and opportunities, income and wealth, and self-respect. Primary goods are thus intended to supply a person with an adequate basis for choosing principles of justice from behind the veil of ignorance but nevertheless to be neutral with respect to specific conceptions of the good.

The parties in the original position must choose principles of justice that will govern the basic structure of society and the distribution of primary goods. Rawls argues that the parties will reject, among other candidates, various forms of utilitarianism. Instead, they will select these principles:

First Principle
Each person is to have an equal right to the most extensive total system of equal basic liberties compatible with a similar system of liberty for all.
Second Principle
Social and economic inequalities are to be arranged so that they are both:
(a) to the greatest benefit of the least advantaged [the difference principle] . . ., and
(b) attached to offices and positions open to all under conditions of fair equality of opportunity.[6]

These principles are subject to certain priority rules. One is the primacy of the first principle; liberty can be restricted only for the sake of liberty, not for social or economic advantages. Another is that fair equality of opportunity takes priority over the difference principle. Rawls does not suggest

6 Rawls, *A Theory of Justice*, p. 302.

that these quite general principles and priority rules will yield immediate solutions to concrete problems. Rather, he contends that these principles are to be elaborated and implemented in later constitutional, legislative, and administrative stages, in which the veil of ignorance is successively lowered and then dropped.[7]

The distribution of property is governed by two principles. The first principle of justice covers *some* kinds of property. It applies to "basic liberties," which include "freedom of the person along with the right to hold (personal) property."[8] "These liberties," Rawls adds, "are all required to be equal by the first principle, since citizens of a just society are to have the same basic rights."[9] It is not wholly clear whether the first principle requires only that people have an equal *right* to hold personal property or that they all have an equal *amount* of it – though the latter reading seems an implausible interpretation. It is, moreover, unclear what Rawls means by "personal property." A lawyer might contrast personal property with, variously, communal, real, or productive property. In a later article, Rawls sheds some light on the matter. There he says that "the right to own certain kinds of property (e.g., means of production) . . .[is] not basic"[10] and thus not protected by the first principle.

The difference principle governs these *other* kinds of property. What the difference principle distributes, put generally, are lifetime expectations with respect to social and economic

---

7   This summary and the following critical examination concentrate almost entirely on Rawls's views as expressed in *A Theory of Justice*. In later essays Rawls has changed his views in various respects. See his "Kantian Constructivism in Moral Theory," *Journal of Philosophy*, 77 (1980): 515–72; "The Basic Liberties and Their Priority," *The Tanner Lectures on Human Values*, vol. 3 (Salt Lake City: University of Utah Press, 1982), pp. 1–87; "Justice as Fairness: Political not Metaphysical," *Philosophy & Public Affairs*, 14 (1985): 223–51.

8   Rawls, *A Theory of Justice*, p. 61.

9   Ibid.

10 Rawls, "A Kantian Conception of Equality," in Virginia Held, ed., *Property, Profits, and Economic Justice* (Belmont, Calif.: Wadsworth, 1980), pp. 198–208, at p. 203.

advantages and the material bases of self-respect. It permits inequalities but only if they maximally advance the position of the least well-off. Property holdings are just one factor among others relating to social and economic position. Hence, unless other factors are in play, the difference principle requires that property be distributed equally unless unequal holdings maximally benefit the least advantaged. If other factors are in play, holdings would be less, or more, nearly equal depending on whether these other factors respectively offset or exacerbate the effect on lifetime expectations.

Two additional features of Rawls's theory complicate the picture. One is that the two principles of justice apply to the design of institutions. Throughout, the principles refer to representative persons holding certain social positions or offices established by the basic structure. Neither principle "applies to distributions of particular goods to particular individuals who may be identified by their proper names."[11] Another feature is that the difference principle does not mandate continual redistributions of property. If it did, it would undercut the long-run expectations of the least advantaged regarding the possibility and worth of ascending to higher social and economic positions. Continual redistribution would not ultimately be to their greatest advantage because in the end under a just regime everyone gains from some measure of stability and order.[12] Instead, Rawls supposes that background economic institutions will include what he calls transfer and distribution branches. Their respective functions are to maintain a social minimum and preserve distributive justice. To perform these functions they will supplement wages and adjust taxes and property rights. The ultimate aim is to maximize the long-run expectations of the least advantaged.

11 Rawls, *A Theory of Justice*, p. 64.
12 See Allen Buchanan, "Distributive Justice and Legitimate Expectations," *Philosophical Studies*, 28 (1975): 419–25, at 421–24; Stephen R. Munzer, "A Theory of Retroactive Legislation," *Texas Law Review*, 61 (1982): 425–80, at 478–80.

A Rawlsian view of property likely favors a much more nearly equal distribution than prevails in most countries. It is possible, though unlikely, that the principle of equal basic liberties requires strictly equal holdings of a few kinds of property. For other kinds, the difference principle requires a substantial narrowing of inequalities. The guiding idea is not merely to ensure a threshold amount of property. It is to reduce the gap between the life prospects of the least well-off and everyone else.[13] Is this position defensible?

One feature of Rawls's position is sensible but unsatisfactorily developed. This is the idea that some kinds of property are more central than others to human life. The first principle of justice protects such property as a "basic liberty." So far, so good. But the protection offered is unclear. As observed earlier, the scope of "personal property" is undefined. There is also the question of whether the first principle ensures only an equal *right* to or an equal *amount* of such property. If it ensures only the former, then it would be compatible with any inequalities not ruled out by the difference principle. If it ensures the latter, then Rawls's position would be identical with strict egalitarianism for all "personal property." Such a position would be philosophically implausible for reasons given in § 9.2, at least unless "personal property" covers very little. More seriously, the protection offered by the first principle is, in a different way, excessively rigid. Deep problems exist with Rawls's view that one must resolve conflicts between basic liberties solely in terms of the extent or amount of liberty. It will often be

---

13 A later essay contemplates a more qualified, background role for the difference principle with a less determinate effect on distribution. "Thus the difference principle holds, for example, for income and property taxation, for fiscal and economic policy; it does not apply to particular transactions or distributions, nor, in general, to small scale and local decisions, but rather to the background against which these take place. No observable pattern is required of actual distributions, nor even any measure of inequality . . . that might be computed from these. What is enjoined is that the inequalities make a functional contribution to those least favored." Rawls, "A Kantian Conception of Equality," p. 205.

necessary to consider as well the competing interests and ends of different persons and actions. Nor need rational persons agree with Rawls that those kinds of property qualifying as a basic liberty always have priority over fair equality of opportunity and the social and economic advantages covered by the difference principle.[14]

Another, highly problematic feature of Rawls's position concerns the interplay between the first principle of justice and the difference principle and their bearing on equality. At first blush the difference principle, though strongly egalitarian, would still seem to permit fairly substantial inequalities. If, however, that is so, then the inequalities thus allowed would impair social stability, erode the worth or effectiveness of civil and political rights, and indeed undermine the equality of basic liberties.[15] In that case, either the first principle and the difference principle conflict, or the apparent conflict between them must somehow be resolved.

The literature suggests some replies in Rawls's behalf.[16] One might reply that Rawls's view is conditional: If the parties assume that their basic liberties can be effectively exercised, then they will agree to the priority of the first principle over the difference principle. Or one might reply that the functions of Rawls's transfer and distribution branches, which include taxation and redistribution, may help to secure the worth or effectiveness of the basic liberties.

These replies, though helpful, lead to the conclusions that, surprisingly, the lexical priority of the first principle is the driving force behind Rawls's social and economic egal-

---

14 See H. L. A. Hart, "Rawls on Liberty and its Priority," in Norman Daniels, ed., *Reading Rawls* (Oxford: Basil Blackwell, 1975), pp. 230–52. For a response, see Rawls, "The Basic Liberties and Their Priority."

15 See Norman Daniels, "Equal Liberty and Unequal Worth of Liberty," in Daniels, ed., *Reading Rawls*, pp. 253–81.

16 See Allen E. Buchanan, *Marx and Justice: The Radical Critique of Liberalism* (Totowa, N.J.: Rowman & Littlefield, 1982), pp. 149–52. Buchanan's conditional reading (p. 151) relies on a passage in Rawls, *A Theory of Justice*, pp. 151–52.

itarianism,[17] and that his position turns out to be much more egalitarian than initially appears. In the event that one adopts the conditional reading suggested above, the "if" clause of the conditional sentence either will almost never be satisfied, which would render the theory of scant practical import, or will be satisfied only if one secures very much more nearly equal economic and social conditions than currently prevail. The end results are to expose some underlying tensions in Rawls's position and perhaps to leave him with a position that is so egalitarian as to seem counterintuitive.

Even if one adopts the more orthodox interpretation that the difference principle is the chief source of Rawls's social and economic egalitarianism, that egalitarianism is still sufficiently strong to be open to criticism. Many philosophers believe that the original position fails to generate the difference principle. Even if it does so, it must be because of a presumption in favor of equality that is embedded in the original position. The presumption, stated roughly, is that the preferences of each person, no matter what their content, are entitled to equal priority.[18] This proposition may seem innocuous but is in fact questionable. If the earlier position on the moral status of preferences is sound (§ 9.2), then it is sometimes proper to exclude or discount some preferences on ground of content. Further, this proposition supposes that an equal distribution, unlike an unequal distribution, requires no special justification. Yet if the later discussion of labor as a basis for desert is sound, then both distributions call for special justification. Hence, if one gives weight to these discussions, then it is appropriate to question both the

---

17 Buchanan, *Marx and Justice*, p. 152, correctly attributes this interesting conclusion to Daniels's argument.
18 For the view that acceptance of the original position entails acceptance of the difference principle, see Steven Strasnick, "Social Choice and the Derivation of Rawls's Difference Principle," *Journal of Philosophy*, 73 (1976): 85–99. Strasnick's derivation is unsatisfactory. See, for example, Robert Paul Wolff, "On Strasnick's 'Derivation' of Rawls's 'Difference Principle'," *Journal of Philosophy*, 73 (1976): 849–58.

presumption in favor of equality latent in the original position and the difference principle itself.

This criticism suggests that the difference principle should seem counterintuitive closer to the surface. In fact it is, for reasons that are familiar. First, the difference principle, and the maximin economic reasoning that underlies it, implies that the parties in the original position will care little, if at all, about gains above the minimum.[19] But it is false to say that they will not care at all. And even if they are much more interested in the minimum than in gains above it, it does not follow that they lack keen interest in the additional gains. One can greatly prefer sports to the theater, but still have a passion for the theater. Second, the difference principle would allow enormous losses by most people if that would produce even a slight gain for the least well-off. In some instances, this will be both counterintuitive and counter to utility. It also assumes that the parties are highly risk-averse. For it presupposes that they will not want, after obtaining a minimum, to take much of a chance on getting rather more, and will instead fix almost entirely on securing the highest minimum. Thus this counterintuitive consequence is related to the previous one.

Furthermore, the difference principle would permit enormous gains by the best-off if that would yield a very small, but in the circumstances highest possible, gain for the least well-off. Rawls anticipates this possibility.[20] He responds that the difference principle is not intended to govern such cases, and in any event presupposes the existence of other principles and institutions that make such cases highly improbable. This response has some merit. But if it is allowed, then a parallel response is available to many utilitarians and to those who combine utility with other principles – namely, that they can provide a supporting cast of principles and institutions that make spectacularly unlikely whatever cases give *them* trouble.

19 Rawls, *A Theory of Justice*, p. 154.
20 Ibid., pp. 157–61.

Since Rawls does not offer an explicit account of property, it is hard to be confident that only the account constructed here squares with his views on justice. But if this account is plausibly ascribed to Rawls, then, though it has much to admire, it suggests that he cannot treat satisfactorily the issue of distributive equity in property holdings.

9.4 THE FLOOR THESIS

One admirable feature of Rawls's theory is the light that it sheds on achieving a minimum. This section presents a different argument for a minimum. The argument differs from Rawls's because, among other things, it does not use maximin economic reasoning or the device of an original position. This section seeks to justify the first clause of the combined principle of justice and equality – namely, that everyone should have a minimum amount of property. This is the Floor Thesis.

To launch the argument it is necessary first to understand the content of this thesis. Some will ask: Minimum *for what?* The answer is: For a decent human life in society. In order to have such a life, it is necessary to meet certain basic needs and to ensure the development of certain basic capabilities (§ 9.1). For purposes of a theory of property, relevant basic needs include food, clothing, shelter, and health care. Similarly, relevant basic capabilities include being able to appear in public without shame, to read, write, and do arithmetic at a rudimentary level, and to work at a job.

Interested readers can pursue the literature for extended arguments regarding the basic character of these needs and capabilities.[21] Here one can observe informally that persons

21 This section draws heavily on, but does not entirely follow, David Braybrooke, *Meeting Needs* (Princeton: Princeton University Press, 1987); Amartya Sen, "The Standard of Living: Lecture I, Concepts and Critiques" and "The Standard of Living: Lecture II, Lives and Capabilities," and Bernard Williams, "The Standard of Living: Lives and Capabilities," in Amartya Sen et al., *The Standard of Living* (Cambridge: Cambridge University Press, 1987), pp. 1–38, 94–102; Henry Shue, *Basic Rights: Subsistence, Affluence, and U.S. Foreign Policy*

lack a decent human life if they are starving or mal-
nourished, if they do not have garments or housing sufficient to keep them warm and dry, or if they suffer from
easily treatable serious diseases or medical conditions. They
also lack a decent human life if they are ashamed to be in the
company of others because, say, they are beggars or homeless, if they are uneducated and illiterate, or if they cannot do
any work that is worth doing. Of these needs and capabilities, the need for food is absolute. It applies in all societies
and times and to children and the aged as well as to adults.
The ability to appear in public without shame is only nearly
absolute, for newborns and the comatose cannot experience
shame. Notice, however, that how much food is enough
varies, as do the personal conditions that count as shameful.
But many basic needs and basic capabilities are not absolute
or near-absolute in this way. For example, clothes may be
dispensable in tropical climates, and the ability to read and
write would not have been basic in ninth-century England.
Notice, too, that some items on the list pertain to the physical condition of persons – consider food – while others relate
to their social situation – consider the ability to do a job.

Several points will help to locate basic needs and basic
capabilities in a theoretical context. First, these needs and
capabilities mark out interests of persons that are so fundamental to human existence in society that it makes sense
to secure them by rights. They are essential to self-respect
and sometimes even to staying alive. They are not the sorts
of things that, if a society can provide them for all, it properly
may deprive some persons of them in order to advance

(Princeton: Princeton University Press, 1980), especially chs. 1, 4–6.
Braybrooke explicates and defends the concept of needs (pp. 5–79),
and relates needs to both justice and preferences (pp. 131–60, 189–
230). Sen explores the idea of capabilities and their relation to wealth
and absolute and relative standards (pp. 14–19, 24–31, 36–38), and
Williams connects capabilities with rights and self-respect (pp. 100–
01). Shue presents a powerful case for a right to subsistence, though
some aspects of his argument are vulnerable to criticisms raised by
James W. Nickel and Lizbeth L. Hasse, Book Review, *California Law
Review*, 69 (1981): 1569–86.

the utility of others. Second, these basic needs and basic capabilities are somewhat akin to Rawls's primary goods (§ 9.3). But unlike his primary goods, they are less abstractly stated and do not place much weight on a view of rationality. Even so, they attest to the soundness of the general idea that some things are essential to a decent human existence. Third, basic needs and basic capabilities are not identical with preferences. They are, of course, things that people typically strongly prefer. Yet this is not always so; people may desperately need treatment for malaria but not have a preference for it if they are unaware of such treatment or their need for it. More important, basic needs and basic capabilities are central to a Kantian perspective because of their indispensability to continued, self-respecting existence in society, not because people have preferences for them. Fourth, basic needs and basic capabilities, like preferences, underscore the wisdom of a combined will and interest theory of rights (§ 3.3). The soundest theory of rights protects both interests – for example, in having adequate food and shelter – and choices – for instance, to have enough education to make an informed choice of how to lead a life.

Even if the content of a decent human life in society is clear enough in theory, some practical pitfalls remain in specifying the minimum amount of property needed to attain such a life. For example, it is implausible to set a cross-cultural minimum solely by an objective yardstick. Ownership of specific resources, such as so many clothes or a home with so many rooms, will be too high a threshold for some societies and too low a threshold for others. Likewise, having certain assets or annual income – say, $10,000 in 1990 dollars – will be too high or too low depending on the society in question, even assuming constant prices. Or, to give another example, it is implausible to set a universal minimum – that is, the same minimum level of property for all within a society. Some persons have greater, or at least different, needs – for food, education, health care, and so on – than do others in order to have a decent human life. Still, some fairly standardized, albeit not universal, minimum is defensible, and not only for administrative convenience. Some persons may be so disabled or so catastrophically ill that it would be either impossible or extraordinarily expensive to provide them with the resources for a decent human life. Again, as yet another example, the minimum is likely to differ across time as well as place. As the economic output, social standards, and cultural level of a society change, the kinds and amounts of property required for a decent human life are apt to change as well. Suppose, however, that one avoids these and other pitfalls. Perhaps, in light of § 5.3, one might specify the minimum for a society using both objective elements (say, the amount normally needed for subsistence) and relative elements (say, the average amount needed for acceptable self-respect given the cultural and material circumstances of the society).

In light of this discussion, the argument for the Floor Thesis is as follows. If one avoids pitfalls of the sort just described, then a minimum amount of property is necessary for a decent human life in society. The exact amount, and kind, of property thus necessary will vary from one society to another. Now a decent human life in society requires that certain basic needs be met and that the development of certain basic capabilities be ensured. These needs and capabilities are not reducible to preferences. Rather, they identify morally justifiable individual advantages – in self-respect and in continued life – that are essential to a minimally decent human existence, and so are appropriately protected by rights rather than merely set as goals or aspirations. They involve, indeed, rights that should not be traded even for substantial gains in utility. A salient background assumption is that one is dealing with societies that have sufficient resources to provide the minimum level for all persons (§ 9.1). Of course, a society need not force minimum property on anyone who wishes to decline; ascetics are permitted. But, ascetics aside, all societies having sufficient resources would violate a person's rights if they failed to provide a minimum and so are required to provide it. Therefore, in these societies, all persons should have a minimum amount of property.

The first clause of the combined principle justifies some public and some private property. The relevant considerations follow in part and differ in part from those advanced under the heading of utility and efficiency (§ 8.6). As to public property, the first clause supports materials for national defense, public facilities of many kinds, natural resources, and cash and emergency food, clothing, and shelter. But whereas the principle of utility and efficiency responds to persons' preferences, the clause requiring minimum property responds to the things necessary for a decent human life in their society. As a result, the emphasis is different. The first clause of the combined principle stresses the wherewithal to meet basic needs and develop basic capabilities: schools, medical facilities, resources for future generations, and cash and in-kind items necessary to deal with natural disasters, economic dislocations, and personal upheavals. As before, a possible counterargument is that it is not necessary for the government to own these things but only to have the power to raise revenue in order to pass help through to individuals. Yet, as before, a response is that the government can best respond promptly and effectively if it already owns or has other substantial property rights in many of the necessary items. It does not, of course, make sense for the government to have huge stockpiles when they are unlikely to be needed; so a great many practical details remain.

Likewise, the first clause justifies some private property through considerations that partly track and partly diverge from those encountered in § 8.6. Once more, people should have private-property rights in clothing, grooming equipment, modest furniture, and cash and other resources to obtain what they need. But though the principle of utility and efficiency bases this conclusion on persons' preferences, the minimum property clause bases it on the things essential to a decent human life in society, and consequently the emphasis is different. Thus, the first clause underscores those things over which private control is necessary for a decent human life: not only personal articles, food, and shelter but also funds for or other secure access to education and health care. It is not possible to say exactly which things are necessary without knowing what sort of economic system a society has (§ 5.5). It is clear, however, that the minimum property clause, unlike the principle of utility and efficiency, will not respond to preferences for dispensable things, except insofar as a society has such a high level of resources that assuring such things counts as part of a decent human life.

One should notice that the argument of this section justifies more than access to goods and services. Some opponents of private property might claim that such access is enough. A society could, after all, provide people with goods and services through a dispensing and lending system. People could get food at the state cafeteria, check out clothes in the proper size each week at the government laundry, and return on a standard-issue bicycle to a warm and clean bunk in a dormitory. This system meets some basic needs, and something like it prevails in prisons and the armed forces. Yet it is not adequate for an open society. A key shortcoming is that a dispensing and lending system allows no scope for the development of one's own personality (§ 4.7). In order best to meet basic needs and develop basic capabilities, it is vital to have personally chosen (as opposed to government-issue) clothes, utensils, furniture, books, mementos, religious articles, and art objects. Such things facilitate control, privacy, and individuality, and underscore Rawls's sound sense in including "personal property" among the "basic liberties" (§ 9.3). In the theory of property advanced by this book, liberty is derivative rather than basic (§ 8.6). It derives in part from the first clause of the principle of justice and equality. Not only is liberty implicit in having personally selected items of property of the kinds just listed, but the exercise of basic capabilities also often involves choices of the life one is to lead – for instance, in deciding to pursue a certain line of work.

So much for the first clause of the combined principle, or Floor Thesis. The second clause, or Gap Thesis, is a taller order. It constrains inequalities of wealth so that they do not undermine a fully human life in society. It is harder to offer a convincing argument for this constraint. Many will object that once a minimum is achieved, society need do no more. This section cannot offer a knockdown proof, but it does try to make the Gap Thesis plausible. Since many thinkers advocate a minimum, the idea that inequalities should be narrowed after a minimum is attained is the more distinctive feature of the combined principle.

To begin the argument, one must clarify the content of the thesis. What is a "fully human life in society"? The answer, insofar as it relates to property, is: a life freed from the conditions that undermine the ability to live with self-respect and healthy self-esteem in society. Part II of this book illustrates some of these conditions. One is the inability to have appropriately equal personal goods, such as control, privacy, and individuality. Another is the inability to develop the positive character traits – especially the property-related moral virtues – that are possible in a given society. Yet another is the inability to have meaningful work for an appropriate wage because of alienating or exploitative circumstances or large differences in economic power in the labor market. Conditions such as these conflict with a basic human need – namely, to live with self-respect and healthy self-esteem with other people. Thus, the idea of a fully human life in society has a Kantian foundation, but the foundation includes, if you will, some Aristotelian and Marxian bricks.

Abstractly stated, the argument for the Gap Thesis runs as follows. Even if everyone in a society has at least the minimum amount of property, that fact is compatible with large extremes of wealth. If the extremes are sufficiently large, then the gap interferes with appropriate amounts of control, privacy, and individuality, with the development of property-related virtues, and with the opportunities for meaningful work. This interference undermines a fully human life in society for at least some persons. A Kantian perspective requires a society to treat persons as equal in moral worth. To treat them in this way is to ensure a fully human life in society for all willing to accept it (ascetics are still allowed), provided that it is reasonably possible to do so. Hence, if a society exhibits wealth inequalities that are wide enough to disrupt or render impossible this sort of life, then it is not ensuring a fully human life for all, and it traverses the Kantian injunction to treat persons as equal in moral worth. Therefore, inequalities are justifiable only if they do not undermine a fully human life in society.

Several points help to clarify the theoretical status of this argument. First, the argument does not move from equal moral worth to equal treatment in the way disapproved toward the end of § 9.2. Rather, it moves from equal moral worth to a constraint on the width of inequalities in property holdings. Second, the argument partly resembles but also partly diverges from Rawls's difference principle (§ 9.3). The resemblance lies in the sound thought that the gap between the rich and others, not merely achieving a minimum, is important. But the present argument, unlike the difference principle and Rawls's case for it, need not require the highest minimum that is possible, does not appeal to maximin economic reasoning, and invokes from the beginning the complex social background of property as set forth in Part II of this book. Invoking this background avoids some of the problems that bedevil Rawls's account of the difference principle and his "basic liberties." Third, as in the argument for the Floor Thesis, one is dealing with basic needs and basic capabilities that are appropriately secured by rights. These needs and capabilities are not equivalent in moral status to mere preferences, and they bring into play both will and

248

interest perspectives on rights. The Gap Thesis, though highly egalitarian, need not exhaust the case for equality. Even after that thesis is met, the principle of utility and efficiency could justify a still more nearly equal distribution if people's preferences so require.

Some readers may agree with the abstract argument for the Gap Thesis but desire some concrete illustration. In fact, one can sketch different ways in which a property distribution can undermine a fully human life in society and so violate a Kantian understanding of equal moral worth. For example, inequalities that are extreme and visible can wound self-esteem and create justified moral resentment. If some people live in luxury not through their own efforts but from large inheritances, then resentment is understandable on the part of those who have a minimum amount of property but still far less than those who have inherited. Social structures and other nonmarket mechanisms can also create extreme inequalities of this sort and can also lead to resentment.[22] The root basis for protest is not the disutility of resentment, or even that resentment can spawn crime, violence, and social instability. It is that the wide inequalities rest on no differences in moral merit and are instead an affront to equal moral worth. It may be objected that if those who have less were of extraordinary character, they would ascribe the disparities to the rough and tumble of life and so take them in stride. But the objection asks too much of human beings. A defensible principle of justice and equality must not assume that those whose sense of equal moral worth is undermined have a duty to act with extraordinary self-command and forbearance.

Or again, even if extreme inequalities fail to provoke resentment, they can distort the legal and political process and reinforce myths offensive to equal moral worth.[23] Con-

---

22 Wounded self-esteem and resentment need not, but can, involve class differences. For this possibility, see, for example, Richard Sennett and Jonathan Cobb, *The Hidden Injuries of Class* (New York: Random House/Vintage Books, 1973 [1972]).

23 See, for example, Charles E. Lindblom, *Politics and Markets* (New York: Basic Books, 1977).

sider a feudal or a caste society. There it would be unsurprising to find that wealthy persons have disproportionate access to and success in the courts and a disproportionate impact on elections and legislation. There it is common for those occupying upper positions in the hierarchy to see their status as a matter of right. Those disadvantaged by these arrangements may voice, and see, no objection. All the same, their equal moral worth is affronted by the wide inequalities in property and their associated social structures.

It may be objected that this situation need not violate the Gap Thesis; for low-caste persons might claim that, though they have much less wealth and are treated as inferiors, they are nevertheless of equal moral worth, just called to a different station in life, and hence suffer no impairment of self-respect or self-esteem. This objection is unsound. It incorrectly supposes that persons cannot be mistaken about their levels of self-respect and self-esteem. As these concepts are explained at the end of § 5.4, people are generally aware of these levels – but not always. In fact, the situations of low-caste persons, slaves, women in sexist societies, and subordinate races in racist societies are prime examples of likely misassessments of self-respect and self-esteem. These concepts, then, are not identical with particular psychological states. Lest one risk legitimating obnoxious societies, it is vital that people not only *feel* but also *be* unimpaired in regard to the self-respect and healthy self-esteem pertinent to the Gap Thesis.[24]

24 Ronald Dworkin, "What is Equality? Part 2: Equality of Resources," *Philosophy & Public Affairs,* 10 (1981): 283–345, advocates a threshold-level criterion for equality of resources. Dworkin creates an auction as an abstract market for distributing resources. He complicates this market by introducing insurance to compensate individuals for certain kinds of bad luck. Dworkin then transmutes the insurance arrangement into a graduated tax scheme with the same effect. A market-derived strategy, he holds, will generate a threshold-level criterion for distributing resources. It will not, however, narrow inequalities merely because of their width.

In the present context, the central difficulty with this proposal is that it lacks an adequate account of how property and other resources are connected with a fully human life. It therefore fails to come to

This is not a book on race relations, but it would be inexcusable to overlook the fact that race can make a difference. In the United States, to be, say, black and poor, or black and (though not poor) much less well-off materially than whites, is not just to experience violations of the Floor and Gap Theses, respectively. It is to suffer a special blow to your humanity. Karst writes eloquently of race and poverty and in effect addresses mainly what this chapter calls the Floor Thesis. To be black and to fall below the community minimum

> is to subject yourself to the community's judgment that you are indecent, outside the community of persons entitled to respect. . . .
>
> Failure in the role of breadwinner reproduces itself as failure in the other roles, with predictable harms to the man's sense of personal worth. . . .
>
> What hurts the most? Not that you have a low income, or even that your furniture and clothes are shabby. What really hurts is that you are denied the self-respect that

grips with the shortcomings of providing only a minimum, and neglects the Kantian argument of § 9.5 for reducing inequalities when they impair a fully human life in society. For other difficulties with Dworkin's views, see, for example, John G. Bennett, "Ethics and Markets," *Philosophy & Public Affairs*, 14 (1985): 195–204 (Dworkin does not show that markets have any special moral significance); John E. Roemer, "Equality of Talent," *Economics and Philosophy*, 1 (1985): 151–88 (*pace* Dworkin, under certain conditions equality of resources and equality of welfare are equivalent); John E. Roemer, "Equality of Resources Implies Equality of Welfare," *Quarterly Journal of Economics*, 101 (1986): 751–84 (technical demonstration of the same).

The argument of Harry Frankfurt, "Equality as a Moral Ideal," *Ethics*, 98 (1987): 21–43, is ineffective against the case for the principle of justice and equality. Insofar as Frankfurt understands "economic egalitarianism" (at 21) as "strict equality" (§ 9.2), there is no disagreement that it is an unappealing moral ideal. But if the "doctrine of sufficiency" (at 22) that Frankfurt favors is the same as the Floor Thesis (§ 9.4), then that doctrine is incomplete. It represents only the first clause of the combined principle. The chief difficulty here, as with Dworkin, is that Frankfurt lacks an account, of the sort facilitated by Part II of this book, of how the narrowing of wealth inequality relates to a fully human life in society.

251

comes from supporting a family, from being a producing member of society.[25]

In a similar vein, Rodes writes in a way that effectively suggests that race – given that slum dwellers come disproportionately from racial minorities – can exacerbate violations of what this chapter calls the Gap Thesis:

> The fact that an American slum dweller eats better, dresses better, or has more gadgets than a rich Eskimo, a nineteenth-century farmer, or a medieval squire does not console him if he lacks the wherewithal for what his own society regards as a fully human existence.[26]

In conclusion, notice a practical and an intellectual consequence of accepting the second clause of the combined principle. Practically, this clause justifies more public and private property. Since the narrowing of inequalities will often require greater government intervention, it supports more public property. It supports, for example, public ownership of the resources needed for a taxation and welfare distribution system that ensures a fully human life in society.[27] Furthermore, since the narrowing of inequalities will often require that individuals have additional kinds and amounts of things, it supports more private property. To say how much more, one needs to know a great deal about the level

25 Kenneth L. Karst, *Belonging to America: Equal Citizenship and the Constitution* (New Haven: Yale University Press, 1989), pp. 126, 129, 140.
26 Robert E. Rodes, Jr., *The Legal Enterprise* (Port Washington, N.Y.: Kennikat, 1976), p. 149.
27 The work of Frank I. Michelman suggests that the welfare rights involved may be constitutional as well as moral rights. See his "The Supreme Court, 1968 Term – Foreword: On Protecting the Poor Through the Fourteenth Amendment," *Harvard Law Review*, 83 (1969): 7–59; "Constitutional Welfare Rights and *A Theory of Justice*," in Daniels, ed., *Reading Rawls*, pp. 319–47; "Welfare Rights in a Constitutional Democracy," *Washington University Law Quarterly* (1979): 659–93. For criticism, see Robert H. Bork, "The Impossibility of Finding Welfare Rights in the Constitution," *Washington University Law Quarterly* (1979): 695–701.

of wealth and the cultural characteristics of a society. If, for example, a society has great wealth and its culture facilitates the benign use of personal goods (§ 5.2) and the development of a sound character (§§ 6.3–6.5), then a more nearly equal distribution of private property is needed for a fully human life in society. In both cases, to say that the second clause justifies "more" public and private property is to say that it justifies a different amount and a different distribution of property than does the principle of utility and efficiency alone. Like that principle, however, applying the principle of justice and equality requires empirical information and intermediate stages of assessment and decision (§ 11.3).

This last remark brings one to an intellectual consequence of the combined principle – namely, that this principle qualifies the principle of utility and efficiency. It does so because the prerequisites of a decent and fully human life in society generally take precedence over maximizing preference-satisfaction. The word "generally" is important, for the combined principle is rarely so powerful as to overcome massive shortfalls in preference-satisfaction. Moreover, it is a mistake to suppose that conflicts between the two principles must be both numerous and sharp. Preferences for the prerequisites of a decent and a fully human life in society are likely to rank high in the preference orderings of most individuals. And no one conversant with the literature on utilitarianism can fail to be aware of attempts to show that utility rarely diverges from defensible moral intuitions or considered judgments.[28] Chapter 11 takes up such matters in detail, but provisionally one can conclude that, in cases of conflict that are likely to be neither frequent nor violent, the principle of justice and equality generally has a higher priority than the principle of utility and efficiency.

28 See, for example, R. M. Hare, *Moral Thinking: Its Levels, Method, and Point* (Oxford: Clarendon Press, 1981), pp. 131–35, 180–82, and the comments in Munzer, "Intuition and Security in Moral Philosophy," at 751–54.

Chapter 10

Labor and desert

10.1 OVERVIEW

There is a tendency to distort the force of desert by labor in the theory of property. Some thinkers exaggerate it. Others repudiate it. In fact, desert based on labor should play a significant, though by no means the only, role in justifying rights of private property.

This chapter tries to show what that role is. Section 10.2 constructs an initial labor theory of property on the basis of some rather strong assumptions. Section 10.3 revises that theory by modifying the assumptions in order to make them realistic. Section 10.4 clarifies the revised labor theory. Section 10.5 assesses its significance. Here and in other chapters, the revised labor theory is also referred to as the principle of desert based on labor, or the labor-desert principle.

The overall picture looks like this. Even though the revised theory shows that labor and desert play a role in property rights, the two other principles previously discussed bear more importantly on the justification of private property: the principle of utility and efficiency, and the principle of justice and equality. Desert is part of justice, but it is not all of it; the principle of justice and equality is concerned only with the nondesert aspects of justice. A major aim of the revised theory is to identify some of the places where desert based on labor must be qualified by these other two principles. Some connected aims are to explain why some thinkers exaggerate and others underestimate the force of desert

254

claims, and to show how the labor theory, with its emphasis
on the individual, can be adapted for and transposed into a
modern social context. This chapter shows that there is a
cogent version of the labor theory that does not have to rest
on unrealistic assumptions about picking up acorns in a state
of nature, and instead illuminates and helps to justify some
private-property rights in a rich social context.

Some connections between the initial and revised labor
theories are as follows. Both theories involve certain premises that support, though they do not entail, a certain
conclusion. The premises of the initial theory are some rather
unrealistic assumptions that are highly favorable to rights of
private property. The premises of the revised theory are
much more realistic assumptions that are produced by systematically modifying the premises of the intitial theory and
that are, at first blush, less favorable to rights of private
property. The conclusion of the initial theory is that a prima
facie justification exists for a set of private-property rights in
a version of the state of nature. The conclusion of the revised
theory is that a prima facie justification exists for a somewhat
different set of private-property rights in a modern society.
The connections just described do not rest on a broad claim
that if theory T rests on unrealistic assumptions, then T
supports a different theory, T', that rests on realistic
assumptions. That claim is overly broad and false. The point
is rather that enough parallels exist between the assumptions
of the initial theory and the systematically modified assumptions of the revised theory to allow the former theory to lend
support to the conclusions drawn in the latter theory.

Three important asymmetries exist between the revised
labor theory (labor-desert principle) on the one hand and the
principles of utility and efficiency and of justice and equality
on the other. First, the labor-desert principle is merit-based,
whereas the other two principles are worth-based (§ 8.1).
Second, the labor-desert principle has closer connections
than the other principles with the projection theory of Chapter 4 and some property-related virtues discussed in Chapter
6. The former principle rests on a conception of persons as

agents who, by their actions in the world, are responsible for changes in the world and deserve or merit something as a result. Though not all labor involves projection, and though not all projection involves labor, many varieties of labor do involve projection. This involvement ties labor to the transcendental features of property elucidated in § 4.4. Similarly, though not all labor involves property-related virtues, and though not all property-related virtues involve labor, some varieties of labor are apt to involve such positive character traits as persistence, industriousness, and probity in business dealings. Third, whereas the principles of utility and efficiency and of justice and equality justify some private and some public property, the labor-desert principle justifies only some private property. At least this is so under the most obvious way of interpreting the revised labor theory. This theory relates each laborer to private-property rights in a product or in wages. Of course, laborers could agree, before or after working, to transfer some of their rights to a public entity. In addition, if everyone who wishes to work should have an opportunity to do so, and if this requires the government to have resources in order to intervene in the labor market or to serve as an employer of last resort, then some of these resources may take the form of public property. Still, apart from worker agreement and government intervention, no direct path exists between the labor-desert principle and public property.

10.2 THE INITIAL LABOR THEORY

This section sketches an argument, based on desert by labor, for rights of private property.[1] Here "labor" means the exer-

---

1 It is not claimed that Locke makes this argument. See John Locke, *Second Treatise of Government* [1690] §§ 25–51, in *Two Treatises of Government*, ed. Peter Laslett 2d ed. (Cambridge: Cambridge University Press, 1967). The argument in the text has little in common with Locke's views about gaining property rights by mixing one's labor with

tion of effort in order to make or physically appropriate something. "Desert" means worthiness of some recompense because of some personal feature or action. The conclusion of the labor-desert argument is the initial labor theory of property. The argument depends on certain assumptions. They fall into four rough groups: background conditions, features of the laboring situation, physical and psychological effects of laboring, and evaluative or normative features of the effects of laboring. These are very strong assumptions, but it is not an easy task to construct, even on them, a cogent labor-desert argument. And if such an argument cannot be mounted on any assumptions, the rest of the chapter would be a waste of paper. After listing the assumptions and presenting the argument, this section makes some remarks on desert, replies to a trio of objections, and describes the impact of adjusting several assumptions. In what follows, the words "labor" and "work" are used interchangeably, as are "laborer" and "worker."

The background conditions depict a fragment of the state of nature. There is no society or government. The thing

unowned things. See ibid. § 27. It is, however, somewhat related to his thought that since no one would labor without expecting some benefit, it would be unfair to let the idle take the benefit of the laborer's pains. See ibid. § 34. This chapter refers to Locke's views in passing, but it takes no position on the overall interpretation of his theory of property. Compare, for example, C. B. Macpherson, *The Political Theory of Possessive Individualism: Hobbes to Locke* (Oxford: Clarendon Press, 1962) (Locke as possessive individualist), with, for example, James Tully, *A Discourse on Property: John Locke and his Adversaries* (Cambridge: Cambridge University Press, 1980) (Locke as natural lawyer). The initial labor theory in the text is perhaps closest to the desert argument in Lawrence C. Becker, *Property Rights: Philosophic Foundations* (London, Henley and Boston: Routledge & Kegan Paul, 1977), pp. 48–56, though this theory is more explicit and copious – and sometimes different – in its assumptions than his argument. On Becker's general treatment of the labor theory (pp. 32–56), see the review by Stephen R. Munzer, *Minnesota Law Review*, 63 (1979): 531–43, at 532–36. See also Anthony Fressola, "Liberty and Property: Reflections on the Right of Appropriation in the State of Nature," *American Philosophical Quarterly*, 18 (1981): 315–22.

sought to be acquired is unowned. Things of that sort (or near replacements), sufficient in both quantity and quality, are available for acquisition by others. The laborer has an exclusive liberty to use his body in the way called for by the work he does.

Certain features of the laboring situation are important. The laborer has no moral duty to work. His intention in working is to acquire enduring control over some thing. He works solely for himself and entirely on his own. His work involves physical contact with the thing he seeks to acquire. The work reflects nothing about how he sees himself in relation to others. All laborers work with equal intensity and effectiveness.

There are, moreover, various physical and psychological effects of laboring. The laborer produces a product, not a service. The "product" is something that he gathers (say, potatoes by digging them up) or makes (say, a table made from wood). The product is not beyond his needs, wasted, or allowed to spoil. Others lose nothing by being excluded from the product. Nor do they experience any adverse sociocultural consequences, such as loss of self-esteem or prestige. No changes in the situation arise after the product is gathered or made.

Finally, there are some evaluative and normative features of the effects of his labor. Its products are good in some general sense.[2] The work done does not benefit anyone besides the laborer. In the event that property rights are justified, there are, subjunctively, certain characteristics that these rights would have. They would not be transferable. They would be exclusive rather than shared. They would last indefinitely. They would be commensurate with the work done and the most fitting benefit for the laborer's work. And they would not infringe any rights held by others.

2   If a person worked mindlessly to produce things that were not "good" in any sense, then though he might have a right to them, it would be odd to say that he "deserved" them. If desert applies, typically the things produced are needed or wanted by the worker and others.

In outline, the labor-desert argument is this: If the background conditions exist, then the laborer may use his body to gain control over some thing. If, further, there exist the features of the laboring situation and the physical and psychological effects described, then the laborer is responsible for a product that he does not misuse and over which his enduring control has no adverse impact on others. If, finally, the evaluative and normative features are as specified, then recognizing his enduring control is the most fitting benefit for his labor and does not infringe the rights of others. Such recognition is the acknowledgment of property rights.

The initial labor theory is the claim that if all of these assumptions hold, then the laborer deserves property rights in the product. This claim and the conditional sentences in the argument sketched for it express relations of support rather than of entailment. If the laborer digs potatoes or makes a table from wood, then he deserves property rights in the potatoes or the table. Now, following Feinberg, the general form of a desert statement is "S deserves X in virtue of F," where S is a person, X is a thing or mode of treatment, and F (the "desert basis") is some feature of or action by S assessed in relation to its surrounding circumstances.[3] Hence, if someone works as described and conforms to the assumptions, then he deserves moral property rights in the product in virtue of his labor. To determine which rights are fitting, one should assess the relative importance of effort, ability, persistence, industriousness, luck, time spent, achievement, the difficulty, unpleasantness, or danger of the work, and other working conditions.[4] These rights can, in

---

3 See Joel Feinberg, "Justice and Personal Desert," in his *Doing and Deserving* (Princeton: Princeton University Press, 1970), pp. 55–87, at p. 61.

4 Literature bearing on this assessment includes George Sher, *Desert* (Princeton: Princeton University Press, 1987), especially chs. 2, 4, and 6; Michael Walzer, *Spheres of Justice: A Defense of Pluralism and Equality* (New York: Basic Books, 1983), pp. 108–09, 165–83, 260; Michael A. Slote, "Desert, Consent, and Justice," *Philosophy & Public Affairs*, 2 (1973): 323–47.

turn, serve as a prima facie justification for legal property rights. The rights include, in Hohfeld's terminology (§ 2.2), a set of moral claim-rights, liberties, powers, and immunities. They are weaker than the property rights recognized in most legal systems because there is no power to transfer.

The initial theory is a labor-desert prima facie-theory, rather than a labor-desert entitlement-theory. To deserve something is a prima facie reason to have it. To be entitled to something implies that reasons, all things considered, dictate having it.[5] Even in the fragment of the state of nature depicted by the background conditions of the initial theory, other reasons might exist for recognizing, or denying, moral rights to private property. Hence the initial theory, as developed here, generates prima facie moral rights, not moral rights all things considered. To develop it at this point into a labor-desert entitlement-theory would take the inquiry too far afield. However, § 10.3 shows how other considerations enter in and thus provides a way to bridge the gap between desert and entitlement.

This argument involves relative, rather than absolute, desert in two respects. First, the laborer's desert rests on actions taken by him, and not by others, in relation to the product in question. So far as this product and his labor are concerned, he is more deserving than those who did not work to produce the product. The argument does not show that other people fail to deserve property rights in the product on some other basis – for example, their high moral character. A necessary condition of the laborer's deserving the rights absolutely is that other persons do not deserve them. Still, as a partial foundation for an institution of private property, labor is more plausible than any other desert basis.

---

5   Thus, "entitlement" as used here is broader than in Nozick's "entitlement" theory of justice. Robert Nozick, *Anarchy, State, and Utopia* (New York: Basic Books, 1974), pp. 150–82. "Entitlement" as used here applies to what persons should have, all things considered, even if the reasons are not rights-based or if they come from a "patterned" theory of justice.

Let anyone who doubts this try to describe an institution resting on, say, moral virtue and see how frustrating the task is. Labor as a desert basis furnishes difficulties enough.

Second, the laborer's desert rests on actions that in turn rest on characteristics that enable and dispose him to work. The argument does not show that he deserves these work-facilitating characteristics – for example, good health, intelligence, strength, stamina, industriousness, and so on. A necessary condition of the laborer's deserving property rights absolutely is that he deserves these characteristics. Still, in this context it is beside the point to claim, on certain grounds, that relative desert is no desert at all. The phrases "in this context" and "on certain grounds" are meant to exclude some general problems about God and human freedom. Someone might say: Human beings do not deserve anything because they owe everything to God. But a secular work on political theory can ignore this theological perspective. Or someone might say: All human actions are determined; freedom and determinism are incompatible; only free human actions can be a basis for desert; since there are no such actions, human beings do not deserve anything. Yet this book, like almost all political writing, can assume that not all human actions are determined or that, if they are, determinism does not rule out desert.

The labor-desert argument will provoke at least three objections. The first is that even if one sets aside general problems about God and human freedom, people do not deserve property rights.[6] Desert of all sorts requires not only a desert basis. It requires also that people do something to deserve the desert basis. If a desert basis is not deserved, people do not deserve anything that results, directly or in-

6 The objection is prompted by Rawls's view that people do not deserve their natural endowments or the advantages achievable with them. See John Rawls, *A Theory of Justice* (Cambridge, Mass.: Harvard University Press, 1971), pp. 15, 75, 103–04, 310–15. The reply owes much to Sher, *Desert*, ch. 2; Alan Zaitchik, "On Deserving to Deserve," *Philosophy & Public Affairs*, 6 (1977): 370–88.

directly, from that desert basis. Since people do not deserve their work-facilitating characteristics, they do not deserve property rights in the product of their work.

The objection is overdrawn. It leads to an infinite regress, cannot rule out universal necessary conditions of desert, and risks depersonalizing those who work. If all desert rests on a desert basis, and if that desert basis must rest on some further desert basis, and so on, then the search for an ultimate desert basis must continue ad infinitum. Eventually one comes to universal necessary conditions of desert, and it is hopeless to claim that these are deserved. For example, to deserve anything one must be born, but no one deserves to be born. Thus, the objection insists on a requirement for desert that is too stringent because it could never be met. Finally, the objection tends to depersonalize workers. It effectively converts into a common asset those work-facilitating characteristics that, even if not deserved, are uniquely theirs and partly constitute the self.[7]

If one repairs the objection to avoid excessive stringency, then it fails to show that workers cannot deserve property rights. As the first remark about desert intimates, desert involves a fittingness often traceable to a comparison between persons – here, between workers and nonworkers.[8] One might, then, repair the objection by weakening its premises as follows. Work-facilitating characteristics need not be deserved provided either that they are distributed equally or that, if distributed unequally, they cause no one to lose. But this weakened premise does not exclude property rights based on desert by labor. On the one hand, if A and B

---

7 On this last point, see Charles R. Beitz, *Political Theory and International Relations* (Princeton: Princeton University Press, 1979), pp. 138–39; Walzer, *Spheres of Justice*, pp. 260–61; Anthony T. Kronman, "Talent Pooling," in J. Roland Pennock and John W. Chapman, eds., *NOMOS XXIII: Human Rights* (New York: New York University Press, 1981), pp. 58–79, at pp. 71–77.

8 See generally Feinberg, *Doing and Deserving*, pp. 65–67; James P. Sterba, "Justice and the Concept of Desert," *Personalist*, 57 (1976): 188–97, at 191–95.

have equal work-facilitating characteristics, and if A works and B does not, then, in the event that anyone is to receive property rights, it is fitting that A have them. After all, B can work but chooses not to. On the other hand, if A and B differ in work-facilitating characteristics, and if the difference causes no loss, then, in the event that anyone is to receive property rights, it is fitting that each should have them in the product of his or her labor. After all, if apples are as good as potatoes, B has no sound objection if A's strong back facilitates digging potatoes and B's climbing ability facilitates gathering apples. One assumption of the labor-desert argument is that no loss occurs through a nonworker's being excluded from a given product. How some version of the no-loss requirement might be met in the real world gets attention in § 10.3. But so far the repaired objection fails to show property rights not to be deserved under the assumptions of the initial labor theory.

A second objection holds that the labor-desert argument begs the question of how one can justify property. The argument assumes that persons have a right to acquire property rights by their labor. Rights have correlative duties. Just as property rights involve a duty on others, so must a right to acquire property rights by labor. But whether others have such a duty is the point at issue.

This objection is mistaken because it confuses different senses of the word "right." In Hohfeld's terminology, "property rights" consist of a cluster of normative modalities, including claim-rights with correlative duties on others. But the "right" to acquire property rights is much narrower. It includes just two elements. One is a liberty to acquire – an absence of a duty not to acquire. The other is a power to acquire. The correlatives are, respectively, the absence of a claim-right held by others to interfere with acquisition, and a liability or susceptibility on the part of others to having their moral position altered. Hence, the "right" of acquisition imposes no duty on others to assist in the laborer's acquisition or to refrain from trying to acquire property rights in the same things. It only allows one person to alter the moral position of himself and others in relation to things in the world.

A third objection begins where this reply ends. It questions the moral defensibility of a right of acquisition. Suppose a nonworker says to the worker: "Why should I respect your so-called property rights? I never asked you to work, and you have done nothing for me." Proudhon makes something like this objection when he writes:

> "The rich," exclaims Jean Jacques, "have the arrogance to say, 'I built this wall; I earned it by my labor.' Who set you the task? we may reply, and by what right do you demand payment from us for labor which we did not impose on you?" All sophistry falls to the ground in the presence of this argument.[9]

This objection raises two distinguishable issues. One is whether lack of consent matters ("I never asked you to work"). But even if universal consent would suffice for property rights, it is implausible to make it necessary for them. To require consent would grant nonconsenting nonworkers a moral immunity against being affected by the worker's labor. It would also give them a moral liberty to help themselves to the product of this labor since the worker, lacking property rights, would have no moral power to exclude them. The other issue is whether the worker's failure to benefit the nonworker matters ("You have done nothing for me"). But it is implausible to require such a benefit. On the assumptions of the labor-desert argument, the nonworker suffers no loss. Even if the nonworker is envious, feelings of envy are not a "loss" in any sense relevant here, for, at least in this fragment of the state of nature, the worker is not answerable for any envy felt by others. Hence the nonworker needs no compensating benefit. To mandate a noncompensating

---

9 Pierre-Joseph Proudhon, *What is Property?*, trans. Benj. R. Tucker (New York: Humboldt, n.d.), p. 84. Contrast Becker, *Property Rights*, p. 41; John Stuart Mill, *Principles of Political Economy* [1848], ed. William Ashley (Fairfield, N.J.: Augustus M. Kelley, 1976), p. 233.

benefit is to shield extortion. For it allows the nonworker to say: "If you will not do something for me, I shall block your claim to any property rights in the product of your labor, no matter how hard you work."

By adjusting some assumptions one can see more clearly the nature of the initial labor theory. These adjustments are not the modifications that yield the revised labor theory of § 10.3. They are minor and produce only variants of the initial theory.

First, suppose that persons exploit unowned resources with different levels of intensity or effectiveness. For example, A works moderately hard on a large amount of land to produce a low-quality wheat crop, while B works extremely hard on a smaller plot to produce excellent grapes. The unadjusted initial labor theory would give A property rights to the wheat and B property rights to the grapes. Yet if B is more deserving than A, one could adjust the initial theory to give B stronger property rights in the grapes than A has in the wheat. This change would in turn require some adjustment in the property rights available, such as by giving B a limited power to transfer. As the revised labor theory will bring out more fully, in practice it is hard to calibrate property rights to desert.

Second, suppose that the laborer has some moral duty to work. The duty may be natural (for example, that of a parent to provide food for his or her children) or voluntary (for example, one arising from a promise to someone to store potatoes). The duty circumscribes the worker's property rights because now the product must be used in a certain way – to feed the children or to be stored. Yet it does not obliterate these rights. The worker still has the same rights vis-à-vis those to whom no duty is owed. And even those owed a duty must respect a lesser package of rights. For example, the promisee may not divert all the stored potatoes to his own use. The point of this adjustment is to show that the initial labor theory need not regard individuals as so atomistic that they can have no natural or voluntary moral duties to one another. As a corollary, notice that such duties also modify slightly the earlier assumption of nontransfer-ability.

Third, suppose that the work benefits some but not all other people.[10] It may, for instance, benefit the worker's children or a promisee. This adjustment complicates the initial labor theory. On the one side, it seems to strengthen the theory by making available a more powerful answer to the third objection considered above. Suppose that A's work benefits both himself and B but neither benefits nor harms C. C repeats the nonworker's lament. Yet since C suffers no loss, to allow C to block the acquisition of property rights not only affects A as before but also deprives B of a benefit. On the other side, this adjustment seems to besmirch the purity of the labor-desert argument, for the answer just given brings in benefit to others. From there it may seem a short step to the social utility of labor – which threatens to trans-form the labor-desert argument into an argument of utility. To this apparent difficulty there are two solutions. One is that to dispose of C's complaint, one need not mention the benefit to B. The effect on A suffices. Another solution is that even if one mentions the benefit to B, doing so does not impair the nature of the theory as a labor-desert argument. The desert basis is still the worker's labor. It is not the worker's individual utility, the joint utility of A and B, or social utility. So even if an institution of private property founded on desert by labor best promotes utility, that does not contaminate the initial reason furnished by desert based on labor.

10.3 THE REVISED LABOR THEORY

The initial labor theory is an unsatisfactory theory of prop-erty, for it rests on unrealistic assumptions. The next step, therefore, is to see what happens if those assumptions are

---

10 Becker's desert argument, unlike the unadjusted initial labor theory, assumes that the worker "adds value" to the lives of others. Becker, *Property Rights*, p. 51.

made more nearly realistic. This section does not go through them one by one, nor does it get to all of them. But it does modify most of them in the following half-dozen subsections. The claim is that something significant survives the process of modification. What survives is the revised labor theory of property.

Rights of and duties to others. A variant of the initial labor theory, introduced near the end of § 10.2, showed that a natural or voluntary duty could qualify the laborer's property rights. If the laborer had broader duties, or if nonlaborers had broader rights, that would further qualify the laborer's property rights. It is hardly possible to settle here what those broader duties or broader rights, if any, are. Yet one can identify two plausible candidates and describe the impact of recognizing them on the laborer's property rights.

One candidate is a right of everyone to have the necessities of life (§ 9.4).[11] People who are physically or mentally unable to work, whether permanently or temporarily, should be able to invoke this right. These handicaps traverse the disjunctive assumption that people have equal work-facilitating characteristics or that unequal characteristics of this kind occasion no loss. The right to life may not involve a correlative duty on assignable individuals. More likely, the duty is owed by the set of individuals who are able to work. If so, then to recognize a right to life is to qualify the property rights of workers in the products of their labor in the following way. They may, as members of the set of working individuals, have to give up some portion of their products to those who need them to live.

A second candidate is a duty on laborers neither to use nor

---

11 "[N]o Man could ever have a just Power over the Life of another, by Right of property in Land or Possessions; since 'twould always be a Sin in any Man of Estate, to let his Brother perish for want of affording him Relief out of his Plenty." John Locke, *First Treatise of Government* [1690] § 42, in *Two Treatises of Government*, ed. Peter Laslett 2d ed. (Cambridge: Cambridge University Press, 1967).

to fail to use products in a certain way. The initial theory assumed that the product is not beyond the laborer's needs, wasted, or allowed to spoil.[12] But if this assumption does not hold, then a question arises as to whether the laborer violates a duty. A duty is hardest to justify in the first case. So long as no loss results to others and their needs are met, perhaps no duty exists for the laborer to stop at the level of need.

Violation of duty is, however, more plausible in some, but not all, cases of waste and spoilage. If, for example, the laborer produces plenty of food and allows it to spoil in full view of a starving person, the laborer violates a duty. But if the laborer unexpectedly has a bumper crop, and no person needing food is around to help consume it, the laborer violates no duty in case some of the crop spoils. There may also be some intermediate situations in which, even if the laborer violates no duty, other forms of moral criticism may be in order. Perhaps he does something that he ought not to do or reveals a deficient moral character. In any event, if one recognizes a duty or other moral stricture regarding the use of products, then the laborer's property rights are further qualified.

Finally, notice that one may have to step outside the labor theory to justify avoidance of a no-spoilage limitation. One way to avoid the limitation is to exchange things that spoil (for example, potatoes or apples) for things that do not (for example, metals, jewels, or land). To vindicate this avoidance, however, one must first justify a power to transfer – of which more momentarily. And to allow such a power is not to endorse a common argument that purports to justify all resulting inequalities.[13] Even if people consent to placing a value on, say, gold in order to facilitate exchange, it does not follow that they consent either to the risk of inequality or

12 "As much as any one can make use of to any advantage of life before it spoils; so much he may by his labour fix a Property in. Whatever is beyond this, is more than his share, and belongs to others." Locke, *Second Treatise of Government*, § 31.
13 Locke seems to make this argument. See ibid. § 50.

to whatever inequalities actually arise through exchange and accumulation. It is plausible to think that if unequal accumulations are defensible, the defense hinges on the capacity of large accumulations to redirect resources to produce more for everyone or at least to raise average or total utility.

The process of acquisition. The initial labor theory assumes that things of the sort that the laborer seeks to acquire, or near replacements, are available in sufficient quantity and quality for acquisition by others. It also assumes that others lose nothing by being excluded from the laborer's product. If these assumptions do not hold, then the laborer's property rights are qualified though not extinguished. Attempts by Locke, Nozick, and Gauthier to handle this problem are not wholly satisfactory.[14] A better way is possible.

Locke restricts his version of the labor theory with a proviso: There must be "enough, and as good left in common for others."[15] Yet if Locke's proviso bars worsening the position of others, then no acquisition is permissible in case there is ever a lack of "enough" or "as good" for even one person. Suppose that at some point there is a person Z for whom there is not enough or as good left to acquire. Then, as Nozick argues,[16] the last person Y to acquire left Z in a worse position. If so, Locke's proviso barred Y's acquisition. But then, in turn, the last person X to acquire before Y worsened Y's position. Hence X's acquisition runs afoul of the proviso. In that case, whoever acquired immediately before X worsened his position and so on back to the very first person to acquire. Therefore, the proviso can never be satisfied.

---

14 Regrettably, space prevents discussion of other views of Locke's proviso (for example, Jeremy Waldron, "Enough and as Good Left for Others," *Philosophical Quarterly*, 29 (1979): 319–28) and indeed of other work on property inspired by Locke (for example, Rolf Sartorius, "Persons and Property," in R. G. Frey, ed., *Utility and Rights* (Minneapolis: University of Minnesota Press, 1984), pp. 196–214).
15 Locke, *Second Treatise of Government*, § 27.
16 Nozick, *Anarchy, State, and Utopia*, pp. 175–76.

Nozick's efforts to amend the proviso are unsatisfactory. In one place, he suggests that a prior acquisition relevantly worsens someone's position only if he is "no longer . . . able to use freely (without appropriation) what he previously could."[17] In fact, however, someone is worse off if previous acquisitions have generated powerful rights of *ownership* while he can now obtain only rights of *use*. For if, as Nozick supposes, rights of ownership include an exclusive interest that is generally unlimited in duration and can be transferred to others, then such rights are much more valuable than mere temporary rights to use things not earlier reduced to ownership. His amended proviso, so understood, is too anemic to prevent substantial worsening by some of the position of others.

There is no obvious way out of this problem. Either a substantial difference in value exists between ownership and rights of use or it does not. If it does, then, as above, Y (who gets ownership) will unduly prejudice the position of Z (who gets only rights of use). If it does not, then Z (who gets rights of use) will unduly prejudice the position of Z' (who gets either nothing or a substantially less powerful form of rights of use). Or at least this will be true of some successor of Z – call him Z_i – and some successor of Z_i – call her Z_j. It will not do to say that there is an indefinite series of ever so slightly less powerful rights of ownership or use such that the rights acquired by any given acquirer will not unduly prejudice the position of his or her immediate successor. There is no reason to believe that acquisition takes place in a linear series. Even if it did, the combination of prior acquisitions would at some point be such as to prejudice unduly the position of some acquirer-come-lately.

Later, however, Nozick amends the proviso in a different way: "A process normally giving rise to a permanent bequeathable property right in a previously unowned thing will not do so if the position of others no longer at liberty to use the thing is thereby worsened."[18] Whereas the previous

17 Ibid., p. 176.
18 Ibid., p. 178.

amendment allows rights of use to be substituted for ownership, this one does not and therefore is not beset by the
problem just described. Instead, the present amendment
would allow rights of use as well as ownership to be barred
to others so long as the position of these others is not "thereby worsened."

This amendment is more plausible than the first, but it is
important to clarify what it does and does not show. It does
show, given some defensible empirical propositions, how
one can meet the no-loss requirement. The propositions relate to the advantages for each person of "a system allowing
appropriation and permanent property"[19] over a situation in
which no property exists. It does not show, even given these
propositions, how one can defend the very strong private-
property rights in Nozick's entitlement theory over competing arrangements of private or shared property rights.[20] To
mount such a defense, one would have to establish some
further empirical propositions. These propositions relate to
the advantages of very strong property rights over other

19 Ibid., p. 177.
20 See G. A. Cohen, "Self-Ownership, World-Ownership, and Equal-
    ity," in Frank S. Lucash, ed., *Justice and Equality Here and Now* (Ithaca,
    N.Y., and London: Cornell University Press, 1986), pp. 108–35, at pp.
    126–33. One aspect of Cohen's instructive discussion is open to ques-
    tion. Cohen interprets the sentence quoted in the text from p. 178 of
    Nozick's book to require that "*A* must not cause *B* to lose the opportu-
    nity to improve his situation by appropriating something, unless *B* is
    adequately compensated for any such loss of opportunity" (what
    Cohen calls S' on p. 121 n. 17). This interpretation reads a lot into
    Nozick's language, because no-worsening with respect to a situation
    in which no property exists differs greatly from no-shortfall-from-
    maximum-improvement with respect to all possible property systems.
    It underlies Cohen's criticisms of Nozick because they use counterfac-
    tual situations. Nevertheless, even if Cohen's interpretation dubious-
    ly reformulates what Nozick said, it accurately formulates what
    Nozick must say if he is to have a suitable restriction on acquisition,
    except insofar as Cohen elides the difference, mentioned presently in
    the text, between an acceptable and the best possible system of prop-
    erty.

property arrangements.[21] Though Nozick need not establish that his property rights are superior to all other arrangements, he must establish that they are not markedly inferior to some other possible arrangement. An acceptable system of property need not be the best possible. But a system cannot be acceptable if it falls well short of the best possible.

In Gauthier's theory of "morals by agreement," two principles are pertinent to this discussion. One is the principle of maximin relative benefit. This principle requires that returns from a cooperative surplus be proportionate to each person's contribution.[22] The other principle is Gauthier's version of the Lockean proviso: It prohibits bettering one's own situation through interaction that worsens the situation of another. Gauthier's version applies not only to the acquisition of external things but also (unlike Locke's) to persons themselves. In the latter capacity, it defines each person's initial rights and duties and so each person's initial position for cooperative interaction.[23] Gauthier's theory favors a rather idealized competitive market society. Paraphrased into the language used here, the theory qualifies the property rights in what the laborer produces. He may receive only such rights as are proportionate to his contribution to the cooperative surplus and as avoid bettering his position by worsening that of others.

Although Gauthier's theory may show how some version of the no-loss requirement can be met in principle, his position has theoretical and practical difficulties. Theoretically, Gauthier's principles do not guarantee that persons will par-

---

21 On empirical premises in Nozick's theory, see Cohen, "Self-Ownership, World-Ownership, and Equality," pp. 130–33; Hal R. Varian, "Distributive Justice, Welfare Economics, and the Theory of Fairness," *Philosophy & Public Affairs*, 4 (1975): 223–47, at 237–39.
22 David Gauthier, *Morals by Agreement* (Oxford: Clarendon Press, 1986), ch. V, especially p. 155. See also David Gauthier, "Justice and Natural Endowment: Toward a Critique of Rawls's Ideological Framework," *Social Theory and Practice*, 3 (1974): 3–26, at 20.
23 Gauthier, *Morals by Agreement*, ch. VII.

take of benefits in proportion to their contributions.[24] A distinct difficulty is the practical impossibility of ascertaining the cooperative surplus.[25] Suppose that one can identify the work-facilitating characteristics that are part of persons' extrasocial endowment. Suppose also that people can produce more by cooperation than by individual production. On these suppositions there will be *some* cooperative surplus. Yet one can rarely say *how much*. In limited circumstances, such as a game-theoretic problem or an artificially sequestered social situation, one might be able to calculate the cooperative surplus. Any such calculation is out of the question in a world with several billion people, complex institutions, and thousands of years of history.

In fact, the practical difficulty can go deeper. It seems likely that, contrary to a supposition above, no water-tight separation exists in practice between extrasocial and socially generated work-facilitating characteristics. Without such a separation, it will be indeterminate how much individual production will yield. This indeterminacy not only compounds the difficulty of ascertaining the cooperative surplus but also casts doubt on measurements of individual contributions. If it is practically impossible to ascertain individual contributions and the cooperative surplus, then one cannot apply the principle of maximin relative benefit.

A more promising way to constrain the acquisition process rests on the principles of utility and efficiency and of justice and equality that were defended in the last two chapters. These principles address actual social situations and can be made determinate. When made determinate, they limit the acquisition of property rights. So the strategy here is this. Desert by labor makes sense in principle and within limits,

---

24 See Jean Hampton, "Can We Agree on Morals?," *Canadian Journal of Philosophy*, 18 (1988): 331–56, at 333–44 (the principle of minimax relative concession, which is closely related to the principle of maximin relative benefit, does not ensure proportionality and may not be rationally preferable to a principle of proportionality).
25 For other possible difficulties, see David Braybrooke, "Social Contract Theory's Fanciest Flight," *Ethics*, 97 (1987): 750–64.

but it seems impossible to construct limits derived entirely from the labor theory itself that are applicable in modern societies. The limits should also come from outside the theory and take account of social complexities. The principles of utility and efficiency and of justice and equality are important limits on acquisition.

Post-acquisition changes. The initial labor theory assumes that no changes in the situation arise after the product is gathered or made. This assumption is often false. Sometimes its falsity stems from the consequences of prior acquisitions; the previous subsection in effect considered this sort of change. At other times its falsity comes from a change in climate or other physical condition. The change not only can make any later acquisition morally indefensible. It also can have a moral impact on prior acquisitions. In general, if a person has by labor acquired property rights in a thing, then those rights may be qualified if later on things of that kind could not be acquired without traversing some moral restriction.

Scarcity is the chief illustration. Suppose, for example, that at one time a person clears land in a sparsely populated area. She grows, harvests, and stores a great deal of wheat. A year later no one could come to own wheat in this way because drought and famine lead to a situation in which acquiring title to wheat by labor would violate, say, the principle of justice and equality. In light of this restriction, the person who acquired wheat a year earlier might have her rights diminished in any wheat in storage now needed for food by others. Applicability of this restriction rests on at least two presuppositions. The now-scarce commodity is essential to life – say, basic food but not truffles or ortolans. And no near replacement exists for the now-scarce commodity. So if wheat were newly scarce but there were plenty of corn and rice, property rights in wheat might not be weakened. But if these presuppositions were satisfied, the wheat farmer would not be within her rights to exclude others from the wheat or to charge them an exorbitant price for it.

It may be objected that this restriction conflicts with the usual understanding of the labor theory and indeed retroactively deprives the wheat farmer of her rights. The reply to this objection brings out some further differences between the initial and revised labor theories. The objection, like the initial theory, assumes that any labor-generated property rights are exclusive and last indefinitely. This assumption is unwarranted if there are post-acquisition changes in situation. For the initial labor theory contemplates a situation in which things are plentiful and available to all for acquisition. This situation creates an implicit constraint that follows the property rights thus acquired into the future. When plenty becomes scarcity, the rights can be diminished. Perhaps the restriction advocated here departs from the labor theory as usually understood. Yet if that is so, then the usual understanding is indefensible.[26] Neither is the restriction retroactive, for it does not change the moral, legal, or social status of any earlier act of acquisition.[27] It only calls attention to a now-matured restriction on the exclusiveness and duration of the property rights previously acquired.

The qualification shows that property rights can, not that they must, be diminished in this way. There are reasons for this both within and apart from the labor theory. Even within the revised labor theory, the qualification does not mean that the farmer occupies a position regarding the wheat that is indistinguishable from that of everyone else. The now-matured restriction may create a duty to share the wheat with others. But if so, sometimes she should have a right to oversee the sharing and to get back any surplus if the drought and famine subside. Again, sometimes she should have a right to compensation from those with whom she

26 See generally Allan Gibbard, "Natural Property Rights," *Noûs,* 10 (1976): 77–86, at 84–85; A. M. Honoré, "Property, Title and Redistribution," in Virginia Held, ed., *Property, Profits, and Economic Justice* (Belmont, Calif.: Wadsworth, 1980), pp. 84–92.
27 For this understanding of retroactivity, see Stephen R. Munzer, "Retroactive Law," *Journal of Legal Studies,* 6 (1977): 373–97.

shares. Furthermore, moral considerations apart from the labor theory may have an impact. Desert based on labor generates prima facie moral rights, not moral rights all things considered. If, for example, a full theory of property also includes a principle of utility and efficiency, it will affect how far, if at all, the original acquirer's property rights are diminished. That principle seems almost certain to call for some diminution. But the amount of diminution might be greater or less than that dictated by the revised labor theory alone.

Transfer. The initial labor theory assumes that property rights are not transferable. This assumption makes the resulting package of property rights less powerful and therefore easier to justify. Yet it is an unrealistic assumption, for an important feature of most legal property rights is transferability. One may, though, drop this unrealistic assumption without precluding transfer so long as certain moral restrictions, which derive from the revised labor theory itself and from the principles of utility and efficiency and of justice and equality, are imposed. Empirical factors partly determine how to restrict transferability. Since these cannot be set out here, this subsection can sketch only the main ideas.

Under the revised labor theory, a transfer is, as a general rule, valid only if whatever constraints apply to acquisition continue to be satisfied. As just shown, post-acquisition changes in situation can affect property rights acquired earlier. Transfer does not sidestep this point. Hence, even if transfer is allowed in principle, desert by labor does not create property rights so powerful that, when transferred, all existing and future claims against them are deactivated. Once again, the idea is that implicit constraints follow the property into the future. This idea may depart from the usual understanding of the labor theory. But if it does, the usual understanding is indefensible.

In order to see how the qualifications work out, it helps to discriminate among different transfers. Consider the taxonomy of transfers represented in Table 2. Now suppose that

TABLE 2. *A Taxonomy of Transfers*

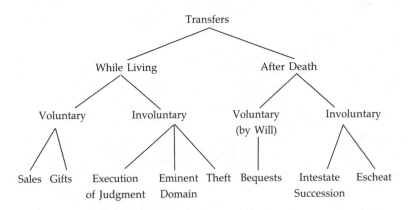

property rights in a certain kind of thing were acquired by labor. Suppose also that later the laborer transfers the property to someone else. Suppose finally that later still, owing to scarcity, things of the relevant kind can no longer be acquired by labor. Does the newly-arisen constraint follow the property so as to diminish the rights of the transferee?

To answer the question properly, bear two points in mind. Scarcity differs from wrongful acquisition. And gratuitous transfers (gifts, bequests, and intestate succession) differ from voluntary transfers for value (sales). Now if the situation involves scarcity and a gratuitous transfer, then the arguments of the previous subsection apply. Ordinarily, the transferees should not be treated differently from original acquirers who retain their property when post-acquisition changes arise. At least two factors can render the situation no longer ordinary. One is that transferees may be unaware of the circumstances of the acquisition and so build up a reliance interest which the original acquirer could not. The other is that in some ways the original acquirer occupies a stronger position than an immediate and, still more, a successor transferee. Consider, for example, a sequence of bequests from A, the original acquirer, to B, and then from B to C. The bequest from A to B may be justified if none of the restrictions described earlier applies. The bequest from B to

277

C is another matter. Since only A worked to obtain the property in question, B has no power founded on his own labor to bequeath it to C. The power of bequest that the labor theory can support is at best a one-shot affair.[28] A corollary is that A cannot transfer everything he has to B, since a power of bequest based on labor is not included in what B receives. There are, of course, other justifications for expanding or contracting the power of bequest – namely, the principles of utility and efficiency and of justice and equality.

If the situation involves scarcity and a sale, then the principle of utility and efficiency plays an especially large role. For example, suppose that if only the original acquirer has a power to transfer, then would-be transferees generally would offer a lower price (since they could make no further transfers of their own). Such a system of constrained transfer would reduce the likelihood that unowned things would be reduced to private ownership and therefore retard the utility of everyone. Or, to take a different example, suppose that not protecting transferees in arm's-length contract sales would forestall useful commerce in commodities that might afterward become scarce. These transferees should not suffer the same diminution of their property rights that original acquirers would if there were no transfer. In general, utility favors unconstrained transferability. Furthermore, it seems plausible that an involuntary transfer in execution of a legal judgment, such as in satisfaction of a debt, should be treated similarly to sales.

If, finally, one is dealing with wrongful acquisition rather than scarcity, somewhat different considerations apply. Where the wrong is theft, the transfer should be disallowed altogether. Where some lesser infraction of the moral restrictions on acquisition by labor is involved, the appropriate treatment hinges not only on the revised labor theory but also on the principle of utility and efficiency. For instance, if

---

28 Compare Locke, *Second Treatise of Government*, §§ 72, 182–84 (supporting bequests), with Mill, *Principles of Political Economy*, pp. 226–27 (restrictions on inheritance).

the transferee has no notice of the wrongdoing, then for purposes of commerce it may well be important to protect the transferee. Indeed, it might sometimes be sensible to give the transferee greater rights than the transferor, as the legal doctrine of holder in due course illustrates. Good-faith reliance may make it unwise to upset the transfer. Even when such reliance is lacking, if a great deal of time passes after the wrongful acquisition, the transferee may build up a reliance interest that counsels against upsetting the transfer. Statutes of limitation can exemplify this possibility. In any case, even if a transfer is upset, it does not follow that the transferee is to be left completely out in the cold. She may be entitled to some compensation from the transferor or from others. In all of these situations involving wrongful acquisition, the details of the limitation on transmissibility must be settled mostly by reference to factors alien to the revised labor theory.

General scarcity. The initial labor theory assumes that sufficiently many and good things are available for acquisition. In the actual world, however, general scarcity prevails – that is, there are few unowned or unrestricted things left to acquire. Even things not reduced to private ownership may be restricted by social or legal rules imposing communal ownership, holding in common, or a public trust. Exceptions exist; for example, air is unowned, and one can compress it in tanks and sell it. Still, *general* scarcity is a radical departure from the isolated or occasional scarcity implicit in the treatments of the acquisition process, post-acquisition changes, and transfer.

Because of general scarcity, labor-generated property rights are rarely product-tied in the same way as in the initial theory. Under the initial theory, the laborer obtains property rights in the product solely because of his labor. Under the revised theory, he does not, save in rare cases like the compressed air example. Rather, if he obtains property rights in the product, it is because of some factor in addition to his labor – for instance, because he purchased raw material (say, wood to make a desk) or entered into a contract (say, part of the crop in return for farming the land). Furthermore, in many cases the laborer will receive wages rather than any rights in the product (say, most factory work). Finally, in many cases there is no "product" at all, but rather a service (say, mowing someone's lawn or giving a massage) for which the laborer receives a wage. In all of these cases, the revised theory requires that, *pro tanto*, the recompense received by the laborer be commensurate with the work done. This commensurateness is difficult to ensure, especially in markedly different social situations from that contemplated by the initial theory.

Work as a social activity. The initial labor theory views work as an individual activity. If this view is inaccurate, and if instead work is a social activity, the laborer's property rights are further qualified. To identify the qualifications, one must see which assumptions of the initial theory cease to hold.

Two assumptions have been implicitly and slightly modified by previous discussion but now must be explicitly and radically modified. One assumption is that no society or government exists. The preceding subsection on transfer tacitly adjusted this assumption. For some qualifications of the laborer's property rights turned on at least rudimentary social or legal rules regulating transfer and compensation. The present subsection supposes explicitly that work occurs in a complex society with a modern government. Another assumption of the initial labor theory is that property rights in the product are commensurate with the work done. The last three subsections to some degree undermined this assumption. For even though post-acquisitions changes in situation would usually diminish the property rights of an original acquirer, it did not follow that the diminished rights would tally exactly with his labor. Even simple transfers might not leave transferors and transferees in positions that square precisely with the work done. And once workers' recompense is no longer product-tied as in the initial theory, commensurateness is harder to achieve. This subsection supposes explicitly that in most modern economies, the workers' property rights might be even less commensurate with the work they do.

Other assumptions of the initial labor theory now also fail to hold. It assumes that the laborer works entirely on his own and solely for himself. But if work is a social activity, people frequently work in the company of others. Consider assembly lines, restaurants, and mines. Furthermore, even when people work alone, they almost always work for or in relation to others. A person who does knitting piecework at home does so for company buyers and distributors and ultimately individual consumers. A lawyer who drafts a will contemplates a secretary who will type it, a client who will pay for it, and presumed heirs who will be affected by it as a probate court determines. So rare as to be exotic are cases in which someone works without relation to others – say, a hermit living on a remote mountainside who raises small crops for private consumption.

The initial theory also assumes that the laborer produces a product, not a service. His production involves, moreover, physical contact with unowned things over which he intends to acquire enduring control. Yet if work is a social activity, these assumptions often fail. As noted above, few things now are unowned. And since labor sometimes provides services, the word "labor" in the revised theory has a broader meaning than it does in the initial theory. Furthermore, what is a fitting recompense for labor falls into a sequence of intellectual – not necessarily historical – stages. In a first stage of independent production the laborer gets sole property rights in the product. A second stage involves group production and shared ownership of the product. In a third stage workers exchange their property rights in the product for wages. A fourth stage allows that wages are also a fitting recompense for labor that produces no tangible product, as in most service industries.

Lastly, the initial theory assumes that work reflects nothing about how the laborer sees himself in relation to others, and has no adverse sociocultural consequences on others. But if work is a social activity, these assumptions may not hold. Today work is often the principal ingredient in a person's self-esteem. Important here are not only income from work but also the actual and perceived interest and prestige of the task itself. Similarly, if some people have high-paying and prestigious jobs, others with lesser jobs or no jobs at all may be envious or lack self-esteem. Thus a job may say a good deal about how its holder and others assess his position in the socioeconomic order.[29]

If viewing work as a social activity alters assumptions as just described, then there will be an impact on workers' property rights. First, workers deserve property rights in their wages. If they use wages to buy things, then they deserve property rights in those things. As a general matter, property rights in clothes, automobiles, and houses stem from exchange rather than original acquisition.

Second, if wages are not commensurate with desert, a wage policy may try to bring them into line. Both government agencies and business firms can set up wage policies. Wages may be incommensurate for at least a pair of reasons. One is that wages depend partly on the price of what is produced. Prices are subject to market fluctuations or centralized manipulation. In a market system, demand may change and so increase or decrease wages. In a socialist economy, centralized decisions relating to output and accounting prices may affect wages. Another reason is that, even given constant prices, it is impossible to separate the labor of one person from other factors of production and assign that labor a definite worth. It is sometimes possible to isolate the "marginal product" of one factor of production – that is, how much extra output results from one unit of that factor. But it does not follow that such isolation carves out for that factor its actual share of the total output. Thus, a wage

---

29 For elaboration, see James W. Nickel, "Is There a Human Right to Employment?," *Philosophical Forum*, 10 (Winter–Summer 1978–79): 149–70, at 158–59.

policy can at most *try* to make wages commensurate with desert, for these reasons cast doubt on the notion of any true or objective worth of labor. Comparative assessments of desert are possible, but the revised theory cannot mathematically calibrate wages to desert in individual situations. Even so, it can sometimes bring them closer together, and can play a role in designing a system that responds to desert.

Third, there are several components to wage and labor policies. Some components stem from the revised labor theory and bear on desert. For example, given the sociocultural consequences of work, perhaps people should have the opportunity to use their talents and abilities to perform certain types of jobs – rather than have that opportunity depend on luck or the market. Other components must come from different parts of a full theory of property. If that theory includes a principle of utility and efficiency, the principle may provide for higher wages than could be justified on the basis of desert in order to give an incentive for work that needs to be done. Again, if that theory includes the principle of justice and equality argued for earlier, the principle may favor redistributive taxation of income and gratuitous transfers, even if desert based on labor would not support such taxation.

To sum up: The revised labor theory is the claim that if the assumptions of the initial theory are modified as described in this section, there remains a qualified justification for property rights founded on desert by labor. This theory may also be called the *labor-desert principle*. Under it desert based on labor is still an anchor of prima facie moral property rights. And these rights can still serve, in turn, as a prima facie justification for legal property rights. The rights are, however, qualified compendiously by the restrictions discussed above. Those restrictions stemming from the altered role of labor are part of the revised labor theory. Other restrictions derive from different areas of a full theory of property – for instance, principles of utility and efficiency and of justice and equality. These restrictions are not part of the revised labor theory. But the revised theory identifies some of the places where such restrictions are apt to apply.

The chief restrictions, by way of recapitulation, are these. (1) If everyone has a right to life, and if workers have a duty not to waste, allow to spoil, or accumulate beyond their needs, then their rights in the products of their labor are qualified. (2) Property rights are justifiable only if the net effect on others during the process of acquisition is defensible. The principles of utility and efficiency and of justice and equality limit acquisition in this way. (3) Existing property rights can be diminished if post-acquisition changes in situation have the result that acquisition would traverse some moral restriction. (4) Under the revised labor theory itself, a transfer of property is generally valid only if the constraints applicable to acquisition remain satisfied. However, the principle of utility and efficiency favors a stronger power to transfer. (5) Because of general scarcity, laborers sometimes obtain property rights in wages rather than in a product, and when they do obtain property rights in a product, it is not owing to their labor alone. Such rights should, *pro tanto*, be commensurate with the work done. (6) In light of the fact that work is a social activity, one should formulate a wage policy to make wages somewhat commensurate with desert. But the policy cannot be completely successful, and it may be qualified by nonlabor components in a full theory of property.

Obviously, the labor-desert principle is specific to property. It is not a general principle of morality. Yet the claim that some sort of broadly stated principle of desert or merit is a general principle of morality seems plausible. For people commonly suppose that a wide range of things can be deserved – both desirable things, such as rewards, prizes, and gratitude, but also undesirable things, such as punishment or condemnation for crimes. This merit-based way of looking at persons seems quite different from any view of equal worth. At any rate, the property-specific character of the principle of desert based on labor is a feature that it shares with the principle of utility and efficiency (§ 8.5) and the principle of justice and equality (§ 9.1), and it carries a similar other-things-being-equal rider. Like them, the labor-desert principle requires empirical information and intermediate stages of deliberation in order to be applied intelligently (§ 11.4).

10.4 UNDERSTANDING THE REVISED LABOR THEORY

In order to grasp the revised labor theory accurately, it will help to contrast its nature with that of the initial labor theory, to identify some relations among these theories and actual property rights, to clarify the role of liberty in the revised theory, and finally to compare that theory with libertarian positions.

(1) Whereas the initial theory is a labor-desert prima facie-theory, the revised theory is partly a labor-desert entitle-ment-theory. In the revised theory, desert plays a fun-damental role. The theory shows how the highly in-dividualistic desert of the initial theory can become a socially qualified desert. But it also contains some elements that do not relate to desert. These elements are not the principles of utility and efficiency and of justice and equality; those princi-ples qualify, but are not part of, the revised theory. The pertinent elements, rather, are qualifications on desert that lie within the revised theory itself. Examples are the restric-tion on post-acquisition changes in situation, the require-ment that initial constraints continue to be satisfied after transfer, and some qualifications stemming from general scarcity and the social nature of work. If Locke's proviso or Nozick's or Gauthier's emendation were sound, then it too would qualify desert from within a labor theory. None of these qualifications, viewed accurately, bears on what the laborer *deserves*. Instead they are reasons, extraneous to his desert, that bear on what his labor *entitles* him to. Because some reasons lie outside the revised theory altogether, that theory is not a full account of entitlement.

(2) The next point involves the relations among the initial and revised theories and actual property rights. The initial

theory is a foundation of the revised theory. If the initial theory, or something like it, were not valid, then one should have small confidence that desert by labor plays any role in justifying actual property rights. Yet it is not supposed that the moral property rights of the initial theory stand, even now, as shadowy forms behind actual property rights. Although the initial theory illuminates the moral status of actual property rights, one should acknowledge that its property rights differ from actual ones in several ways. The former are moral rights, analyzable as Hohfeldian normative modalities, with respect to other persons. The initial theory creates no means to enforce these rights. Nor does it show that other persons will actually recognize them. In contrast, actual property rights involve institutional enforcement and social recognition. Because of these differences, some thinkers may contend that the moral rights of the initial theory are not property rights at all.[30]

If there is a dispute here, it may be largely verbal. The issue is whether, despite the differences, rights under the initial theory have enough in common with actual property rights to warrant the title "property." In fact, the former rights presuppose the existence of other persons, make room for natural and voluntary duties, deal with the possession and use of external things, arguably permit voluntary arrangements for enforcement (for example, through Nozickean protective associations),[31] and do not prevent other persons from recognizing these rights. These facts may suffice to merit the appellation "property." Anyone who is willing to acknowledge these facts, yet insists that "property" requires more robust enforcement and recognition, may be allowed to go in peace.

(3) The revised theory assigns a prominent, but still derivative, role to liberty. The revised theory attaches central

---

30 See, for example, Alan Donagan, *The Theory of Morality* (Chicago: University of Chicago Press, 1977), pp. 97–100.
31 See Nozick, *Anarchy, State, and Utopia*, pp. 12–17.

importance to the laborer's choosing to work and deserving property rights and wages as a result. It thereby calls upon the account of projection and agency of Chapter 4, which understands persons as autonomous entities who initiate changes in the world, including changes caused by labor, that can merit private property. Although the normative force of all desert claims may not stem from autonomous action that produces expected consequences,[32] this is usually true of the desert claims generated by the revised theory. Besides, many details of that theory, such as the discussion of transfer, recognize human liberty. Finally, that theory is lodged in a broader account of property that includes a principle of utility and efficiency and a principle of justice and equality; these principles explicitly make room for liberty (§§ 8.6 and 9.4). As before, liberty is not a basic principle in the theory advocated here; rather, it derives from the three principles that are basic. To be sure, this book seeks to bar exercises of liberty in regard to property rights that interfere with the rights and interests of others, and so favors a moderate egalitarianism that endeavors to prevent the worst abuses of private property. Nevertheless, liberty remains a significant, though derivative, feature of the revised theory.

(4) The preceding comment suggests an answer to the objection that even though the initial labor theory is unsatisfactory, a better revision would have restated the labor theory along libertarian lines. Libertarian theories abound. The most prominent is that of Nozick. But his views have already received some attention in § 10.3, and the large critical literature that has grown up around his theory makes further progress here unlikely.[33] Other libertarian theories

---

32 See Sher, *Desert*, ch. 3. Sher contends that no single principle or value grounds all the varieties of desert (pp. xii, 20, 110, and generally in chs. 7–8). The specific case of desert by labor, as presented in this chapter, does not require one to agree or disagree with this contention.

33 See, for example, Jeffrey Paul, ed., *Reading Nozick: Essays on "Anarchy, State, and Utopia"* (Totowa, N.J.: Rowman & Littlefield, 1981).

vary widely and require a book in their own right. Yet if these theories have a common core, it is a dual concern with liberty and rights to property in some form or other.[34]

If that is indeed the core, then a salient feature of the revised labor theory, and the larger pluralist position of which it forms a part, is a concern with the consequences of the exercise of "liberty" and "rights." If one person exercises them, then it is necessary to think about the impact on others. That concern emerges dramatically in the discussion of alienation, exploitation, and large differences in economic power in Chapter 7. It is present, too, in the attention given to the preferences of each person by the principle of utility and efficiency, and in the case for a decent, and a fully human, life in society offered by the principle of justice and equality. Similarly, the full social context that gives rise to the labor-desert principle attends to the impact of work on the worker and on others. To say all this is not to reiterate a criticism of Nozick by Cohen – "that 'libertarian' capitalism sacrifices liberty to capitalism, a truth its advocates are able to deny only because they are prepared to abuse the language of freedom."[35] For not all libertarians endorse capitalism, and in any case the mistake is often not the abuse of

---

34 See, for example, Ellen Frankel Paul, *Property Rights and Eminent Domain* (New Brunswick, N.J.: Transaction Books, 1987), pp. 224–39; Richard A. Epstein, "Possession as the Root of Title," *Georgia Law Review*, 13 (1979): 1221–43.

   Two brief comments are in order on Epstein's article. First, though its views are libertarian, one may question whether Epstein's views are always purely libertarian or, if not, whether he combines libertarian and other views consistently. See Margaret Jane Radin, "Market-Inalienability," *Harvard Law Review*, 100 (1987): 1849–1937, at 1868 n.66. Second, Epstein neglects adequately to distinguish first-possession and labor theories. A first-possession theory says that one can come to own something by being the first person to possess it. It differs from a labor theory because it requires no exertion of effort to make or acquire something. The difference is indeterminate at the margin, for there is no precise amount of effort that the labor theory requires. For cogent criticism of first possession, see Becker, *Property Rights*, pp. 24–31.

35 G. A. Cohen, "Robert Nozick and Wilt Chamberlain: How Patterns Preserve Liberty," *Erkenntnis*, 11 (1977): 5–23, at 21 (footnote omitted).

language but the inadequate reckoning of the impact on others of the "free" exercise of one's supposed "rights."[36] These brief comments are not likely to persuade libertarians. Yet they do explain why the revised labor theory, though it gives scope to liberty, is not a restatement along libertarian lines.

10.5 ASSESSING THE SIGNIFICANCE OF THE REVISED LABOR THEORY

So far this chapter has made a case for the proposition that desert by labor should play a role in justifying private-property rights. But how important is that role? The answer is that it is significant but less important than the roles of utility and efficiency and of justice and equality.

Someone might argue, in contrast, that desert by labor plays no, or virtually no, justificatory role. For the revised theory is supplemented and sometimes even trumped by utility and efficiency and by justice and equality. Actual property rights are rarely product-tied as in the initial theory. And, so far as wages are concerned, no precise correlations exist for desert claims.

This argument has some merit but is overstated. First, to supplement or trump is not to obliterate. Thus, the fact that the two other principles qualify the revised theory does not prevent that theory from playing a significant role. Furthermore, since the revised theory has some nondesert elements, that theory is not identical with desert based on labor. Even if desert claims were to play only a tiny justificatory role, the same need not be true of the revised theory.

Second, the product-tying point is less far-reaching than might appear. Because of general scarcity, it is true that property rights are not tied to products *in the same way* as

36 For an intelligent and witty libertarian account of property rights, written after Cohen's criticism of Nozick, see Loren E. Lomasky, *Persons, Rights, and the Moral Community* (New York and Oxford: Oxford University Press, 1987), ch. 6. One can guess that Lomasky would resist the charge of "mistake."

under the initial theory. Yet it fails to follow that they are tied in no way at all. In fact, a tie exists whenever someone buys new material and fashions something out of it (for example, desk making) or contracts for a portion of the product in return for labor (for example, sharecropping). A tie can also exist in some cases of joint production. Worker cooperatives are a prime illustration.[37] Though cooperatives are not a major part of United States industry, in countries such as Yugoslavia and Spain they are more important. At all events, since wages are generally a good substitute for rights in the product (what worker can use his or her share of the ball-bearings or clothes that the factory produces?), the absence of a product tie usually makes little difference. And even here there is some indirect linkage because wages are apt to reflect the worth of the product to others.

Third, although commensurateness is a problem, comparative assessments of desert claims based on labor are feasible. The tasks are to identify relevant features of a worker's performance and to arrive at a fitting recompense. The revised theory preserves the relevance of factors specified by the initial theory – namely, the relative importance of effort, ability, persistence, industriousness, luck, time spent, achievement, the difficulty, unpleasantness, or danger of the work, and other working conditions. The social nature of work emphasized in the revised theory allows one to capture other relevant factors, such as the responsibility, leadership, or motivating capacity displayed by one worker in relation to others. Using these factors, one then compares the case of one worker (or type of job) with the case of other workers (or types of job) and so tries to arrive at some relative fitting recompense for each. This procedure does not generate

---

37 Although cooperatives need not be based on a labor theory, that possible basis is advocated in David P. Ellerman, "Theory of Legal Structure: Worker Cooperatives," *Journal of Economic Issues*, 18 (1984): 861–91. His version of the labor theory, in any case, differs markedly from that advanced here. See David P. Ellerman, "On the Labor Theory of Property," *Philosophical Forum*, 16 (1985): 293–326.

absolute values, disclose the "inherent worth" of labor, or yield a "just price" for labor. Nor is it suggested that government-set wages should supplant the labor market; after all, wages set by the market are likely to reflect utility and efficiency to a substantial extent. Still, this procedure does provide comparative appraisals of desert by labor. Its feasibility is demonstrated by the fact that many government agencies and large firms use some variant of it to assess the comparative worth of different tasks and to arrive at relative wages. Although such procedures have limitations, they can in some contexts supply comparative assessments of desert claims in regard to wages.[38]

These reflections help to explain why some thinkers exaggerate and others underestimate the force of desert claims. Exaggeration stems from focusing on something like the initial labor theory and failing to appreciate the realistic assumptions needed for the revised theory. Underestimation derives from hastily concluding that realistic assumptions spell the end of desert. It is true that the implications of general scarcity, the social nature of work, and the problem of commensurateness suggest that the consequentialist and patterned considerations supplied by the principles of utility and efficiency and of justice and equality are more important than desert claims in a pluralist theory of property. Even so, desert by labor performs a significant role in justifying rights of private property.

---

38 For a balanced discussion, see Paul Weiler, "The Wages of Sex: The Uses and Limits of Comparable Worth," *Harvard Law Review*, 99 (1986): 1728–1807, at 1756–79.

Chapter 11

Conflict and resolution

This book has now argued for three principles that justify, and limit, public and private property: utility and efficiency, justice and equality, and desert by labor. As § 1.2 observes, although these may not be the only principles that make up a satisfactory moral, political, and legal theory of property, they are by far the most important. Yet since this is a pluralist theory, conflicts can occur between or among the principles.

To make the topic of conflict more concrete, imagine that a legislature has asked a social planner to formulate an income policy based on the three principles. The planner has a staff that includes economists, demographers, statisticians, and social psychologists. She and her staff first survey the incomes of all persons in the state, and break down income from employment by type of job, employer, region, sex, race, and other factors. She then attempts to determine whether her findings are justifiable under the three principles. Her preliminary determination is that most incomes square well with the principles and that little reason exists to disturb income from other sources such as investment.

However, several problem areas come to light. Because of imperfections in the labor market, many executives and upper-level managers in manufacturing receive incomes well in excess of those justified by the labor-desert principle and the principle of utility and efficiency. In contrast, members of a few mid-income groups, such as nurses, do not receive as

292

much as they should according to the labor-desert principle. And there is a small minority of recent immigrants who work as unskilled laborers whose income fails to give them even the decent life required by the principle of justice and equality. Still, the labor market appears to operate efficiently as far as the nurses and unskilled workers are concerned. So the issue of potential conflict presented to the social planner is: Can she formulate an income policy that will tally with the three principles so far as executives, upper-level managers, nurses, and unskilled immigrant workers are concerned without throwing out of kilter some other feature of the distribution of income?

The purpose of this chapter is not to solve this specific problem, but to take up generally the matters of conflict, moral pluralism, and guidelines for applying the theory. One would need to add far too many empirical details to make this hypothetical problem determinate enough to admit of a "solution," but referring to this problem in the course of the inquiry will illustrate what is at stake. Instead, the actual inquiry is both theoretical and practical. Theoretically, the chapter considers the frequency and variety of possible conflicts (§ 11.2), and wrestles briefly with some problems of logical consistency, moral realism, and theory acceptance (§ 11.3). Practically, it tries to formulate general guidelines for applying the three principles to real-world problems (§ 11.4).

The picture that emerges yields a deeper understanding of the pluralist theory of property advanced here. As Becker has explained, pluralist moral theories are not second-class citizens, temporary truces, or weary compromises whose interest stems entirely from their components.[1] Rather, they are often the only way to deal honestly with the complexity and uncertainty of moral and political life. In certain situa-

1 Lawrence C. Becker, "Comments on Stephen Munzer's 'A Pluralist Theory of Property'," unpublished paper presented at the American Philosophical Association, Central Division Meeting, Cincinnati, Ohio, April 29, 1988.

tions, morality seems to pull in different directions. Only a pluralist theory can accommodate this fact, for unitary theories are unable to capture the complexity of our considered judgments. In the case of property, a pluralist theory is sounder than any unitary competitor.

Pluralist theories need not be rife with conflict. The specific pluralist theory offered here allows for some priority rules. It also permits mutual revision of particular moral judgments, of the background normative, psychological, and socioeconomic theory advanced in Part II, and of the three principles formulated in Part III. This combination of priority rules and mutual revision resolves most conflicts. Any irresolvable conflicts, it will be argued, create no logical infirmity and confirm that the theory is genuinely pluralist.

The inquiry deals with a genuine, not a mere seeming or pretend, pluralist theory. In order for a theory to be genuinely pluralist, not only must it have more than one principle, but its principles must also be irreducible. So if someone were to show that the three principles could be reduced to a single, more fundamental principle, then the theory would not be genuinely pluralist after all. A rigorous demonstration of irreducibility is too arduous philosophically to be attempted here. Yet two brief reflections suggest that the theory that this book offers is in fact pluralist. One is that the philosophical foundations of each principle are quite different from those of the others. Utility and efficiency proceed from an understanding of equal moral worth in regard to the recognition of preferences. Justice and equality derive from a different understanding of equal moral worth that invokes rights to basic needs and basic capabilities. Desert by labor rests on a view of differential moral merit that stems from persons' actions in the world. Given these marked differences in foundations, it would be astonishing if the three principles were reducible to any single principle. A second reflection is that, as argued in the next section, the three principles sometimes conflict – perhaps even irresolvably. The existence of irresolvable conflict is not a necessary condition of irreducibility, for difference in foundations, and perhaps even in scope, would be enough.[2] Still, if there are irresolvable conflicts, that would indicate that the principles are irreducible.

The inquiry addresses "conflicts" in the following sense. A *conflict* exists if two or more principles are applicable and if it is not possible for a person or society to conform to them simultaneously.[3] A conflict *between* principles is a conflict involving a given pair of principles. For instance, the social planner might find that she can raise the income of the unskilled immigrants sufficiently to eliminate a violation of the principle of justice and equality, but that doing so leaves the other two principles in conflict. A conflict *among* principles is a conflict involving all three principles such that either a conflict exists for each combination of two or, if not, it is still impossible to conform to all three principles simultaneously. Thus, the social planner might discover that all three principles conflict. The target, then, is conflict between or among principles, since that is the issue peculiar to pluralist theories. Rarely, of course, will conflict come solely from the wording of the principles. Rather, if conflict arises at all, it will almost always come from the principles together with empirical premises. If the social planner encounters a conflict, it results partly from the empirical conditions that she has identified.

2 James Lamoureux has argued to me that it is possible to identify in pluralist theories features that correspond to features exhibited by some social-choice procedures and then to show, in light of Arrow's Impossibility Theorem (see Chapter 8, note 15, and accompanying text), that all pluralist theories *must* contain irresolvable conflicts. I cannot assess his argument here.

3 Since the three principles do not have the same scope, they might not all be applicable. For instance, the labor-desert principle is applicable only if the situation is work-related in some way. The characterization in the text in effect takes the impossibility of joint conformity to be the hallmark of conflict. The joint-conformity test will do for present purposes, even if one needs a subtler analysis for other purposes. See Stephen Munzer, "Validity and Legal Conflicts," *Yale Law Journal*, 82 (1973): 1140–74, at 1140–48.

Although the inquiry does not focus on possible conflicts *within* any one of the principles, a brief word on conflicts of this sort is in order. Conflicts within a principle arise if the principle is applicable and if it is sometimes not possible for a person or society to conform to it. As a general matter, these conflicts arise when a principle has more than one part or its formulation is such that, in a given – usually contrived – situation, one cannot conform to the principle no matter what one does. Though the pluralist theory proposed here would have to be made more precise in order to say that conflicts of this sort cannot arise, they do seem unlikely. The principle of utility and efficiency has two parts; yet, as explained in § 8.5, efficiency is the junior partner in the combination and can be an index of utility. The principle of justice and equality also has two parts; but, since the narrowing of inequalities comes into play only after a minimum is achieved, the first clause or part, which requires minimum property, has priority over the second, which can require narrowing. The labor-desert principle is more complicated because it involves a half-dozen restrictions on labor-generated property rights. These restrictions, however, derive in the main from separate areas – for example, the process of acquisition and subsequent transfers. Different restrictions tend to apply in different situations. As a result, the likelihood seems small of situations in which two or more restrictions cannot be met together.

Nevertheless, conflicts within one or more of the three principles *might* be possible. After all, recent work suggests that conflicts could lurk even in utilitarianism – the theory that seems least likely to generate them.[4] Here it seems that the utilitarian could always say, "Do whatever best promotes

---

4   See, for example, Isaac Levi, *Hard Choices: Decision Making under Unresolved Conflict* (Cambridge: Cambridge University Press, 1986), ch. 10; Terrance C. McConnell, "Utilitarianism and Conflict Resolution," *Logique et Analyse,* no. 94 (1981): 245–57; Michael Slote, "Utilitarianism, Moral Dilemmas, and Moral Cost," *American Philosophical Quarterly,* 22 (1985): 161–68.

utility," and, if two incompatible actions each promote utility equally, "Do either." At any rate, if conflicts were to arise within any of the three principles, it would be necessary to ask whether the principle should be revised or whether the conflict could be resolved in ways analogous to those suggested in the next section.

11.2 THE FREQUENCY AND VARIETIES OF CONFLICTS

In returning to conflicts between or among principles, one must first understand why some philosophers view such conflicts as problematic. These philosophers contend that conflicts occur too often, take unpredictable forms, and lend themselves only to ad hoc, indefensible resolution. This section argues that if one analyzes conflicts as follows, this contention is mistaken and the appearance of a problem vanishes.

Several features of the pluralist theory of property advocated here significantly reduce the frequency of conflicts between and among principles. First, previous chapters have formulated the principles so as to limit the chance of conflict. Chapter 9 suggested how, and why, the principle of justice and equality qualifies the principle of utility and efficiency. Chapter 10 pursued, in greater detail, how, and why, both of these principles qualify the labor-desert principle. The reasons given in those chapters rebut the charge that the overall formulation is ad hoc. Thus, the social planner may find that it is possible to devise an income policy that dissolves all appearance of conflict. Second, if one takes a broad view of the matter, it is at once obvious why conflicts will not be ubiquitous. Suppose that the justifiability of a certain type of property is at issue. Often all of the principles will support it, or all of them will reject it, or at least two of them will have nothing to say one way or the other. In such cases, no conflict arises. Third, in many instances the principles complement rather than compete with each other. For example, sometimes one may be confident that a certain sort of property is essential to a decent life in society but uncertain of persons' preferences on the matter. In that instance, though the principle of utility and efficiency helps little, the minimum-property clause of the principle of justice and equality supports the sort of property at issue. Or, to take a different example, sometimes one may have good econometric data pertaining to a possible rule of property law, but the rule is unrelated to the laboring process. In that case, one may ignore the labor-desert principle and apply the principle of utility and efficiency. In sum, the pluralist theory that this book advocates is hardly conflict-ridden, and thus should be more palatable to those who worry about continually having to resolve conflicts in pluralist theories.

Yet even if conflicts are infrequent, it is implausible to claim that they will never arise under the theory proposed here, and so it is important to predict what forms conflict will take. To do that, it will help to identify various conflicting combinations. Table 3 lists these combinations given the principles of utility and efficiency (U/E), justice and equality (J/E), and desert based on labor (D/L). This is only a list of possible combinations; some of them may not exist outside the philosopher's study. The next-to-last combination involves only incompatibility between the labor-desert principle and the principle of utility and efficiency. The previous chapter addressed this issue and no need exists to comment on it further.

The first two combinations pit justice and equality against a single competing principle. Case (1) is likely to involve sharp conflict, for it involves a collision of property rights based respectively on equal worth and equal merit. Case (2) would be thought quite numerous by most antiutilitarians but nearly a null class by some defenders of utilitarianism. Perhaps the more important issue is not how frequently conflicts of this second sort resist resolution but how best to think about them when they are at least apparent. As argued elsewhere,[5] different sorts of substantive moral judgments

---

5 See Stephen R. Munzer, "Intuition and Security in Moral Philosophy," *Michigan Law Review*, 82 (1984): 740–54, at 743–47, 753–54.

TABLE 3. *Conflicting Combinations*

(1)	J/E vs. D/L
(2)	J/E vs. U/E
(3)	J/E vs. (D/L & U/E)
(4)	(J/E & D/L) vs. U/E
(5)	(J/E & U/E) vs. D/L
(6)	D/L vs. U/E
(7)	J/E vs. U/E vs. D/L

or intuitions are properly available for use, not only as rules of thumb or in popular moral thought, but also in critical moral reflection. Accordingly, if the bearing of utility were unclear or utility calculations were quite difficult, one might resort straightway to the principle of justice and equality. If that principle were unclear in scope or small in weight under given circumstances, one might employ the principle of utility and efficiency.

The next three combinations raise some additional points. One is that they all pit two principles against a third. As such, they would be amenable to a rule of resolution that prescribes, absolutely or presumptively, that two principles override one. Though an absolute rule is silly, a presumptive rule, which might seem to make more sense, may not be sound either, given that the principles are incommensurable. Even then, questions arise as to how strong the presumption is and what considerations can override it. Obviously no mechanical answers are possible. Another point is that these cases involve different combinations of the various perspectives on distributive equity. In cases (3) and (4) principles deriving from equal worth and assertedly unequal merit are arrayed against a principle deriving from equal worth (§ 8.1). Only the alignment differs. This pair of cases, along with case (2), confirms that utility and Kantian perspectives on equal worth can assess situations differently. Case (5), on the other hand, involves the two principles deriving from equal worth pitted against a principle deriving from assertedly unequal merit. This case, along with cases (1) and (6), will occur frequently in the eyes of many libertarians – who believe that rights prevail over utility and reject a nonlibertarian account of justice and equality.

The final combination involves three-way conflict. It may appear to identify nothing new, for the points made about the preceding half-dozen combinations, *mutatis mutandis*, hold where pertinent. Yet the last combination underscores that conflicts need not always be of a two-valued either-or character, because sometimes *each* of the principles may point in a *different* direction. It therefore gives importance to the idea of conflict among, and not only between, principles. At a practical level, the social planner struggling with an income policy may encounter just such a three-way conflict.

If one or more of these possible cases of conflict occur, is that an objection to the pluralist theory proposed here? To answer this question, one should first draw a distinction pertaining to the genesis of the conflict. The distinction is between those cases in which the theory has been followed and a conflict nevertheless arises and those cases in which the theory has not been followed in the past and the present conflict has arisen only because of previous violations of one or more of the principles.[6] The former cases might at least seem to pose a serious objection (more on them momentarily). But the latter cases are not a theoretical objection in the sense that the *ideal theory* gives rise to the conflict or involves logical inconsistency in its principles; the conflict comes from

6   The distinction follows Aquinas's distinction between moral perplexity *simpliciter* and moral perplexity *secundum quid*. See St. Thomas Aquinas, *Summa Theologiae*, IIa 2ae Q.62 a.2, IIIa Q.64 a.6, in *Summa Theologiae* (London: Blackfriars, 1964–75), respectively, vol. 37, pp. 104–09; vol. 56, pp. 118–23; St. Thomas Aquinas, *Quaestiones Disputatae de Veritate*, Q.17, art. IV, a.8, in *Truth*, 3 vols. (Chicago: Henry Regnery, 1952–54), vol. 2, p. 334 (trans. James V. McGlynn, S.J.). See the contemporary exposition in Alan Donagan, "Consistency in Rationalist Moral Systems," *Journal of Philosophy*, 81 (1984): 291–309, at 305–06. Aquinas and Donagan view moral perplexity *simpliciter*, though not *secundum quid*, as objectionable; § 11.3 argues that "irresolvable conflicts," which would be roughly equivalent to moral perplexity *simpliciter*, need not be objectionable.

the fact that the theory has not been followed in the past. For example, the social planner may determine that only because of past violations of one or more of the principles is there now even the appearance of a conflict. One must acknowledge that a serious problem of choice has arisen. Being in a fix, one may agonize in working out what seems to be the best resolution of the conflict. Since one may experience some regret or distress however one resolves it, the latter cases are indeed thorny. And these cases do identify a *nonideal* theoretical problem concerning transitions, compensation, and rectification in the justification of property rights – a problem that will arise, of course, for any theory that does not validate everything that has happened in the past.

The distinction between these two groups of cases is not just a philosopher's distinction. It is important in practice. As the end of § 8.6 points out, one is not working with a clean slate. Existing property arrangements may diverge sharply from what the theory offered here requires. To correct those divergences, one may sometimes, though not often, find oneself in a predicament where it is impossible now to satisfy all of the principles in the theory. For instance, if an existing distribution of wealth in a society were unjustifiable, and if that distribution arose only because of past violations of the theory, one might find now that, to restore justice and equality, one would have to diverge either from utility and efficiency or from desert based on labor, or both. Some cases discussed in Part IV of this book may exemplify this possibility. One would certainly be well advised to avoid such conflicts in the future if it is possible to do so.[7] Yet these cases are hardly objections to the ideal theory represented by the three principles.

7 See Ruth Barcan Marcus, "Moral Dilemmas and Consistency," *Journal of Philosophy*, 77 (1980): 121–36, at 121. On the status of a principle of avoiding conflict in the future, compare Lyle V. Anderson, "Moral Dilemmas, Deliberation, and Choice," *Journal of Philosophy*, 82 (1985): 139–62, with Terrance McConnell, "More on Moral Dilemmas," *Journal of Philosophy*, 83 (1986): 345–51, at 349–51.

Suppose, however, that one faces a case of the former sort – in which a conflict arises even though the theory has been followed. Once more, the existence of a conflict need not pose an objection. It will not do so if one can defensibly resolve the conflict. Such resolution involves defensibly adjusting the scope of one or more principles, creating an exception to one or more principles, devising a priority rule to resolve the conflict, or revising the background normative, psychological, and socioeconomic account of property in Part II. The word "defensibly" is important here. In order for the moves to be defensible, one must rethink, quite possibly from the ground up, each of the principles and the background theory, and then decide whether some conflict-avoiding change is philosophically justifiable. The principles continue to exert pressure in the rethinking, however, for no reason exists to suppose that they have spent their force and are out of play entirely. And there is no objection in principle to employing considered judgments or "intuitions" in making the decision; for, as § 1.3 mentions, one can sometimes properly have more confidence in a discrete intuition than in some antecedent formulation of an abstract principle. In any case, a coherence approach to conflict resolution allows for the mutual revision of different elements in the pluralist theory as a whole. One is not, however, likely to find "balancing" an effective strategy for resolving conflicts. No method exists to weigh all opposing considerations. And their intersection is apt to be sufficiently complicated to make metaphors of "balancing" and "weighing" oversimple and unhelpful – at least as a general technique. Nor is it easy to draw up a cogent system of presumptions for resolving conflicts.[8]

8 On the use of presumptions, compare Lawrence C. Becker, *Property Rights: Philosophic Foundations* (London, Henley and Boston: Routledge and Kegan Paul, 1977), pp. 99–118, with Stephen R. Munzer, Book Review, *Minnesota Law Review*, 63 (1979): 531–43, at 541–43. For accounts of the intersection of reasons and moral appraisal, see, for example, Joseph Raz, *Practical Reason and Norms* (London: Hutchinson, 1975), pp. 37–48; Robert Nozick, "Moral Complications and Moral Structures," *Natural Law Forum*, 13 (1968): 1–50.

To make this line of argument less abstract, one can reflect, for example, on how to devise defensible priority rules based on type of property. If the property in question is important for the development of personality in the sense of moral and political personhood, then it is tied to equal worth in the Kantian sense, and the principle of justice and equality prevails. Next, if the property is the fruit of work covered by the revised labor theory, then it is tied to the potentially unequal merit of persons, and the principle of desert based on labor prevails. Lastly, if the property is important for the economic functioning of an organization, then the property is linked to equal worth in the sense of equal counting of preferences of equal strength, and the principle of utility and efficiency prevails.

These highly simplified priority rules need much refinement. They are rules of thumb rather than priority rules in Rawls's sense (which specify lexical precedence).[9] They are, moreover, rules that depend on the ability to characterize property unambiguously. Sometimes such characterizations will be possible, or at least cannot be rejected out of hand as fatuous. Perhaps basic clothes, a copyright protecting a painting, and a restaurant franchise, respectively, count as the property in question for the three priority rules just given. But plainly, much property does not fall neatly into these categories. Consider, for example, a patent for an invention developed by someone working on his or her own for several years. One can view the patent as connected with personality development, as the fruit of labor, and as central to the economic performance of a company that the inventor sets up to build and market the patented device. Here the rules do not help much in deciding how strong the inventor's property rights in the patent ought to be. Yet that does not mean they fail to help altogether or that they are ad hoc, for they are lodged within the account of property, persons, and society developed in Part II.

9 John Rawls, *A Theory of Justice* (Cambridge, Mass.: Harvard University Press, 1971), pp. 42–45, 243–51, 298–303, 541–48.

At this stage, a skeptical reader might agree that even for conflicts arising when the theory has been followed, no objection exists to the theory if the conflicts can be defensibly resolved, and that it is *sometimes* possible so to resolve them, but still claim that it will not *always* be possible to do so. How should one respond to this claim? In two ways: First, the existence of such conflicts in the theory has yet to be proved, and till proved or at least made plausible, the claim hardly need be accepted. Second, if such irresolvable conflicts did exist, they would not pose a serious objection to the theory unless either the skeptic could formulate an otherwise equally attractive theory of property that is conflict-free, or the conflicts showed the theory to be logically inconsistent. This book leaves it to others to formulate an alternative theory; the next section considers the issue of logical consistency.

11.3 LOGICAL CONSISTENCY, MORAL REALISM, AND THEORY ACCEPTANCE

Up to this point it has been shown that (defensibly) *resolvable* conflicts pose no problem for a pluralist theory of property. But what about *irresolvable* conflicts? Would such conflicts indicate that the theory is logically inconsistent? It may seem that the answer has to be affirmative.

Yet this is not so, for at least two reasons. First, irresolvable conflicts may involve prima facie obligations rather than obligations all things considered.[10] Consider a moral principle requiring that persons keep their promises and another moral principle requiring persons to tell the truth. A case might arise in which a person could keep a promise only by

10 See W. D. Ross, *The Right and the Good* (Oxford: Clarendon Press, 1930), ch. II. There is a large secondary literature on the distinction. Recall that not even the labor-desert principle is a *full* account of "entitlement" – that is, of obligation or justification all things considered. See § 10.4 and Chapter 10, note 5.

lying or tell the truth only by breaking the promise. Many moral philosophers would analyze this as a case of conflicting prima facie obligations. Which obligation ought to override could turn, for example, on the respective consequences of keeping the promise or telling the truth. Similarly, one could regard the three principles as each generating only a prima facie obligation regarding, or, if you prefer, a prima facie justification of, certain property rights. In the absence of conflict, or upon the resolution of a resolvable conflict, one could say what the theory requires, all things considered. The existence of an irresolvable conflict would not involve conflicting obligations, or justifications, all things considered, and hence would not show the theory to be logically inconsistent. The theory would simply fail to generate an answer in such a case.

Second, even if irresolvable conflicts do involve conflicting obligations or justifications, all things considered, it does not follow that logical inconsistency exists. To suppose that it does is to assimilate the logic of principles, rules, and norms to the logic of statements and sentences. In technical parlance, it is to assimilate deontic logic to indicative logic. But the assimilation is unwarranted, for it is possible to construct systems of deontic logic that do not take conflicting principles, rules, or norms to be logically inconsistent. In fact, the literature suggests at least three different ways in which irresolvable conflicts can be seen to involve no logical inconsistency.[11] Here as elsewhere in philosophy, unanimity

---

11 The moves relate to a standard argument that conflicts do involve logical inconsistency. The argument requires the premise that "ought" implies "can" and a rule of inference sometimes called the agglomeration principle. See Munzer, "Validity and Legal Conflicts," at 1165. One way to avoid inconsistency is to reject the premise that "ought" implies "can." See E. J. Lemmon, "Deontic Logic and the Logic of Imperatives," *Logique et Analyse,* no. 29 (1965): 39–71, at 43–51. A second way is to restrict that premise so as to allow moral conflicts. See Marcus, "Moral Dilemmas and Consistency," at 133–35. A third way is to repudiate the agglomeration principle. See Bernard Williams, "Ethical Consistency," in his *Problems of the Self* (Cambridge:

is hard to come by,[12] but it is fair to say that there are strong arguments, offered by highly regarded philosophers, for rejecting the claim that moral conflict involves logical inconsistency. Thus a basis exists for holding that even if a pluralist theory of property were to generate irresolvable conflicts, that is not a logical objection to the theory.

Someone might respond that a serious objection could arise in a different way. Even if irresolvable conflicts do not involve logical inconsistency, they are incompatible, it might be said, with the nature of morality correctly understood. Morality is objective, real, and knowable. It could not be so if it contained irresolvable conflicts. Therefore, a pluralist theory of property, advanced here as part of morality, is unsatisfactory.

This argument against the theory will not do, for several reasons. First, as the end of § 11.2 points out, the existence of irresolvable conflicts in the theory has not been established, and until established or rendered plausible, the argument in question does not get off the ground. Second, though it is not immediately clear what is meant by describing morality as "objective," "real," and "knowable,"[13] one can resist these descriptions. Many philosophers reject such views of morality.[14] This book need not take a position on this controversial matter, and in fact § 1.3 is careful to say that there may not be anything that people can correctly regard as objective moral truth. Third, even if morality is objective, real, or knowable, that may be compatible with the existence

---

Cambridge University Press, 1973), pp. 166–86, at pp. 179–84; Bas C. van Fraassen, "Values and the Heart's Command," *Journal of Philosophy*, 70 (1973): 5–19, at 15–17.

12 See, for example, Donagan, "Consistency in Rationalist Moral Systems," at 297–301, for critical comments on the moves mentioned in the preceding note.

13 See, for example, R. M. Hare, *Moral Thinking: Its Levels, Method, and Point* (Oxford: Clarendon Press, 1981), pp. 206–12, who distinguishes many senses of "objective."

14 See, for example, J. L. Mackie, *Ethics: Inventing Right and Wrong* (Harmondsworth: Penguin, 1977).

of irresolvable moral conflicts. For example, Foot has suggested that irresolvable moral conflict involves a kind of incommensurability, and has argued that this incommensurability can be compatible with the reality of moral values (one sense of "moral realism") and with the capacity of human beings to know those values (one sense of "cognitivism").[15] As with moral conflict and logical consistency, one should not pretend that knockdown arguments exist, but plainly there is no swift and uncontested passage from the irresolvability of moral conflicts to the incompatibility of this theory of property with moral realism or moral cognitivism.

The objection that the theory is incompatible with moral realism might take a more specific form. The exposition of the theory indicates that each of the principles responds to a different conception of persons. The principle of utility and efficiency rests on a conception of persons as equally morally worthy in terms of their preferences. The principle of justice and equality conceives of persons as equally morally worthy in terms of basic needs and basic capabilities. The labor-desert principle conceives of persons as agents who, by their actions in the world, are responsible for changes in the world and deserve or are entitled to something as a result. Yet, if moral realism is true, it must conceive of persons in some unique way. Hence it is incompatible with the pluralist theory suggested here.

This specific form of the objection is likewise unacceptable. The problem is not merely that the objector must show some version or other of moral realism to be correct. It is that the objection requires a particular version of moral realism to be correct – namely, a version that has as a consequence that

15 See Philippa Foot, "Moral Realism and Moral Dilemma," *Journal of Philosophy*, 80 (1983): 379–98, especially at 394–98. See also Samuel Guttenplan, "Moral Realism and Moral Dilemmas," *Proceedings of the Aristotelian Society*, 80 (1979–80): 61–80. Even if some version of moral realism is correct, its applicability in legal contexts is debatable. See Stephen R. Munzer, "Realistic Limits on Realist Interpretation," *Southern California Law Review*, 58 (1985): 459–75.

one must conceive of persons in one and only one way. Such a requirement is a tall order. Until the objector meets it, a pluralist theory can be compatible with moral realism. The theory advocated here does not claim that persons *are* a certain sort of entity only. Rather, it claims that, for different purposes, one can *conceive* of persons in different ways. These different conceptions, though, can each capture part of the truth about the way persons are. Recall Foot's suggestion that moral conflict involves a kind of incommensurability that is nevertheless compatible with moral realism. Transposed into this context, the suggestion would be that the different ways of *conceiving* of persons may represent a complex and indeed incommensurable vision of the way persons *are*. To represent persons in this way need not run afoul of moral realism.

Finally, one comes to the issue of theory acceptance: Even if conflicts in a pluralist theory pose no problems of logical consistency or of compatibility with moral realism, what grounds does one have for accepting such a theory? Perhaps the best answer to this question involves a method of wide reflective equilibrium.[16] This method seeks coherence in a set of moral judgments, a set of moral principles, and a set of background theories. In the pluralist theory of property advocated here, the moral judgments are the considered judgments ("intuitions"), of various levels of generality, about public and private property that strike one as correct. The moral principles are the principles of utility and efficien-

---

16 The following sketch draws heavily on Norman Daniels, "Wide Reflective Equilibrium and Theory Acceptance in Ethics," *Journal of Philosophy*, 76 (1979): 256–82. The idea of reflective equilibrium has its roots in Rawls, *A Theory of Justice*, pp. 20–21, 46–53, 120, 432, 434, 579; John Rawls, "The Independence of Moral Theory," *Proceedings and Addresses of the American Philosophical Association*, 48 (1975): 5–22. These difficult issues are pursued in David Copp and David Zimmerman, eds., *Morality, Reason and Truth: New Essays on the Foundations of Ethics* (Totowa, N.J.: Rowman & Allanheld, 1985), pp. 27–190; Michael R. DePaul, "Two Conceptions of Coherence Methods in Ethics," *Mind*, 96 (1987): 463–81.

cy, justice and equality, and desert based on labor. The background theories are the accounts of persons and property in an ever-widening social context as set forth in Part II of this book. Thus, the method tries to get these sets of judgments, principles, and background theories to hang together. It is a bit narrow to model this procedure on linguistic competence.[17] For this method does not try to systematize only particular moral judgments and moral principles. Rather, it attempts to systematize theory-based views of property institutions as well, and allows for mutual revision in the members of each set. If there is such a thing as a "true" moral, political, and legal theory of property, convergence in wide reflective equilibrium is not sufficient for having found it, for one might have converged in error. Neither is it necessary for the truth of the moral component of the theory, for one might have identified that component without having formulated a sound theory of property institutions. All the same, since the question at hand is what grounds one has for accepting the pluralist theory advocated here, an answer is that convergence in wide reflective equilibrium supplies relevant grounds.

It remains to clarify the sense in which this pluralist theory is "intuitionist" (§ 1.3). It *is not* intuitionist in the sense that it supposes that some psychological faculty exists to intuit moral truths, or that particular moral judgments have an epistemically privileged position. In fact, as noted in § 1.3, though the theory does not assume that there is such a thing as objective moral truth, neither does it rule out moral truth, moral objectivity, or moral realism.[18] All the same, the theory *is* intuitionist in Rawls's sense, for it contains a family

17 M. B. E. Smith, "Ethical Intuitionism and Naturalism: A Reconciliation," *Canadian Journal of Philosophy*, 9 (1979): 609–29, seems to endorse such a view. For reservations, see Daniels, "Wide Reflective Equilibrium and Theory Acceptance in Ethics," at 258 n.4; Norman Daniels, "On Some Methods of Ethics and Linguistics," *Philosophical Studies*, 37 (1980): 21–36.
18 See also Daniels, "Wide Reflective Equilibrium and Theory Acceptance in Ethics," at 273–82.

of principles that are irreducible, the principles sometimes conflict, and, though priority rules resolve some conflicts, they may not resolve all of them.[19] In addition to the general philosophical arguments for intuitionism of this sort,[20] it is to be observed that, so far as can be told, neither the current state of moral theory nor available accounts of property institutions in actual social contexts show how to eliminate irresolvable conflicts or to reduce a moral theory of property to a single principle.

11.4 GUIDELINES FOR APPLICATION

Some readers will have come to this chapter with a practical rather than a theoretical concern: How does one apply a pluralist theory of property? The most concrete response is to tackle specific problems and use the theory to solve them. Part IV of this book does just that. It is, though, possible to formulate here some guidelines for applying the theory.

First, the theory is to be applied in stages and in the light of appropriate empirical evidence.[21] It is not intended, for example, that a judge deciding a wage dispute under a union contract should be squinting directly at the labor-desert principle to see what it commands in the case at bar. Rather, applying the theory will generally involve intermediate stages of deliberation and assessment. Institutions and situations differ so widely, and so many varieties of property exist, that it seems impossible to decree precise stages. Help-

---

19 See Rawls, *A Theory of Justice,* p. 34. For a searching examination, see M. B. E. Smith, "Rawls and Intuitionism," in Kai Nielsen and Roger A. Shiner, eds., *New Essays on Contract Theory, Canadian Journal of Philosophy,* Supplementary Volume III (1977): 163–78.

20 See, for example, Munzer, "Intuition and Security in Moral Philosophy"; Christine Swanton, "The Rationality of Ethical Intuitionism," *Australasian Journal of Philosophy,* 65 (1987): 172–81; J. O. Urmson, "A Defence of Intuitionism," *Proceedings of the Aristotelian Society,* 75 (1974–75): 111–19.

21 Sections 8.6, 9.5, and 10.3 mentioned this point in passing but deferred discussion of it till now.

ful suggestions, however, come from rule-utilitarianism, which uses the principle of utility not directly but to justify subordinate principles or institutions; from Rawls, who specifies a four-stage sequence involving the original position and later constitutional, legislative, and administrative stages;[22] and from Nickel, who adapts Rawls's stages to the justification of specific rights and looks to additional information about contemporary institutions and resources.[23]

What counts as appropriate empirical evidence will vary from one deliberative stage to the next. For instance, the social planner who is trying to formulate an income policy surveys the incomes of all persons in the state in order to make sure that she has the facts straight. Similarly, a legislature considering an inheritance tax on land transfers at death needs statistical information about the predictable effects of such a tax, but should not get bogged down in the details of individual cases. In contrast, a court applying such a law can usually ignore the general statistics, since the legislature has already used them to determine the provisions of the tax; yet the court needs to be careful that it has correctly ascertained relevant facts – such as the cost or other tax basis.

The problems addressed in Part IV will illustrate some of the deliberative stages and empirical factors. The discussion of business corporations, for example, distinguishes how the three principles apply to corporate enterprise as a whole from how they apply to individual corporations. It uses the extensive empirical literature on corporate performance – especially as performance relates to the separation of ownership and control. The chapter on the justifiability and taxation of gratuitous transfers takes up a different, essentially legislative problem and, using data on inequalities of wealth and their causes, formulates a moderately detailed tax pro-

---

22 See Rawls, *A Theory of Justice*, pp. 195–201.
23 See James W. Nickel, *Making Sense of Human Rights: Philosophical Reflections on the Universal Declaration of Human Rights* (Berkeley: University of California Press, 1987), pp. 43–44, 107–08, and, generally, chs. 6 and 7.

posal. Finally, the treatment of government taking and regulation of private property involves two different stages. One is a preconstitutional stage that constructs, on the basis of the three principles, a moral and political theory of takings. The other is a constitutional inquiry; it shows the extent to which the United States Constitution countenances, and diverges from, that moral and political theory. Here the inquiry attends to the sorts of tests that judges can apply in actual disputes, and the "empirical" element consists not in statistical data but in the rich lode of past judicial decisions.

Second, it will help to distinguish between a method of intellectual inquiry and a strategy of exposition for writing up the results of that inquiry. Consider once again the social planner who is trying to formulate an income policy. As to method, she need use no particular order in applying the theory. Here is *one* order that she might follow: Step A: If the Floor Thesis of the principle of justice and equality is unsatisfied, then make sure that whoever needs the minimum gets it. Step B: If the minimum is secured but the Gap Thesis of that principle is unsatisfied, then narrow the inequality. Step C: If the labor-desert principle applies because someone works to make a product or provide a service, then make sure that their compensation is, so far as possible, commensurate with the work done. Step D: If the previous principles are inapplicable or already met, then implement the principle of utility and efficiency. Step E: If any conflict seems to exist, then try to resolve it by appealing to the arguments for the respective principles.

Suppose that the social planner follows these steps and arrives at a conflict-free income policy. She now must have a strategy of exposition for preparing her report to the legislature. Just as no particular order is required as a method of inquiry, so no particular order is required in presenting the results of the inquiry. In fact, whatever order was followed in the inquiry need not be repeated in the report. In writing the report she will have to consider which sequence of exposition is the clearest and most persuasive. Part IV of this book actually uses different strategies of exposition. The

treatment of takings and of business corporations first presents an interim solution based on the principle of utility and
efficiency, and then shows how the remaining principles
modify that interim solution. In contrast, the discussion of
gratuitous transfers applies all three principles more or less
simultaneously, though it suggests that the labor-desert
principle plays a relatively small role.

Third, one should take advantage of the theoretical points
made in §§ 11.2 and 11.3. For almost any problem, one
should ask how, if at all, each principle bears on it. Since the
scope of the principles varies, all principles need not be
applicable to all problems. If all principles point in the same
direction – say, by favoring some plan of income redistribution – no conflict exists to be addressed. Similarly, in any
given context, one principle may give more definite guidance
than the others; one should then, other things being equal,
follow that principle. If a conflict has arisen, one should
attempt to identify its origin. If it stems from a past violation
of the theory, one should avoid repeating the violation. If it
stems from a conflict within the theory itself, one should use
the method of wide reflective equilibrium to see whether one
can defensibly adjust the scope of a principle, create an
exception, or devise a priority rule. In all of these situations,
it is important to obtain the best empirical evidence.

Fourth, one should understand what sort of property is at
stake. As much is apparent from the discussions of the
minimum, the narrowing of inequalities, and the resolution
of conflicts. It may be added that cultures vary in the sorts of
property relevant to the development and retention of personality – in the sense of moral and political personhood.
Commonly, clothes, tools, and dwellings are relevant and
portfolios of stock are not.

Fifth, if redistribution is required, the best mode of
redistribution will ordinarily be some system of taxation and
transfer. The reason is that, though higher taxes can also be
unpopular, the shifting of particular items of property from
one person to another is especially likely to cause resentment
and unrest. One need take no position on the best system of

313

taxation – whether to base it on income, wealth, consumption (expenditures), some other index, or some combination of these. Nor need one take a position on the best sort of transfer. It seems likely, though, that a sensible arrangement will use income supplements, subsidies for housing and education, and welfare programs in a broad sense. It is, however, an important condition on the system of taxation and transfer that it not be conceived as a one-shot or spasmodic operation. It must ensure over time that everyone has access to a minimum amount of property and that inequalities do not undermine a fully human life in society for each person.

There is one major exception to the rule preferring taxation and transfer to shifts of particular items of property. The exception is land reform. There it will often not be possible to achieve the desired effect by taxation and transfer. Some system of government takings of private landholdings will be needed – with the amount of compensation to be set on the basis of factors discussed in Chapters 14 and 15. This applies not only in underdeveloped countries but also, sometimes, in developed ones.

Sixth, redistribution is not a talisman for a humane system of property. One cannot solve problems simply by throwing money at them. Two things in particular must be borne in mind. One is production. Those who work need some significant amount of control over this part of their lives. Otherwise they will be alienated or discontented, no matter how equal their income and wealth. Another is the promotion of communal values. It will not help as much as it should if a program merely redistributes, so that more people have more to spend in the same old spiritless way. That may reduce inequalities, but it is not a full solution.

Part IV

Applications

Chapter 12

Business corporations

So far this book has proposed what will be called the basic theory of property. It consists of the analysis of the concept of property in Part I; the background theory of property in Part II; and, in Part III, the principles of utility and efficiency, justice and equality, and desert based on labor, together with the account of the relations and the resolution of conflicts between or among the principles. The task now is to apply the basic theory to specific problems. Though the theory illuminates all problems of property, this Part IV will discuss a few problems in at least moderate depth rather than aim the theory in a scattershot fashion at a host of problems.

This chapter applies the basic theory to a general problem of economic organization: How should business corporations be structured and operated in both a private-property economy (§ 5.1) and a socialist economy? This problem, though quite broad, is narrower than it might have been. For

The material in Part IV is so varied and sometimes so specialized that I am fortunate to have had many astute commentators on various portions of it. I wish to thank Richard L. Abel, Martin Barrack, Raquelle de la Rocha, Jesse Dukeminier, Richard A. Epstein, Kenneth W. Graham, Jr., William A. Klein, Christine A. Littleton, Thomas Morawetz, Christopher W. Morris, Gregory J. Ramirez, and John Shepard Wiley, Jr. Special thanks go to Margaret Jane Radin and Carol M. Rose, who served as commentators, on a version of Chapter 14, at a session of the American Society for Political and Legal Philosophy at the meeting of the Association of American Law Schools, New Orleans, Louisiana, in January 1989.

this chapter does not consider either nonbusiness corporations, such as charitable corporations, or noncorporate business entities, such as partnerships or individual proprietorships. Furthermore, it does not deal with issues pertaining to business corporations other than "structure" – ownership and control – and "operation" – standards of corporate behavior and responsibility. Nevertheless, if the chapter is sound, it may shed indirect light on other issues, such as securities regulation, and on charitable corporations or noncorporate firms.

The chapter has four specific aims and a pair of underlying themes. The first aim is to show that even if one were to accept efficiency as the sole normative principle for evaluating business corporations, the separation of ownership and control is, despite much economic opinion to the contrary, a significant issue at several levels. The second aim is to argue that if one accepts the basic theory of property, one can offer a promising response to that issue. In both cases, the issue posed by the separation of ownership and control is: In whose interests or behalf should corporations be run? The third aim is to extend the account of ownership and control to standards of corporate behavior. The final aim is to show that essentially the same conclusions hold for socialist as well as private-property economies.

The underlying themes suggest approaching business corporations somewhat differently from the way many thinkers today actually do. One underlying theme is that just as it will repay political philosophers to devote more time than they generally do to economic and business writing on the firm and to the empirical literature on corporate performance, so it will benefit academic lawyers and economists who study corporations to step back from the minutiae for a while and to consider what general moral and political principles should govern the separation of ownership and control and corporate standards. The other theme is the usefulness of looking at economic organization from the standpoint of property. Currently, many economists and academic lawyers view corporations from the perspective of interlocking contracts and the costs of agency. This chapter includes that perspective within a broader view of corporations as a topic in the theory of property rights. In this respect, the chapter repairs to an older tradition of thinking about property and economic enterprise – a tradition that embraces such diverse thinkers as Adam Smith, Proudhon, Marx, and Mill.

Here is the itinerary. Section 12.2 pursues the first aim just described. It explains what the separation of ownership and control is and why some economists do not regard that separation as a significant issue. It then distinguishes three levels of significance and shows why these economists are mistaken – for each level of significance and for manager-controlled firms, owner-controlled firms, and employee-oriented firms. These interim conclusions are important because they put only efficiency in play, and so meet the economic arguments on their own turf. This section identifies, at the end, the intellectual results of applying the principle of utility and efficiency to ownership/control structures.

Section 12.3 pursues the second aim. It builds on the interim conclusions by displaying the impact on ownership and control of the principles of justice and equality and of desert based on labor. It then uses all three principles systematically to supply criteria for acceptable ownership/control structures.

Section 12.4 pursues the third aim. It addresses mainly what corporations may, rather than what they must, do. It considers, and rejects, two extreme positions on corporate standards. It then argues that the intermediate position proposed by the American Law Institute, though an improvement on the extreme positions, is too closely tied to prevailing standards of right and wrong as they relate to the conduct of business. Lastly, it contends that the basic theory of property yields systematic guidance for standards of corporate behavior in a private-property economy.

Section 12.5 pursues the final aim. It rebuts claims that the separation of ownership and control and corporate standards are concerns only under some form of capitalism. Rather, much the same requirements and restrictions apply in all developed economies.

319

12.2 EFFICIENCY, UTILITY, AND THE
SEPARATION OF OWNERSHIP AND CONTROL

Separation of ownership and control. The classic formulation of the separation of ownership and control is by Berle and Means.[1] Holders of private property, they argued, have three functions in business enterprises: providing capital for the enterprise, having power over it, and acting with respect to it. Before the Industrial Revolution, all three functions were performed by the same individual. After it, throughout most of the nineteenth century and in the closely held corporation even today, the "owner" of the enterprise performed the first two functions, and hired managers performed the third. With the rise of the modern publicly held corporation in the late nineteenth and early twentieth centuries, the "owners" came to be widely dispersed and performed only the first function. The managers of the corporation performed the second and third functions. The separation of ownership and control is the separation between the performance of the first function ("ownership") and the performance of the second and third functions ("control").[2]

Berle and Means thought that this separation leads to a conflict. On one side stands the "traditional logic of property,"[3] which would allocate all of the profit to the shareholders. On the other side stands the "traditional logic

1 Adolf A. Berle, Jr. and Gardiner C. Means, *The Modern Corporation and Private Property* (New York: Commerce Clearing House, 1932). Anticipations of their account include Adam Smith, *An Inquiry into the Nature and Causes of the Wealth of Nations* [1776], ed. Edwin Cannan and pref. George J. Stigler (Chicago: University of Chicago Press, 1976), vol. 2, bk. V, ch. I, pt. III, art. I, pp. 264–65; Karl Marx, *Capital* [1867], ed. Frederick Engels and trans. Samuel Moore and Edward Aveling (New York: International Publishers, 1967), vol. 3, bk. III, pt. V, ch. XXVII, pp. 435–41.
2 Berle and Means, *The Modern Corporation and Private Property*, pp. 119–25. The text substitutes "providing capital for" for Berle and Means's phrase "having interests in" (p. 119). Their phrase, strictly speaking, does not describe a function. The substitution describes a function and appears to capture what they meant to say.
3 Ibid., pp. 333–39.

of profits,"[4] which would allocate only some of the profit to the shareholders. Although Berle and Means's resolution of the conflict is beyond the scope of this chapter, they believed that both traditional theories are inadequate because both theories rely on an outdated picture of economic life – a picture painted by Adam Smith and touched up by later economists.[5] Berle and Means contended that profits should not go entirely either to the shareholders or to the managers. But neither should they be divided entirely between the two groups, for the community at large has an interest, too. The modern corporation, Berle and Means concluded, should "serve not alone the owners or the control but all society."[6]

The characterization of the separation of ownership and control, as given at the end of the first paragraph of this section, will suffice for present purposes. A more thorough treatment, however, would have to attend to at least three additional points. First, it might be more accurate to substitute "property rights" for "ownership." Some might argue that shareholders in a publicly held corporation do not "own" corporations in the sense that the classical entrepreneur had, or the shareholders of a close corporation have, ownership. Even if one were to accept this argument, one could conclude that some weaker notion of ownership is involved here, or certainly that shareholders have property rights even if they lack ownership. So at least a question would remain about the separation of property rights from control. This chapter, in keeping with most of the literature, will continue to speak of ownership. Readers who find this troubling may substitute "property rights" for "ownership" and will find the conclusions unaffected.

Second, for some purposes it may be useful to draw the

---

4 Ibid., pp. 340–44. Some economists may prefer to avoid the word "profit" in favor of "economic rent" and "returns" to shareholders, managers, labor, and so on. However, in order to report the literature in its own terminology, this chapter will use "profit" when the source does.

5 Ibid., pp. 345–51.

6 Ibid., p. 356.

distinction between ownership and control differently or to examine various aspects of each separately. For example, if one wished to study organizations such as partnerships, financial mutuals, and nonprofit organizations as well as business corporations, one might distinguish, as do Fama and Jensen, between "decision management" (which involves initiating and implementing a decision) and "decision control" (which involves ratifying and monitoring a decision).[7] Such purposes are outside the scope of this chapter.

Third, in order to bring Berle and Means into contact with later economic and business writing, one would need to explore their connections with the so-called managerialists.[8] Briefly stated, the managerialists contend that in publicly held corporations, managers pursue maximum growth of the firm or other ends rather than maximum profits. This contention is akin to Berle and Means's views, for if growth maximization is in the interests of managers and profit maximization is in the interests of shareholders, and if one cannot maximize both growth and profits simultaneously, then managerial and shareholder interests conflict to some extent. This chapter will not trace connections between Berle and Means and the managerialists in any detail, but it bears notice that some of the empirical literature cited in this section addresses various managerialist hypotheses rather than the older formulation of Berle and Means.

A common economic response. A common, perhaps orthodox, response to Berle and Means is an abstract argument to the effect that the separation of ownership and control is a nonissue. The argument usually partakes of one or both of two

7 Eugene F. Fama and Michael C. Jensen, "Separation of Ownership and Control," *Journal of Law & Economics*, 26 (1983): 301–25.
8 See, for example, William J. Baumol, *Business Behavior, Value and Growth*, rev. ed. (New York: Harcourt, Brace & World, 1967); Robin Marris, *The Economic Theory of "Managerial" Capitalism* (London: Macmillan, 1964); Oliver E. Williamson, *The Economics of Discretionary Behavior: Managerial Objectives in a Theory of the Firm* (Englewood Cliffs, N.J.: Prentice-Hall, 1964).

similar background positions: that corporations arise from voluntary agreement, and that contract is central to understanding corporations. Its proponents call it a set-of-contracts or nexus-of-contracts perspective on, or a series-of-bargains model of, corporations. It is unclear how fully reductionist this view is. Proponents seem to hold, variously, that corporations *are* sets of contracts; that all talk about corporations can be paraphrased without remainder into talk about interrelated sets of contracts; that corporations can usefully be analyzed as sets of contracts, even though in a few contexts it may still be convenient to think of them as entities. At any rate, such proponents as Demsetz, Fama, and Klein regard concern about the separation of ownership and control as "meaningless,"[9] "irrelevant,"[10] or "vacuous."[11]

The argument from the nexus-of-contracts perspective to this conclusion does not always take the same course, but the following steps are the core of it. If nothing constrained managers, nonmanagers would have cause for concern. Yet if the corporation is seen as a set of contracts, constraints abound. The constraints come from the contracts that the

9   "A broader perspective on the problem of the optimum ownership structure makes the fears of Berle and Means meaningless." Harold Demsetz, "The Structure of Ownership and the Theory of the Firm," *Journal of Law & Economics*, 26 (1983): 375–90, at 377. For citations to the perspective to which Demsetz appeals, see at 376 n.3.

10 "In this 'nexus of contracts' perspective, ownership of the firm is an irrelevant concept." Eugene F. Fama, "Agency Problems and the Theory of the Firm," *Journal of Political Economy*, 88 (1980): 288–307, at 290.

11 This view is more guarded: Under the "series-of-bargains approach, . . . [t]he descriptive separation of risk of loss, return, and control, for example, makes *much* of the discussion of separation of ownership and control seem vacuous." William A. Klein, "The Modern Business Organization: Bargaining Under Constraints," *Yale Law Journal*, 91 (1982): 1521–64, at 1526 (emphasis added, footnotes omitted). Klein's model contains enough noncontract elements that he is not fully a member of the nexus-of-contracts school, though his work reflects its influence. For criticism of the agency cost and nexus-of-contracts approach, see Victor Brudney, "Corporate Governance, Agency Costs, and the Rhetoric of Contract," *Columbia Law Review*, 85 (1985): 1403–44.

participants make against the background of the market and existing law. The participants include not only shareholders and managers but also lenders, distributors, employees, and others. Managers may desire and even successfully bargain for some measure of control. And managers have institutionally legitimate interests in control. Hence shareholders have no entitlement to all control.

More to the point, plenty of constraints reduce managerial freedom to act contrary to shareholder interests. The usual litany includes later adjustment of managers' compensation according to performance, internal monitoring of some managers by other managers, supervision by the board of directors, the outside managerial labor market, and the specter of a hostile takeover. These constraints make the large publicly held corporation an efficient form of business organization. More precisely, they lead to an efficient ownership/control structure that allows all participants to pursue their own self-interests. If all goes well, it is as idle to worry about the separation of ownership and control as to worry about getting a sunburn at night. If all does not go well, the constraints allow shareholders to reassert their control in one way or another. Asks Demsetz, "How could it be otherwise? In a world in which self-interest plays a significant role in economic behavior, it is foolish to believe that owners of valuable resources systematically relinquish control to managers who are not guided to serve their interests."[12]

Efficiency, corporate performance, and levels of significance. In order to appraise this economic argument, it is necessary to explain how the notions of efficiency, corporate performance, and levels of significance will be used. Economists use the word "efficiency" in various senses – including Pareto-superiority, Pareto-optimality, and Kaldor-Hicks efficiency (§ 8.4). Actually, for the purposes of this section, it will work well enough to treat efficiency in a general and nontechnical sense as the production of desired effects with a minimum of

12 Demsetz, "The Structure of Ownership and the Theory of the Firm," at 390.

effort and waste. However, some of the literature cited occasionally focuses on specific understandings of efficiency, and the end of the section uses the principle of utility and efficiency defended in Chapter 8. Similarly, though examination of corporate performance is central to this undertaking, there is no single test for efficient corporate performance. Some of the tests used are productivity, profits, profitability, and returns to equity, debt, and retained earnings.

The matter of levels of significance is more complicated. Suppose that one can distinguish between factual propositions – that something *is* the case – and normative propositions – that something *should* or *ought* to be the case. Suppose also that, in the present context, one is concerned with the factual proposition that all existing firms, whether controlled by owners, managers or employees, *are* efficient; that is, that each firm, whatever its existing ownership/control structure, is performing as well as it could if it had a different ownership/control structure. At level one, an issue is significant if, even if existing firms *are* efficient, one can ask whether firms *should* be efficient – that is, whether efficiency is the sole normative criterion by which one should judge firms. At level two, an issue is significant if it is significant at level one and if, while manager-controlled (MC) firms sometimes are efficient, at other times owner-controlled (OC) or employee-oriented firms outperform MC firms. At level three, an issue is significant if it is significant at level two and if there is a practical possibility for change.

The differentiation of levels of significance, which at first may seem stilted, is the key to appraising economic arguments that concern about the separation of ownership and control is meaningless or vacuous. Such arguments may appear to deny significance at level one, but they are not really denying that. If the separation poses the normative issue of how corporations should be run, and if one accepts Hume's Law (no "ought" from an "is"),[13] then this issue is

---

13 See David Hume, *A Treatise of Human Nature*, ed. L. A. Selby-Bigge (Oxford: Clarendon Press, 1960 [1888]), bk. III, pt. I, § I, p. 469.

plainly significant at level one. Some might wish to attack Hume's Law; but one would be very hard pressed to find an economic writer who has opposed Berle and Means on that ground; so there is no need to pursue that avenue of attack here. Instead, the economic arguments deny significance at level two or three. Such a denial will strike philosophers as somewhat confused. For levels two and three raise in part empirical questions about how the world of corporate business operates rather than questions about meaning, and therefore a claim that the separation is "meaningless" may seem muddled. As will emerge, the economic arguments against Berle and Means do have a point, but they are mostly unsuccessful and in any case are not best expressed in terms of lack of meaning.

Empirical evidence: manager-controlled versus owner-controlled firms. Although one might attempt to give an abstract reply to the economic argument outlined earlier, this chapter will pursue a different strategy. It will ask what the empirical evidence shows.[14] Berle and Means's book would be boring if it were merely a statement that management control (separation of ownership and control) and shareholder control (unity of ownership and control) are analytically distinct or reflect different patterns of share ownership. If one assumes that, under the latter, shareholder-managers act in their own interests, the claim must be that, under the former, managers have a propensity to act, and sometimes do act, contrary to the interests of shareholders. This claim will be referred to as Berle and Means's claim. The contrary claim implicit in some economic writing seems to be that the market generates both MC and OC firms, that each long-surviving firm of either sort has an efficient ownership/control structure, and that no empirical evidence exists that any given long-

14 Here I owe a large debt to Martin Barrack. He identified most of what we needed to read; we read and discussed it together; and he commented on successive drafts summarizing and interpreting the empirical literature.

surviving firm would have performed better had it been an OC firm rather than an MC firm.

How might one test these claims? Obviously it would be difficult to do so by drawing a sample of corporations identical except for the fact that half involve separation and half unity of ownership and control. The difficulty is not merely finding corporations that are identical, or nearly so, in all relevant respects. It is that management control typically occurs where ownership is widely dispersed. Such dispersion occurs chiefly in large publicly held firms in which capital is assembled from many sources. Shareholder control typically occurs in the opposite situation. Even though some small firms are not closely held, most closely held firms are small.

Nor can one easily test the claims by comparing motives. Here the difficulty is not merely ascertaining motives. Nor is it merely that shareholder motives vary, given that some shareholders seek dividends paid out of profits, others seek growth, and still others seek deferred income or tax advantages. The chief difficulty is that even if shareholder motives and management motives differ, it does not *follow* that managers' actions will be contrary to shareholders' interests. Suppose that shareholders seek high dividends paid out of profits. Suppose that managers seek job stability and increased professional reputation inside and outside the firm. The motives differ. All the same, managers acting on the latter motives might well generate high profits and distribute them as dividends. Berle and Means were fully aware of this point. The outcome, they believed, depends on "the degree to which the self-interest of those in control may run parallel to the interests of ownership and, insofar as they differ, on the checks on the use of power which may be established by political, economic, or social conditions."[15] If managers seek personal monetary gain, they may well act counter to the interests of shareholders. If they seek something else, it is harder to speculate on the consequences for shareholders.

15   Berle and Means, *The Modern Corporation and Private Property*, p. 121.

327

If these reflections are on the right track, then one must test these claims indirectly by trying to control for the variables that affect MC and OC firms. The notes summarize much of the empirical literature of the last two decades. This literature, though its details are of transitory importance, indicates the kind of empirical fact gathering that is relevant to applying the basic theory. The statistical studies, which control for such variables as size[16] and which use various

---

16 Other things being equal, one would expect small corporations to be OC firms and large corporations to be MC firms, and that it would therefore be hard to confirm or reject Berle and Means's claim. Actually, however, there is some crossover, and steps can be taken to control for size.

Some studies focus on either large or small corporations. An example is a study of large corporations – namely 360 firms from the Fortune 500 – in Peter Holl, "Control Type and the Market for Corporate Control in Large U.S. Corporations," *Journal of Industrial Economics*, 25 (1977): 259–73 (10 percent ownership criterion for "weak" control and 30 percent ownership criterion for "strong" control). After attempting to control for size and structure, Holl found that MC firms were 4.53 percent less profitable than OC firms. He concluded that although a market for corporate control exists, its discipline is imperfect and the imperfection probably increases with firm size. This result favors Berle and Means's claim. (As a practical matter, less than complete or even majority ownership of shares suffices for control. Most studies use figures ranging from 10 to 20 percent. In the following references, the classificatory criteria are, where available and relevant, indicated parenthetically.)

Subsequent literature, however, has questioned some aspects of Holl's approach. See, for example, Michael L. Lawriwsky, "Control Type and the Market for Corporate Control: A Note," *Journal of Industrial Economics*, 28 (1980): 439–41; William A. McEachern, "Corporate Control and Growth: An Alternative Approach," *Journal of Industrial Economics*, 26 (1978): 257–66. But see Peter Holl, "Control Type and the Market for Corporate Control: Reply," *Journal of Industrial Economics*, 28 (1980): 443–45.

In contrast, small corporations were examined in B. J. Campsey and R. F. DeMong, "The Influence of Control on Financial Management: Further Evidence," *Review of Business and Economic Research*, 18, no. 2 (Winter 1983): 60–70 (20 percent ownership criterion for OC firms). They drew a sample of 54 firms from the over-the-counter market that was evenly divided between MC and OC firms. They found that the two sorts of firms had few significant differences in financial management and none in profits, which cuts against Berle and Means's claim.

Other studies deal with corporations of various sizes. One way to

criteria of corporate performance,[17] reveal a complicated pattern. Some studies indicate that MC firms sometimes out-

do this is to examine firms of different sizes in the same industry. For example, a sample consisting of the largest bank in each of 1,406 bank holding companies was drawn in Cynthia A. Glassman and Stephen A. Rhoades, "Owner vs. Manager Control Effects on Bank Performance," *Review of Economics and Statistics*, 62 (1980): 263–70 (tested various percentages of ownership). They found that, overall, OC banks had higher profit rates than MC banks. Still, profit rates were about the same for the 200 largest banks, and higher profit rates for OC banks were evident only after a relatively high level of ownership. However, a study of the food and beverage industry found that whereas OC firms tended to have a higher average product of labor than MC firms, MC firms had a higher rate of return than OC firms. See Robert F. Ware, "Performance of Manager- Versus Owner-Controlled Firms in the Food and Beverage Industry," *Quarterly Review of Economics and Business*, 15, no. 2 (Summer 1975): 81–92 (ownership criteria for OC firms of 15 percent with representation in management or on board of directors or 25 percent without being active in the firm). These two studies send somewhat conflicting messages; the former supports and the latter tends to undermine Berle and Means's claim. Ware's study only tends to undermine Berle and Means's claim because, as he suggests, "the theory of the managerial firm is really the theory of the large bureaucratic firm and a large firm's behavior may be primarily a function of its size rather than entirely of separation of ownership and control" (at 89) (footnote omitted).

17 In fact, even the way performance is reported suggests some support for Berle and Means's claim. See E. Daniel Smith, "The Effect of the Separation of Ownership from Control on Accounting Policy Decisions," *Accounting Review*, 51 (1976): 707–23 (10 percent ownership criterion for OC firms). Since there are many acceptable reporting alternatives, those who control a firm can select among them for a range of possible profit figures for a given period. Smith investigated whether MC firms and OC firms differed in the use of changes in accounting policy to smooth income. He found that MC firms smoothed income more often than OC firms. He also found that smoothing-change periods are consistently different from no-change periods. Smoothing changes occur in periods in which the deviation from the target before the change is greater than the deviation from the target in no-change periods. These findings support Berle and Means's claim because OC firms will have less reason to avoid fluctuations in reported profit, whereas the managers in MC firms benefit from being able to report a smoothed income stream, in particular a stream that indicates gradually rising performance. See also Shu S. Liao, "The Effect of Separation of Ownership from Control on Accounting Policy Decisions: A Comment," *Accounting Review*, 54 (1979): 414–16; E. Daniel Smith, "The Effect of the Separation of

perform OC firms.[18] Other studies find no particular difference in performance.[19] But many studies indicate that OC firms sometimes outperform MC firms – whether the test for performance is profitability,[20] profitability with adjustment for risk,[21] use of retained earnings,[22] return on investment,[23] or productivity.[24]

Ownership from Control on Accounting Policy Decisions: A Reply," *Accounting Review*, 54 (1979): 417–20.

18 See, for example, Ware, "Performance of Manager- Versus Owner-Controlled Firms in the Food and Beverage Industry."

19 See, for example, Robert L. Conn, "Merger Pricing Policies by Owner-Controlled versus Manager-Controlled Firms," *Journal of Industrial Economics*, 28 (1980): 427–38 (no significant differences exist between MC and OC firms in regard to merger pricing policies); Gerald P. Madden, "The Separation of Ownership from Control and Investment Performance," *Journal of Economics and Business*, 34 (1982): 149–52 (no significant differences exist between performances of portfolios of stock in MC and OC firms).

20 See, for example, Holl, "Control Type and the Market for Corporate Control in Large U.S. Corporations."

21 See James L. Bothwell, "Profitability, Risk, and the Separation of Ownership from Control," *Journal of Industrial Economics*, 28 (1980): 303–11 (support exists for the managerialist position that managers may depart from profit-maximizing behavior when market constraints and owner control are weak); David S. Krause, "Corporate Ownership Structure: Does It Impact Firm Performance?," *Akron Business and Economic Review*, 19, no. 2 (Summer 1988): 30–38 (support exists that OC firms clearly outperform MC firms on a risk-adjusted basis).

22 For example, William J. Baumol, Peggy Heim, Burton G. Malkiel, and Richard E. Quandt, "Earnings Retention, New Capital and the Growth of the Firm," *Review of Economics and Statistics*, 52 (1970): 345–55, found that managers of MC firms use retained earnings less effectively than debt or new equity. The comparison suggests that managers may be somewhat lax in their use of retained earnings because such funds are less exposed to market discipline. It also suggests that a firm will use more expensive funds – debt or new equity – only if it has an investment project that is sufficiently promising to justify the higher cost. These findings tend to support Berle and Means's claim. For later work, compare G. Whittington, "The Profitability of Retained Earnings," *Review of Economics and Statistics*, 54 (1972): 152–60, with W. J. Baumol, P. Heim, B. G. Malkiel, and R. E. Quandt, "Efficiency of Corporate Investment: Reply," *Review of Economics and Statistics*, 55 (1973): 128–31. See also Donald G. McFetridge, "The Efficiency Implications of Earnings Retentions," *Review of Economics and Statistics*, 60 (1978): 218–24; Daniel M. Shapiro, William A. Sims, and Gwenn Hughes, "The Efficiency Implications of Earnings Retentions: An Extension," *Review of Economics and Statistics*,

These various studies are partially conflicting. *All* the evidence does not point the same way. Yet it is important to locate the nature of the conflicts. Surveying the literature virtually never turns up a pair of studies that reach inconsistent conclusions using exactly the same data base. Neither does it reveal studies that are applying wholly incompatible methodologies to different data bases. Rather, the data bases almost always differ. And though methodologies differ, they tend to be overlapping and at most only partially incompatible. So the studies cited are not mutually canceling; it would be implausible to hold that they reveal nothing about the separation of ownership and control. Instead, they provide *enough* evidence to conclude that though sometimes MC firms are efficient, at other times OC firms outperform MC firms. Enough studies, performed on reliable data and with defensible methods, show that OC firms are sometimes superior, in some respect or other, to MC firms. Accordingly, there is credible support for Berle and

65 (1983): 327–31 (distinguishing foreign-controlled firms as well as MC and OC firms).

23 See, for example, R. Joseph Monsen, John S. Chiu, and David E. Cooley, "The Effect of Separation of Ownership and Control on the Performance of the Large Firm," *Quarterly Journal of Economics,* 82 (1968): 435–51 (OC firms produced a 75 percent higher ratio of net income to net worth, and thus a better return on investment, than MC firms). Some related studies, such as those by Radice and Boudreaux, yield similar results. Others, such as a study by Hindley, support this sort of conclusion but rather more weakly. See, respectively, H. K. Radice, "Control Type, Profitability and Growth in Large Firms: An Empirical Study," *Economic Journal,* 81 (1971): 547–62 (OC firms have higher profit and growth rates than MC firms) (Radice expresses some reservations about these results at 561–62); Kenneth J. Boudreaux, "'Managerialism' and Risk-Return Performance," *Southern Economic Journal,* 39 (1973): 366–72; Brian Hindley, "Separation of Ownership and Control in the Modern Corporation," *Journal of Law & Economics,* 13 (1970): 185–221 (only weak support exists for the hypothesis that MC firms and a lower ratio of potential to actual value are positively correlated).

24 See Charles W. L. Hill and Scott A. Snell, "Effects of Ownership Structure and Control on Corporate Productivity," *Academy of Management Journal,* 32 (1989): 25–46 (strong support exists that the level of stock concentration in a firm directly and indirectly affects productivity).

331

Means's claim and some aspects of the managerialist position.[25] Furthermore, the contrary economic claim is undermined, since the controls on some statistical studies suggest that some long-surviving firms would have performed better had they been OC rather than MC firms. Therefore, the separation of ownership and control poses, so far as MC and OC firms are concerned, an issue that is significant at level two.

One should beware of missing the point here. The point is *not* the anemic idea that no clear *general* superiority can be found for MC firms over OC firms or vice versa. This idea is sound, but it is a pretty benign finding. Given that both MC and OC firms have survived in the marketplace, it is unsurprising that no clear general superiority exists for one sort of firm over the other. Such a finding is parallel to the idea that though people communicate by both speaking and writing, no clear general superiority exists for either form of communication, since each possesses virtues that the other lacks.

Rather, the point of the empirical evidence is the more robust idea that *sometimes* MC firms are superior to OC firms and *sometimes* OC firms are superior to MC firms, and that it is possible, by examining the studies, to try to identify the

---

25 This assessment disagrees with that of Frank H. Easterbrook, "Managers' Discretion and Investors' Welfare: Theories and Evidence," *Delaware Journal of Corporate Law*, 9 (1984): 540–71. Easterbrook concludes that to "the extent the evidence permits the rendition of a verdict, it is that the Berle-Means-ALI hypothesis may confidently be rejected" (at 570) and that "markets operating under current legal rules . . . have been quite successful in aligning the interests of investors and managers" (at 543). Easterbrook's conclusions are unwarranted. First, his article omits many of the empirical economic studies dealing specifically with ownership and control that this section discusses. Hence he lacks an adequate basis on which to reject Berle and Means's claim. Second, once the missing evidence is supplied, Berle and Means's claim has credible support. Third, as a result, one should not view "current legal rules" as sanguinely as does Easterbrook, for the reasons adduced in the next subsection. Finally, Easterbrook's article is myopic in focusing entirely on MC and OC firms. As the end of § 12.2 argues, employee-oriented firms sometimes offer the best ownership/control structure.

factors that make one sort of firm better in specific instances and make another sort of firm better in other specific instances. It is beyond the scope of this chapter to conduct any such detailed examination. However, one can see that this more interesting finding is parallel to the claim that by examining instances of communication, it is possible to ascertain when speaking is more effective than writing (say, with young children who cannot yet read) and when writing is more effective than speaking (say, for keeping a permanent record).[26]

Economic replies and rejoinders. This subsection considers two economic replies that might be made to the empirical evidence. That evidence indicates that, in actual corporations, constraints on managerial behavior do not function wholly effectively. One may speculate about the reasons. Later wage revision may "close the door" too late. Social and personal ties may inhibit intramanagerial monitoring. Directors may lack the information and expertise to supervise well. Highly adept managers may sometimes find it hard to acquire and process accurately information about compensation in other firms. Hostile takeover attempts may result not in a new management but in the existing management's disposing of valuable corporate assets to make the target corporation less attractive, or buying the insurgents' shares at a premium, both of which can harm shareholders. Whatever the reasons, it is clear that market constraints on managerial behavior are not entirely effective.

The first reply, suggested in effect by Demsetz, is almost a definitional stop. "It is a mistake to confuse the firm of economic theory with its real-world namesake. The chief mission of neoclassical economics is to understand how the price system coordinates the use of resources, not to un-

---

26 These remarks, as well as those at the end of the next subsection, were prompted by some comments of Richard A. Epstein, who may well disagree with the use made of them here.

derstand the inner workings of real firms."[27] The idea, then, is that the idealized firm of economic theory has an efficient ownership/control structure.

One may rejoin that this reply misses the point – namely, what happens in the real world. In effect, the reply tacitly acknowledges significance at level one but contends that significance is lacking at level two because the idealized firm of economic theory is efficient. However, since the chief concern of this chapter is real-world corporations, Demsetz's contention, even if it were true of idealized firms, is beside the point. The empirical evidence, which Demsetz is not entitled to ignore if he is to say anything pertinent to actual firms, shows that the issue of separation is significant at level two for actual MC and OC firms.[28]

A second reply, suggested in effect by Klein and Coffee, is that the conclusions drawn in the preceding subsection rely on a "mythical ideal of the owner-managed firm."[29] Even if some MC firms are outperformed by comparable OC firms, and even if those MC firms would have done better had they been OC firms, not all firms can be OC firms. The root error

---

27 Demsetz, "The Structure of Ownership and the Theory of the Firm," at 377 (footnote omitted). Although Demsetz is right to say that it would be a mistake to confuse these two sorts of firms, his article oscillates between the two. In the passage just quoted, he is concerned mainly with the firm of neoclassical economic theory. In the passage (at 390) quoted earlier, he is concerned with real-world firms; indeed, he would have to be in order to claim that constraints on managerial behavior enable shareholders effectively to reassert control if they wish to do so.

28 A later co-authored article adduces some empirical evidence for his position. See Harold Demsetz and Kenneth Lehn, "The Structure of Corporate Ownership: Causes and Consequences," *Journal of Political Economy*, 93 (1985): 1155–77. However, this article neglects to consider much of the relevant evidence cited above. In addition, it fails to control for differences among various industries in regard to return on assets, and subsequent researchers using the same data base as Demsetz and Lehn have found support for Berle and Means's position. See Hill and Snell, "Effects of Ownership Structure and Control on Corporate Productivity," at 43.

29 William A. Klein and John C. Coffee, Jr., *Business Organization and Finance: Legal and Economic Principles*, 3d ed. (Westbury, N.Y.: Foundation Press, 1988), p. 34 (emphasis omitted).

of those who make a fuss about the separation of ownership and control is that they falsely suppose that there is a practical possibility of change. In the terminology used here, even if the separation is significant at the first two levels, it poses no significant issue at level three. Some such reasoning seems to underlie views that concern about the separation is meaningless, irrelevant, or vacuous.

Though this reply does not succeed in the end, it contains an element of truth. That element is the fact that, in an economy such as that of the United States, it is neither possible nor desirable for all firms to be OC firms. It is not possible because that economy has many very large MC firms that it is unfeasible to restructure as OC firms. It is not desirable because MC firms offer access to capital and opportunities for investment that OC firms generally do not – financing through equity (rather than debt) without the burdens of control. The element of truth here, put somewhat differently, is that from the standpoint of efficiency it is overblown to maintain that MC firms should be systematically replaced by OC firms. Yet it is confused to state this element in terms of adjectives such as "meaningless" or "vacuous," for the truth concerns what is feasible in the world of business rather than what has meaning. Furthermore, the empirical evidence cited earlier was never claimed to show that *all* MC firms would do better as OC firms. This chapter subscribes to no "mythical ideal of the owner-managed firm."

Still, the evidence indicates that *some* MC firms would do better as OC firms, and that some of these can feasibly reform their ownership/control structures. One technique for doing this is the leveraged buyout, in which the management of an MC firm or others use debt to gain a controlling interest.[30] But one need not limit alternatives to restructur-

---

30 For critical evaluations, see Victor Brudney and Marvin A. Chirelstein, "A Restatement of Corporate Freezeouts," *Yale Law Journal*, 87 (1978): 1354–76; Harry DeAngelo, Linda DeAngelo, and Edward M. Rice, "Going Private: Minority Freezeouts and Stockholder Wealth," *Journal of Law & Economics*, 27 (1984): 367–401.

ings that convert MC firms into garden-variety OC firms. One can also investigate giving employees some control or ownership interest that enables a firm to do better; the next subsection discusses this possibility. For now, however, it is clear that there is some middle ground between complacent acceptance of existing real-world firms and some mythical ideal of the owner-managed firm. The reply under consideration fails to show that there is no practical possibility for desirable change. As this rejoinder makes clear, the separation of ownership and control is, as regards MC and OC firms, a significant issue at level three.

One should be careful not to miss the force of significance at level three. It is tempting to make a point relating to transaction costs: Even given that some MC firms would have done better as OC firms and vice versa, the reason inefficient organizational forms persist is that the costs of changing them exceed the expected gains. One should resist the temptation. It is true that sometimes the transaction-costs point holds. But it is farfetched to claim that it always holds, and in fact one cannot say how often it holds without doing the requisite empirical work to see if the costs of change exceed the expected gains. Furthermore, often one is not seeking to change existing corporate forms but rather to decide which form is best for a new corporate venture. In that case, there are no costs of change, and the point about transaction costs is irrelevant. Finally, even when one is considering exchanging one corporate form for another and so must take the costs of change into account, it behooves the legal system to create rules that minimize such costs when a change of form for an existing firm would otherwise promote efficiency. For example, if evidence were to show that leveraged buyouts of MC firms generally lead to more efficient OC firms, then it would make sense to have legal rules that hold down the costs of such buyouts.

Empirical evidence: employee-oriented firms. This subsection deals with business enterprises in which employees have a more substantial role than in traditional MC or OC firms.

The leading examples are worker cooperatives and corporations with employee stock ownership plans (ESOPs).[31] The discussion is not exhaustive. Nor is it a brief for cooperatives or ESOPs as *general* alternatives to prevailing forms of corporate enterprise. Rather, it describes cooperatives and ESOPs, cites some evidence on their performance, explores two explanations for their success in cases where they have been successful, and explains their relevance to this chapter.

Many possibilities exist for substantial employee involvement in business enterprise. Worker cooperatives are one possibility. In cooperatives, the workers own the enterprise and are entitled to what the enterprise produces. Ellerman contrasts cooperatives with the usual corporation in the following way.[32] In the usual corporation, ownership has three components: voting rights, rights to profits distributed as dividends, and rights to the net book value. All are property rights held by the shareholders. In cooperatives, voting rights and rights to profits are personal rather than property rights. They are tied to the worker's membership in the cooperative and are not transferable. Usually each member has one and only one vote. Rights to net book value, in contrast, are property rights. They are rights to the paid-in capital and the net retained profits, less the liabilities of the enterprise. Such rights are transferable. Future members of the cooperative are not entitled to any portion of the existing

---

31 Worker cooperatives are usually organized legally as corporations, but with special bylaws. A few states have statutes that create a special corporate structure for worker cooperatives. See, for example, the Massachusetts Employee Cooperative Corporations Act, Ann. Laws Mass. ch. 157A (Law. Co-op. Supp. 1989). ESOPs are financing devices established by the Employee Retirement Income Security Act of 1974, Pub. L. No. 93–406, 88 Stat. 829 (1974) (codified in scattered sections of 5, 18, 29, 31, 42 U.S.C. and I.R.C.). Business enterprises with associated ESOPs are almost always organized as corporations.
32 David Ellerman, "Workers' Cooperatives: The Question of Legal Structure," in Robert Jackall and Henry M. Levin, eds., *Worker Cooperatives in America* (Berkeley: University of California Press, 1984), pp. 257–74; David P. Ellerman, "Theory of Legal Structure: Worker Cooperatives," *Journal of Economic Issues*, 18 (1984): 861–91.

net book value.[33] There is no necessary connection between the cooperative form and the size of an enterprise. In fact, however, most cooperatives are small.

Employee stock ownership plans differ significantly from worker cooperatives. ESOPs are arrangements in which a trust purchases shares in the employer corporation for the benefit of employees and employees gain a collective voice in its operation. It is usually the existing company that sets up the trust. ESOPs have two main functions. First, healthy companies can use them in a way similar to pension plans, since corporate contributions to buy stock are tax deductible and income earned by the trust is not taxed until distributed to employees. Second, troubled companies can use them as a way of transferring ownership from existing shareholders to employees who have a stake in the continuation of the enterprise in its existing form.[34] Although conversion to an ESOP is generally amicable so far as existing management is concerned, it is often done to ward off a hostile takeover by outsiders. It is disputed whether ESOPs are more a creature of the tax laws than a splendid way to foster employee participation and ownership.[35] Tax treatment aside, corpora-

---

33 The description of cooperatives in the text applies to Mondragon-type cooperatives in which an internal account separates net book value from voting and profit rights. In traditional worker cooperatives, membership shares continue to carry net book value. If this value increases, then the price of membership shares increases, and it becomes more difficult for new workers to purchase membership shares. Thus, traditional cooperatives can exhibit share-transfer problems in practice.

Ellerman views cooperatives as the outcome of a labor theory of property. Although this view is open to question, the matter need not be decided here. In any case, Ellerman's version of the labor theory is not the same as the labor-desert principle argued for in Chapter 10.

34 See, for example, Christopher Eaton Gunn, *Workers' Self-Management in the United States* (Ithaca and London: Cornell University Press, 1984), pp. 132–52 (Rath Packing Company).

35 For criticism that ESOPs cause inefficiency, distort the market, and fail to provide the nontax benefits often claimed for them, see Richard L. Doernberg and Jonathan R. Macey, "ESOPs and Economic Distortion," *Harvard Journal on Legislation*, 23 (1986): 103–57. For positive assessments, see Joseph Raphael Blasi, *Employee Ownership: Revolu-*

tions with ESOPs are basically similar to the usual publicly held corporation. Share ownership is proportional to the amount invested. Employees have ownership rights because they own shares rather than merely because they work. Profits are distributed in proportion to the shares owned. Although some ESOPs have a one-vote-per-member rule, generally there is one vote per share owned.

At this point two questions arise. Do cooperatives and corporations with ESOPs ever outperform MC firms? If and to the extent that they do, what explains their superior performance? The available empirical evidence, limned briefly here, comes more from cooperatives, which have existed for a long time, than from ESOPs, which are quite recent.

The evidence indicates that some employee-oriented firms sometimes outperform traditional MC and OC firms.[36] For example, in the soft-plywood industry, many firms are cooperatives. Although every cooperative has not outperformed every noncooperative plywood producer, plywood cooperatives on average have had higher labor productivity than other plywood producers and have given their members higher wages than the union average.[37] When cooperatives or other employee-oriented firms have outperformed MC firms, the most plausible explanations are participation and ownership. The participation hypothesis is that if employees

tion or Ripoff? (Cambridge, Mass.: Ballinger, 1988); Michael Quarrey, Joseph Blasi, and Corey Rosen, *Taking Stock: Employee Ownership at Work* (Cambridge, Mass.: Ballinger, 1986); Corey M. Rosen, Katherine J. Klein, and Karen M. Young, *Employee Ownership in America: The Equity Solution* (Lexington, Mass. and Toronto: Lexington Books/D.C. Heath, 1986), chs. 2–7.

36 See generally Derek C. Jones and Jan Svejnar, eds., *Participatory and Self-Managed Firms: Evaluating Economic Performance* (Lexington, Mass.: Lexington Books/D.C. Heath, 1982); Frank H. Stephen, ed., *The Performance of Labor-Managed Firms* (London: Macmillan, 1982).

37 See Katrina V. Berman, "The United States of America: A Cooperative Model for Worker Management," in Stephen, ed., *The Performance of Labor-Managed Firms*, pp. 74–98, at pp. 79–81. On the difficulties of comparing the economic performance of plywood cooperatives and conventional firms, see Katrina V. Berman, *Worker-Owned Plywood Companies: An Economic Analysis* (Pullman, Wash.: Washington State University Press, 1967), ch. 12.

participate in the decision making in the firm, then they will be better motivated and more committed and therefore will tend to outproduce otherwise similarly situated employees in other sorts of firms. Research on plywood cooperatives[38] and other sorts of cooperatives[39] supports this hypothesis. The ownership hypothesis is that if employees own shares in the firm, then they will be better motivated and more committed and therefore will outproduce otherwise similarly situated employees in other sorts of firms. The participation and ownership hypotheses are not inconsistent. Some studies of the plywood industry conclude that employee ownership is less important than participation in the higher performance of cooperatives.[40] Other evidence supports an independent and significant role for employee ownership.[41]

---

38 See also Carl J. Bellas, *Industrial Democracy and the Worker-Owned Firm: A Study of Twenty-One Plywood Companies in the Pacific Northwest* (New York: Praeger, 1972).

39 See, for example, Michael Conte, "Participation and Performance in U.S. Labor-Managed Firms," in Jones and Svejnar, *Participatory and Self-Managed Firms*, pp. 213–37; Daniel R. Fusfeld, "Labor-Managed and Participatory Firms: A Review Article," *Journal of Economic Issues*, 17 (1983): 769–89. See also Avner Ben-Ner, "Labor-Managed and Participatory Firms: A Note," *Journal of Economic Issues*, 18 (1984): 1189–95; Daniel R. Fusfeld, "Labor-Managed and Participatory Firms: Reply," *Journal of Economic Issues*, 18 (1984): 1195–98.

40 See references in notes 37 and 38 above.

41 For example, one study, using a nonrandom sample of companies with ESOPs, found that the amount of stock received each year was by far the most important factor in explaining the superior commitment and performance of employees. See Rosen, Klein, and Young, *Employee Ownership in America*, pp. 9–11, 101–68, 201–02. Another study surveyed ninety-eight companies – sixty-eight with ESOPs and thirty with direct employee ownership. See Michael Conte and Arnold S. Tannenbaum, "Employee-Owned Companies: Is the Difference Measurable?," *Monthly Labor Review*, 101, no. 7 (July 1978): 23–28. Employees in about three-fourths of the companies studied owned at least half of the equity. The researchers collected data on such variables as percentage of equity owned by workers, presence of workers on the board of directors, voting, and so on. Of these variables, the first was the only significant variable when regressed on pretax profitability. This result suggests that ownership, not participation, matters. See also Samuel J. Davy, "Employee Ownership: One Road to Productivity Improvement," *Journal of Business Strategy*, 4 (Summer

The relevance of this discussion to the first aim of this chapter is as follows. That aim, it will be recalled, is to suggest that even if one were to accept efficiency as the sole normative principle for evaluating business corporations, the separation of ownership and control poses a significant issue at several levels. This subsection indicates that firms in which employees play a larger role sometimes outperform traditional MC and OC firms. The word "traditional" is important here. In the traditional MC firm, shares are owned entirely or almost entirely by persons who are not employees – except, perhaps, managerial employees. Thus, even large companies with ESOPs that hire professional managers are not traditional MC firms, since nonmanagerial employees own a substantial percentage of shares. In the traditional OC firm, a controlling group of shares is owned by a party who is either a managerial employee or not an employee at all. Hence, cooperatives and companies with ESOPs are not traditional OC firms, for no single party has control and the shareholders are generally employees and indeed generally nonmanagerial employees.

Yet it is vital to see that these employee-oriented business enterprises capture and recombine some key features of traditional firms. Cooperatives and smaller companies with ESOPs typically emphasize participation. In this way they seize

1983): 12–21; Richard J. Long, "The Effects of Employee Ownership on Organizational Identification, Employee Job Attitudes, and Organizational Performance: A Tentative Framework and Empirical Findings," *Human Relations*, 31 (1978): 29–48. A more qualified conclusion is reached in Richard J. Long, "The Relative Effects of Share Ownership vs. Control on Job Attitudes in an Employee-Owned Company," *Human Relations*, 31 (1978): 753–63, at 761–62. A regression analysis of data secured from a questionnaire administered to employees suggested a difference in the way that ownership and participation affect workers. Commitment appeared to be a function of ownership and to be unrelated to participation. Satisfaction and motivation appeared to be determined by participation in decision making and to be unrelated to ownership. See also J. Lawrence French and Joseph Rosenstein, "Employee Ownership, Work Attitudes, and Power Relationships," *Academy of Management Journal,* 27 (1984): 861–69; Richard J. Long, "Job Attitudes and Organizational Performance Under Employee Ownership," *Academy of Management Journal*, 23 (1980): 726–37.

on a salient feature of MC firms – namely, that those who make decisions and implement them will have a keen interest in the outcome. In addition, employee-oriented business enterprises of all types commonly stress ownership. By doing so they replicate a key feature of OC firms – namely, that the equity owners will display a special interest in the performance of the enterprise. These two features – participation and ownership – are, of course, the prime candidates for explaining why employee-oriented business enterprises sometimes outperform traditional firms. Consequently, so far as these enterprises are concerned, the separation of ownership and control poses a significant issue at level two.

Is the separation significant at level three for these business enterprises? In order to be so, there must be some practical possibility for desirable change. The empirical evidence cited in this subsection does not show that *all* existing MC and OC firms can or should become employee-oriented business enterprises. This chapter subscribes to no "mythical ideal" of the employee-owned or employee-managed firm. Still, the empirical evidence suggests that *some* existing MC and OC firms can give employees a greater role, and the controls on some statistical studies indicate that some long-surviving MC and OC firms would have performed better had they done so. Thus it is sometimes feasible and desirable for traditional MC and OC firms to revise their ownership/ control structures to create more employee ownership or participation or both. Furthermore, even if the transaction costs of change sometimes are high for existing firms, legal rules should hold them to a minimum, and in any event new business ventures can avoid such costs by selecting the best form of organization at the outset. This observation completes the argument that the separation of ownership and control is a significant issue at all three levels for all business corporations.

As a corollary, it is myopic to see the issue of the separation of ownership and control solely as a contest between traditional MC and OC firms. The myopia may spring partly from the fact that the literature on traditional MC and OC firms is at the present time fairly separate, and in fact generally appears in different journals, from the literature on employee-oriented firms. Whatever the cause, the nearsightedness is unjustified. Indeed, sometimes the best ownership/control structure is some variety of employee-oriented business enterprise.

Interim conclusions. One can distill three key points from this discussion, even if one uses efficiency – in a general and nontechnical sense as the production of desired effects with a minimum of effort and waste – as a sole criterion. First, despite the claims of some economists, the separation of ownership and control poses a significant issue at several levels. The issue is: In whose interests or behalf should corporations be run? Second, it is myopic to see the issue of separation solely as a contest between traditional MC and OC firms. Rather, sometimes the best ownership/control structure is some variety of employee-oriented business enterprise. Third, no single type of business enterprise is the best in all circumstances. A private-property economy should make room for all of the types discussed here, because for each type there are some circumstances in which it will be best.

If one uses the specific principle of utility and efficiency defended in Chapter 8, one can expand matters in the following way. Although some neoclassical economists overstate the efficiency of existing ownership/control structures,[42] no one claims that existing corporations are thoroughly inefficient, for otherwise they would not survive. As this section brings out, employee participation and ownership can be important in achieving an efficient ownership/control structure. More generally, employee and manager interests, in the form of preference-satisfaction, are a vital component in a well-run business enterprise. In re-

---

42 See, for example, Fama and Jensen, "Separation of Ownership and Control," and the comments in Oliver E. Williamson, "Organization Form, Residual Claimants, and Corporate Control," *Journal of Law & Economics*, 26 (1983): 351–66.

gard to analytical accounts of corporate practice, most traditional discussions of the separation of ownership and control pay attention mainly to the interests of shareholders and managers. Yet some sophisticated recent accounts – for example, that of Klein – emphasize the interests of such additional contractors as employees, lenders, suppliers, and distributors and the importance of such additional contractual terms as duration, rate of return, and risk of loss.[43] If, though, one takes seriously the conception underlying the principle of utility and efficiency, then one should cast the net even more widely to include others – such as consumers and noncontractors – whom corporations affect. Though this will often be difficult to do, it will sometimes be possible, and the possibility lends support to Berle and Means's comment that corporations should serve not only shareholders and managers but also "all society."[44]

Furthermore, the utility component of the principle of utility and efficiency often gives answers to practical questions that are different from, and sounder than, those supplied by the efficiency component. The general and nontechnical sense of efficiency will sometimes be too vague to be helpful. If, instead, one uses a Pareto conception of efficiency, often it will provide no useful guidance because in any complicated situation virtually every change will make *someone* worse off (§ 8.4). Kaldor-Hicks efficiency sidesteps this problem, but, since it requires only *hypothetical* compensation of losers by gainers (§ 8.4), using it could greatly diminish the preference-satisfaction of losers. Thus, some *actual* compensation is likely to be important – whether this is justified by the utility component or by a revised Kaldor-Hicks criterion that sometimes requires actual compensation.

Leveraged buyouts illustrate the point. The jury is still out on whether such buyouts generally advance efficiency in the long run or whether they merely shuffle financial assets. For

---

43 Klein, "The Modern Business Corporation: Bargaining Under Constraints."
44 Berle and Means, *The Modern Corporation and Private Property*, p. 356.

the sake of argument, however, assume that they usually do advance Kaldor-Hicks efficiency. Even so, the impact on preference-satisfaction varies widely. Preliminary figures indicate that investors average returns of 30 percent to 50 percent over two or three years.[45] Still, bondholders often suffer because the increased debt frequently diminishes the value of existing bonds.[46] Middle managers and other employees often suffer much more, for they may lose their jobs.[47] In such cases, the utility component of the principle of utility and efficiency would require some compensation for those who are adversely affected. For example, some profit from the buyout might be used for cash awards to employees or for retraining or relocating employees.

Yet the point is hardly confined to leveraged buyouts, for the utility component is apt to yield systematic guidance, if reliable information is available, on all issues affecting all constituents of a corporation. These issues include the legal rights and duties of directors and managers and of shareholders and bondholders; the treatment of such other participants as suppliers and distributors; methods for changing ownership/control structures, such as mergers, acquisitions, and buyouts; and many aspects of employees' ownership stake in, or control over, the corporation and its activities – for instance, profit sharing, opportunity to buy stock, unionization, wages, training, promotion, and a voice in the work process. These issues are so numerous and varied that no hope exists of treating them here, but the

---

45 See Bill Sing, "Players in LBO Game Often Hit Giant Jackpots," *Los Angeles Times,* Oct. 22, 1988, pt. IV, at 1, col. 3 (estimate of Martin Sikora). In less than two years, the stake of former Treasury secretary William E. Simon rose from $330,000 to $70 million in the Gibson Greetings leveraged buyout. Ibid. For less recent but more detailed discussion, see "Symposium on the Market for Corporate Control: The Scientific Evidence," *Journal of Financial Economics,* 11 (1983): 3–471.

46 See, for example, Eileen V. Quigley, "Big Bondholders Launch Revolt Against Nabisco," *Los Angeles Times,* Nov. 18, 1988, pt. IV, at 1, col. 5.

47 See, for example, Sing, "Players in LBO Game Often Hit Giant Jackpots," at 2, cols. 5, 6.

principle of utility and efficiency, given adequate empirical data, is pertinent to all of them.

12.3 TOWARD A COMPREHENSIVE VIEW OF OWNERSHIP AND CONTROL

The basic theory of property does not, however, end with the principle of utility and efficiency. It also contains a principle of desert based on labor and a principle of justice and equality. The first subsection sketches the impact of the latter two principles on ownership/control structures; the next subsection orchestrates all three principles together. As a whole, this section illustrates the attractiveness of a pluralist theory in dealing with practical issues.

The impact of labor-desert and justice and equality. The labor-desert principle bears in three major ways on ownership/control issues. First, the principle recognizes desert as one basis among others for an appropriate wage. Hence market considerations as played out under utility and efficiency should not be the sole determinant of wages. The labor-desert principle indicates some features of a defensible wage policy (§ 10.3). Yet it acknowledges that implementing such a policy can be difficult, for comparative assessments of desert claims based on labor are often difficult. Even so, such comparative appraisals are sometimes feasible, and in fact government agencies and large firms sometimes use variants of these appraisals to assess the relative worth of different tasks and to arrive at relative wages (§ 10.4).

Second, the labor-desert principle emphasizes that work is often a social activity that bears on the self-respect and self-esteem of employees. As a result, market considerations answering to utility and efficiency are not the sole criterion of ownership/control structures. Rather, in distributing the economic fruits of corporate enterprise, one must be careful not to slight the labor input and favor the capital input. Furthermore, one should give employees some control over the work process. In this context, the labor-desert principle is

not mainly an argument for employee ownership of productive resources or for an important role in making major
decisions on what to produce. It is instead mainly an argument for a significant employee voice in the day-to-day
ordering of the work process.

Third, the labor-desert principle sometimes supports limited property rights for workers in their jobs and in their
corporate employers. That principle recognizes various factors as pertinent to assessing which rights are appropriate.
The factors include effort, persistence, time spent, responsibility, and certain working conditions (§§ 10.2 and 10.5). If
these factors are present in the right way over a sufficiently
long time, they may justify *limited* property rights besides
those that the principle of utility and efficiency can justify –
with, of course, some accompanying responsibilities to
corporate employers. These factors involve a participation by
employees in the aims and interests of their employers, and
so bring moral reciprocity into play.

Recently, Singer has argued, with impressive erudition,
for legal property rights stemming from a "reliance interest"
held by employees and has applied his views to the issue of
plant closings.[48] The arguments differ importantly. His argument invokes much legal detail, and rests chiefly on forms of
"reliance" that exhibit a mutual dependence between employer and employee despite great differences in economic
power. The present argument calls upon a moral and political theory, turns on the underlying case for the labor-desert
principle and specifically on moral reciprocity rather than the
fact of mutual dependence, and covers much more than
plant closings. Consequently, though the present argument
cannot help itself to all of Singer's conclusions, many points
of detail in his argument can be mapped onto that sketched
here. The payoff is not that corporate employees have in-
violate moral rights to their jobs or moral ownership of the
corporation for which they work. It is rather that, in light of

---

48 Joseph William Singer, "The Reliance Interest in Property," *Stanford
Law Review*, 40 (1988): 611–751.

the labor-desert principle, they have some circumscribed moral property rights in their jobs and in the ongoing corporate enterprise, and that these moral rights are part of the case for corresponding legal rights.

As a result, it would be misleading to say that nonmanagerial employees, through voluntary bargains in the labor market, have acceptably relinquished control over the work process and their interest in how the corporation is run. Some economic writing of the nexus-of-contracts school regards employees as one group of participants and their labor contracts as one part of the nexus. This view is true enough so far as it goes. But it does not yield the stronger proposition that choosing to enter such contracts is acceptable – where a choice is "acceptable" only if it is practically possible to persist in an alternative choice. Alchian and Demsetz, for example, suggest that employees can terminate their labor contracts "as readily as can the employer."[49] This suggestion corrects the overemphasis by Coase on the power of the employer to direct the employee.[50] Yet it erases the gains by overreacting in the opposite direction. As the earlier discussion of property and power intimates (§ 7.6), the acceptability of contractual arrangements must be placed in the context of surrounding economic conditions. If there is full employment, and if employees can afford a short time out of work to secure another job, then any bargain they strike is apt to be acceptable (on their side). But if unemployment is high, and if they need wages to survive, then their side of the bargain is less likely to be acceptable. In the latter situation, it may not be practically possible to persist in alternative choices – for example, to quit or to strike for greater control over the work process. This situation raises thorny issues in the law and theory of contracts. The aim here is not to suggest that they have neat solutions. It is merely to block the facile

49 Armen A. Alchian and Harold Demsetz, "Production, Information Costs, and Economic Organization," *American Economic Review*, 62 (1972): 777–95, at 783.
50 R. H. Coase, "The Nature of the Firm," *Economica*, 4 (1937) (n.s.): 386–405, at 403–04.

objection that when nonmanagerial employees have not contracted for control over corporate work regimens, they have somehow acceptably relinquished any precontractual interest they may have had in them.

The scope and mode of employee participation are, of course, open questions. The principle of desert based on labor does not yield determinate answers valid for every employee and every corporation. Possible forms of participation include profit sharing and labor representation on the board of directors. Profit sharing may offer additional incentives to employees and so induce greater productivity. Nonetheless, to reason in this way is to bring in utility and efficiency. That suggests that profit sharing is not best defended on the labor-desert principle alone. Profit sharing also brings with it some responsibility for the performance of the enterprise. If high profits go partly to nonmanagerial employees, then losses may occasion, if not some modest liability, at least reduced wages. The wisdom of labor representation on the board of directors depends on the nature of industrial relations in the company itself, in the industry, and in the economy as a whole. If there is a great deal of friction between labor and management, labor representation may exacerbate the conflicts and impair productivity. If relations are good, labor representatives can supply a knowledge of the process of production that traditional managers might overlook or underemphasize and so enhance productivity. These variables are a good reminder that desert based on labor should not be the sole ingredient in designing the best form of labor participation.

The principle of justice and equality might at first seem to be irrelevant to ownership/control structure, but reflection suggests that it at least has a systemic bearing on corporate enterprise as a whole. The institution of property in any society is a complicated affair. Many factors bear on whether everyone has a minimum amount of property and whether inequalities undermine a fully human life. Hardly any corporation has the power to affect these factors so adversely as to violate the principle of justice and equality for very many people. Thus that principle is chiefly a systemwide constraint. For the most part it does not, in actual economies, apply to each corporation directly. Matters could have been otherwise. If a rather farfetched socialist economy carried out all business enterprise through a single huge corporation, the distinction between each corporation and corporate enterprise as a whole would collapse. In that case, direct application would make sense. But at least in actual private-property economies there are many corporations. Thus it is an important, though contingent, feature of these economies that the principle of justice and equality restricts mainly corporate enterprise as a whole rather than each corporation directly.

Corporations and the interests of all. It is time to bring the different principles of the basic theory together for the central issue of ownership and control in a private-property economy: In whose interests or behalf should corporations be run? The answer is that they should be run in the interests of all – shareholders, managers, employees, other contractors and participants, and the public at large.[51] This answer is not the vague inanity it will seem to some. But to make it precise one must distinguish between how the basic theory applies to corporate enterprise as a whole and how it applies to each corporation. The distinction does not rest on a confusion involving "all" and "each." One can accept that "All persons should keep their promises" entails and is entailed by "Each person should keep his or her promises," and that "All corporations should comply with the basic theory" entails and is entailed by "Each corporation should comply with the basic theory." The distinction relates instead to the implementation of a normative theory in a complex institutional framework. For example, the basic theory may justify regulating corporate enterprise as a whole in

51 In the case of multinational corporations, the "public at large" would include people from many countries, but for simplicity's sake one may assume here that only those within a country's borders are affected by its corporations.

350

certain ways, but it might prove impossible, difficult, too costly, or pointless to try to regulate each corporation in those ways. If so, it is prudent to investigate separately how the basic theory applies to each corporation and to corporate enterprise as a whole.

First: The level of each corporation. From § 12.2 it is clear that no unique ownership/control structure is the optimal structure, under the principle of utility and efficiency, in the case of each corporation. If the market were functioning quite badly, some major government overhaul of the market framework would be in order. But if the market in a private-property economy is functioning well, it will tend to correct departures from the principle of utility and efficiency. Inefficient corporations tend either to change or to go out of business. Thus there is little need to have the government enforce that principle in the case of each corporation, and attempting to do so is apt to be costly, difficult, or pointless. However, some government fine-tuning of the market may be in order. For example, suppose that evidence indicates that many MC firms are unproductive and that more leveraged buyouts converting them into OC firms would increase their productivity. Or suppose that evidence suggests that most hostile takeovers retard rather than promote the efficiency of the target corporations. If so, the government might adjust legal rules regarding buyouts and takeovers accordingly.

This hands-off conclusion for happily functioning markets is subject to one major qualification by the principle of utility and efficiency itself. Such markets do pretty well for shareholders and managers in MC firms and also for employees in employee-oriented firms. Their record is less clear not only for employees in MC firms but also for such participants as lenders, suppliers, and distributors. When it comes to the public at large, the record is sometimes unimpressive. And, of course, the interests of the various members of a corporation's constituency sometimes collide. Since the principle is concerned with the preference-satisfaction of *all* persons, it may justify some government regulation on behalf of constituents whose interests are slighted or ignored by an otherwise satisfactorily functioning market.

More substantial qualification comes from the labor-desert principle. As the previous subsection brings out, that principle bears on wages and control over the work process. Its bearing will sometimes justify government regulation of individual corporations that utility and efficiency do not. Thus, the government may require each corporation to pay a minimum wage. Again, if one reads "wage" more broadly to include all compensation, the government may require each corporation to include certain benefits, such as medical insurance, in its compensation package. By the same token, the labor-desert principle may justify government regulation of the work process in order to enhance employee participation. Under this principle all employees, not merely managerial employees, should have a significant voice in the corporation for which they work. Thus, even if the details of such regulations are left unsettled, and even if one agrees that justice and equality form mainly a systemwide constraint, desert based on labor supports a more thoroughgoing government intervention than currently exists in the United States.

Yet the labor-desert principle does not, at the level of each corporation, license a move from its employees to the public at large. The desert basis is the work of the employees in a given corporation. That is why they should have appropriate compensation and a voice in that corporation. The public at large does not work for that corporation. Hence it has no desert basis, cognizable under the labor-desert principle, for making the corporation serve its interests.

Second: The level of corporate enterprise as a whole. One may now turn to the system of corporate enterprise. At this level, the principle of utility and efficiency is the dominant standard. More precisely, corporate enterprise as a whole need satisfy only that principle, provided that it (1) operates within a system of property that largely satisfies the principle of justice and equality, (2) does not pervasively violate the labor-desert principle, and (3) does not, owing to its size and power, threaten to disrupt a justifiable system of property or a justifiable democratic political system. This criterion and its three-part proviso go beyond the ownership/control issue as usually understood, but they nevertheless pertain to the interests that corporations should serve. The criterion and proviso deserve a closer examination.

The guiding thought behind the independent clause of the criterion is that, other things being equal, corporate enterprise, like business enterprise generally, should promote utility and efficiency. There is much else in the world besides economic activity. But the chief point of such activity, when people do engage in it, is to maximize welfare. That need not be the same thing as maximizing, say, productivity or profits. It will, though, have a good deal to do with them, even if one needs to take other factors – for example, having meaningful work – into account in determining what maximizes welfare. It is in this sense that corporate enterprise as a whole should be run in the interests of all.

Nevertheless, the phrase "other things being equal," used at the beginning of the previous paragraph, signals that there are qualifications. One finds them in the proviso. Its first limb observes that the system of property must largely satisfy the principle of justice and equality. Perfect conformity would be too stringent a requirement. If justice and equality generally have priority over utility and efficiency in cases of conflict, substantial conformity is a defensible requirement. Suppose, however, that this limb of the proviso is not met. It does not follow that corporate enterprise must be run in some inefficient way. For efficient operation may have a neutral impact on justice and equality, or it may advance them. And even if some inefficient manner of operation would help a little, it may be far from the best way to advance justice and equality. Land reform or redistributive taxation, for example, might be better ways. However, if efficient operation would exacerbate existing departures from justice and equality, and if some less than efficient manner of operation would be a particularly good way of correcting those departures, then operating in that way may be required.

The next limb of the proviso holds that the system of corporate enterprise must not pervasively violate the labor-desert principle. Here pervasive violation means substantial disregard of desert based on labor in all or most sectors of the economy. It does not include, for example, absence of employee participation in a single industry. An example of pervasive violation lies in the long hours, harsh working conditions, and low wages of factory employees in the nineteenth century in Great Britain and the United States. Under the revised labor theory, the employees were entitled to a larger share of the fruits of the enterprise. It is highly likely that this state of affairs did not best promote utility, that is, individual preference-satisfaction for all. Even if factory owners reaped large material rewards, a much more numerous group of factory workers had to endure terrible conditions to earn a very modest wage. But suppose that this arrangement really did best promote utility by a small margin. Then the proviso forbids it. It does so because the labor-desert principle has the power to override competing considerations of utility, at least when the gains in utility are not substantially greater. And since the proviso refers to pervasive violation, the difficulties that sometimes beset the application of the labor-desert principle at the level of each corporation do not arise here.

The final limb of the proviso says that corporate enterprise as a whole must not, owing to its size and power, threaten to disrupt a justifiable system of property or a justifiable democratic political system. If it becomes possible to predict that the system of corporate enterprise will have a destructive impact on an institution of property and related areas of social and political life justified by the basic theory, then the basic theory requires modifying the corporate system to prevent this impact – even if modifying it would retard utility and efficiency. What sort of disruption or destructive impact is meant? In part it includes effects that can be described in terms of utility and efficiency, such as risky mutual interdependence of firms in certain areas (for example, banking) or loss of competitive efficiency (for example, price fixing or some horizontal mergers). But some effects are not easily so described without remainder. An example relating to the social and political consequences of large corporations having a substantial share of economic power would be the effects of corporate lobbying or campaign spending. Concern over the growing size and concentration of corporate enterprise is, indeed, a subordinate theme in Berle and Means's study. They found that, in the case of nonfinancial corporations, the 200 largest owned 49.2 percent of all assets owned by such corporations as of January 1, 1930.[52] More recent figures on aggregate concentration show a different, but still potentially worrisome, picture.[53] It requires both sound thinking and solid empirical information to decide whether, and if so what, response this last part of the proviso demands in any given institution of property and system of corporate enterprise.

If this application of the basic theory, at the levels of each corporation and corporate enterprise as a whole, is cogent, it remains to say something about the modes and mechanisms by which the requisite changes could be introduced. Possible modes include constitutional mandate, legislative requirement, judicially imposed requirement, independent action by labor or management, and voluntary agreement between labor and management. A constitutional amendment seems out of place. But most likely some combination of the other modes would be fruitful. Possible mechanisms include labor representation on the board of directors, use of shop stewards, use of a grievance process, consultation between labor and management, requests by management of labor and vice versa, adoption of models used in, say, some Japanese and German corporations, and instituting correlative duties of loyalty on the part of employees. This list, like the first, is not

52 Berle and Means, *The Modern Corporation and Private Property*, p. 28.
53 See, for example, Leonard W. Weiss, "The Extent and Effects of Aggregate Concentration," *Journal of Law & Economics*, 26 (1983): 429–55.

exhaustive. Once again, some combination is apt to be fruitful.

This application of the basic theory will provoke objections. Most of these are left for another day. But it is hard to ignore the objection that potential conflict exists in applying the three principles within and between the two levels. The most likely conflict is between promoting utility and efficiency for each corporation and for corporate enterprise as a whole and satisfying the labor-desert principle for each corporation. For it may be said that substantial worker control and attention to employee interests in each corporation will lower productivity in each corporation. This lowering will in turn impair utility and efficiency at the level of corporate enterprise as a whole.

The reply is twofold. First, the conflict may be more apparent than genuine. Attention to employee interests is apt to result in happier, better motivated employees. It will, therefore, likely increase productivity and advance utility and efficiency. Specifically, even if a positive correlation exists between corporate profits and utility, how those profits are distributed affects the utility calculation. It seems plausible that channeling some profits to employees, either outright or in the form of better working conditions, will increase not only the individual utilities of these employees but also the aggregate utility of everyone connected with the corporation. Amazingly, despite the emphasis by some thinkers that corporations are the nexus of many contracts, much economic writing about ownership and control proceeds as if only the interests of shareholders and managers matter. Thus, if the labor-desert principle is applied as indicated to each corporation, it bids fair to increase the utility and efficiency of corporate enterprise as a whole.

Second, even if this were not so, the labor-desert principle should have priority in this situation, unless giving it priority would create a great shortfall in utility and efficiency. The reason is that the desert-based entitlements generated by the revised labor theory are quite powerful. Thus they should override competing considerations of utility whenever the margin of shortfall is small. Matters would be different if the margin were great. Still, if the argument of the previous paragraph is sound, the probability of a great margin is even lower than the probability of a genuine conflict.

12.4 STANDARDS OF CORPORATE BEHAVIOR

The central issue here is: Given that, in a private-property economy, the legal interests of shareholders and bondholders are forms of property rights, and given that corporate employees can have at least some moral property rights in their jobs or corporate employers, what standards of corporate behavior are in order? The standards relate to the ends of corporate activity and the means of achieving them. The traditional problem of corporate standards or responsibility breaks down into what corporations *may* do and what they *ought* to do. This chapter addresses mainly the former.

The account in § 12.3, if sound, sheds light on both ends and means. It holds that the overarching end is to operate in the interests of all. This end casts doubt on the idea that the sole end of corporate activity should be that of making the highest possible profits. Even at the level of corporate enterprise as a whole, maximizing profits is not likely to be identical with satisfying the principle of utility and efficiency qualified by the three-part proviso. And at the level of each corporation, the labor-desert principle implies that it should be run partly in the interests of employees. Considerations at both levels also affect means. In particular, the labor-desert principle requires that employees have a significant voice in running the corporation for which they work. This requirement inhibits ruthless treatment of employees, though other, more general principles may also come into play here. All the same, previous sections fall short of completely resolving the issue of corporate standards. They do not touch on such questions as whether each corporation should pay employees more than their marginal product, show compassion for them when closing a plant, make gifts to charity, or avoid the imposition of harmful externalities to an extent greater than required by law.

This section aims to resolve the central issue at least a bit more completely. It first considers what one can intelligibly require of corporations, then addresses two extreme positions on corporate standards, and finally defends an intermediate position. The proposed standards apply at the level of each corporation.

Intelligibility. To some it may seem easy to have *intelligible* standards. The difficult part is not *saying,* but *justifying,* that a corporation may or ought to do something – for example, pursue some objective besides maximum profits. If "ought" implies "can," then it makes no sense to say that a corporation ought to observe certain standards if it cannot do so. And verbs such as "observe," "obey," and "conform to" import some mental element. So one must reject any anthropomorphic assumption that a corporation is an entity that has a mental life. To say that a corporation should observe or obey or conform to certain standards is an elliptical way of saying that those who own or manage the corporation should do so, which makes perfect sense.

Yet the matter of intelligible standards is a little subtler than these brief comments indicate. Some writers seem to hold that a corporation is an artificial system designed by its owners for a certain goal. If the goal is, say, to maximize profits, then it makes no sense to require the corporation to do something else. In that case it would no longer be the same corporation. Even within an accepted goal, it is not possible to require a corporation to do everything that a person could be required to do. Consider Victor A. Thompson's remarks on compassion and modern organizations: "There is not only no compassion; there is no way that compassion can be included. Compassion cannot be prescribed. The idea of a designed role of 'administrator of compassion' is ludicrous."[54]

This line of argument for severely constricting the range of intelligible standards does not hold water. First, contemporary corporations are not merely voluntary associations but legal and social creations. As such, the incorporators do not have the only voice in deciding which goals the corporation will pursue and which restrictions it must observe. Thus a corporation does not lose its identity by having additional goals prescribed or constraints placed on existing goals – provided, of course, that the new goals and constraints do not depart too greatly from what was there before.

Second, it is important not to confuse affective and objective aspects of behavior. A corporation, unlike a person, cannot have emotions like compassion or sympathy. Nor can it exhibit the virtue or character trait of compassion or sympathy. But it does not follow that it is unintelligible to instruct corporate managers to act in a way that satisfies whatever objective criteria exist for compassionate or sympathetic action. Suppose that, contrary to the labor-desert argument of § 12.3, corporations have an unlimited right to close manufacturing plants. If so, in a well-known case the shareholders of the United States Steel Corporation might have instructed the directors not to invoke that right and instead to act compassionately. The directors might have displayed compassion by keeping the plant open or by selling it to the steelworkers.[55]

All the same, one should not ignore a spark of sound sense present in this line of argument. The sensible point is that corporations, like other modern organizations, are specialized creations. They typically answer to a narrower range of goals and values than do persons. And persons occupying a

---

54 Victor A. Thompson, *Without Sympathy or Enthusiasm: The Problem of Administrative Compassion* (University, Ala.: University of Alabama Press, 1975), p. 13.
55 See *Local 1330, United Steel Workers of America v. United States Steel Corp.*, 631 F.2d 1264 (6th Cir. 1980).

corporate role typically act on different criteria from those that they do when divorced from the role. These special features seldom bear on the intelligibility of corporate standards of behavior, but they frequently bear on the practicability and justifiability of those standards. How strong that bearing ought to be will occupy the balance of this section. Here it is enough to point out that it is intelligible to suggest that corporations and corporate employees should have different goals and act on different criteria from those that currently govern them.

Two extreme positions. At the start, one should rule out two extreme positions on corporate standards. One is that the sole end of each corporation should be to maximize profits and the only defensible means are those that promote that end. Arguments for this position commonly urge that other standards are not economically viable or that they require managers to act without the legitimacy of universal consent or a political franchise.[56]

Both arguments are ineffective. In regard to economic viability, many economists[57] have doubted that corporations in fact try to maximize profits, and yet corporations survive. Plainly they are not indifferent to profits. But neither are they indifferent to such ends as maximizing or at least increasing sales, obtaining an acceptable return on capital, increasing dividends, and so on. Let it be granted that if standards necessitated higher costs to the corporation, its managers would try to pass on some or all of the costs to

---

56 See, for example, Henry G. Manne, "Should Corporations Assume More Social Responsibilities?," in M. Bruce Johnson, ed., *The Attack on Corporate America: The Corporate Issues Sourcebook* (New York: McGraw-Hill, 1978), pp. 3–8; Donald L. Martin, "Do Corporations Have No Inherent Rights, Only Government-Given Privileges?," in ibid., pp. 151–57.

57 See, for example, John Kenneth Galbraith, *The New Industrial State*, 3d ed. (Boston: Houghton-Mifflin, 1978). The first edition is discussed by Robert M. Solow, "The New Industrial State *or* Son of Affluence," *Public Interest*, 9 (1967): 100–08. For Galbraith's reply and Solow's rejoinder, see ibid., pp. 109–18, 118–19, respectively.

others – as higher prices, lower wages, lower dividends, and so on. Still, so long as the increased costs are not too high, the corporation might well survive anyway.

The argument from legitimacy is astonishing. Surely universal consent is lacking for the proposition that the sole corporate aim should be maximum profits. And surely, except in a libertarian state, a political franchise does not support that proposition. Even with such support, if libertarianism is taken seriously, then those who own and manage the corporation should still be free to choose whatever end they wish – and they might not choose profit maximization. Now the claim is not that the legitimation of corporate ends and means is a meaningless issue. On the contrary, such legitimation must come, at least in part, from an underlying theory of property. The theory advanced in this book, however, does not legitimate profit maximization as the sole standard. And it is implausible that such legitimating moves as universal consent or political franchise would support that standard.

The other extreme position is that each corporation should be run solely in the public interest. In a private-property economy, this position is unattractive, for two reasons at least. First, it is impractical to instruct corporate managers to act solely in the public interest. For it will ordinarily be terribly hard for them to tell what that would involve in all or most situations. They will be much more expert on the interests of the corporation. Consider J. S. Mill. He subscribed to the principle of utility. But he maintained that ordinarily one could best promote utility by taking account of the interests of persons close to oneself in time and space, rather than trying to follow out the furthest temporal and geographical consequences of one's actions.[58]

Second, this extreme position clashes with part of the point of having rights of private property – namely, that one

---

58 J. S. Mill, *Utilitarianism*, ed. Samuel Gorovitz (Indianapolis and New York: Bobbs-Merrill, 1971), pp. 25–26. See also Larry Alexander, "Pursuing the Good – Indirectly," *Ethics*, 95 (1985): 315–32.

does not always and everywhere have a duty of using one's property in the public interest. This feature comes to the fore when private property shelters the control, privacy, and individuality of each person. It has lesser, but not imaginary, force in the case of private ownership of corporations. Warrant exists for abjuring a system of private-property rights that are so strong that they often retard the public interest. The system defended in this book does not allow for the creation of such rights. This does not mean that, at the level of each corporation, corporate actions must always comport with the public interest. Still, private property must be restricted enough so that it is not inimical to the public interest at the level of corporate enterprise as a whole.

An intermediate position. If the foregoing arguments are correct, then it is intelligible and sensible to have corporate standards somewhere in between the extreme positions just rejected. But where? This question can receive a partial answer through modifying a recent tentative proposal by the American Law Institute (ALI). The proposal holds that the basic objective of the business corporation should be to pursue corporate profit and shareholder gain with certain exceptions. The exceptions are that the corporation has a duty to act within the boundaries of law, a permission to "take into account ethical considerations that are reasonably regarded as appropriate to the responsible conduct of business," and a permission to "devote a reasonable amount of resources to public welfare, humanitarian, educational, and philanthropic purposes."[59] The ALI proposal deals else-

---

59 American Law Institute, *Principles of Corporate Governance: Analysis and Recommendations* § 2.01, at p. 25 (Philadelphia: American Law Institute, 1984) (Tentative Draft No. 2, April 13, 1984).
   A comment to this section seems to suggest that general acceptance is the prime determinant of whether an ethical consideration is "reasonably regarded" as appropriate to business:

   One useful indicator of whether account may properly be taken of a given ethical consideration in a given case is whether doing so would be likely to violate the fair expectations of the corporation's shareholders taken as a group. This in turn is likely to depend on

where with possible tension between corporate profit and shareholder gain. The exceptions that the proposal creates reflect a belief that moral and social considerations can qualify pursuit of the basic economic objective.

A virtue of the ALI proposal is that it limits severe losses that might stem from idiosyncratic judgments. Its authors seem to suppose that moral beliefs, as they relate to business enterprise, are generally but not universally concordant. In a diverse society, it may thus appear essential to restrict officers or controlling shareholders who hold moral views that are out of step with those of everyone else. They must not act so as to harm the financial interests of (other) shareholders. This kind of restriction will seem eminently sensible to some moral skeptics. If there is no objective or universally valid moral system, then those who mistakenly subscribe to such a system should be barred from harming the financial interests of others.

> whether the consideration reflects a principle that would be widely recognized as appropriate to the conduct of business by a significant portion of the community. In this connection it should be recognized that new principles may emerge over time, and a corporate official should therefore be permitted to take into account emerging ethical principles, reasonably regarded as relevant to the conduct of business, that have significant support although less-than-universal acceptance.

Ibid., p. 37.

It is difficult to interpret the relation of this comment to § 2.01 itself. On the one hand, the current version of § 2.01 has substituted "reasonably regarded" for the phrase "generally recognized" that was used in the previous version. See American Law Institute, *Principles of Corporate Governance and Structure: Restatement and Recommendations* § 2.01, at p. 17 (Philadelphia: American Law Institute, 1982) (Tentative Draft No. 1, April 1, 1982). On the other hand, the comment to the current version seems to bring in general recognition, albeit in a qualified way, by the back door. This interpretation is reinforced by Illustrations 13 and 20 in Tentative Draft No. 2 (pp. 38–39, 44–45). The reference in the comment to "fair expectations" is ambiguous between institutionally legitimate and morally legitimate expectations as distinguished in § 8.7 of this book, but more likely it means the former. Accordingly, the examination in the text will treat wide or general recognition as extremely important though not decisive.

Upon examination, however, the ALI proposal turns out to be too closely tied to prevailing standards of right and wrong as they relate to the conduct of business. This shortcoming is the vice of its virtue. For example, consider a person who gains a controlling interest in a corporation in Virginia in 1840. The corporation employs – indeed, owns – slaves to work its coal mines.[60] The person who now has a controlling interest intends, on moral grounds, to emancipate the slaves and hire them or other people at prevailing market rates. Doing so would have a negative effect on the short-run and long-run profit picture of the corporation. It would also violate the ALI proposal. Though even in that place and time some moral controversy existed regarding slavery, no "ethical consideration" requiring or even permitting emancipation would have been "reasonably regarded as appropriate to the responsible conduct of business."

As another example, consider a controlling shareholder of a manufacturing corporation in Massachusetts in 1890. The corporation employs both adults and children. They work twelve to fourteen hours per day six days a week for very low wages. The controlling shareholder intends, on moral grounds, to discharge children under sixteen years of age, and to pay adults a much higher wage for working eight to ten hours per day five days a week. He believes that this would be a fair wage and would significantly increase the family income of employees (despite the fact that young children would no longer be working). Still, to do so would depress profits in both the short and the long run. It would also run afoul of the ALI proposal. Under the standards of that place and time, no moral principle on which the controlling shareholder intends to act would have been generally recognized either as "appropriate to the responsible con-

60 Various types of firms, including corporations, often leased and sometimes owned slaves to do industrial work. See Ronald L. Lewis, *Coal, Iron, and Slaves: Industrial Slavery in Maryland and Virginia, 1715–1865* (Westport, Conn.: Greenwood Press, 1979), pp. 20–35, 46, 50–51, 65–74.

duct of business" or as involving a "reasonable amount of resources" for "humanitarian" purposes. These examples show that an appropriate account of corporate standards must not be tied so closely as is the ALI proposal to prevailing standards of right and wrong.

Examples like these may move some people but still leave doubt on whether they answer the moral skeptic. To allay doubt it is important to differentiate varieties of moral skepticism. One variety holds that moral judgments either are meaningless or only express the subjective beliefs or attitudes of the speakers. This book has not dealt with this kind of moral skepticism. However, this kind of skeptic cannot endorse the ALI proposal over any alternative. For he cannot judge that those who hold idiosyncratic moral views should be barred from acting on them and thus doing financial harm to others. The word "should" here can only mean "morally should." If the skeptic holds that moral judgments are meaningless, then so is this moral judgment. If he holds that moral judgments only express the subjective beliefs or attitudes of the speaker, then he must say that no moral disagreement exists between him and someone who criticizes the ALI proposal, since each person is just expressing his or her own beliefs or attitudes and would acknowledge that the other is accurately expressing different beliefs or attitudes. But in fact there is moral disagreement between him and his opponent. The only refuge of this skeptic is to repudiate, as moral views, the ALI proposal and all others.

A different variety of moral skepticism claims that one should not apply a moral judgment to corporate affairs unless it is widely accepted. This kind of moral skeptic could say that the ALI proposal makes sense. If someone makes a moral judgment that is not generally recognized as pertinent to business, then its very idiosyncrasy is strong evidence that it should not be accepted. Only if the later history of moral opinion sides with an originally idiosyncratic moral judgment is the evidence overcome. Such a change actually occurred in the United States regarding slavery, child labor, and wage and hour legislation. No such change has yet occurred here on whether, say, it is morally permissible for a meat-packing corporation to slaughter animals for food.

But this kind of moral skeptic confuses moral argument with empirical evidence. Evidence that people generally subscribe to a particular moral judgment does not show it to be true or well founded. Nor is such evidence in itself a good reason to subscribe to that judgment. One should not, moreover, assimilate this variety of moral skepticism to intuitionism. Intuitionism gives substantial weight to a person's considered moral judgments or opinions or convictions ("intuitions"). And if intuitionism does so for any given person, it seems natural to extend this weight to moral judgments that society will recognize and enforce by requiring that most people have the same moral judgment or opinion or conviction on a particular matter. Yet any plausible version of intuitionism must subject the raw data to examination. It is not simply a matter of cataloguing one's intuitions or taking a poll. For this reason careful intuitionists have insisted on some method for excluding intuitions apt to be based on bias, prejudice, or faulty empirical information. One such method might employ intuitions about which one felt most secure to test others, and use historical and social research to alert oneself to bias, prejudice, or faulty empirical information. Again, one might use the method of wide reflective equilibrium discussed in § 11.3. The point is not that there exists a foolproof intuitionist methodology for sifting moral judgments. It is that one cannot make a swift transition from the general recognition of a moral judgment to its suitability as a corporate standard. Nor can one use its lack of general recognition as an adequate basis for ruling out its use by corporate decision makers.

Other varieties of moral skepticism may merit consideration, but if the basic theory of property makes sense, a more direct response is possible. The basic theory supports the examples given above. For example, Chapter 10 gives an account of the role of labor in acquiring property rights. It provides, in the contemporary context, the beginnings of an account of fair wages and appropriate treatment of employees, which this chapter develops further. This account, in conjunction with the treatment of body rights and autonomy in Chapter 3, is hardly likely to justify slavery. The basic theory thus offers a surrounding moral framework that endorses the conclusions reached in the examples. It therefore cuts against the ALI proposal.

In fact, the basic theory yields systematic, though incomplete, guidance for standards of corporate behavior in a private-property economy. The guidance is incomplete because many moral restrictions on corporate behavior have nothing to do with the theory of property. They stem from other parts of morality. Nevertheless, the principle of desert based on labor has a direct impact at the level of each corporation. That principle constrains a corporation in its treatment of employees – and, perhaps, of other workers with whom it deals, such as some customers, suppliers, and independent contractors. If this line of argument is correct, then certain treatment of employees may be morally defensible, perhaps sometimes morally required, even if it would be too generous under the ALI proposal.

For reasons similar to those given in § 12.3, the principle of justice and equality is unlikely to furnish direct guidance at the level of each corporation. But it does not follow that this principle will be without impact. If current corporate practices have systemic results that run counter to the principle, then one should try to devise rules that avoid these results and secure results more nearly in line with it. If the effort is successful, the impact of the new rules will be mainly at the level of corporate enterprise as a whole. Yet it is hard to see how successful rules could be possible without their issuing some commands and prohibitions to individual corporations. If so, then the rules will have at least an indirect impact at the level of each corporation.

One might wonder whether the standards discussed in this section would be any different if one were talking about individual persons rather than corporations. Some differences stand out. First, very few persons own as much productive property as do many corporations. Corporations are significant in part because socioeconomic consequences follow when those with large productive assets hire others to use them. Second, even in unusual cases where a person owns a great deal of productive property, there may be a unity of ownership and control. If § 12.2 is right, then the separation of ownership and control, which characterizes many corporations, is important. If so, then the principles developed in §§ 12.2–12.3 carry over to the issue of corporate standards. The principles for individual persons *might* be different. Nevertheless, the present section does not claim that the standards for corporations and individuals *must* be different.

12.5 OWNERSHIP, CONTROL, AND CORPORATE STANDARDS IN A REGIME OF PUBLIC OWNERSHIP

The analysis up to this point has dealt only with corporations in private-property economies. Should the analysis differ for economies in which most productive property is publicly owned? This section answers that it should be essentially the same. For property arrangements must still satisfy the basic theory. If so, business enterprise in general must operate in the interests of all. And to make determinate the requisite mode of operation, one must still distinguish between the level of corporate enterprise as a whole and the level of each corporation. Therefore, if the argument of the chapter thus far is correct, it should apply to regimes of public ownership – that is, to socialist economies – even though the application need not be identical to its application in private-property economies.

To test this thought it is necessary to expose it to objections from various socialist perspectives. Answering the objections suggests some differences in detail regarding the application of the argument in the two regimes.

A concern only under capitalism? Some socialists may object that the separation of ownership and control is a serious concern only in a private-property economy. It is a superficial concern in a socialist economy, for by definition socialist corporations are owned by and operated in the interests of all.

Reflection suggests, however, that one cannot eliminate the concern at the drop of a definition. For one thing, defining the term "socialist corporation" does not guarantee that it applies to anything in reality. For another, it is vague to say "in the interests of all." Until one specifies what that means, one has not avoided the concern posed by the separation of ownership and control. Section 12.3 takes that concern seriously and gives an account of the interests of all in this context. A socialist thinker must do the same. Finally, even if all persons in a socialist economy "own" each corporation, and even if the aim is to operate each corporation in their interests, it does not follow that all persons do, or could, control each corporation. That would be chaos. On the contrary, specialist managers must make key decisions and supervise operations. Of course, socialist corporations will not be quite like their capitalist, or even modified capitalist, counterparts. With the former, central planning agencies and labor representatives are likely to constrain managerial options more fully than (or at least differently from) in other economies. Only under corporate anarchism would everyone try to run everything – with the likely result that no one would succeed in running anything. And even if it were possible for all persons to control each corporation, the problem would remain of ensuring that managers operate the corporation in the interests of its intended beneficiaries.

Marx's objection. It may be objected that in Marx's vision of a socialist society, the separation of ownership and control will be unworthy of concern because of changes in human beings. Production under capitalism involves "alienation." It distorts human nature ("species being") and the nature of

369

work. Production under socialism does not involve alienation. It realigns human beings with their species being and
allows work to be truly liberated and expressive of human
nature. These themes from the *Economic and Philosophic Manuscripts of 1844* must be joined to the prescient discussion of
stock companies and cooperatives in the third volume of
Capital.[61] There Marx identifies what writers today call the
separation of ownership and control. He observes that it is a
specific feature of a "money-capitalism" in which the
shareholders have no managerial role. He seems to hold that
this form of capitalism involves increased alienation. This
alienation can be eliminated only through the growth of
cooperative business enterprises. Cooperatives are part of a
mature socialist economy in which "social property" replaces
private property, and alienation vanishes.

This objection is unconvincing, for at least three reasons.
First, as argued in § 7.3, serious difficulties afflict Marx's
account of alienation, species being, and the transition from
capitalism to socialism. Second, Marx's discussion of business enterprise under socialism is extremely vague. As a
result, it is difficult to say what business organizations would
be like. Hence it is also difficult to say that they would pose
no problem of separating ownership from control.

Third, there is a deep ambiguity in Marx's treatment of
stock companies. It can best be brought out in connection
with Clark's perceptive discussion of the "four stages of
capitalism."[62] Clark's four somewhat overlapping stages are
those of the entrepreneur, the professional business manager, the portfolio manager, and the savings planner. Each
shift from one stage to the next is marked by two features.
These are an increased division of labor and a wider
participation in the fruits of business enterprise. Each stage

61 See the chapter entitled "The Role of Credit in Capitalist Production"
   in Marx, *Capital*, vol. 3, pp. 435–41, and the helpful discussion in
   Shlomo Avineri, *The Social and Political Thought of Karl Marx* (Cambridge: Cambridge University Press, 1968), pp. 174–84.
62 Robert Charles Clark, "The Four Stages of Capitalism: Reflections on
   Investment Management Treatises," *Harvard Law Review*, 94 (1981):
   561–82, at 562–75.

after the first separates off a distinct aspect of capital mobilization. It also witnesses the emergence of a new kind of professional to deal with that aspect. The entrepreneurial stage (mainly the nineteenth century) involves the unity of ownership and control. The stage of the professional business manager (early decades of the twentieth century) involves their separation. The stage of the portfolio manager (from the mid-1960s) divides ownership into capital supply and investment. The investment aspect is handled by a professional. Finally, the stage of the savings planner (now in its infancy) further divides capital supply into the holding of a beneficial claim and the decision to save. Savings decisions are made by a professional. The characteristic business institutions of the stages are, respectively, the closely held corporation, the large publicly held corporation, the institutional investor (such as banks, savings institutions, insurance companies, pension plans, and investment companies), and the savings planner (such as the administrator of a corporate pension plan). If a "capitalist" is a person who has a direct or indirect claim on the fruits of business enterprise, then in each stage capitalists have grown more numerous. The term includes – in the fourth stage, for example – all participants in employee benefit plans. Nonetheless, a decreased sharing in power accompanies this wider sharing in benefits. And the wider sharing does not mean that income or wealth is distributed more equally.

The ambiguity in Marx turns on whether the development of capitalism increases or decreases "alienation" and how this development bears on the emergence of socialism. If it *increases* alienation, then later stages do not undermine Marx's objections to alienation under capitalism, but they may make the birth of socialism more mysterious. The following argument can be made for reading Marx in this way. Plainly, Marx thinks that alienation exists in what Clark calls the first stage of capitalism.[63] Less plainly, Marx seems

63 See Karl Marx, *Economic and Philosophic Manuscripts of 1844*, ed. Dirk J. Struik (New York: International Publishers, 1964), especially pp. 106–19, 128–31.

to think that alienation increases in what Clark calls the second stage.[64] For capitalists lose active control of their property, and become mere suppliers of investment funds on which they receive interest. If alienation does increase in the second stage, and if Marx understands alienation as a set of objective relations stemming from production rather than a set of feelings (§ 7.3), one might argue that alienation would increase again in the third and yet again in the fourth stages. Thus although more sophisticated forms of capitalism may increase the number of "capitalists" in Clark's sense, alienation would actually rise rather than decline. Since alienation is a bad thing, the last stage of capitalism, whatever it is, is worse than the first. If, however, one subscribes to this argument, it is less clear than ever how socialism grows out of capitalism.

But one might read Marx differently. It may be that, given some additional assumptions, alienation *decreases* with the progress of capitalism. The argument goes like this. In each new stage, property rights in business enterprise become more dispersed. In the fourth stage especially, capitalists in Clark's sense become quite numerous. Suppose that one also assumes that virtually everyone eventually becomes a capitalist in this sense, that income and wealth are more equally distributed, and that labor gains significant representation

---

64 "Profit thus appears . . . as a mere appropriation of the surplus-labour of others, arising from the conversion of means of production into capital, i.e., from their alienation vis-à-vis the actual producer, from their antithesis as another's property to every individual actually at work in production, from manager down to the last day-labourer. In stock companies the function is divorced from capital ownership, hence also labour is entirely divorced from ownership of means of production and surplus-labour. This result of the ultimate development of capitalist production is a necessary transitional phase towards the reconversion of capital into the property of producers. . . ." Marx, *Capital*, vol. 3, p. 437. Avineri's interpretation is that "[t]he separation of ownership from control and management must also be viewed as the climax of alienation. Not only is the worker alienated from his labour; even the capitalist is alienated, in the more sophisticated form of capitalist society, from his capital." Avineri, *The Social and Political Thought of Karl Marx*, p. 179.

on boards of directors. Then the process seems akin to the growth of what Marx calls "cooperatives." And the end result seems akin to socialism. Since socialism is supposed to reduce or eliminate alienation, so will a highly developed capitalism. Yet if this is true, *one* path to an economic system close to, if not identical with, socialism becomes clearer, but the trenchancy of Marx's objections to capitalism declines.

Skepticism may greet this latter argument, for two reasons. One is that fissioning the functions of ownership seems unlikely to be what Marx means by socialism. Another is that what capitalists receive seems tied to capital rather than to labor. Surely Marx insists that mature communism ensures that the worker will receive full recompense for his labor rather than allowing the capitalist to intercept its "surplus value."[65]

Though the skeptic has a point, there are opposing considerations. First, if the highly developed capitalism just described is not akin to socialism and does not reduce alienation, nettlesome questions arise for Marx. In that case it is unclear what he means by socialism, how it reduces or eliminates alienation, and even why alienation is obnoxious. Second, one might respond that in this highly developed capitalism, the return actually is tied to labor and not to capital, as Marx uses that term. The tie comes from the dispersion of interests in business enterprise, the erosion of inequalities of income and wealth, and the existence of substantial labor representation. These two opposing considerations do not destroy the skepticism, but they render it less appealing.

"Feasible socialism." Some may wish to recast the objection about ownership and control in terms of some contemporary version of socialism. A plausible candidate is what Nove calls

65 However, Karl Marx, *Critique of the Gotha Programme*, ed. C. P. Dutt (New York: International Publishers, 1938), pp. 7–8, apparently allows that, in an initial form of socialism, society appropriates the surplus value.

"feasible socialism."[66] By "feasible" he means a state of affairs that could exist in some part of the developed world within, say, the next half century, without having to make farfetched assumptions about society, human beings, or economic affairs. A "feasible socialism" must, accordingly, reject assumptions that neither scarcity nor the state will exist, that all citizens can meaningfully run the state, and that there will be no division of labor. Instead, Nove means to take human beings and the world largely as they are. He also supposes that there will be a multi-party democracy, with periodic elections to a parliament.

This "feasible socialism" allows five types of business enterprise: centralized state corporations, socialized enterprises, cooperative enterprises, small-scale private enterprises, and individuals. The first three types qualify as "corporations" in a broad sense. Centralized state corporations exist mainly in areas, such as electrical power and steel production, where vast resources are required and a monopoly might be helpful. Socialized enterprises are on a somewhat smaller scale; the means of production do not belong to the workers; the state has residual responsibility for operating losses. Cooperative enterprises, in contrast, are owned by the workers in common. The fourth type – small-scale private enterprises – are somewhat like closely held corporations but are more like individual proprietorships. The owners of such enterprises, each of which employs only a few people, also work in them and have no income that comes simply from the ownership of capital or land. Individuals working alone are the last type; examples would be freelance journalists, plumbers, and artists. "Feasible socialism" includes a high degree of worker self-management, accepts both a horizontal and a vertical division of labor, and severely restricts inequalities of income and wealth.

The question here is not whether Nove's socialism is the

66 See especially Part 5, entitled "Feasible Socialism?," in Alec Nove, *The Economics of Feasible Socialism* (London and Boston: G. Allen & Unwin, 1983), pp. 197–230.

most desirable economic system, but whether it avoids concern about the separation of ownership and control. The answer is that it reduces, but does not avoid, this concern. Nove does not address the question, at least in these terms, but it seems likely that he would agree with the answer. His "feasible socialism" has features that reduce the concern. Among them are worker self-management, restriction of economic inequalities, and prohibition of nonworking capitalists. Indeed, Nove's socialism might be seen as *one* way of articulating what it means to operate business enterprise in the interests of all.

Nevertheless, "feasible socialism" does not entirely avoid concern about the separation of ownership and control, or satisfactorily answer the underlying question of in whose interests corporations are to be run. Nove supposes that most types of economic enterprise will have a vertical division of labor. That is, they will have a hierarchical structure in which some persons set production goals and monitor the performance of others. Some such structure is necessary because the enterprise must operate efficiently and because many will not desire, or be well suited, to manage. Worker self-management will forestall some of the disagreeable features of hierarchical business organizations, but it cannot eliminate them all. Particularly in centralized state corporations and socialized enterprises, many employees are apt to feel that they have insufficient control. Thus, even if they, as part of the public, are regarded as owners, there remains some divorce between ownership and control. So, too, there remains a question about whether corporate operations will adequately reflect their interests.

The situation is more complicated in the case of cooperatives. They may be less likely to rely heavily on a vertical division of labor. If so, they may sidestep some of the difficulties that arise for centralized state corporations and socialized enterprises. Still, cooperatives may encounter a new difficulty. Nove is silent on whether they, like corporations in a private-property economy, have limited liability. If they do not, that will dampen worker enthusiasm for putting up assets for that type of business enterprise. For workers would stand to lose not only their investment but also whatever other assets they have. Enthusiasm is likely to be especially weak if deficiency judgments against cooperatives are not dischargeable in workers' personal bankruptcy proceedings. This would allow judgments against workers to be kept open and satisfied out of future earnings.

If corporations have limited liability, a different problem arises. Suppliers of capital, such as large banks, may be unwilling to invest in a cooperative enterprise where the workers put up only a tiny fraction of the capital and seek to borrow the rest. A parallel point about the rarity, in a private-property economy, of certain corporations is made by Jensen and Meckling.[67] These are large corporations owned by individual entrepreneurs who supply a small part of the capital and borrow the rest; they receive, nonetheless, all of the profits. Such corporations are rare because of undesirable incentive effects, high monitoring costs, and high costs of bankruptcy. To return to Nove's cooperatives, notice that it will not help if large banks and other suppliers of capital are centralized state corporations or socialized enterprises. For these types of business enterprises, if acting rationally, should not make large loans to cooperatives that have limited liability. Even if they made such loans, doing so would not eliminate the risk of loss or bankruptcy. It would merely shift it to capital suppliers.

The upshot of the discussion is this. In a contemporary developed society, most economic activity will involve medium-sized to large business enterprises. In the case of Nove's socialism, such activity would be carried out by his first three types of enterprises. Yet centralized state corporations and socialized enterprises present difficulties of worker control over their working lives. Cooperatives may avoid

---

67 Michael C. Jensen and William H. Meckling, "Theory of the Firm: Managerial Behavior, Agency Costs and Ownership Structure," *Journal of Financial Economics*, 3 (1976): 305–60, at 330–43.

some of these difficulties. However, if they are to be efficient and to avoid causing inefficiency elsewhere, suppliers of capital will have to monitor their performance in ways that impinge on worker control. The diffuse-owner corporation financed by equity claims, which is prevalent in private-property economies, may not be as efficient as Jensen and Meckling claim. Still, at some point Nove must make a trade-off between efficiency and other values, such as having worker control and meaningful work. So, indeed, must other perspectives. The resolution advanced in §§ 12.2–12.3 explicitly does so. Hence, though much is to be learned from Nove's account, it does not avoid difficulties with the separation of ownership and control or with deciding in whose interests corporations should be run.

Standards for socialist corporations. The same analysis applies to standards of corporate behavior under socialism. The objection is that corporate standards pose a problem only in a private-property economy. There a tension exists between the interests of private corporations (and their shareholders) and the public interest. But in a socialist economy no such tension exists. There corporations operate in the interests of all.

If the views expressed earlier in this section are correct, the objection has a ready answer. A socialist economy still faces a problem of separating ownership from control. More fundamentally, it must still articulate what it means to run corporations in the interests of all. If so, a parallel tension exists regarding corporate standards of behavior. Even under socialism one must decide, for example, whether to pay employees more than their marginal product, and whether to show compassion for them when economic conditions make a plant closing desirable. Even under socialism one must adjudicate the sometimes conflicting demands of the labor-desert principle and the principle of utility and efficiency.

It does not follow from this answer that corporate standards will be identical in regimes of private and public ownership. In the former, the chief worry centers on de-centralized corporate choices and their capacity to harm the interests of employees and the public at large. In the latter, it centers on centralized choices by state planners that may disregard or undervalue the interests of workers and the public in pursuit of goals of production set by the state or of planners' political goals. Nevertheless, the basic theory of property must importantly undergird corporate standards.

12.6 CODA

It will distress or annoy some readers, and perhaps amuse others, that the basic theory does not either embrace a mod-ified capitalism and reject socialism, or embrace socialism and reject a modified capitalism. Why does so much ink lead to apparent fence straddling? Discerning readers can readily supply the answer. It is that the basic theory does not uniquely determine a particular economic system as the only morally justifiable system or a particular form of business enterprise as the only morally justifiable form. Some eco-nomic systems and some business enterprises violate the basic theory. Yet if one understands the arguments for the basic theory, one will perceive that they do not dictate unique moral solutions in economic matters. This perception is the deeper meaning of the mutual moral availability of the economic options first sketched in § 5.5.

This moral indeterminacy betokens no conflict between or among principles in the basic theory, but it does raise the possibility of conflict, or incommensurability of choice, in regard to character. Chapter 6 gave an acount of virtue and moral character in relation to property. It observed that not all virtues are equally available in all economic systems (§§ 6.5–6.6). If that is so, then although the basic theory dictates no choice among the range of systems that satisfy it, it leaves open the matter of what sort of people, with what characters, one should want. Thus, in regard to economic systems validated by the basic theory, no given person can develop to the highest degree each of, say, the virtues of kindness, cooperativeness, industriousness, reciprocity, generosity, frugality, charity, and probity in business dealings. No given economic system can allow each person to "maximize" each of these virtues. And, in fact, different systems satisfying the basic theory will encourage some of these virtues and inhibit others. The basic theory is powerless to choose among them, but it clearly shows that fundamental choices are at stake.

Chapter 13

Gratuitous transfers

13.1 TAXATION AND REDISTRIBUTION

This chapter applies the basic theory of property to the justifiability and taxation of gratuitous transfers. A transfer is gratuitous if the recipient obtains nothing through any performance of legal duty by the transferor. Thus, gratuitous transfers differ from sales and other bilateral contractual exchanges and from transfers made to repay a debt or satisfy a court judgment. It does not follow that all gratuitous transfers are unmerited. If a woman takes care of her dying aunt for six months, a bequest of, say, $10,000 may be appropriate even though it is not legally required. In general, such transfers are gratuitous from a legal, but not necessarily a moral or personal, point of view.

Gratuitous transfers fall into two groups: transfers from a living person and transfers from the estate of a person who has died. The former group (*inter vivos* transfers) consists mainly of gifts. The latter group (transfers at death) divides. If the deceased person made a valid will, the transfers are called devises in the case of real property and bequests in the case of personal property. If that person has no valid will, the transfers occur by intestate succession. In all cases of the latter group, the things received may be called inheritances. For simplicity's sake, the term "bequests" will be used for all transfers by will.

This chapter deals with whether it is justifiable to make gifts and bequests, to have intestate succession, and to receive inheritances, and, if so, what sorts of limitations and taxation, if any, are appropriate. The argument is straightforward. Pronounced inequalities of wealth exist in Great Britain and the United States. Powerful, if not the dominant, causes of these inequalities are gifts and inheritances at current levels of taxation. The inequalities, moreover, contravene the basic theory of property. That theory requires a steeply progressive tax on gratuitous transfers. Such a tax is proposed and defended against objection.

To grapple with the issues that this argument raises it is important to bear two points in mind. First, gratuitous transfers have, in addition to their obvious material role, an interpersonal and social dimension. Gifts and inheritances can create or reinforce ties of affection and kinship. They can also produce or intensify divisions between transferors and those who receive nothing. The power to transfer is among the most important components of property rights. Second, people transmit many things to others. Gifts and inheritances involve "material wealth." But people often endow their children and others with "human wealth" in the form of love and security, educational or business opportunity, social status, means for developing character, and so on. The transmission of both is important. Yet on the whole it is easier to regulate the passing of material wealth than human wealth. One should not rule out regulating the latter. But because such regulation poses a great threat to liberty, it makes sense to determine first whether injurious inequalities can be prevented by taxing transfers of material wealth.

The wider context of the argument is likewise important. Heavy transfer taxes and redistribution will not cure all the ills of unequal property holdings. As to taxation, it would be a mistake to concentrate on the reproduction of inequalities of wealth to the neglect of their creation. A sound political theory of property will not make that mistake. If its principles are adopted, then the creation of wide disparities in wealth will be inhibited through a progressive income tax. Thus the need for a gratuitous transfer tax to reduce such disparities should eventually decline. Furthermore, the tax proposed here will tend to break down existing inequalities

381

over several generations. Hence four or five generations after its adoption, the tax, which is not mainly a device for raising revenue, will generate less revenue than at first. It may even come to be seen as banal rather than inflammatory. Finally, the importance of redistribution, though considerable, should not be exaggerated. Worker control over production and the promotion of human values are as important as redistribution. And the nature of effective redistributive programs merits discussion in its own right. Only by attending to all of these factors can a society achieve a humane system of property relations.[1]

1   D. W. Haslett, "Is Inheritance Justified?," *Philosophy & Public Affairs*, 15 (1986): 122–55, contends that inheritance is inconsistent with the fundamental values of capitalism. As a proponent of capitalism, he believes that inheritance should be abolished. Specifically, he thinks that large gifts and bequests should be barred and that upon death a person's estate should pass to the government, subject to three exceptions. The exceptions are for surviving spouses, those dependent on the decedent, and charitable organizations. Although this chapter refers to Haslett's article in passing, its purpose is not to answer it point for point but to propose a different way of dealing with the inequalities caused by gratuitous transfers.

It may help, however, to give advance notice of some leading differences in methodology and substantive position between Haslett's article and this chapter. (1) Haslett provides some statistics on inequalities of wealth, but his figures do not establish convincingly a causal relationship between these inequalities and gratuitous transfers at current tax rates. This chapter appeals to additional data to establish such a relationship. (2) Haslett slights the effect of his proposal on saving and investment. This chapter gives a more balanced picture of the effect under its proposal. (3) Haslett wishes to bar large gifts and bequests, with the three exceptions mentioned above. This chapter is skeptical of such a prohibition, and suggests a more flexible approach that imposes a progressive tax on recipients. (4) Haslett places great weight on abolishing inheritance as the way to restore equal opportunity. In this chapter the regulation of gratuitous transfers is only part of a larger picture designed to achieve a humane economy and system of property relations. (5) Haslett defends his proposal in terms of the ideals of capitalism. This chapter defends its proposal in terms of the basic theory of property.

For other recent discussions, see James O. Grunebaum, *Private Ownership* (London and New York: Routledge & Kegan Paul, 1987) (scattered references to bequest under various theories of property); Andrew Reeve, *Property* (Atlantic Highlands, N.J.: Humanities Press International, 1986), pp. 152–78 (property and time).

13.2 WEALTH INEQUALITY AND ITS CAUSES

Persons differ in income and in property holdings (wealth). In both Great Britain and the United States, the distribution of wealth is more unequal than the distribution of income. But just because inequality of wealth exists, it does not follow that gratuitous transfers cause it. There may be other factors. The British figures merit special attention. Often they are more complete and have received more relevant historical and statistical analysis than the American figures.

The British figures on wealth come mainly from Inland Revenue statistics. The statistics are imperfect. They do not include trusts or, till very recently, pensions ("missing wealth"). Nor do they reflect the wealth of people with assets too small to come to the attention of the Inland Revenue ("missing population"). The various sorts of missing wealth may have offsetting effects. The inclusion of pension rights will broaden the distribution of wealth, and the inclusion of trust property will increase the shares of top percentiles. But even if missing wealth is ignored, estimates of wealth distribution would still vary according to how much wealth the missing population is assumed to have. Table 4 indicates the variation on the assumptions, first, that the missing population has no wealth, second, that it has £500 per head, and third, that it has £1,000 per head.

TABLE 4. *British Wealth Distribution in 1972*

Percent Shares of Percentiles on Assumptions 1–3			
	1	*2*	*3*
Top 1%	29.9	28.8	26.8
2–5%	26.4	26.4	24.6
6–10%	15.6	13.8	12.7
11–20%	17.3	15.4	14.5
21–100%	10.8	15.6	21.4

Source: C. D. Harbury and D. M. W. H. Hitchens, *Inheritance and Wealth Inequality in Britain* (London: George Allen and Unwin, 1979), p. 8, Table 1.1.

This wealth distribution, with some qualifications, has been roughly constant over the last half century. Based on estate duty statistics from various sources, the historical pattern summarized in Table 5 emerges. Table 5 indicates that the most substantial declines were in the shares of the top 10 percent. The shares of the top 20 percent fell rather less markedly. The overall picture, at any rate, reveals a distribution of wealth in which a fifth of the population has a highly disproportionate share. As Table 4 indicates, even with the assumption of £1,000 per head for the missing population, in 1972 the top 1 percent owned 26.8 percent of the wealth, the top 5 percent owned a total of 51.4 percent, and the top 20 percent owned a total of 78.6 percent. The remaining 80 percent of the population had only 21.4 percent of the wealth.

Quite recently, the Inland Revenue has assembled statistics that take into account occupational and state pension rights. Table 6 summarizes the results.

TABLE 5. *Shares in Total Personal Wealth, England and Wales, Selected Intervals, 1923–72*

Year	Top 1%	Top 5%	Top 10%	Top 20%
1923	60.9	82.0	89.1	94.2
1926	57.3	79.9	87.4	93.2
1936	54.2	77.4	85.7	92.0
1956	44.5	71.3	–	–
1966	30.6	55.5	69.2	83.8
1972	31.7	56.0	70.4	84.9

Sources: Harbury and Hitchens, *Inheritance and Wealth Inequality in Britain*, p. 9, Table 1.2; A. B. Atkinson and A. J. Harrison, *Distribution of Personal Wealth in Britain* (Cambridge: Cambridge University Press, 1978), p. 159.[2]

2 Data are not available for all years in the period 1923–72. In 1956, figures for the top 10 percent and top 20 percent were outside the range of estate duty statistics.

TABLE 6. *British Wealth Distribution with Adjustments for Pension Rights, 1971–81*

Marketable Wealth Alone	1971	1974	1978	1979	1980	1981
Top 1%	31	23	23	24	23	23
Top 5%	52	43	44	45	43	45
Top 10%	65	57	58	59	58	60
Top 25%	86	84	83	82	81	84
Top 50%	97	93	95	95	94	94
Marketable Wealth Plus Occupational Pension Rights	1971	1974	1978	1979	1980	1981
Top 1%	27	19	19	20	19	19
Top 5%	46	38	39	38	37	37
Top 10%	59	52	52	51	50	50
Top 25%	78–83	76–82	75–79	75–79	73–77	73–77
Top 50%	90–96	88–92	89–93	89–93	89–93	89–93
Marketable Wealth Plus Occupational and State Pension Rights	1971	1974	1978	1979	1980	1981
Top 1%	21	15	13	13	12	12
Top 5%	37	31	25	27	25	25
Top 10%	49	43	36	37	35	35
Top 25%	69–72	64–67	57–60	58–61	57–60	57–60
Top 50%	85–89	85–89	79–83	79–83	79–83	78–82

Source: W. D. Rubenstein, *Wealth and Inequality in Britain* (London and Boston: Faber and Faber, 1986), p. 97.

Plainly, taking pension rights into account supplies figures only for a portion of heretofore missing wealth. It will be much harder to get accurate figures for trust assets – assets that would almost certainly offset some of the leveling indicated by including pension rights. At any rate, the period since World War II, when pension rights became much more common and important in Britain, has witnessed some wealth redistribution. Rubinstein's useful study puts the matter in this way: "Although there seems little doubt of a continuing and significant redistribution of wealth away from the very wealthiest portion of the population to the less wealthy majority of the population, the bottom portions of the population have been relatively unaffected – again, the thrust of wealth distribution has been from the very wealthiest to the merely wealthy or affluent sections of the population."[3]

The most recent United States figures are for 1984 and were reported by the Census Bureau in July 1986.[4] The survey investigated "households," which can consist of a single person, a family, or several unrelated people. It provided a profile of "net worth," which is derived by totaling the value of assets, such as homes, bank accounts, and securities, and then deducting liabilities, such as mortgage loans and other debts. This survey found that the top 12 percent of households hold 38 percent of all the wealth, that the bottom 11 percent have a zero, or even a negative, net worth, and that another 21 percent have a net worth of less than $10,000. It also found that the typical white household has twelve times the net worth of the typical black household and eight times the net worth of the typical Latino household.

As to trends over time, it would appear that wealth in the United States has become somewhat less concentrated in the last sixty years. The diminution occurred, however, mainly during the Great Depression, when the drop in stock prices decreased the shares of the very wealthy. The broad picture is partly dissimilar to that of Great Britain, for in Britain the

---

3 Rubinstein, *Wealth and Inequality in Britain*, pp. 97–98.
4 U.S. Bureau of the Census, *Household Wealth and Asset Ownership: 1984* (Washington, D.C.: U.S. Government Printing Office, July 1986) (Household Economic Studies, Series P–70, No. 7).

top 10 percent have experienced a sharper drop even though they still have a larger share than the top 10 percent in the United States. But otherwise the picture is similar – wide disparities in wealth between the top 20 percent and the bottom 30 or 40 percent that have remained fairly stable over a long period.[5]

What accounts for these pronounced inequalities? At least three factors are at work: savings from income, entrepreneurial success, and receipt of gifts and inheritances. The controversial issue is how large a role each factor plays. The evidence strongly supports the proposition that gifts and inheritances, under existing levels of taxation, have been a powerful, and perhaps the dominant, cause of inequalities of wealth.

The root idea behind the first factor is sometimes called the "life-cycle hypothesis."[6] It holds that as persons mature and go to work they save a portion of their incomes. Savings here include all forms of conservative (as opposed to entrepreneurial) investment, such as savings accounts, money market funds, certificates of deposits, "safe" stocks and bonds, and "indexed" mutual funds or mutual funds that are less

5 See John A. Brittain, *Inheritance and the Inequality of Material Wealth* (Washington, D.C.: Brookings Institution, 1978), pp. 3–7; James D. Smith and Stephen D. Franklin, "The Concentration of Personal Wealth, 1922–69," *American Economic Review*, 64, no. 2 (1974): 162–67. A Joint Economic Committee Report, using the 1983 Federal Reserve Board figures cited by Haslett, "Is Inheritance Justified?," at 123–24, may indicate that wealth inequality has increased somewhat in the period 1963–83. See Michael Wines, "0.5% of Families Found to Hold 35% of Wealth," *Los Angeles Times*, July 26, 1986, Part I, at 21, col. 1; David M. Gordon, "Concentrated Wealth Poses Threat," *Los Angeles Times*, Aug. 5, 1986, Part IV, at 3, col. 4.

6 The life-cycle hypothesis is discussed in, for example, Brittain, *Inheritance and the Inequality of Material Wealth*, pp. 9–13, 51–72, 94–95; A. B. Atkinson, "The Distribution of Wealth and the Individual Life-Cycle," *Oxford Economic Papers*, 23 (1971): 239–54; Franco Modigliani and Richard Brumberg, "Utility Analysis and the Consumption Function: An Interpretation of Cross-Section Data," in Kenneth K. Kurihara, ed., *Post-Keynesian Economics* (New Brunswick, N.J.: Rutgers University Press, 1954), pp. 388–436; Nicholas Oulton, "Inheritance and the Distribution of Wealth," *Oxford Economic Papers*, 28 (1976): 86–101.

risky than the market as a whole. A person's wealth at any point is his or her savings and the previous return on them. Thus it is reasonable to expect a slow accumulation of material wealth up to the point of retirement and then a slow decline. As a result, unequal wealth stems from a person's age, income, rate of saving, and the market rate of return on savings. Some may use the life-cycle hypothesis to paint a benign picture of inequalities of wealth. For, it may be said, wealth derived from earned income and saving rests on individual character and merit. Moreover, wealth due to a person's being at the peak of his or her savings curve is defensible, for the young will later have their turn. No one should expect a toddler and a person on the edge of retirement to have equal savings.

The life-cycle hypothesis, as an explanation, is vulnerable on at least three grounds. First, actual inequalities of wealth far exceed those for which the life-cycle hypothesis can account. Various economic studies show that, given differences in income and rates of saving, the hypothesis can explain why there should be modest disparities in material wealth – especially at the lower end of the spectrum if pensions are included. But it cannot explain why, especially among the top 20 percent, holdings in both Great Britain and the United States are highly disproportionate.[7] Second, if the life-cycle hypothesis were true, the inequality would be fairly narrow within homogeneous age groups, but in fact the distribution of wealth within most age groups tends to be similar to its distribution among the population as a whole.[8] Third, the life-cycle hypothesis cannot account for aggregate capital formation. If the hypothesis were true, the vast majority of capital accumulation would be due to life-cycle savings. In fact, this is not so. An important paper by Kotlikoff and Summers shows that accurate age-earnings and age-consumption profiles are far too even to yield great life-

7 See Brittain, *Inheritance and the Inequality of Material Wealth*, ch. 3.
8 Ibid.

cycle savings. Rather, on the basis of solid data and a sensible methodology, they conclude that intergenerational transfers of wealth are "the major element determining wealth accumulation in the United States."[9] While there are some voices to the contrary,[10] the Kotlikoff-Summers analysis is highly plausible and receives support from other empirical studies.[11]

Furthermore, it is unconvincing to use the life-cycle hypothesis to give a benign picture of inequalities of wealth. Existing differences in income and wealth often are not morally deserved. True enough, the labor-desert principle recognizes that, with qualifications, persons can deserve the fruits of their labor. The fruits include wages and even different wages for different sorts of work. But existing labor markets often contravene this principle. In addition, some people have income from sources other than work, such as income from gifts or bequests. Hence, even though the basic theory of property can justify some differential incomes, and

9 Laurence J. Kotlikoff and Lawrence H. Summers, "The Role of Intergenerational Transfers in Aggregate Capital Accumulation," *Journal of Political Economy*, 89 (1981): 706–32, at 730. The article has elicited comments and a response. See, for example, Franco Modigliani, "Measuring the Contribution of Intergenerational Transfers to Total Wealth: Conceptual Issues and Empirical Findings," in Denis Kessler and André Masson, eds., *Modelling the Accumulation and Distribution of Wealth* (Oxford: Clarendon Press, 1988), pp. 21–52. But see Laurence J. Kotlikoff and Lawrence H. Summers, "The Contribution of Intergenerational Transfers to Total Wealth: A Reply," in ibid., pp. 53–67. The volume contains many other interesting essays on this topic.

10 See, for example, Michael J. Boskin, Statement in *Hearings before the Subcommittee on Economic Growth and Stabilization of the Joint Economic Committee* (July 1977), 95th Congress (Washington, D.C.: U.S. Government Printing Office, 1978), pp. 245–55, at 246, 251–52. See also Yannis M. Ioannides and Ryuzo Sato, "On the Distribution of Wealth and Intergenerational Transfers," *Journal of Labor Economics*, 5 (1987): 366–85.

11 See, for example, Oulton, "Inheritance and the Distribution of Wealth," at 99 (Great Britain); Betsy Buttrill White, "Empirical Tests of the Life Cycle Hypothesis," *American Economic Review*, 68 (1978): 547–60 (United States).

so give some normative scope to the life-cycle hypothesis, many actual differences in income and wealth do not rest on differences in desert. Neither can these differences generally be justified by the principle of utility and efficiency or the principle of justice and equality.

A different explanation for inequalities of wealth lies in entrepreneurial success: Some persons greatly increase their material wealth by entrepreneurial risk taking that succeeds. There is a good deal of anecdotal and survey literature claiming that about half the persons with extremely large fortunes have earned their wealth themselves.[12] Obviously, the entrepreneurial factor partly accounts for inequalities of wealth. Obviously, too, it complements the life-cycle hypothesis by explaining some extremely large fortunes that could not have been amassed by savings out of earnings and the going rate of return on them. Some may use the entrepreneurial explanation to offer a comforting view of wealth inequality, for it suggests that much wealth results from individual effort and superior risk-taking ability.

Nevertheless, studies favoring the entrepreneurial explanation are too anecdotal, unrigorous, and otherwise methodologically flawed to offer a suitable demonstration. In particular, they fail to account satisfactorily for the relative contributions of inheritance and entrepreneurial accumulation. In some *Fortune* analyses, for example, apparently the *bulk* of the *current* value of the holdings must have been inherited in order for the wealth to count as inherited rather than independently accumulated.[13] In a different survey,[14] responses reflected an instruction that, in evaluating the fractional source of assets, the ratio of the *original* value of the

12   See, for example, the *Fortune* studies cited in Haslett, "Is Inheritance Justified?," at 125 n.7.
13   For this criticism, see Brittain, *Inheritance and the Inequality of Material Wealth*, pp. 14–20.
14   Robin Barlow, Harvey E. Brazer, and James N. Morgan, *Economic Behavior of the Affluent* (Washington, D.C.: Brookings Institution, 1966), ch. 7. See generally Brittain, *Inheritance and the Inequality of Material Wealth*, pp. 9–20.

gift or inheritance to the *current* value of total assets was to be used. These approaches tend to understate the importance of gratuitous transfers and to overstate the importance of subsequent activity. For an original gift or inheritance can be invested so as to earn a high rate of return, and thus can play a large role in current holdings. It may not be possible to separate gifts and inheritances in a watertight way from independent accumulation. But some approach is needed that estimates the shares of gratuitously acquired and independently accumulated wealth immediately after gratuitous transfer. Evidently this will be complicated if a person receives gifts and inheritances at different times.

Even if the entrepreneurial explanation had more empirical support, it would be questionable to use it to give a comforting view of inequalities of wealth. To see this, notice that entrepreneurial risk taking covers a wide range of qualities and situations. Among them are actions based on business shrewdness, market boldness, hunches, and sheer luck. Both the labor-desert principle and the principle of utility and efficiency support, within limits, entrepreneurial success that comes from business shrewdness. And perhaps there is, if not desert or merit, something admirable in market boldness – the courage to take an entrepreneurial risk in the hope that it will pay off. But hunches and sheer luck do not ground desert, merit, or, usually, admiration; in light of Chapter 6, they hardly qualify as virtues. Furthermore, it is an open empirical question whether it promotes utility or efficiency to award property rights when favorable entrepreneurial results come from hunches or sheer luck – or even, perhaps, from market boldness. In fact, it is unclear how much entrepreneurial success comes from business shrewdness or even market boldness. If a great deal of it comes from hunches or sheer luck, or from adventitious factors such as government subsidies or favorable regulation or insider information, then entrepreneurial risk taking is morally less impressive than might at first appear. It will take both philosophical and empirical work to clarify the matter. No hope exists of doing that work here. Still, one should question whether the entrepreneurial explanation, even if empirically powerful, can support a comforting view of inequalities of wealth.

Since the life-cycle and entrepreneurial hypotheses do not, separately or together, appear to explain the pronounced inequalities of wealth in Great Britain and the United States, it makes sense to explore the role of gifts and inheritances. One technique for assessing their role is to relate the wealth of fathers and sons. This can be done by drawing a sample of wealthy sons and tracing back to ascertain the wealth of their fathers. Such a backward-tracing technique has been used in Great Britain, with similar results, by Wedgwood in a study originally done in 1929 and by Harbury and Hitchens in various studies completed since 1962. Wedgwood related the probated wills of two samples of sons to the wills of their fathers. He found that wealthy sons tended to have wealthy fathers and that only a minority of wealthy men built up their capital without aid of inheritance.[15] Harbury and Hitchens examined the wealth of the fathers of three samples of wealthy sons dying in 1956–57, 1965, and 1973. They found that among top wealth leavers there was a high probability that their fathers were also wealthy, but that the relative importance of fathers' wealth declined as the size of sons' estates fell. For example, for sons' estates over £100,000 in 1956–57, 51 percent of the fathers also left estates over £100,000 (in constant prices). For sons' estates between £50,000 and £100,000 in 1956–57, 37 percent of the fathers left estates over £100,000 (in constant prices).[16] The correlations greatly exceed those of a random relationship. To illustrate, in the 1973 sample, 41 percent of fathers whose sons left more than £500,000 themselves had estates over £100,000 (in constant prices). Yet only 0.14 percent of all decedent sons had fathers who were that wealthy.[17] Fathers' wealth is

---

15   Josiah Wedgwood, *The Economics of Inheritance* (Port Washington, N.Y. and London: Kennikat, 1971 [1939]), ch. VI.
16   Harbury and Hitchens, *Inheritance and Wealth Inequality in Britain*, ch. 3, especially p. 44 (Tables 3.3 and 3.4).
17   Ibid., p. 48.

therefore an important correlate of sons' wealth. There are, nevertheless, limitations to these studies by Wedgwood and Harbury and Hitchens. They reflect influences other than gifts and inheritances, including material wealth transmitted by trust and various types of human wealth. Nor have the British studies been duplicated in the United States, though preliminary findings in this country are consistent with them.[18]

A different technique for determining the role of gratuitous transfers is to ascertain the sources of the wealth of married women.[19] In Great Britain, studies by Harbury and Hitchens indicate that the principal sources of their property are their fathers and husbands. For married women dying in 1973 with estates over £100,000, 49 percent of their fathers and 33 percent of their husbands had estates exceeding £100,000 (in constant prices).[20] There was also a strong, but lesser, correlation between the wealth of married women and that of their fathers-in-law.[21] If £25,000 is used as a watershed for "rich," fully 92 percent of rich women had rich fathers or rich husbands or both; very few were "self-made."[22] In the United States, Brittain concluded that the wealth of wealthy married women stems primarily from intergenerational transfers. He found this to be especially true of women with a net worth over $100,000 (in 1972 dollars). He also found that *inter vivos* transfers from husbands and independent accumulation played but a small role in the wealth of such women.[23] All of these statistical results

---

18 Brittain, *Inheritance and the Inequality of Material Wealth*, pp. 87–88.
19 Ibid., ch. 2; Harbury and Hitchens, *Inheritance and Wealth Inequality in Britain*, ch. 5. Such evidence as is available (Harbury and Hitchens, ch. 4) indicates that nonpaternal sources of inheritance reinforce paternal patterns of inheritance but are not often a powerful independent factor. This indication probably does little more than confirm that in Anglo-American society inheritance mainly is interspousal or runs along bloodlines.
20 Harbury and Hitchens, *Inheritance and Wealth Inequality in Britain*, p. 89 (Tables 5.1 and 5.2).
21 Ibid., p. 91.
22 Ibid., pp. 90–91.
23 Brittain, *Inheritance and the Inequality of Material Wealth*, ch. 2.

must, of course, be understood in light of patterns of socialization of and discrimination against women. These patterns do much to explain why, at least until very recently, most wealthy women owed their wealth to gratuitous transfers rather than employment or entrepreneurial success.

The overall conclusion, supported by evidence on both sides of the Atlantic, is that gratuitous transfers are a powerful, and perhaps the dominant, cause of inequalities of wealth. Harbury and Hitchens conclude that "acquisition of even a moderate level of wealth appears strongly dependent upon having a father who is at least well into the top half of the wealth distribution."[24] In their view, "inheritance has been the most important single source of wealth inequality in the fairly recent past in twentieth-century Britain."[25] Likewise, Brittain concludes that inheritance plays a strong role in perpetuating inequalities of wealth in the United States.[26]

It is possible to differ over details in the analytical techniques and over shortcomings in the data. Inclusion of poverty assistance, unemployment compensation, social security old-age benefits, and life insurance will make the distribution of wealth less unequal. Inclusion not only of trust assets but also of gratuitous transfers effected by trusts, close corporations, joint ventures, sale-and-leaseback arrangements, long-term loans and leases, sweetheart employment deals, private charitable foundations, and some will substitutes such as life insurance and pension accounts will make it more unequal. It is difficult to know whether including these two categories would be precisely offsetting. Moreover, the situation of the two countries is not fully parallel, for class differences play a larger role in Britain than

24 Harbury and Hitchens, *Inheritance and Wealth Inequality in Britain*, p. 129.
25 Ibid., p. 136.
26 Brittain, *Inheritance and the Inequality of Material Wealth*, p. 88. Although the role of inheritance differs in the various strata that make up the wealthy, a recent Forbes survey found that 154 of the 400 wealthiest persons in the United States control fortunes that were mostly or entirely inherited. *Forbes*, Oct. 24, 1988, 140, no. 9, at 347.

in the United States.[27] All the same, the strong bearing of gratuitous transfers on unequal material wealth is not seriously deniable.

13.3 JUSTIFYING THE REDUCTION OF INEQUALITIES OF WEALTH

The basic theory of property includes a principle of utility and efficiency, a principle of justice and equality, and a principle of desert based on labor (§ 12.1). If the basic theory is sound, and if gratuitous transfers at current tax levels play the causal role in inequalities of wealth claimed in § 13.2, then a justification exists for reducing wealth inequality by restricting gifts and bequests. This section leaves it an open question whether restriction should take the form of prohibition, limitation, taxation, or some combination of these.

Someone might contend, to the contrary, that the labor-desert principle undercuts any justification for restricting gratuitous transfers. If people deserve property rights by virtue of their labor, then they may do with their property as they wish. In particular, they may give or bequeath it to others.

In fact, however, the labor-desert principle does not support such a robust power of gift and bequest, for several reasons. First, the property rights generated by labor have many restrictions. The labor-desert principle is not the same as, for example, classic versions of the labor theory of property (say, Locke's account or Nozick's entitlement theory). The principle does support, with limitations, a power to exchange some of one's property rights for those of someone else (a transfer for value received). But it is quite another matter to show that it justifies unfettered gratuitous transfers.

Second, the labor-desert principle, like most other versions of the labor theory of property, involves the work done

---

27 For a discussion of class and demographic factors that is as solid as it is fascinating, see W. D. Rubinstein, *Men of Property: The Very Wealthy in Britain since the Industrial Revolution* (London: Croom Helm, 1981).

by the laborer. Thus, even if this principle shows why the *laborer* should have property rights, it does not show why *someone else* should have them by gratuitous transfer from the laborer. Or, to make a more cautious point, the labor-desert principle can support at most a one-time power of gift or bequest. Assume *arguendo* that the laborer (the original owner) can gratuitously transfer certain property to someone else. It does not follow that the transferee in turn can do so. For the transferee did not work to produce the property, and so cannot claim any right founded on his or her labor to give or bequeath it to a third party.

Third, nothing in the notion of labor-generated property rights excludes legitimate taxation. Indeed, so long as the aggregate tax is fair, taxes may be assessed in two steps (on income and on transfer) rather than in one step (on income alone). Hence, a common double-taxation argument against transfer taxes is flawed.

The principle of utility and efficiency, given some plausible empirical propositions about human beings, supports the reduction of inequalities of wealth (§ 8.6). One proposition is that money and other material goods have diminishing marginal utility – that is, capacity to satisfy preferences. Even if interpersonal comparisons of utility are not possible, the efficiency component of the combined principle holds. If they are possible, the utility component also holds. In what follows, it will be assumed that such comparisons are possible. Another proposition is that wide differences in wealth cause some persons to experience preference-dissatisfaction. Common forms of such dissatisfaction include resentment, hopelessness, and social malaise. Yet another proposition is that, even apart from actual dissatisfaction, a more nearly equal wealth distribution will produce increased satisfaction if existing preferences are rationally altered. So even if current wealth inequalities do not make those who are poorly off feel dissatisfied because they fail to understand their situation (owing, say, to self-deception), one must consider the satisfaction they would have were their preferences changed (say, by education).

Moreover, given some additional propositions, utility and efficiency prima facie support reducing inequality by restricting gifts and bequests. One further proposition is that the inequalities of wealth described in § 13.2 are pronounced enough to have an adverse impact on utility and efficiency. Another is that it is at least possible to reduce inequality by restricting gratuitous transfers in some way – whether by taxing them, limiting them, or prohibiting them altogether. These propositions seem plausible, but the support they offer is prima facie rather than conclusive. For one must see what the principle of justice and equality requires. And eventually, even if inequalities of wealth should be reduced, one must consider whether some way of going about it other than restricting gratuitous transfers would, all things considered, be better.

The principle of justice and equality also supports the reduction of inequalities of wealth. The combined principle, it will be recalled, maintains that unequal property holdings are justifiable if (1) everyone has a minimum amount of property and (2) the inequalities do not undermine a fully human life in society. The property minimum pertains to the basic things needed by nearly everyone for a decent life – food, clothing, shelter, education, health care, and job and old-age security. The minimum will vary from one society to another, and cannot be set solely by an objective yardstick, such as owning certain assets or having a certain income. Justice does not require that the minimum be forced on anyone who wishes to decline; ascetics are permitted.

Yet even when the minimum is satisfied, there can be a wide gap between the rich and those who are least well-off. This gap involves pronounced economic class lines and can sometimes undermine a fully human life in society. A wide difference is cause for concern because of its effects on rich and poor alike. In the rich, there can be a diminished sense of common humanity. The wealthy may develop a distorted sense of self-esteem and undesirable traits such as smugness, haughtiness, and unconcern. The account of property and moral character in Chapter 6 would regard these traits as vices. The wealthy may overestimate how much they merit their material good fortune and underplay the human nature they share with others. But the effects on those having only the minimum amount of property are apt to be more deleterious. Their condition may breed damaged self-esteem – leading sometimes to servility and at other times to envy and resentment. The concern here is not with unpleasant feelings as episodes of preference-dissatisfaction but with the dehumanizing consequences of wide inequalities.

Moreover, with some additional plausible propositions, justice and equality also prima facie support reducing inequality by restricting gifts and bequests. One proposition, argued for in § 13.2, is that gratuitous transfers at current levels of taxation play a causal role in existing inequalities of wealth. Another proposition is that the current distributions of wealth in Great Britain and the United States leave some persons with less than a minimum amount of property. The many who are homeless or chronically unemployed, for example, lack some of the things needed for a decent human life. Yet another proposition is that these inequalities of wealth impair the capacity of some persons to have a fully human life in society – even if one were, implausibly, to suppose the property minimum to be satisfied. For current distributions give some persons a very favorable, and others a very poor, start in life. Wealth is important not just for the manifold pleasures of consumption. It also provides unearned income, confers security and many sorts of power, and serves as a material foundation of opportunities and self-esteem. In light of the startling disproportion between, say, the top 10 percent and the bottom 10 percent in both Great Britain and the United States, it is no surprise that the inequalities can wound self-esteem, create justified moral resentment, distort the legal and political process, and reinforce myths offensive to equal moral worth.

The net result is that the basic theory of property prima facie supports restrictions on gratuitous transfers. The principles of utility and efficiency and of justice and equality both favor such restrictions; desert based on labor does not cut against such restrictions. More precisely, the former principles bear in two different ways on the narrowing of inequalities. On the one side, they underscore the importance of ensuring a minimum level of wealth for all. Those below it are apt to have a low level of preference-satisfaction and to lack the things needed for a decent human life. On the other side, the principles make clear the need to reduce the wealth of some of those who are best-off. At least this is so except in the rare situation in which it is possible to raise the level of wealth of a large fraction of society without lowering that of those who are best-off. The labor-desert principle, to be sure, can under some circumstances justify high income and substantial wealth for a small percentage of the population. But it cannot do so very well in the case of unearned income and wealth, particularly when they are obtained by gratuitous transfers. The narrowing of inequalities, then, comes from two different directions – raising the wealth level of some (through various redistributive programs) and lowering the wealth level of others (through restrictions on gratuitous transfers).

A strong justification exists, therefore, for reducing inequalities of wealth by restricting gifts and bequests. On a philosophical plane, the case for taxing such transfers is admittedly contingent. If all actual differences in income were justifiable under a sound theory of property, and if gratuitous transfers would not disturb the resulting distribution, an income tax would suffice. Or if actual differences in income were not justifiable, but gratuitous transfers, miraculously, corrected the disutilities and injustices at all points in time, an income tax would suffice. But, as the world is, not all differences in income are justifiable. And gratuitous transfers at current tax levels perpetuate distributions that are unjust and counter to utility. If such distributions are avoidable, that will help to prevent concentrations of wealth from exerting an undue influence on other areas of social life – for example, political representation, civil rights, and access to educational and cultural opportunities.

It may be suggested that even if inequalities of wealth

should be reduced, the reduction should not, all things considered, be accomplished by restricting gratuitous transfers. A common suggestion is that an income tax would suffice. The reply is that both strategies are needed. A progressive tax on income will not by itself reduce inequality enough. For it will not erode existing inequalities of wealth (as distinct from income) and, if sufficiently progressive, will even hinder the making of new fortunes. Still, it is unwise to rely entirely on restricting gratuitous transfers. Even a rather progressive transfer tax, for example, is unlikely to generate sufficient revenue for needed government programs and services, let alone projects for redistributing wealth.[28]

It may be retorted that there are independent arguments defending the role of inheritance in the current distribution of wealth. So there are, but they do not survive inspection. Little time is needed for the argument that large gifts and inheritances create a leisure class that consciously or unconsciously performs a useful function. As Wedgwood pointed out over a half century ago,[29] it is hard to grasp why the sight of riches gratuitously obtained should stimulate members of society better than riches gained by work. Furthermore, historical arguments that achievements in art and science came largely from members of a leisure class are unsound. Most great thinkers and artists did not, in fact, inherit significant wealth. And even if some did, it is doubtful that inheritance best promotes art and science. It makes more sense to support education and research so that those who demonstrate the ability, energy, and productive capacity to make advances receive support than to rely on those who by chance are born into wealthy families.

28 "The progressive income tax alone, no matter how steep the progression, tends to preserve and magnify the advantages of inherited wealth." Walter J. Blum and Harry Kalven, Jr., *The Uneasy Case for Progressive Taxation* (Chicago: University of Chicago Press, 1963) (edition with added introduction), p. xviii. They add: "Conversely, a progressive transfer tax alone without a progressive income tax could do little by way of redistribution in our society." Ibid.
29 Wedgwood, *The Economics of Inheritance*, pp. 208–12.

A more interesting argument, advanced by Bentham,[30] invokes utility. More precisely, it involves the utility of meeting needs and upholding expectations and the disutility of leaving needs unmet and disappointing expectations. In Bentham's view, gratuitous transfers, especially at death, are necessary to provide subsistence for the rising generation and to prevent disappointment.

This argument has some merit, but to ascertain its force it must be dissected carefully. No doubt hardship can result if those dependent on decedents are cut off entirely upon death. Dependent survivors should therefore have some claim on the resources of decedents. To recognize this claim, however, is also to circumscribe the rights of decedents. For instance, they may have no right to disinherit a dependent spouse or child. At all events, the survivors' needs relate only to the avoidance of hardship and extend only during the period of dependency. They do not, by themselves, justify the transfer of wealth beyond that needed to avoid hardship. Nor do they justify the continuation of benefits after the need has passed; this limitation is important, as most intergenerational transfers are received after the beneficiaries have attained adulthood, even comfortable middle age, and so can do well enough on their own. It is, moreover, important to restrict gratuitous transfers so as not to encourage dependency.

So far as the prevention of disappointment is concerned, it is helpful to separate the expectations of would-be transferors of a power to make gifts and bequests from the expectations of would-be transferees of a right to receive them. Both sets of expectations derive not only from the wealth of potential benefactors but also from the various laws that determine the validity and taxation of gifts and bequests. If the laws change, the expectations will change. Thus the more important issue, as Sidgwick saw nearly a century

30 Jeremy Bentham, *The Theory of Legislation*, ed. C. K. Ogden (London: Routledge & Kegan Paul, 1931), pp. 177–87.

401

ago,[31] is not whether the law should prevent the disappointment of expectations, but whether it should create such expectations in the first place. Of course, it is not now possible to start from scratch. Laws are on the books that have shaped expectations. As a result, the factor of disappointment should influence how those laws are altered. It may counsel, for example, in favor of a phase-in approach.

The disappointment factor may carry more weight in the case of would-be transferors. After all, their expectations that they can give or bequeath may spring from noble motives. But their motives are varied,[32] and sheltering their expectations seems less attractive to the extent that they hold out the carrot of gratuitous wealth to exert undue influence on, say, the behavior of their children. It is harder to feel solicitous for would-be transferees. Sometimes new laws may disturb the expectations of the fawning parasite more than those of the loving relative. It would be unkind and unwarranted to ascribe only greedy motives to relatives; inheritance does support some diffuse arrangement of reciprocity that facilitates humane care for the elderly. Although these sets of current expectations differ somewhat, their existence should not prevent a society from eventually so structuring any expectations of gifts and inheritances as to avoid unjustifiable reliance on the idea of receiving gratuitous wealth. To do otherwise simply perpetuates inequalities of wealth on a fragile base of inequity.

These arguments hardly exhaust those brought against the idea of restricting gifts and bequests. But the other arguments are not mainly intended as justifications for an unfettered right of gratuitous transfer. They direct themselves instead to the supposed adverse impact of restricting gratuitous transfers. As such it is better to confront them after specific restrictions have been suggested.

31 Henry Sidgwick, *The Elements of Politics* (London: Macmillan, 1891), p. 98.
32 For an economic discussion, see B. Douglas Bernheim, Andrei Shleifer, and Lawrence H. Summers, "The Strategic Bequest Motive," *Journal of Labor Economics*, 4 (1986): S151–S182.

13.4 A PLAN FOR REDUCING INEQUALITIES
OF WEALTH

The task now is to show how best to restrict gifts and bequests. This section suggests a plan to limit gifts, bequests, and intestate succession and to tax gratuitous transfers. It also compares this plan with current United States law and argues that it would be a bad idea to prohibit gratuitous transfers altogether.

The plan aims to reduce inequalities of wealth to the point at which they no longer contravene the principles of utility and efficiency and of justice and equality. Several factors constrain this general aim. One is the labor-desert principle. This principle, however, supports very few inequalities of wealth whose reduction is otherwise desirable. Another factor is protecting liberty when its exercise does not harm others. This factor allows some freedom of gift and testation. A final factor is a set of goals and constraints for a comprehensive tax system. These include raising revenue, preserving incentives to maximize social wealth, obtaining a fair contribution from all, and promoting consistency and administrative convenience.

The aim just described and the constraints on it are quite general. It is therefore unlikely that any particular plan will satisfy them uniquely. Still, one can try to be specific. If people are free to make some bequests, then they should at least be able to arrange for continued care of a dependent spouse or dependent children. Also, it would be counter to utility and efficiency, other things being equal, to limit gifts and bequests in ways that would destroy or disrupt natural ties of human affection. What counts as natural varies from one culture to another. In contemporary Western cultures, gratuitous transfer along family lines, especially to spouses and children, is natural. The legal system should avoid the extremes of encouraging obsequiousness, which would be a vice under Chapter 6, and requiring would-be benefactors to treat everyone alike, which would require an unnatural and probably unhealthy degree of impartiality. Since most per-

403

sons who fail to make a will have natural affections similar to those of persons who do, intestate succession reflecting these affections should be allowed.

If these assumptions are correct, the substantive law can plausibly include these rules among others. Persons have the rights to make gifts and bequests and to set up trusts. Exercise of these rights is subject to tax. A benefactor – donor, testator, settlor – may not completely disinherit a dependent spouse or dependent minor children. Such persons are entitled to one-half the share that they would obtain by intestate succession. The rules for intestacy are as follows: one-half to the surviving spouse and one-half to surviving children; entire estate to the surviving spouse if there are no surviving children, or to the surviving children if there is no surviving spouse; if neither spouse nor children survive, then, in order, to other surviving issue, surviving parents, surviving brothers and sisters (or, if dead, their surviving issue), or surviving grandparents (or, if dead, their surviving issue); entire estate to the state if none of the above survives.[33]

These rules cut off intestate succession after descendants of grandparents. Some might favor cutting off intestate succession even earlier. But escheat – particularly escheat of small estates – is heartily disliked and therefore apt to retard utility. And it should be remembered that the rich are likely to have wills and that the poor more often die intestate. These rules single out those persons most likely to be the natural objects of the decedent's affection in Western culture. Other cultures may require different rules. Finally, the rules transmit full ownership – in lawyer's language, a fee interest rather than an interest measured by the recipient's life. The reason is that to give only a life interest would unduly hinder the marketability of property.

The general aim described earlier favors, with one qualification, a tax on transferees rather than transferors. Since the aim is to reduce inequalities of wealth, what matters is

---

33 These rules by and large follow the *Uniform Probate Code* (St. Paul, Minn.: West, 1969) §§ 2–101 et seq. The Code is, of course, considerably more detailed.

how much persons receive – more precisely, how much they receive over their lifetimes. Hence the tax should be imposed on the gifts and inheritances that each individual obtains during his or her entire life.[34] A transferee-based tax cleaves in spirit to Mill's views on property. Mill believed that a power of bequest, though not a right of inheritance, was part of the idea of private property founded on labor.[35] Even the power of bequest, he thought, could be limited if its exercise conflicts with the "permanent interests of the human race." For the ultimate end of arrangements of property is, in his view, utility or social welfare, and "property is only a means to an end, not itself the end."[36] But he was even more concerned to limit the right of inheritance. As a practical matter, he preferred "to restrict, not what any one might bequeath, but what any one should be permitted to acquire, by bequest or inheritance."[37] The plan suggested here is considerably more detailed than anything suggested by Mill, and embraces gifts as well as transfers at death.

Though the plan is mainly interested in the gratuitous receipt of very large amounts over a lifetime, it has a subordinate, but not trivial, interest in the gratuitous transfer of very large amounts over a lifetime by any given transferor. This is the lone qualification to the transferee-based tax. Suppose that a very wealthy woman makes many gifts and bequests to a large number of persons. Then the recipients may pay little or no tax. But it does not follow that nothing of

34 Some might wish to extend this to a wealth (asset-based) tax, but the extension is problematic. Assets are difficult to measure and monitor. Moreover, though assets that are earned need not be morally deserved, in general they present a more questionable target for redistributive taxation. For a balanced general discussion, see A. B. Atkinson, *Unequal Shares: Wealth in Britain* (London: Allen Lane The Penguin Press, 1972), chs. 6–9.

35 John Stuart Mill, *Principles of Political Economy* [1848], ed. William Ashley (Fairfield, N.J.: Augustus M. Kelley, 1976), p. 221. Notice, however, that if a society restricts inheritance, it indirectly restricts bequest to some extent.

36 Ibid., p. 226.

37 Ibid., p. 227. See also John Rawls, *A Theory of Justice* (Cambridge, Mass.: Harvard University Press, 1971), pp. 277–78, who suggests a transferee-based tax.

moment or concern has happened. In the pattern of the transferor's gifts and bequests may lie something affected with a public interest. For example, she may have enriched a wide circle of her extended family and its employees. Or she may have enriched a number of distinct "charitable" entities having the same purpose. Very large concentrations of wealth are not merely funds for consumption but sources of corporate, cultural, and political power. Hence in some cases it may be appropriate to tax the transferor as well as the transferee.

At this point, it is vital to distinguish between the foregoing general structure and a specific proposal for tax rates, deductions, exclusions, and exemptions. The structure is strongly, though not uniquely, supported by the general aim and its surrounding constraints. But any specific proposal is less well supported. Such a proposal requires a good deal of empirical information that is not presented here. Empirical studies of the operation of relevantly similar proposals in relevantly similar countries and econometric studies of the impact of specific provisions on behavior would be particularly helpful. Since such studies have not been done, the following proposal is advanced more tentatively than the foregoing general structure.

The core of the proposal is, after an exclusion, to tax the remainder of the amounts received at steeply progressive rates. The tax is based on the lifetime total value, for each transferee, of gifts, inheritances, and trust proceeds. Each transferee has a lifetime exclusion of $100,000 (in 1990 dollars) – that is, the first $100,000 received, whether at once or over many years, whether from one transferor or many, is untaxed. Above $100,000, the tax rate begins at 20 percent, rises by increments to 40 percent at $300,000, rises again by increments to 50 percent at $600,000, and finally rises by increments to 65 percent at $1,000,000. Amounts exceeding $1,000,000 are taxed at 65 percent. If a transferor gives or bequeaths more than $5,000,000 during his life, the excess is subject to a supertax of 5 percent. Charitable contributions are exempt from both the transferee tax and the supertax.

Interspousal transfers are also exempt. No other deductions, exclusions, or exemptions are permitted.[38]

Several observations on this proposal are in order. (1) The dollar figures and tax rates are illustrative, not sacrosanct. The numbers should be adjusted to allow just those wealth inequalities that are consonant with utility and justice. Once rates for a transferor-based tax exceed 50 percent, affected potential transferors tend to move their assets to foreign countries. It is unclear whether such flight of capital would occur in the case of a transferee-based tax, but that possibility is a reason for not setting the top rate higher than 65 percent. Utility and justice would probably support a higher top rate if it could be imposed without provoking a flight of capital. (2) The marital exemption stems from the idea that a husband and wife should be thought of as an economic partnership.[39] (3) The exclusion and the tax rate up to $300,000 are set so as to minimize the impact on the standard of living of surviving dependent spouses and minor children. It may be possible to specify the exclusion and rate in some other way – for example, as some factor of average or median annual wage or average or median personal assets. (4) The supertax on transferors reflects the concern with the power stemming from extremely large concentrations of wealth. (5) Redistributive programs are a separate matter. To earmark transfer-tax revenues for the least well-off is a respectable gesture, but most of the revenue needed for redistribution will come from a progressive income tax and

38 Only in revising the final typescript, I am embarrassed to say, did I encounter similar proposals for an "accessions tax" by Andrews and by Halbach and for a "lifetime capital receipts tax" by Atkinson. See William D. Andrews, "The Accessions Tax Proposal," *Tax Law Review*, 22 (1967): 589–633; Edward C. Halbach, Jr., "An Accessions Tax," *Real Property, Probate and Trust Journal*, 23 (Summer 1988): 211–74; Atkinson, *Unequal Shares*, ch. 9, who generously describes related proposals by J. E. Meade, C. T. Sandford, and O. Stutchbury (pp. 172–74). Readers who are basically sympathetic to my proposal but object to some of its provisions may profit from examining these more detailed proposals.

39 See Haslett, "Is Inheritance Justified?," at 138.

from other taxes. (6) The proposal leaves out many details, such as integration with or concomitant modification of federal and state income taxes, and the exact handling of in-kind transfers and capital assets. For present purposes, it is better to streamline than to clutter.

This proposal differs markedly from current federal and state taxation of gratuitous transfers. The present federal tax is on gifts and estates. The transferor pays it. The basic arrangement is that a person pays a tax on the entire amount of gratuitous transfers that he or she makes in a given year. A welter of exclusions, deductions, and credits complicates the arrangement. The tax rates are nominally progressive, but the effective tax rates are not very progressive once exclusions, deductions, and credits are taken into account. Thus the system proposed here is simpler and effectively much more progressive, taxes (mainly) the transferee instead of the transferor, and cumulates over the transferee's lifetime rather than annually.[40]

As to state taxation, only twelve states tax gifts, but all states except Nevada tax transfers at death. In taxing the latter, fifteen states use estate taxes (transferor-based) and thirty-four states use inheritance taxes (transferee-based). Tax rates, exclusions, deductions, and credits all vary considerably. The system proposed here is once again simpler and effectively much more progressive and applies to the transferee's entire life. If states desire to have a concomitant system of taxation, it would make more sense for them

---

40 The most recent significant changes in the federal estate and gift tax occurred in 1981. See Economic Recovery Tax Act of 1981, Pub. L. 97-34, §§ 401 et seq., 95 Stat. 172, 299–323, codified in scattered sections of I.R.C. §§ 2001 et seq. (West 1989). The changes increased the annual gift tax exclusion from $3,000 to $10,000 per donee, reduced the top estate tax rate from 70 to 50 percent, granted an unlimited marital deduction, and now exempts all estates worth $600,000 or less. As a result, most unrealized appreciation passing through estates escapes both income and estate tax, and the estate tax applies to less than one percent of all estates. For detailed figures, see Michael J. Graetz, "To Praise the Estate Tax, Not To Bury It," *Yale Law Journal*, 93 (1983): 259–86.

simply to take a (progressive) percentage of the federal levy (that is, a kind of surtax).

A word on alternative mechanisms may be helpful. This proposal retains a salient feature of current state and federal law – namely, that gifts, bequests, and inheritances are not included in income but are subjected to separate transfer taxation. If they were included in income, the result might be called an integrated income tax. It is no simple matter to devise such an integrated tax.[41] But if it can be done, the proposal advanced here should not be seen as hostile to it, provided that inequalities of wealth are appropriately narrowed. The proviso requires that, in an integrated income tax, income from gratuitous transfers must ordinarily be taxed at higher rates than other sorts of income. More precisely, income from gratuitous transfers, once it passes a threshold, should be taxed quite heavily because it is not earned by work and can reinforce pernicious inequalities of wealth. Income from work that observes the strictures of the labor-desert principle should be taxed less heavily. Varieties of income in between the two require some intermediate treatment. These observations also apply, *mutatis mutandis*, to other tax mechanisms that might be devised to deal with the effects of gifts and bequests.

The next section will grapple with the claim that the foregoing plan goes too far. Consider now, however, the claim that it does not go far enough. Gratuitous transfers, it might be said, should not be limited and taxed; they should be prohibited altogether. Haslett says exactly that – subject to exceptions for spouses, dependents, and charities.[42]

Either Haslett's proposal can be effectively implemented or it cannot. Assume that implementation is effective if and only if gratuitous transfers, save for the three exceptions he

---

41 An integrated income tax is proposed in Joseph M. Dodge, "Beyond Estate and Gift Tax Reform: Including Gifts and Bequests in Income," *Harvard Law Review*, 91 (1978): 1177–1211. For relevant economic discussion, see Alan J. Auerbach and Laurence J. Kotlikoff, *Dynamic Fiscal Policy* (Cambridge: Cambridge University Press, 1987), ch. 8.

42 Haslett, "Is Inheritance Justified?" See note 1 above for a summary of Haslett's account.

lists, do not occur within the United States. If it is known in advance that the proposal cannot be effectively implemented, and if its implementation is therefore never attempted, then discussing it further is unnecessary. If it is not known in advance that the proposal cannot be effectively implemented, and if an attempt at implementation therefore fails, then the failed attempt will likely have adverse consequences. The consequences include the money wasted in the attempt and the deleterious effect on public confidence in the legal system. Of course, the plan suggested here might fail, too; yet, because it is much less radical than Haslett's proposal, the risk of failure is much lower.

Suppose, however, that Haslett's proposal can be effectively implemented. In that case, its implementation is also likely to have adverse consequences. Under one scenario, impermissible gratuitous transfers will take place not in but outside the United States. For instance, those with even moderate assets may invest in foreign real estate or securities, or purchase annuities or life insurance policies payable in foreign countries. They may then make gifts and bequests using the foreign assets. If they do, it will be very costly to prevent the repatriation of those assets by transferees. And if the assets do not return to this country, there will be problems relating to the balance of payments and many other difficulties for the United States economy.

Under a different scenario, no impermissible gratuitous transfers will occur within or outside the United States, but the very success of the proposal will have undesirable effects. For example, the abolition of inheritance is apt, over time, to undermine reciprocity between generations. A common, though not unique, way to express love and affection for the next generation is through gifts and bequests. This practice stems from powerful human desires and plays some role in humane care for the elderly by children and grandchildren. Or, to take another example, the unavailability of intergenerational transfers may distort the pattern of charitable giving. Transferors may favor "charities" that represent their class interest or that support idiosyncratic projects.

410

Although the government can restrict what counts as a charity, such restriction poses some threats to transferors' liberty, and in any case transfers to government-sanctioned charities may divert wealth from projects that utility and justice favor.

It may be replied that precisely these consequences will accompany the effective implementation of the plan suggested here. This reply is seriously overstated. For there is a vast difference between not being able to do something at all – namely, make gifts or bequests in the United States – and knowing that, if you do it, *some* of your transferees *may* have to pay *some* tax. As a result, the suggested plan is unlikely to have the consequences described above. Its tax component is intended to be flexible. If econometric studies suggest that the rates are so high as to lead to these consequences, then the rates should be lowered accordingly, for otherwise the tax will not satisfy the principles of utility and efficiency and of justice and equality. Furthermore, this plan, like many significant departures from existing law, may require a sophisticated transition strategy.[43] In contrast, Haslett's call for the abolition of inheritance is so inflexible that it seems highly likely to have some of the adverse consequences detailed earlier.

13.5 MORE CHARGES OF ADVERSE IMPACT

So much for the claim that the plan suggested here does not go far enough. One may turn now to some objections that it goes too far. The objections relate, variously, to social impact, economic effect, enforceability, and motivation for adoption.

Social impact. One objection here is that to tax gratuitous transfers heavily enough to reduce inequalities of wealth will blunt benevolent motives and acts – which would be a bad thing. In reply, observe that the suggested plan does not tax

---

43 A useful general treatment is Louis Kaplow, "An Economic Analysis of Legal Transitions," *Harvard Law Review*, 99 (1986): 509–617.

charitable contributions. Nor does it remove the effective possibility of transfers of material wealth to private persons. Many such transfers will be tax-free, since the tax applies only when a transferee has received more than $100,000 in a lifetime. Many others will not be heavily taxed, since between $100,000 and $300,000 of lifetime receipts, the rate begins at 20 percent and does not exceed 40 percent. It is far from clear that transfers to one person above these amounts would not occur or, to the extent that they would not, that their nonoccurrence would be a bad thing (given their propensity to perpetuate inequalities of wealth). In the end, the objection simply forgets that benevolence can take many forms. Do not people show their love and fondness for others in many ways besides transfers of substantial material wealth? Do not many parents try to provide for their children a secure and supportive home and to endow them with educational and other opportunities? It would indeed be unfortunate to fetter the benevolent instincts of human nature. But the plan put forward here does not do so, unless it be supposed that benevolence can manifest itself only in the transmission of very large amounts of material things.

A subtler objection is that the plan will weaken family and social structure. This objection takes note of a point made in § 13.1 – namely, that gratuitous transfers play an important role in reproducing interpersonal relations and structuring the social system. If such transfers are taxed so as to reduce inequalities of wealth, then they will be diminished in their capacity to reinforce family and social structure.

This objection raises two distinct questions. One is: Will the plan have the effect charged? The other is: If so, is that a bad effect? As to the first, the assertion that the proposal would weaken family and social structure is vague. In families where the transfers to be received would be less than $100,000 per person, there would be little effect. Indeed, where the total amount to be transferred is less than $100,000, there would be no effect at all, since the transferor would have no tax reason to transfer in a way different from that in which he or she would have before (assuming that the intended transferees would have received no transfers from anyone else). If the total amount to be transferred exceeds $100,000, the tax consequences would counsel only in the direction of making transfers more nearly equal – so that no transferee would receive more than $100,000. Thus, in families of low to moderate levels of wealth, there would be little or no effect. Consequently, if there were any discernible impact, it would be on rather wealthy families, in which the proposal would induce a different pattern of gratuitous transfers or in which the recipients would receive less because of the new tax. All that would result even for these families, however, would be some effect on wealth transferred or received. The tax plan would not necessarily have any impact on family or social structure.

Still, it must be allowed that there could be such an impact. One way is that in very wealthy families, those who stand to receive a good deal may become more independent of their benefactors. Another way is that diffuse class or social relations may be affected in succeeding generations. E. P. Thompson once wrote that "over time, family fortunes rise and fall; what is inherited is property itself, the claim on the resources of a future society; and the beneficiary may be, not any descendant of that particular family, but the historical descendant of the social class to which that family once belonged."[44] Hence the plan *might* have an impact on class or social relations that spring from great disparities in wealth.

These remarks lead to the second question of whether such effects on family and social structure are bad. It is hard to see that they are in light of justice and utility. To the contrary, it would appear to be a good thing for children of very wealthy families to become more self-reliant, and for class and social relations dependent on great wealth inequalities to be broken down and replaced by a more equitable social structure.

---

44 E. P. Thompson, "The Grid of Inheritance: A Comment," in Jack Goody, Joan Thirsk, and E. P. Thompson, eds., *Family and Inheritance: Rural Society in Western Europe, 1200–1800* (Cambridge: Cambridge University Press, 1976), pp. 328–60, at p. 360.

More troubling, however, is the claim that the plan might solidify social stratification in a different way. Given the tax consequences of transfers of material wealth, the wealthy might divert their resources to the transmission of human wealth – especially education. The shift might create an even more homogeneous class of the children of the well-to-do. It is difficult to assess this claim. The effect envisaged might not occur. For the wealthy might transfer human wealth in widely different ways, so that their children would form a heterogeneous group. Or their children's capacity to absorb and profit from education might vary sufficiently that no wealth-based educated elite would result.

If, however, the effect claimed did occur, or threatened to occur, it might be necessary to regulate the transmission of human wealth. Such regulation merits extended discussion in its own right, and here one may merely offer two suggestions. (1) Regulation should be attempted only as a last resort because of the risks it poses to liberty. When it is attempted, it should, for the same reason, most likely take the form of taxation rather than prohibition or severe limitation. It seems unwise to forbid private schooling, for its elimination would interfere too drastically with the freedom of parents to educate their children. (2) Only some human wealth transfers are fit targets of taxation. Any plan to tax, say, the love, affection, attention, and character development that good parents give their children is highly implausible. It might, however, be possible to tax the value of some transfers – especially the cost of private education. Any such tax should be sensitive to the income and wealth of the parents. It makes little sense to thwart the efforts of people of modest means who reduce their own consumption in order to give their children a better education than they otherwise would have received.

Economic effect. Surely the most common objection is that steep progressive taxation of gratuitous transfers diminishes the incentive to work, save, and invest, and thereby impedes the formation of capital and lowers economic output. Haslett has some useful replies to this charge that one can happily incorporate.[45] He observes that persons work, save, and invest from many motives besides a desire to make gifts and bequests, and that persons can partly satisfy that desire in any event through transfers to charities. He suggests that other measures can stimulate investment. For example, the government can tax consumption, or subsidize investment in private enterprise. Anyway, much investment already comes from retirement plans and undistributed corporate profits rather than from individual investors.

It is unnecessary to rehearse Haslett's discussion in detail, but it will help to make two additional points. First, his replies to the objection aid his proposal less than they do the plan suggested in § 13.4. His proposal is quite radical in that, with exceptions for spouses, dependents, and charities, gratuitous transfers are abolished. Their abolition is apt to have a far-reaching impact on the economy. In contrast, the suggested plan only limits and taxes gratuitous transfers. It is more modest and flexible and its economic effects are more predictable.

Second, pursuing one form of the objection is instructive.[46] Assume that wealth disposition falls into two categories – consumption and gratuitous transfers. Assume also that people have certain preferences (utility curves), which vary from person to person, for consumption and gratuitous transfers. If neither category of wealth disposition is taxed, the "price" of each is equal. If, however, the government taxes gratuitous transfers, their price rises. So, for example, if the applicable tax rate is 20 percent, it costs $1.25 to ensure that a transferee obtains an after-tax amount of $1.00. Some persons will have utility curves such that, if the tax rate is high enough, they will redirect some or all of their wealth disposition from gratuitous transfers to consumption. It might now be suggested that the government can tax

---

45 Haslett, "Is Inheritance Justified?," at 145–48.
46 Here the plan adapts, but does not agree with the conclusions expressed by, Michael J. Boskin, "An Economists' Perspective on Estate Taxation," in Edward C. Halbach, Jr., ed., *Death, Taxes and Family Property* (St. Paul, Minn.: West, 1977), pp. 60–65.

consumption. Doing so increases the price of consumption. The problem is that if the government taxes both consumption and gratuitous transfers, then at some point some people will produce less – because they prefer leisure to both consumption and gratuitous transfers at tax-influenced prices. Further, reduced consumption can ultimately depress demand to a point where an economy stagnates.

Drawing out the objection in this way is instructive for several reasons. (1) It brings out that production, consumption, gratuitous transfers, and leisure are interrelated. One cannot alter one element in the set, say by taxation, and assume that everything will work out satisfactorily. (2) One should not, however, assume *tout court* that more leisure and lower production are all bad. As a matter of common sense, some people may enjoy life more if they work less hard and attend to other things that life has to offer. (3) In any case, the guiding criteria for the suggested plan are the principles of utility and efficiency and of justice and equality. The utility considerations are obvious. The applicable requirement of justice and equality is that inequalities of wealth stemming from gratuitous transfers must not undermine a fully human life in society for all. If a scheme of gift and estate taxation impairs incentives to a point at which productivity falls, and if the decline in productivity does not, even in the light of greater equality of wealth, benefit those whose capacity for a fully human life is impaired, then the taxation scheme should be changed. If justice and equality require adjustments in the exclusion level or the tax rate, they should be made. Not to do so undercuts the guiding aim of the proposal.

Enforceability. It may be objected that the plan will not be effective because of lack of compliance. Noncompliance may stem from illegal behavior to escape the tax (evasion), alteration of behavior (legal tax avoidance), or exploitation of imperfections in drafting (loopholes).[47]

---

47 For these distinctions, see Wedgwood, *The Economics of Inheritance*, pp. 240–44.

In reply, it is important to mark these points. First, any tax system must deal with the problem of noncompliance. The plan does not present a greater problem of compliance than some others. With all of them it is a matter of staying one jump ahead of the taxpayer. It would be a technical, but important, undertaking to extend this treatment of gifts and bequests to other forms of material wealth transfer: trusts (particularly generation-skipping trusts), close corporations, joint ventures, sale-and-leaseback arrangements, long-term loans and leases, sweetheart employment deals, private charitable foundations, and some will substitutes.[48] Second, legal tax avoidance is all right so long as it does not cause or shelter the inequalities of wealth that the proposal seeks to reduce. If it does, the tax proposal should be amended accordingly. Third, use of loopholes shows that the drafting must be done more carefully. As loopholes become evident, they should be closed. Fourth, outright evasion should be monitored and reduced. Of course, reducing evasion is not costless, and it is not suggested that it is worthwhile to try to reduce evasion to zero. All the same, the criterion is not that evasion should be reduced to the point at which further reducing it does not yield revenue great enough to repay the additional costs of reduction. The chief aim of the proposal is to reduce inequalities of wealth, not to generate revenue. Thus, the appropriate standard is that evasion (and, indeed, all forms of noncompliance) should be reduced to the point at which further reduction is not worth the gains in both equality and revenue. Admittedly it will be controversial to assess how much of a "gain" is involved in incremental reductions in inequality of wealth.

Motivation. A final objection raises a problem of motivation: Even if the plan is sound, people will not favor it because

---

48 A step in the right direction is the relatively recent tax on generation-skipping transfers. See Tax Reform Act of 1986, Pub. L. 99–514, §§ 1431 et seq., 100 Stat. 2085, 2717–32, codified in I.R.C. §§ 2601-2663 (West 1989). The act taxes all generation-skipping transfers at a flat rate equal to the highest rate applicable under the federal estate tax (which is now 55 percent but will decline to 50 percent in 1992).

they will perceive that it is not in their self-interest. In response, it should not be conceded that people act only out of perceived self-interest. Yet the concession would harm the plan not at all, for assuming one person, one vote, the plan is in fact in the self-interest of enough people to merit passage. Perhaps this would not be so if the proposal were so radical as to bar gratuitous transfers altogether or to limit them severely. But under the plan defended here, comparatively few would lose. The potential losers are those who are now quite wealthy, will be quite wealthy in the future, or hope to receive very large sums from someone who is quite wealthy. All other people – some 80 to 90 percent of the population – would benefit or be unaffected. At least 20 to 30 percent, perhaps more, would definitely benefit.

There may, it is true, be a diffuse belief that the current system respects equality, for those who are wealthy can pass on their riches as they see fit. This belief, though, is really a myth that, in the current scheme of things, panders to the false hopes of many people to become rich and in the end serves but a small fraction of the population. No doubt some political opposition to the plan would stem from general resistance to government intervention. The plan would have to respond to this attack and others that space prevents considering here.

The plan is, in any case, part of a wider restructuring of property relations and society, and the wider endeavor will reinforce the good sense of this treatment of gratuitous transfers. If the true condition of wealth inequality and its causes were exposed, and if the advantages of the plan were carefully explained, most could come to see that they would benefit. Or, to put the matter cautiously, if they were also disabused of relevant myths and misinformation, which could well be a difficult undertaking, they could come to see the benefit. And in all this "benefit" means "material benefit." Once the nonmaterial advantages that proceed from living in a just society are taken into account, the appeal to rational self-interest should be easier still.

Chapter 14

A moral and political theory of takings

14.1 TAKINGS AND TAXINGS

Government takings of private property pose at least two problems. One is a legal problem: How should a legal system deal with situations in which government action adversely affects private holdings? In many countries, this is a problem mainly of constitutional law rather than statutory or common law. In the United States, it centers on the command of the Fifth Amendment, known as the takings clause, that "nor shall private property be taken for public use, without just compensation."[1] The other problem is one of moral and political theory: How should a society deal with situations in which government action adversely affects private holdings? It is important to distinguish the two problems because the adoption of constitutional and other institutionalized legal norms can affect the applicability of any abstract solution offered by moral and political theory. The moral and political problem is more fundamental because an answer to it should guide an answer, and if necessary correct an existing answer, to the legal problem.

This chapter applies the basic theory of property to the moral and political problem of takings. The next chapter extends the answer to that problem to the legal problem of takings under the United States Constitution. A "taking," in this context, is thus an adverse effect on private property

1   U.S. Const. amend. V.

caused by government action. Obviously, the answers to these problems are of greatest interest for a private-property economy as defined in § 5.1, because it has private ownership of the means of production. But the answers are of interest as well for economic systems that allow private property of any kind, for in all such systems government action can adversely affect private holdings.

These final chapters lay to one side a pair of problems that are at least adjacent to these two problems of takings. One concerns government action that affects persons' freedom over their bodies. Examples include laws requiring military service or restricting abortion. Some people may find it bizarre that anyone would even imagine that such laws take private property. But if, as argued in Chapter 3, persons have limited property rights in their bodies, then government action adversely affecting these rights might be a taking. If there were a taking, then the government might have to pay compensation or even abandon its action. Space does not allow pursuit of these controversial issues here. This chapter deals only with government action that adversely affects property rights that people have in external things.

The other adjacent problem involves taxation. Some may find it astonishing that anyone would maintain that to tax is to take. Yet many libertarians argue that taxation is morally and politically legitimate only to support minimal functions of the state such as police protection and national defense. Other taxation unjustifiably takes private holdings without compensation. Indeed, those libertarians who assimilate property rights in external things to property rights in the body might argue that unjustifiable taxation is not only a taking but also a kind of forced labor or slavery.

To clarify the difference between takings and taxings, it will help to distinguish between unfixed and fixed distributions of property. A distribution is unfixed if it is vulnerable to a legitimate tax on income or wealth and fixed if it is not thus vulnerable. Assume, just for illustration, that a society has legitimate taxes on income and decendents' estates. Then adjusted gross earnings prior to withholding are unfixed; they become fixed once income tax is paid. Again, holdings fixed in an owner become unfixed on his or her death until estate tax is paid. The point of the distinction is this: The moral, political, and legal problems of takings arise only insofar as a distribution is fixed because there is no private property in a full sense to be taken except insofar as legitimate income and wealth taxes have been paid. The standard background for takings, then, presupposes that legitimate taxation is no longer in the picture.

The distinction between fixed and unfixed distributions suggests that legitimate taxings are not takings, but it does not resolve any substantive or every conceptual issue, for three reasons at least. First, the distinction does not determine which taxes, if any, are legitimate. Though the basic theory has many implications for taxation, it is hardly a full-blown theory of taxation, which would require a book of its own. The distinction functions as a set-aside rather than a dodge. Second, in some instances taxes on income and wealth may amount to a taking. Possible examples are a gross-receipts tax set so high that it destroys a business, or a property tax on Indian real estate that was exempted by treaty from land taxes.[2] It may be difficult to say whether these taxes are illegitimate, or, though legitimate, are takings. Anyway, there is not always a clear line between taxes and takings. Third, if one believes that a legitimate tax can have a redistributive purpose, then one might allow that a taking could also have such a purpose. In fact, most takings that occur in the United States legal system lack any clear redistributive purpose. And even if a taking were intended to redistribute, it would not follow that it would *be* a tax. But if redistribution is sometimes legitimate, and if takings can redistribute, then one cannot rule out certain takings simply

2 On whether taxings can ever amount to takings, see A. Magnano Co. v. Hamilton, 292 U.S. 40 (1934); Alaska Fish Salting & By-Products Co. v. Smith, 255 U.S. 44 (1921); Swimming Turtle v. Bd. of County Comm'rs of Miami County, 441 F. Supp. 374 (N.D. Ind. 1977). See also City of Pittsburgh v. Alco Parking Corp., 417 U.S. 369 (1974) (combination of taxing and direct competition by taxing authority).

on the footing that they aim to redistribute income or wealth. Contextual factors determine whether taxation is a less intrusive, more efficient, or morally better means of redistribution than taking. So even if as a general matter taxes on income and wealth are preferred means, this will not always be so. In a country with grossly unjust and disproportionate land holdings, land-reform measures classifiable as takings may be in order,[3] and no moral or political justification may exist for providing full, or perhaps any, compensation.

The subject of this chapter, therefore, is government action that adversely affects private-property rights[4] in external things, prescinded from issues of taxation. Sometimes the government may acknowledge such impact, as when it condemns private land by eminent domain to build a school. At other times it may dispute the impact or at least any duty to compensate, as when it conserves wetlands or preserves architectural landmarks. This chapter first considers how to approach the moral and political problem and then tries to solve it.

14.2 AN APPROACH TO THE MORAL AND POLITICAL PROBLEM

If one accepts the basic theory of property, one should try to build a moral and political theory of takings on it. In saying this, one need not claim that it would be impossible to

---

3 For an interesting examination of this issue, along the lines of the republican themes of § 6.4, see Gia L. Cincone, "Land Reform and Corporate Redistribution: The Republican Legacy," *Stanford Law Review*, 39 (1987): 1229–57, especially at 1235–46.

4 This chapter ignores the infrequent cases where one government unit seeks to take or regulate the property of another government unit. See, for example, City of Temple Terrace v. Hillsborough Ass'n for Retarded Citizens, Inc., 322 So. 2d 571 (Fla. Dist. Ct. App. 1975), aff'd, 332 So. 2d 610 (Fla. 1976) (zoning). When the United States government condemns the property of other government units, issues of federalism arise. Thus, the justifications for compensating public condemnees may differ to some extent from the justifications for compensating private condemnees. See Michael H. Schill, "Intergovernmental Takings and Just Compensation: A Question of Federalism," *University of Pennsylvania Law Review*, 137 (1989): 829–901.

construct a portion of a theory of takings without the basic theory. Some legal scholars have in fact done much useful work on takings while attempting to remain uncommitted on the philosophical underpinnings of property. The attempt may spring in part from doubts that there are, or at least that they can find, suitable underpinnings. But since the basic theory provides these philosophical underpinnings, it would be a poor strategy to theorize about takings while remaining silent, or explicitly trying to keep options open, on the soundest general theory of property. Such a strategy would yield an account of takings that is at best incomplete.

With the basic theory in hand, one must first make some fundamental background judgments about government power and private property. The judgments rest on the finitude of government resources and the desirability of both some private property and some government action. Since, under the principle of utility and efficiency, some government projects advance preference-satisfaction, the government should at least be able to purchase private property on the open market to pursue those projects. Often market transactions are cheaper than forced transactions (eminent domain), and in fact about 80 percent of federal land acquisitions in the United States use the market.[5] But should the government have any power of eminent domain? Some will find tempting the suggestion that since private land developers often assemble large parcels by using agents, options, and straw transactions, the government can do the same. The temptation should be resisted. As Merrill convincingly argues,[6] this suggestion is overly broad. Market mechanisms do not always yield optimal land assembly when very large tracts are needed or when only one or a few sites will do. Highways, wilderness areas, and urban renewal are cases in point. Furthermore, acquiring land through the market re-

5 See Comptroller General, *Federal Land Acquisitions By Condemnation – Opportunities To Reduce Delays And Costs* (Washington, D.C.: General Accounting Office, 1980), p. 81.
6 Thomas W. Merrill, "The Economics of Public Use," *Cornell Law Review*, 72 (1986): 61–116, at 81–82.

quires secrecy to prevent holdouts and strategic bargaining, and in an open society governments are less good than private developers in keeping secrets. The first background judgment, then, is that a power of eminent domain, carefully employed, is justified. This judgment holds even if one uses only the principle of utility and efficiency. It is even more secure if one recalls that the labor-desert principle and the principle of justice and equality may favor some government projects that utility and efficiency alone do not.

Next, one should reject two extreme positions on takings and compensation. On the one hand, it is implausible to hold that the government should *never compensate*. For takings, as defined in § 14.1, include government acquisition of private titles to land. A rule offering no compensation would undermine the stability of private holdings. It would thus conflict with the fact that some private property is justifiable under the basic theory. Indeed, from the standpoint of efficiency and utility alone, never to compensate is bound to be undesirable, since at least sometimes the preference-dissatisfaction experienced by those whose land is condemned and by those who occupy similar positions will outweigh the gains from the government project.

On the other hand, it is implausible to maintain that the government should *always compensate*. Takings, as defined in § 14.1, include all adverse effects on private property caused by government action. Often the action takes such undramatic forms as closing a street for a week to make road repairs or taking several hours to make a safety or health inspection – which can cause minor losses in revenue to affected businesses. Thus, even from the perspective of utility and efficiency alone, to compensate in every case would be undesirable. Of course, if the government action is Kaldor-Hicks efficient (§ 8.4), then gainers theoretically could compensate losers, and if it is not, then one can question the action. But Kaldor-Hicks efficiency does not require that gainers compensate losers, and indeed one point of this criterion of efficiency is that the transaction costs of compensation may be too high to make compensation worth-

while. One needs more detailed arguments to establish con-
clusively that these two extreme positions are misguided.
Still, the foregoing arguments strongly support the second
background judgment – namely, the cautious conclusion
that the government should *sometimes compensate*.

14.3 UTILITY, EFFICIENCY, AND TAKINGS

One must now turn to the business of deciding when government action is justifiable and when the government
should compensate for takings. The basic theory of property
contains principles of utility and efficiency, justice and equality, and desert based on labor (§ 12.1). Since it could be
messy or unwieldy to develop simultaneously all three principles as they relate to takings, one might elaborate first the
component of utility and efficiency and see later what difference desert based on labor and justice and equality make.
Fortunately, for the first stage of the inquiry, one has an
excellent guide – a utilitarian approach offered by Michelman.[7]

The basic utilitarian strategy is to maximize net gains and
minimize net losses. To pursue this strategy, Michelman
defines three special terms.[8] "Demoralization costs" (D) are
the disutilities to uncompensated losers and their sympathiz-
ers and the lost future production from impaired incentives
or social unrest that would arise if no compensation for
government action were paid. "Settlement costs" (S) are the
costs, chiefly the administrative costs of operating a compensation program, that must be borne to avoid demoralization. "Efficiency gains" (E) are the excess of the gains pro-

---

7   Frank I. Michelman, "Property, Utility, and Fairness: Comments on
    the Ethical Foundations of 'Just Compensation' Law," *Harvard Law
    Review*, 80 (1967): 1165–1258, at 1214–18. Michelman's efforts to devel-
    op a fairness theory of takings (ibid. at 1218–24) based on Rawls's
    theory of justice are unsuccessful, for the reasons given in Stephen R.
    Munzer, "A Theory of Retroactive Legislation," *Texas Law Review*, 61
    (1982): 425–80, at 477–80, and will not be pursued further here.
8   Michelman, "Property, Utility, and Fairness," at 1214.

duced by a government action over the losses inflicted by it, not including D or S. Michelman's term "efficiency gains" is somewhat misleading because the value of E involves interpersonal comparisons of gains and losses; "utility gains" would be more accurate (§ 8.4). The relative magnitude of these three quantities is an empirical matter in any given situation.

Any time a government action is proposed, it is vital to assess the costs and benefits of the action itself and the costs and benefits of paying compensation to demoralized losers. This assessment yields conclusions on two issues of public policy. First, if the costs of demoralization and of settlement both exceed the efficiency gains of the government action, then the action is unjustifiable. It should not be undertaken at all because the efficiency gains of the measure will not be worth its costs. In other words, the proposed action should be rejected altogether in case D> S> E or S> D> E. Thus utility sets a limit to the defensible use of the power of eminent domain.[9] Second, if the government action is justifiable – that is, if the efficiency gains exceed the costs of either demoralization or settlement – then the utilitarian approach is to pay the lower of these two costs. Hence, the government should compensate if demoralization costs exceed settlement costs. Compensation is to be paid, then, in the event that E> D> S or D> E> S. On the other hand, the government should not compensate if settlement costs exceed demoralization costs. It is not worthwhile to compensate if the costs of administering payment are higher than the demoralization to be avoided – namely, where E > S > D or S > E > D. Given strict inequalities and a way of valuing gains and losses, Michelman's utilitarian approach seems to solve, for each of the six possible orderings of gains and costs, the problem of whether a proposed

9   It is only *a* limit. Even if the proposed action is justifiable, the government should use the market when doing so is cheaper than using eminent domain. For the view that, under one model, the government in effect generally chooses the cheaper alternative, see Merrill, "The Economics of Public Use," at 101.

government action is justifiable and, if so, whether compensation should be paid.

It is, however, possible to refine and improve on this approach. Michelman in effect defines S as the costs that must be borne to reduce D to zero. Given this definition, a government action will be unjustifiable if both D> E and S> E. However, it might still be the case that E would exceed the sum of the costs of allowing some demoralization to result by the use of a less expensive settlement program. Call the revised values D' and S', respectively. A government action will then be improper just in case D > E and S > E *and* there is no minimal sum of D' and S' such that E > (D' + S'). Hence Michelman's first conclusion – that the proposed action should be rejected where D > S > E or S > D > E – is overly simple. It should be accepted nonetheless if E > (D' + S'). This observation has an effect on whether to compensate, and, if so, how much to compensate, when the government action is justifiable. Once again, demoralization and settlement may be related in such a way that (D' + S') is lower than D taken alone or S taken alone. When this occurs, it makes sense to compensate by just that value of D' such that the sum of D' and S' is as low as possible. This is another way of saying that partial compensation is an eligible solution under the principle of utility and efficiency. In fact, it would appear to be the standard solution except where both (D' + S')> D and (D' + S')> S.

The reality is more complicated than the appearance because much depends on how one elaborates the utility component of this principle. If one adopts an act-utilitarian strategy that even bars use of "rules of thumb," then partial compensation will indeed be the standard solution. Yet if one adopts a strategy derived from rule-utilitarianism, or from a version of act-utilitarianism that uses "rules of thumb,"[10] then partial compensation will be an eligible, but

10 See, for example, J. J. C. Smart, "An Outline of a System of Utilitarian Ethics," in J. J. C. Smart and Bernard Williams, *Utilitarianism: For and Against* (Cambridge: Cambridge University Press, 1973), pp. 3–74, at pp. 42–57.

not the standard, solution. In these last two cases, one must be able to state and apply a rule that promotes utility. Such a rule would have to specify actions, programs, and situations in which partial compensation maximizes net gains. To frame such a rule does not seem impossible. But it does not promise to be easy. Thus, one should regard partial compensation only as an eligible solution.

Another refinement clarifies the variables in Michelman's calculus. Some of his definitions are unclear or unduly narrow. The labeling, if not the definition, of E should be changed. Because E contemplates interpersonal comparisons of utility, but because such comparisons may not always be possible (§§ 8.4 and 8.5), it would be better to speak of "utility/efficiency gains" (U/E). For D one substitutes "noncompensation costs" (N), which are all costs incurred if no compensation is given. N includes D. But the new term frees the analysis from the unduly psychological overtones of the word "demoralization." Also, it includes all costs stemming from risk aversion, even if they are not part of D. For S one substitutes "compensation costs" (C), which are all costs that are paid if full compensation is given. Full compensation is in turn defined as the amount needed to reduce N to zero. C includes the various administrative costs mentioned by Michelman. But the new term also includes costs that one does not usually consider administrative. Here are three examples: If the availability of full compensation induces persons to invest in risky property more than they would do otherwise, then the over-investment retards the efficient allocation of resources ("incentive effect costs"). Again, if the availability of full compensation induces persons to affect the probability or magnitude of an event that triggers compensation, as by lobbying or bribery, then their actions retard efficiency ("moral hazard costs"). Yet again, if raising the revenue for full compensation causes economic distortion or evasion, then such effects retard efficiency ("revenue costs"). Given strict inequalities and a way of valuing gains and costs, the six possible orderings of gains and costs described earlier still hold, substituting U/E for E,

N for D, and C for S throughout. Similarly, one can construct revised values, called N' and C', which affect the justifiability of government action and the matter of partial compensation in the ways described above.

One may now introduce three further refinements that stem from the principle of utility and efficiency as elaborated in Chapter 8. The first refinement observes that to maximize utility, in this context, is to maximize the satisfaction of preferences, especially those preferences that involve rational and institutionally legitimate expectations concerning material things (§ 8.7). Thus, one should not give equal weight to all expectations of equal strength or intensity in assessing utility/efficiency gains and costs of compensation or noncompensation. Instead, one should favor expectations that are part of a web of concordant expectations supported by social and legal institutions. More precisely, one should insist that, as a general matter, only expectations that are both rational and institutionally legitimate present a strong structural claim for protection. This insistence will reduce costs associated with incentive effects, moral hazard, and raising revenue for compensation. Hence, in determining values for U/E, N, C, and (N' + C'), one should look beyond the expectations held by an individual person to whether the expectations satisfy the criteria for rationality and institutional legitimacy.

Consider contrasting hypothetical illustrations that involve expectations and rezoning. Assume that the basic theory justifies government power to zone and, because land use needs can change, to change existing zoning classifications. In one community, unimproved land was rezoned from commercial to single-family residential. The owner claimed that the rezoning destroyed his expectations of a large profit from building a shopping center. However, he had not engaged an architect or contractor or sought a building permit. In this case, if the zoning authority has done its work well, the new classification is sound. Thus, the utility/efficiency gains favor the rezoning. No compensation, or at least very little, is in order. Noncompensation costs are apt to

429

be low where an owner has taken no concrete steps to develop his property. If the government had to compensate in relevantly similar situations, it would make sensible use of the power to rezone very expensive and hence would retard utility. Such considerations should be built into legal or social rules on zoning. The owner of the rezoned property has, then, no rational and legitimate expectations sufficient to require compensation.

Suppose, though, that in a similar community an owner claimed that rezoning from commercial to single-family residential destroyed her expectations of a large profit from a shopping enter. In this case, she had engaged an architect two years earlier, obtained a building permit a year ago, and now her contractor has the shopping center half completed. Here one might well wonder if conditions have changed so radically as to make the rezoning wise. If they have not, the rezoning is counter to utility and should be abandoned. But suppose that conditions are radically different and that utility/efficiency gains favor the rezoning. Then full compensation, or something close to it, is required. Noncompensation costs are likely to be high when the owner has taken several concrete steps over a two-year period to develop the property. The costs stem not merely from the keen disappointment and financial loss to the owner. They derive as well from the fact that, if no compensation is paid, similarly situated property owners will not develop their land in ways that would be useful (high costs from risk aversion). Moreover, if the government does not have to compensate, it may overuse the power to take and may not take into account the full consequences of its action ("fiscal illusion"). Such deterrent considerations should be part of the legal and social order. Thus in this case the owner of the rezoned property does have rational and legitimate expectations that make compensation desirable.

The second refinement is that one should hold that takings policy must enlist the rational alteration of preferences (§ 8.6), and hence must look to the long run. From the standpoint of utility, one should move to the set of preferences and expectations that it is possible to satisfy and that, if satisfied, will yield the most satisfaction. This thought, applied to takings, means that the government should adjust its practice of regulation and compensation to accommodate new conditions and to inhibit the entrenchment of preferences and expectations whose satisfaction would not maximize utility. In economic terms, the adjustment pays special attention to incentive-effect costs over time. It seeks to restructure incentives.

Consider the introduction of zoning in the early decades of this century.[11] It may well have been the case that owners of newly zoned land expected compensation. To have compensated might have best promoted utility in the short run. But cities were becoming more crowded. Conflicting land uses were creating problems. Thus it made sense, in the long run, not to compensate certain owners of newly zoned land. Had their expectations of compensation been upheld, it would have been too expensive for most cities to do as much zoning as was desirable. It is true that cities could have borrowed and amortized the loans needed to compensate; in fact, cities sometimes issue bonds for one-shot projects such as sewers. Yet, in the case of initial zoning, this course of action would have been expensive because it would only have spread over time the costs of compensating for one instance of zoning and might not have provided the flexibility necessary to rezone in the face of future changes in circumstances. To have postponed a change – for example, by saying that twenty years hence all loss in value from new zoning would go uncompensated – would have been unsatisfactory. That would probably have been too late. And postponement would have fostered the undesirable expectation that the government would regulate land use only when those favored by the existing system were not disturbed. Hence, a policy of uncompensated initial zonings for a certain range of situations, over time, altered what counted as

11 Here the lawyer will think of the famous case of Village of Euclid v. Ambler Realty Co., 272 U.S. 365 (1926).

rational and legitimate expectations about land-use regulation.[12]

The third refinement is that one should insist, to the consternation of some critics of utilitarianism, that room exists for both property *interests* and property *rights* (§ 8.8). A "property interest" is an entitlement to property that is just as powerful in given circumstances as can be justified on grounds of utility and efficiency alone. A "property right" is a property entitlement that has some threshold capacity to withstand competing claims of utility and efficiency. The phrase "in given circumstances" signals that one is invoking some strategy derived from rule-utilitarianism or from a version of act-utilitarianism that allows rules of thumb.

This distinction between property interests and property rights applies to takings as follows. An anti-utilitarian may object that one can, in the utility component of the theory, recognize only property interests. One cannot support morally the enforcement of property rights against the government when, in given circumstances, it would advance utility not to enforce them. The concept of a right includes the power to trump some competing considerations of utility and efficiency. Here one should reply that sometimes a property interest falls under a rule that affects the calculation of utility. If one views the interest in the given circumstances only, as an extreme act-utilitarian would, no property right exists. But if one views it not merely in the actual circumstances given but as falling under some rule undergirded by utility, then a property right, as defined above, might well exist. The case of Martin in § 8.8 illustrates this possibility. One can acknowledge that the property rights that this version of utility supports might be less powerful than those

---

12　This argument in terms of expectations overlaps, but is not identical with, the argument that because of imperfections in the market zoning sometimes promotes efficiency better than other courses of action. For insightful criticisms of zoning – too detailed to consider here – see Robert C. Ellickson, "Alternatives to Zoning: Covenants, Nuisance Rules, and Fines as Land Use Controls," *University of Chicago Law Review*, 40 (1973): 681–781.

supported by rival philosophical traditions. Yet rights supported by utility will not necessarily be less powerful. Rival traditions generally allow rights of property to be qualified by other considerations, and the qualifications might be more stringent than those imposed by this version of rule-utilitarianism.

With these three refinements in hand, one can summarize the utility and efficiency component of the moral and political theory of takings in this way. First make sure that the government action creates utility/efficiency gains that exceed the costs of either compensation or noncompensation (or of some minimal sum of these costs). If it does not, then reject the action. If it does, approve the action and pay the lower of the two costs. In ascertaining these costs, pay special attention to incentive effects, moral hazard, revenue costs, fiscal illusion, rational and legitimate expectations, long-range rational alteration of preferences, and the desirability of some property rights as distinct from property interests. The impact of this theory cannot be determined without empirical information about the factors influencing the costs just listed. But it seems almost certain that, despite gains that are Kaldor-Hicks efficient (§§ 8.4 and 14.2), the costs of compensation will sometimes be high enough to rule out full compensation. It also seems likely that sometimes utility will favor no compensation for government actions that adversely affect private property.

A final note: One should be cautious, but not hidebound, about substituting private insurance for government compensation. Someone might argue that if persons are risk-averse, if there is full information and markets are perfectly competitive, and if the cost of an insurance policy equals its expected value (actuarially fair insurance), then persons will want to insure fully against the risk of government action adversely affecting their property. Even if there are departures from full information, perfect competition, and actuarially fair premiums, many persons will want to buy some insurance, provided that the departures are not too great. If one assumes also that private markets are more efficient than government intervention, private insurance is better than government compensation.

One should neither flatly reject nor wholeheartedly endorse this argument. One possibility is that insurance companies have overlooked a new area of business. If they can do a better job than government compensation, delight is in order. At least this is so for the utility component of the theory; one should be skeptical that the private market can do better once nonutility components are introduced (§ 14.4).

Another possibility, however, is that insurance companies have overlooked nothing. In fact, "takings" insurance is virtually unavailable in the United States. Although some writers have professed to know why this is so,[13] their explanations are not wholly convincing. Moral hazard is an unsatisfactory explanation. For insurance companies could use deductibles or coinsurance, exclude recovery in certain cases, or lower premiums for actions that reduce moral hazard – as with insurance for homes, automobiles, and medical care. Also unsatisfactory is the explanation that the practice of government compensation antedated private insurance and thus made such insurance superfluous. Many adverse effects of government action still go uncompensated. And antedating has not foreclosed private suppliers in other areas; the postal service has existed for centuries, yet companies like United Parcel Service and Federal Express do well. A more helpful, but still not wholly satisfactory, explanation appeals to an asymmetry of information –

13   See Lawrence Blume and Daniel L. Rubinfeld, "Compensation for Takings: An Economic Analysis," *California Law Review*, 72 (1984): 569–628, at 592–97 (moral hazard and adverse selection); William A. Fischel and Perry Shapiro, "Takings, Insurance, and Michelman: Comments on Economic Interpretations of 'Just Compensation' Law," *Journal of Legal Studies*, 17 (1988): 269–93, at 286 (adverse selection); Louis Kaplow, "An Economic Analysis of Legal Transitions," *Harvard Law Review*, 99 (1986): 509–617, at 539 n.84 (government compensation antedating private insurance markets); Schill, "Intergovernmental Takings and Just Compensation," at 855–56 (adverse selection and moral hazard).

that would-be insureds have a better idea of the risks than would-be insurers ("adverse selection"). This explanation helps, because in some situations would-be insureds actually may have better information that would-be insurers. Interestingly, there is some private and some government-sponsored insurance against expropriation for United States investors in foreign countries;[14] in this situation, insurers may have as good information as insureds. But the explanation is not wholly satisfactory. For even if there were no informational asymmetry, one needs more evidence and argument to show that it is sufficiently great to preclude altogether a market for "takings" insurance. Also, the government could negate the asymmetry by requiring everyone to insure (compare mandatory automobile insurance). In sum, the argument is unconvincing that market failure explains the absence of private insurance against takings, or that government insurance would not be a possible substitute.

14.4 THE IMPACT OF LABOR-DESERT AND JUSTICE AND EQUALITY

At this point, one is at best halfway to a solution of the moral and political problem. One must now integrate the perspective of utility and efficiency on takings with the rest of the basic theory of property. That theory also includes a principle of desert based on labor and a principle of justice and equality. To apply the remaining principles, one should first ascertain whether the society to which the moral and political theory of takings will apply conforms, in its property arrangements, to the basic theory. Obviously, conformity is a matter of degree, and perfect conformity is quite unlikely. To simplify matters, assume that there are just two possibili-

---

14 See, for example, Joseph P. Griffin, "Transfer of OPIC's Investment Insurance Programs to Private Insurers: Prospects and Proposals," *Law and Policy in International Business*, 8 (1976): 631–56; Vance R. Koven, "Expropriation and the 'Jurisprudence' of OPIC," *Harvard International Law Journal*, 22 (1981): 269–327.

ties. Either the society conforms very well (full conformity), or it fails to conform in a number of major respects (partial conformity). The difference between full and partial conformity affects, first, the justification for exercising the power of eminent domain, and, second, the compensation offered, if any, to adversely affected property owners. The simplifying assumption elides no issue of principle. But it makes the following argument less complicated than it would be otherwise.

Suppose that a society fully conforms to the basic theory. In that case, justification of the proposed government action turns solely on considerations of utility and efficiency. *Ex hypothesi* no corrective or backward-looking adjustment is needed. Thus the use of eminent domain rests on the forward-looking ground that reallocating resources will promote utility and efficiency. Only the principle of utility and efficiency is relevant. Hence, the utility/efficiency gains of the proposed action must exceed at least one of the following: the noncompensation costs, the compensation costs, or the minimal sum of such costs under a revised compensation program.

To handle issues of compensation under full conformity, one must ascertain the ground of the property entitlements adversely affected by the government action, and distinguish between degenerate and nondegenerate cases. The degenerate cases are those in which the entitlements rest on utility alone; on all three principles, but desert based on labor and the principle of justice and equality offset each other; or on a combination such that utility offsets any competing principles with force to spare. The identification of these cases is apt to be controversial. It may be hard to show, as in the first case, that only utility is in play. It may be harder to do the moral mathematics contemplated by the last two cases. Given these difficulties, identification will most likely have to proceed by social or legal rules classifying different situations. But if one can identify such cases, then the decision whether to compensate and, if so, how much, will turn solely on the utility component of the moral and political theory of takings. These cases are degenerate because they involve no moves beyond those described in the previous section.

The nondegenerate cases arise when utility and efficiency do not exhaust the force of or limitations on property entitlements. Utility and efficiency need not, but ordinarily still will, be in play. But here the principle of desert based on labor and the principle of justice and equality support, or limit, entitlements in a way not reducible to considerations of utility and efficiency. If they do, then the case for compensation is, respectively, stronger or weaker. For example, imagine that the government appropriates the right to manufacture and distribute a new vaccine from a person who discovered it after years of solitary research. The principle of desert based on labor strengthens the case for full compensation to the discoverer. No suggestion is made, in this example or in others, that a single scale or gradient exists for being entitled to compensation. The claim is only that one can appreciate, in some less precise way, how considerations other than utility can strengthen or weaken the case for compensation.

One may now shift attention to cases involving only partial conformity to the basic theory. The initial move is to ascertain the purpose of the government action. Does it aim to promote utility by reallocating resources, or to correct some shortcoming in existing property arrangements, or some combination of the two? Some may assume that if the existing arrangements are deficient, then the government's purpose must be to correct them. But one should not assume this. Nor should one assume that the government must be deemed to have a corrective purpose. The reason is that takings may not be a good corrective means. As pointed out in § 14.1, taxation is ordinarily better than takings as a method of redistribution. Takings are ordinarily too haphazard or ill-tailored to correct systematically. There are exceptions, as will emerge. And there would be something wrong with a society if it failed to conform to the basic theory in major respects and never tried to correct the deficiencies.

Prolonged failure to come to grips with the deficiences might justify ascribing a corrective purpose. At all events, one should first ascertain purpose. One need adopt no particular view of discovering or ascribing purpose. One can select whichever view best suits the task.

Suppose that one finds that the government action aims only to promote utility by reallocating resources. Suppose further that no aggravating circumstances exist; the government has not, for example, been ignoring departures from the basic theory for a long time. In this situation the use of eminent domain, subject to a proviso, is justified exactly as before – namely, if the efficiency gains exceed the costs of compensation, noncompensation, or some minimal sum of the two. The proviso is that the government action must not exacerbate the shortcomings of the existing property arrangements. One can resolve the issue of compensation in parallel fashion. Whether compensation is offered and, if it is, how much, will proceed in accordance with the degenerate and nondegenerate possibilities discussed under the heading of full conformity. But there is a proviso: The compensation paid or withheld must not exacerbate existing deficiencies. One makes these choices because, since no correction is sought, the pertinent considerations are, with one exception, the same as in the case of full conformity. The exception is that neither the government action nor the compensatory practice may exacerbate current departures from the basic theory. In fact, even the exception has an exception. Should the utility/efficiency gains be sufficiently great, they can override the proviso. But this is not likely and is not merely a matter of balancing.

Suppose, however, that the government action aims to correct some shortcoming in existing property arrangements. Variables abound. The corrective purpose may be avowed or ascribed. The need for correction may stem from past wrongdoing or from a change in circumstances that caused a formerly acceptable property arrangement to become unacceptable under the basic theory. The ground for correction may be utility or not.

438

Though even a schematic discussion of all the possibilities would be lengthy, the following general points stand out. First, the government action must be a better corrective mechanism than taxation. Otherwise one should opt to tax and redistribute. Second, it matters whether the need for correction proceeds from past wrongdoing in connection with the property at issue. If it does, then, other things being equal, action becomes more urgent. If the government takes such action, then, other things being equal, the case for compensation, or at least full compensation, diminishes in the event that those whose property is adversely affected are themselves wrongdoers or profited from past wrongdoing. Third, if the ground of correction is utility, this will affect prior calculations of utility. The problems are apt to be especially knotty when nonutility considerations undergird or limit the property entitlements in question. The treatment of nondegenerate cases under full conformity indicates some of the problems. Fourth, if the ground of correction is not utility, a different problem can arise – namely, conflict among the three principles of the basic theory. For the nonutility ground sometimes can justify exercises of eminent domain even though the utility/efficiency gains fail to offset the costs. And it can sometimes justify more, less, or no compensation in cases where a different amount of compensation would advance utility.

An illustration that involves the labor-desert principle may bring closer to earth this unavoidably abstract discussion of corrective action under partial conformity. Imagine that a century ago a small group of industrialists owned most of the productive resources in heavy manufacturing. They paid employees an extremely low wage, market conditions gave employees no effective opportunity to work elsewhere, and industrialist profit margins were very high. With only minor changes, these conditions have prevailed down to the present day. Descendants of the original industrialists hold sway over heavy manufacturing through either close corporations or control of sufficient shares in corporations that have gone public. Descendants of former employees work in the plants. Wages are higher but still low. Employees have little control over conditions in the workplace. As a result of these and other factors, productivity sags.

Accordingly, the government proposes a compulsory buyout of the manufacturing plants. Ownership is to be transferred first to the government and gradually over the next fifty years to present and future employees. The program is ultimately to be self-funding. Initial capital for the purchase comes from the government. The government investment is to be gradually retired from anticipated increased productivity deriving from better incentives to employees. Current shareholders will receive compensation, some of it deferred, that amounts to about ninety cents on the dollar for the market value of their holdings.[15]

One would have to add many details to this rather stylized illustration before it would be possible to judge the proposal securely, but here is how to go about it. One should first decide whether this is an appropriate exercise of eminent domain. Not only must one determine whether some tax program that leaves ownership of the plants undisturbed is superior to the government proposal. One must also decide whether the plan has a good chance of success. Yet one's criterion of success is not that the efficiency gains must exceed the minimal sum of compensation and noncompensation costs. One must recognize that utility is not the sole aim of the proposal. It has also a corrective aim based on a nonutility consideration. The government is in part trying to adjust for past violations of desert based on labor that were involved in the low wages and high profits over the last century.[16]

15 For general discussion from a republican perspective, see Cincone, "Land Reform and Corporate Redistribution," at 1247–56.
16 The text assumes that it is possible to elaborate the notion of a "group" such that the original employees and their descendants are members of the same group over time and that the buyout program is corrective rather than merely redistributive. No attempt is made to justify this assumption here, but it will be important to do so eventually in light of Christopher W. Morris, "Existential Limits to the Rectification of Past Wrongs," American Philosophical Quarterly, 21 (1984): 175–82.

Suppose that one concludes, on these and additional facts, that eminent domain is justifiable. One must move next to judge the compensatory aspects of the plan. On the one hand, the lack of full compensation should be troubling, because the precedent, if not firmly cabined, may destabilize expectations regarding other forms of productive property. On the other hand, full compensation would exacerbate problems of funding and leave past wrongdoing un-corrected. The assessment will turn significantly on how well one can control the political and social repercussions of the program. One could add further details in many different ways. It seems plausible that, on some set of further details, less than full compensation would be justifiable.

A pair of warnings may forestall some misguided objections to this integrated moral and political theory of takings. First, the theory is not a formula or a calculus. It is a set of distinctions, together with reasons for them, that enables someone who accepts the basic theory to think more systematically and effectively about takings. Second, the theory is susceptible of development. One method of development is to conjoin it with an account of institutional competence. Some judgments about takings may be better made by legislatures and others better made by courts. Another method is to elaborate subordinate rules that comport with the theory of takings but are easier to apply directly than is the theory itself. These warnings suggest that to develop the theory, one should consider the legal problem of takings.

Chapter 15

Takings and the constitution

15.1 SOME TRADITIONAL JUDICIAL TESTS

Even if the moral and political theory developed in Chapter 14 is sound, it hardly follows that it is part of federal constitutional law. Justice Holmes once observed that the United States Constitution did not enact Herbert Spencer's *Social Statics*.[1] It did not enact the basic theory of property either, or the moral and political theory of takings constructed on it. Still, the latter theory has constitutional implications, and this chapter tries to explain them. The itinerary is as follows. This section examines some traditional judicial tests for takings. The next discusses some academic approaches to takings. Later sections elaborate and apply a new constitutional perspective. The chapter as a whole shows how the account of property developed in this book can be translated into concrete legal applications.

The present examination is limited to judicial doctrines relating to the takings clause of the Fifth Amendment – "nor shall private property be taken for public use, without just compensation."[2] Its language raises constitutional questions

---

1 Lochner v. New York, 198 U.S. 45, 75 (1905) (Holmes, J., dissenting).
2 U.S. Const. amend. V. The Constitution does not list a power of eminent domain. Such a power is presupposed or tacitly recognized. See United States v. Carmack, 329 U.S. 230, 241–42 (1946); Kohl v. United States, 91 U.S. 367 (1875). The takings clause is so read that the power can be exercised *only* for a "public use." The "public use" requirement has on the whole become less stringent over nearly two centuries. See note 46 below.

concerning what is "private property," whether it has been "taken" for a "public use," and what counts as "just" compensation. The constitutional inquiry typically becomes a search for a "test" – that is, a standard that affords clear and definite guidance to a competent lawyer or judge after careful examination – for the existence of a taking and, to a lesser extent, for the proper compensation.

The results of the inquiry are mixed. Since the nineteenth century the Supreme Court has developed several "tests" for takings. Yet each raises difficulties if offered as a sole test. The scholarly reconstruction of these tests by Michelman, though it sheds light on their underlying sense, has little predictive value. The brief discussion to follow will provide little that is new for the informed lawyer, but should aid the lay reader.

The earliest federal takings tests are physical invasion and noxious use.[3] The physical-invasion test says that if the government physically invades private property, than a "taking" has occurred and compensation must be paid. Examples of physical invasion include occupation, acquisition of title, flooding of private land as a result of a government dam, and very low government airplane flights directly over private land. The complementary noxious-use test holds that if the government controls or prohibits uses of property that are

---

The usual standard for "just" compensation under the Fifth Amendment is fair market value. See, for example, United States v. 564.54 Acres of Land, 441 U.S. 506 (1979); United States v. Fuller, 409 U.S. 488 (1973); Almota Farmers Elevator & Warehouse Co. v. United States, 409 U.S. 470 (1973). The standard is not employed when fair market value cannot be determined or when its application would "result in manifest injustice to owner or public." See United States v. Commodities Trading Corp., 339 U.S. 121, 123 (1950).

3   The classic formulation of the complementary tests of physical invasion and noxious use is Mugler v. Kansas, 123 U.S. 623 (1887). For instances of physical invasion, see United States v. Causby, 328 U.S. 256 (1946) (direct overflights); Pumpelly v. Green Bay Co., 80 U.S. (13 Wall.) 166 (1871) (flooding). Examples of noxious use include Hadacheck v. Sebastian, 239 U.S. 394 (1915) (brickyard); L'Hote v. New Orleans, 177 U.S. 587 (1900) (brothel); Mugler v. Kansas, 123 U.S. at 623 (brewery); Fertilizing Co. v. Hyde Park, 97 U.S. 659 (1878) (fertilizer works).

injurious to public health, safety or welfare, then a "mere regulation" is involved and no compensation need be offered. Examples of noxious use include the employment of land for prostitution, fertilizer plants, liquor manufacture, and brickmaking in a residential area.

Familiar problems arise with these tests, whether employed individually or together, as a touchstone for takings. Some government actions have been held to be takings even though there was no physical intrusion. This may occur, for instance, when a city government rezones property for school purposes to get what it wants without paying for it, or imposes height restrictions on land near an airport to avoid using eminent domain.[4] Again, a few physical invasions have been held noncompensable. An example is the subdivision exaction (mandatory dedication), under which a developer must, say, construct a water or sewer line and then transfer title to the city government.[5] Finally, it may seem silly to find a taking when the physical occupation benefits the property and is extremely slight, as when a state law requires apartment owners to allow wires and junction boxes for cable television on their buildings.[6]

The noxious-use test also falters. As Sax observes, often it is difficult to identify one use as "noxious."[7] Instead there

---

4   See, for example, City of Plainfield v. Borough of Middlesex, 69 N.J. Super. 136, 173 A.2d 785 (1961) (rezoning for school purposes requires compensation); Yara Engineering Corp. v. City of Newark, 132 N.J.L. 370, 40 A.2d 559 (1945) (height restrictions near airport require compensation).

5   See, for example, Associated Home Builders, Inc. v. City of Walnut Creek, 4 Cal. 3d 633, 484 P.2d 606, 94 Cal. Rptr. 630 (parks and fees), appeal dismissed, 404 U.S. 878 (1971); Ayres v. City Council of Los Angeles, 34 Cal. 2d 31, 207 P.2d 1 (1949) (streets); Crownhill Homes, Inc. v. City of San Antonio, 433 S.W.2d 448 (Tex. Civ. App. 1968) (water mains). A different and more dramatic example is United States v. Caltex (Philippines), Inc., 344 U.S. 149 (1952) (wartime government destruction of oil refinery requires no compensation).

6   See Loretto v. Teleprompter Manhattan CATV Corp., 458 U.S. 419 (1982) (found taking and remanded on issue of amount of compensation).

7   Joseph L. Sax, "Takings and the Police Power," Yale Law Journal, 74 (1964): 36–76, at 48–50.

may be two uses that are individually innocent or desirable but that conflict.[8] Furthermore, as Sax also observes,[9] the test works well for police-power regulations, common in the nineteenth and early twentieth centuries, that affected uses of land for prostitution, liquor manufacture, and the like. It falters for contemporary forms of regulation, involving zoning, conservation, scenic easements, landmarks, and historic-district preservation, which are often held noncompensable.[10]

A different and slightly later test is diminution of value. This test holds that if government action excessively diminishes the value of property, then there is a taking and compensation must be paid, and, if it does not, then no taking has occurred and no compensation need be paid.[11] Put this way, the test is inaccurate as a description of the outcome of many cases. In consequence, the test might be reformulated to apply only where there is neither a physical invasion (almost always compensable) nor a restriction on a nuisance (never compensable). Yet even thus confined, the test appears open to objections made by Sax.[12] It pre-

8   The classic case of innocent conflicting uses is Miller v. Schoene, 276 U.S. 272 (1928) (cedar-apple rust).

9   See Sax, "Takings and the Police Power," at 39–40.

10 Contemporary forms of regulation not involving noxious uses have been upheld in, for example, Penn Central Transp. Co. v. New York City, 438 U.S. 104 (1978) (landmarks); Village of Euclid v. Ambler Realty Co., 272 U.S. 365 (1926) (zoning); Just v. Marinette County, 56 Wis. 2d 7, 201 N.W.2d 761 (1972) (wetlands conservation).

   Of course, such regulations are not always upheld. For extensive discussions of the cases, see, for example, Bruce A. Ackerman, *Private Property and the Constitution* (New Haven: Yale University Press, 1977); Richard A. Epstein, *Takings: Private Property and the Power of Eminent Domain* (Cambridge, Mass.: Harvard University Press, 1985); Frank I. Michelman, "Property, Utility, and Fairness: Comments on the Ethical Foundations of 'Just Compensation' Law," *Harvard Law Review*, 80 (1967): 1165–1258.

11 The diminution-of-value test is usually traced to Justice Holmes's opinion in Pennsylvania Coal Co. v. Mahon, 260 U.S. 393 (1922), though Holmes did not propose it as a sole test for takings. The test is discussed critically in Michelman, "Property, Utility, and Fairness," at 1190–93, and Sax, "Takings and the Police Power," at 50–60.

12 See Sax, "Takings and the Police Power," at 50–60.

supposes some fairly expansive definition of "property," according to which all legally acquired economic values are property. In fact, however, many cases can be found that hold such values not to be "property." Nor, he argues, should they. The history of the compensation principle and of the framing of the takings clause indicates that only those losses inflicted by arbitrary or unfair government action are to be compensated.

The diminution-of-value test also involves a difficult problem of definition. Presumably an "excessive" diminution is to be viewed as an excessively high percentage of the value of a parcel of property, not a fixed sum or a percentage of the owner's total wealth. But how high is excessive? There is no obvious solution to this definitional problem in general. Still less is there in troublesome cases. Michelman's example is a nontrespassory devaluation resulting from public development, and the issue is whether there is a total destruction of part of the parcel or partial destruction of the whole.[13] The problem assumes special force when the "parcel" is split into layers, as with surface rights and mining rights, or surface rights and air rights. At all events, the force of the case launching the diminution-of-value test may have been eroded to some extent, since a 1987 case held, on very similar facts, that no taking had occurred.[14]

Michelman has made a masterful effort to rehabilitate these tests, in combination, in light of his utilitarian and "fairness" perspectives on takings. To use his language (§ 14.3), demoralization costs are apt to be high when there is a physical invasion because it is a great shock to the security of expectations lodged in things. The physical-invasion test thus marks off at least one class of clearly compensable cases and holds down settlement costs. It cannot, however, discern which cases are clearly noncompensable. Again, if an activity involves a nuisance, then from the standpoint of

---

13 Michelman, "Property, Utility, and Fairness," at 1191–93.
14 See Keystone Bituminous Coal Ass'n v. DeBenedictis, 480 U.S. 470 (1987) (5–4 decision).

fairness no compensation is warranted for government restriction or prohibition of that activity. Nevertheless, this observation hardly provides, of itself, an account of when an activity is a "nuisance." Lastly, the utilitarian framework can make sense of diminution of value. Demoralization costs are likely to be high if value is greatly diminished. The importance of an identifiable parcel of property now becomes clearer. Without it there is difficulty in explaining why expectations will be disrupted in a way that involves great demoralization. Still, to elaborate diminution of value in terms of utility is to recognize that, as argued in § 14.3, partial compensation is an eligible utilitarian solution. This recognition does not square with the all-or-nothing cast of most takings law: Either a taking has occurred or it has not, and if it has, then full compensation must be paid.

Michelman's efforts give insight into the joint and several merits of these traditional takings tests. But they do not yield much by way of predictive value. The rehabilitation often will not aid the lawyer much in determining, in a case not clearly covered by precedent, whether a taking will be judged to have occurred. So, for instance, the rehabilitation would not obviously have yielded the result that a landmark designation decreasing the value of a building by prohibiting the erection of a large office tower atop an existing structure would be held not a taking.[15] Nor could it have been anticipated that the government takes property when it decrees a public right of access to a former inland pond, now dredged and opened to the ocean by a private developer, even though the pond was "navigable water" subject to regulation under the commerce clause.[16] To put it mildly, no "set formula"[17] is used in, or explains, the Supreme Court's decisions. Thus a good part of the characteristic function of a "test" – namely, to yield clear and definite guidance to a

15 See Penn Central Transp. Co. v. New York City, 438 U.S. 104 (1978).
16 See Kaiser Aetna v. United States, 444 U.S. 164 (1979). See also Vaughn v. Vermillion Corp., 444 U.S. 206 (1979).
17 Goldblatt v. Town of Hempstead, 369 U.S. 590, 594 (1962).

competent lawyer or judge – is not performed under Michelman's rehabilitation.

15.2 SOME OTHER ACADEMIC APPROACHES

If reconstruction of traditional tests falls short in this way, it seems reasonable to inquire whether some test or theory based on a rethinking of the concept of property, yet tied to the Constitution, might do better. Academic writing on takings is distinguished and voluminous.[18] For brevity's sake, this section will discuss only a few of the better known theoretical approaches.

Sax has offered two such theories. The first asserts that property is not something fixed by existing economic values, but is the outcome of a process of competition between incompatible economic values. Since the process is continuing, the outcome will vary over time. Under this conception of property, the constitutional problem of takings turns on what kinds of competition existing economic values may be exposed to and from what kinds they should be protected. Sax's suggested solution rests on a distinction between government as enterpriser and government as arbiter or mediator. If government causes economic loss while acting in its enterprise capacity, then a taking has occurred and compensation is due. But if government acts in its arbitral or mediating capacity, then economic losses are noncompensable. The theory fits nicely classic examples of government as enterpriser (such as road building, in which compensation is paid) and as arbiter (such as environmental or safety laws, in which no compensation is paid). Sax gives two arguments for the theory. One is that the history of the compensation clause reflects concern, not with all legally acquired economic values, but only with "arbitrary" or "unfair"[19] govern-

18 See, for example, the many excellent articles in "The Jurisprudence of Takings," *Columbia Law Review*, 88 (1988): 1581–1794.
19 These terms are used interchangeably in Sax, "Takings and the Police Power," at 57–60. It can be argued that they do not stand for equivalent concepts.

ment action that interferes with such values. The other is that when the government acts as enterpriser, there are special risks of discrimination, excessive zeal, and unlimited exposure to loss.

Despite its substantial explanatory and critical power, the theory is not wholly satisfactory. First, the distinction between enterpriser and arbiter is often hard to apply. Hence the theory frequently cannot discharge the main function of a test – namely, to provide clear and definite guidance that is accessible to a competent lawyer or judge upon careful inquiry. Suppose that a city imposes a very high gross-receipts tax on commercial parking lot operators.[20] The purposes of the tax are to reduce traffic congestion and to promote environmental quality, which are arbitral functions. However, the city owns parking lots that compete for business with commercial lots, which suggests that the city is also acting in an enterprise capacity. The fact is that many complex government activities, such as that involved here, mix enterprise and arbitral functions. Consequently, they cannot be placed firmly on either side of Sax's distinction.

Second, the distinction between enterpriser and arbiter sometimes is not merely hard to draw but also mainly a matter of form.[21] Consider the famous case in which the city of Los Angeles ordered a brickyard to cease production.[22] The brickyard had formerly been outside city limits. But as Los Angeles grew it annexed more land, and the brickyard was brought within city limits. The city banned brickmaking in order to spare homeowners who had built nearby from noise and dust. The ban was an arbital decision, but it likely caused every bit as much demoralization as if the government had taken the land for a school. The underlying difficulty about form is that whether the government acts in its

20 See Alco Parking Corp. v. City of Pittsburgh, 453 Pa. 245, 307 A.2d 851, 863–64 and n.14 (1973) (purporting to apply Sax's distinction), *rev'd*, 417 U.S. 369 (1974).
21 See Note, "Developments in the Law – Zoning," *Harvard Law Review*, 91 (1978): 1427–1708, at 1475.
22 Hadacheck v. Sebastian, 239 U.S. 394 (1915).

enterprise capacity, as by building schools, roads or military bases, or its arbitral capacity, as by prohibiting brickyards or restricting strip mining or the development of wetlands, it characteristically does so in behalf of some competing interest that is merely diffuse rather than discrete.

Third, it is not clear that, whatever the true constitutional history of the takings clause, its historical or original meaning should be decisive today. In many areas, judges and others substantially extend or even modify original meaning. Judicial "interpretations" of the commerce, contract, and equal protection clauses are conspicuous examples. Since conceptions of property and of legitimate limitations on it have evolved substantially over the last 200 years, perhaps the takings clause now no longer means, or should mean, what it once meant.[23] It is possible that the risks to property by government action that troubled the framers may not be the same risks that do, or should, trouble people today.

Fourth, although special risks may be associated with enterprise activity, there is no necessary or universal connection. Perhaps the test should be reversed for cases where mediation carries high risks and enterprise activity low risks. Or perhaps sometimes a wait-and-see attitude should be adopted and compensation paid only if the risks materialize.

These seemingly isolated objections in fact fall into a pattern. It is possible to think of Sax's theory as involving both a surface operation and an underlying purpose. The enterpriser/arbiter distinction belongs to the surface level. The underlying purpose of the theory is to ferret out those cases involving "arbitrary" or "unfair" government action, for they pose special risks of discrimination and excessive zeal. The two levels of the theory are linked because the surface labels of "enterpriser" and "arbiter" are correlated, respectively, with the presence or absence of these special risks. If this reconstruction of Sax is accurate, the objections

---

23 See Stephen R. Munzer and James W. Nickel, "Does the Constitution Mean What It Always Meant?," *Columbia Law Review*, 77 (1977): 1029–62.

are also linked. The first two objections raise a difficulty with the surface level of the theory – namely, that the enterpriser/arbiter distinction often cannot be easily and convincingly applied. This difficulty signals that something is amiss with the ostensibly neat correlation between the surface level and the underlying purpose of Sax's theory. The last two objections then pinpoint the difficulty with the correlation – namely, that it is highly problematic to identify the constitutionally relevant risks and to tie them to any straightforward surface test that lawyers and judges can use.

Concern that the distinction between enterpriser and arbiter might sometimes be mainly a matter of form, together with a sympathy for the growing environmental movement, may have spurred Sax to offer a second, more radical theory.[24] Once again, he conceives of property as involving competition. But this time he emphasizes that property is an interdependent network of competing uses. Property cannot ultimately be understood as isolated, physically definable parcels. Instead, the use of any given parcel of property is frequently a use of or demand upon property beyond the border of the parcel. Moreover, the effects that spill beyond the border may fall very broadly onto many others. Hence under this conception of property, the constitutional problem of takings turns, as before, on the kinds of competition to which existing economic values may be exposed or from which they should be protected. Yet this time it also turns on a view that economic values can, unlike property rights as traditionally conceived, be diffusely held claims. These claims, Sax holds, amount to public rights. They are entitled to equal consideration with traditional property rights in legislative or judicial resolution of competing uses.

Sax's solution to the reconceived problem of takings involves the notion of a spillover effect, of which he recognizes three types. First are cases where use of one person's land physically restricts the uses of other land, as where strip

24 Joseph L. Sax, "Takings, Private Property and Public Rights," *Yale Law Journal*, 81 (1971): 149–86.

mining of coal causes drainage problems for lower-lying land. Next are cases where the use interferes, as by pollution, with a "common" (air, water overlying a wetland, visual prospect) to which another landowner has an equal right. Last are cases where the use affects the health or well-being of another. Government still need not compensate when acting in its arbitral capacity. For it is then, by definition, regulating the spillover effects among competing uses. The operational difference between the first theory and the second is that, under the latter, the government must compensate when acting in its enterprise capacity in only two situations. One is where it devalues property that has no spillover effects on a competing use. An example is where a farmer is compelled by the government to devote a portion of his farmland to a new runway for an airport. Here farming has no spillover effects at all. The other situation is where the government proceeds against one of several parcels of property when it could equally well proceed against any of the others. This is a sort of discrimination exception. Sax's revised theory of takings is quite radical because it will offer compensation in many fewer cases than does current law.

Someone might object that the revised theory rests on an inconsistent understanding of property. A particular use of property has no spillover effects and is eligible for compensation only if it stays within its "domain,"[25] and "domain" presupposes a physical, metes-and-bounds conception of property. Yet the rest of the theory rejects this conception and holds that one parcel of property is inextricably bound up with other parcels.[26] This objection is unsound because it conflates the different purposes for which these conceptions of property are used. The physical, metes-and-bounds conception is employed only to determine whether spillover effects exist. The inextricable-network conception is used only for the purpose of providing a new foundation for the jurisprudence of takings.

25 Ibid., at 165–66.
26 Ibid., at 152.

Even so, the new theory seems vulnerable to criticism. There is, for a start, inadequate justification for making almost all government action – whether in an enterprise or arbitral capacity – noncompensable. That no compensation need be offered results from the fact that virtually all uses of property have spillover effects. Even if this result were ultimately sound, one would have to defend it by reference to the *justifications* for and *limitations* on private property, not merely to the *concept* of property. Although the concept of property is such that virtually all uses of property have spillover effects, there may be either justification for those effects (or some of them) or no justification for government action that devalues property on the footing that such effects exist. It is one thing to say that property uses have spillover effects. It is quite another to say that therefore the government can interfere with those uses. True, the anti-discrimination exception is important here. But under the basic theory of property advanced in this book, there is much more to justification than that.

Allied with this criticism is another: Even if a use of property has spillover effects, that use and its effects merit further analysis. Two connected difficulties arise here. One is that some uses of property may have priority over other uses. Here Sax seems to confuse two distinct propositions: (1) It is true that neither of two uses is entitled a priori to priority over the other.[27] (2) It is a priori true that neither of two uses is entitled to priority over the other.[28] If "a priori" is used in the Kantian sense of independent of experience, the first proposition is plausible. But the second proposition does not follow from the first, and is in fact false or at least highly debatable. In the light of experience of different uses of property in different social and legal systems, one use of property may have priority over another. For instance, if residential property is scarce and farmland plentiful, then

27 "[N]either is a priori entitled to prevail." Ibid., at 161.
28 "[B]oth are a priori equal in status." Ibid., at 163.

use of land for homes may well have priority over agricultural use. Again, justification may exist for giving priority to the historically first of two conflicting uses.

The second difficulty is that Sax neglects to take account of the relative seriousness of different spillover effects. Assume that two uses of property conflict. The first use interferes seriously with the second. The second use has effects that pass the threshold for being accurately styled "spillover effects" in Sax's sense, but it impinges only in a minor way on the first. Here it would seem, other things being equal, unjustifiable to curtail the second use. If the government restricts either use, then it ought, other things being equal, to restrict the first. Sax's exception for discrimination by the government is irrelevant here because the two uses are not, in view of the difference in gravity of spillover effect, "similarly situated"[29] or regulated with equal justification by the government.

It remains to ask why both judicial doctrines and scholarly proposals have failed to provide a satisfactory test for takings. One simple answer is that takings situations differ so greatly that there can be no test that grapples adequately with the variety and also affords clear and definite guidance to a competent lawyer or judge. This answer has both brevity and a large measure of truth in its favor. Yet it does not offer a very penetrating diagnosis of the shortcomings of available doctrines and proposals.

A subtler answer is given by Ackerman.[30] He suggests that traditional doctrines rest on principles (derived from "Ordinary Observing") that order judicial holdings pretty well but cannot clarify the deeper problems of takings law. On the other hand, scholarly proposals like those of Sax (derived from "Scientific Policymaking") try to adjust legal concepts and rules so as to further some comprehensive view (for example, utilitarianism) that should govern the legal system, but they cannot make sense of judicial doctrines. As a result,

29   Ibid., at 169.
30   Ackerman, *Private Property and the Constitution*.

takings laws is commonly perceived to be incoherent and its principles mysterious.

Though this answer is helpful, it relies on dichotomies between "Ordinary Observing" and "Scientific Policymaking" and between "ordinary talk" and "scientific talk" about property. In consequence, such categories do not help much in classifying actual thinkers and are apt to distort as much as they illuminate. More fundamentally, Ackerman overemphasizes the linguistic or conceptual, as opposed to the justificatory, aspects of takings. The mistake, committed in a different way by Sax, is to suppose that the key to the constitutional problem of takings lies in the language persons use, or the conceptions they employ, regarding property. Here Michelman's insight is superior. He correctly perceives that not even the constitutional issue can be confronted adequately without referring to underlying justifications of private property. A shortcoming of Michelman's position is that though he offers a survey of theories of property, the only existing theory he finds directly helpful is utilitarianism, which is only part of the story (§§ 14.3 and 14.4), and the pseudo-Rawlsian account that he suggests is misguided.[31]

From this critical discussion one should distill three broad conclusions. First, any constitutional perspective on takings must attend carefully to the justifications for and limitations on private property and not overemphasize the concept of property. Sax's later theory and Ackerman's theory do not adequately observe this point. Second, there is no easy transition from a moral and political theory to a constitutional theory of takings. The criticisms of Sax's earlier theory should be seen in this light. Third, no constitutional theory is likely to yield a litmus test for when the government must compensate. Even Michelman's reconstruction of traditional takings doctrine does not yield such a test.

31 Michelman, "Property, Utility, and Fairness," at 1219–24, attempts to adapt Rawls. The result is criticized in Stephen R. Munzer, "A Theory of Retroactive Legislation," *Texas Law Review*, 61 (1982): 425–80, at 477–80.

15.3 TOWARD A NEW CONSTITUTIONAL PERSPECTIVE

If one accepts the moral and political theory of takings proposed in Chapter 14, and if one also accepts the criticisms of
certain judicial tests and academic approaches offered in
§§ 15.1 and 15.2, then a new constitutional perspective is
possible. Yet these two conditions do not, by themselves,
determine a new perspective. One also needs an account of
how a background moral and political theory can become
part of federal constitutional law. Obviously, a constitutional
amendment could make it part, but that is rather farfetched.
More realistic is some account explaining how, in the process
of deciding cases, the moral and political theory could be
adopted. In short, one needs a theory of constitutional interpretation.

This section makes use of an account of constitutional
interpretation and change formulated in a joint article with
Nickel.[32] The account, in brief outline, is as follows. The
Constitution is best understood as a text-based institutional
practice. It is therefore neither just an ancient text with an
accretion of precedents nor just a complicated political institution involved in the process of governing. It is, indeed,
important that constitutional argument involves preoccupation with the language of the document and a search for
original understandings – two features that one might call
the "textual focus." But there is tension between the textual
focus and change in constitutional norms. The best way to
understand and resolve this tension is to realize that the
Constitution has a special sort of meaning. As a result, authoritative interpretations can modify this meaning, and the
present content of the document stems from the interaction
over time of framers, judges, legislatures, and executive officials. Constitutional change through interpretation is both
necessary and desirable, and the functions of the Constitution furnish some guidance as to when such change is in
order.

32 Munzer and Nickel, "Does the Constitution Mean What It Always
    Meant?"

This section employs the foregoing account, but two warnings are in order. First, though not every view of constitutional interpretation will allow the new perspective described below, the account just sketched may not be the only way to reach it. An original-intent-only view of interpretation, which is one sort of historical approach, will not permit the new perspective, but there are decisive reasons for rejecting such a theory of constitutional interpretation.[33] Conversely, other views of interpretation might yield a similar perspective on takings. For example, Dworkin's distinction between "concepts" and "conceptions" might allow judges to say that the framers proposed some concepts of "takings" and "just compensation," but that their conceptions of these concepts are not controlling and that judges today should use the best available conceptions, or theories, of what takings and just compensation really are.[34] Difficulties may afflict this distinction.[35] Still, if the distinction is sound, then it, or some other interpretive theory proposed by Dworkin[36] or other thinkers, may nevertheless generate the same, or at least a highly similar, perspective on takings. Second, the new perspective does not furnish a test for takings or recommend a different decision for most famous cases decided in the past. It therefore differs only partly from its predecessors.

The schematic formation of a different perspective might

---

33 Munzer and Nickel, "Does the Constitution Mean What It Always Meant?," at 1030–33. The view of constitutional interpretation in Epstein, *Takings*, is a variant of the historical approach, and is vulnerable to similar criticisms. See also Note, "Richard Epstein on the Foundations of Takings Jurisprudence," *Harvard Law Review*, 99 (1986): 791–808, at 793–97.

34 Ronald Dworkin, *Taking Rights Seriously* (Cambridge, Mass.: Harvard University Press, 1978) (paperback ed.), pp. 134–36.

35 See Munzer and Nickel, "Does the Constitution Mean What It Always Meant?," at 1037–41; Stephen R. Munzer, "Realistic Limits on Realist Interpretation," *Southern California Law Review*, 58 (1985): 459–75, at 464–65.

36 See Ronald Dworkin, *A Matter of Principle* (Cambridge, Mass.: Harvard University Press, 1985), especially pp. 48–57; Ronald Dworkin, *Law's Empire* (Cambridge, Mass.: Harvard University Press, 1986).

proceed in this way. Assume that the moral and political theory of takings is correct. Then its introduction into a legal system depends on how much of a legal framework already exists. It one were starting from scratch, with a constitution and some legislation but no explicit provision in regard to takings, the moral and political solution would be only marginally constrained. The constraints would stem, in the United States, from the federal form of government and the executive, legislative, and judicial spheres of authority embodied in the Constitution. That would have been the situation in 1790.

But in 1990 one is not starting from scratch. The takings clause is in the Bill of Rights (1791). One has the framing of that clause and its intellectual inheritance. One might hold, with Sax, that it aimed to prevent arbitrary and unfair government action against private property. One has also the subsequent constitutional development of the takings clause. This development includes, *inter alia,* principles of institutional competence and subordinate constitutional rules. An example of the former is the principle that if the legislature in exercising eminent domain judges that its action is for a "public use," a court will not substitute a different judgment of its own unless it believes that the legislature is blatantly mistaken. Examples of the latter include the rules that make up the doctrines of physical invasion, noxious use, and diminution in value. In line with the account of constitutional interpretation and change just sketched, the subsequent constitutional development can modify as well as expand the takings clause as originally framed. Thus, the meaning of the clause today can differ from what it once was. Suppose that the *received constitutional doctrine* is the existing product of the framing, intellectual inheritance, and subsequent constitutional development of the takings clause. Then the introduction of the moral and political solution into the United States legal system is significantly constrained by the received constitutional doctrine. The constraints in 1990 are more substantial than the constraints were in 1790.

458

Yet the moral and political theory also constrains the received constitutional doctrine. The former is a basis for criticizing and revising the latter. Since constraint is a two-way street, a nettlesome question arises: Under what circumstances does one constrain the other? Logic is powerless to supply an answer. If the moral and political theory and the received constitutional doctrine are partially incompatible, then one can eliminate the incompatibility by revising either or both.

Although this section has no full answer to this troublesome question, two points will help. First, the received constitutional doctrine should ordinarily constrain the moral and political theory in cases of *indirect incompatibility*. The argument is this. The moral and political theory is a foundation for a solution to the constitutional problem of takings. The moral and political solution need not, even applied to a given legal system in a given historical setting, generate a unique constitutional solution. Suppose that it generates at least two constitutional solutions. One is incompatible with the received constitutional doctrine. The other is not. Here the moral and political solution is indirectly incompatible with the received constitutional doctrine. It would be directly incompatible only if either the moral and political solution itself is incompatible with the received constitutional doctrine or all constitutional solutions it generates are incompatible with that doctrine.

In cases of indirect incompatibility, one should hold that the received constitutional doctrine ordinarily bars incompatible constitutional solutions. The reason is that the doctrine represents an institutional choice entitled to substantial weight. To choose one solution is to foreclose other solutions. The choice is a substantial, though not decisive, reason. This reason is not available in cases of direct incompatibility. For there the received constitutional doctrine can generate no compatible solution.

Second, the moral and political theory should ordinarily constrain the received constitutional doctrine when the former involves a *fundamental commitment on principle*. To make this vague recommendation somewhat more precise, contrast the following. On the one hand, fundamental to the moral and political theory are the distinction between full and partial conformity and the idea that government action in situations of partial conformity can have a corrective purpose. Such corrective action can affect both the scope of eminent domain and the matter of compensation. If these features of the moral and political solution were incompatible with the received constitutional doctrine, they would be reasons for criticizing and revising that doctrine.

On the other hand, slight differences in valuation rules are not fundamental to the political solution. Suppose that the moral and political solution generates two possible valuation rules for situations in which fair market value cannot easily be determined. The received constitutional doctrine contains a third rule that conflicts with each of them. This is a case of direct incompatibility. Suppose further that the differences among the rules are slight, but that the third rule is so embedded in the received constitutional doctrine that its removal would disrupt adjacent compensatory rules. Here one might say that, direct incompatibility notwithstanding, the received constitutional doctrine should constrain the political solution. The doctrine should retain its existing valuation rule.

15.4 APPLICATIONS

What practical difference does the new constitutional perspective make? This question might spawn a series of law review articles. This section, in order not to try the reader's patience, will apply the new approach only to two recent cases. One was correctly decided, and the new approach indicates how to rebut criticisms of the decision. The other was incorrectly decided, and the new approach shows why it should have come out differently.

In *Hawaii Housing Authority v. Midkiff*,[37] the Supreme Court

37   467 U.S. 229 (1984).

upheld a Hawaii land redistribution statute.[38] The factual background is complex. Before Hawaii became a state, it had a feudal system of land tenure that led to highly concentrated land ownership. As of 1967, the seventy-two largest private landowners owned 47 percent of the land in the state, the state and federal governments owned 48.5 percent, and only 4.5 percent was left for the rest of the population. The large landowners usually sold long leases rather than fees simple. The Hawaii legislature concluded that this situation led to artificially high land prices and was generally inimical to the public welfare. It passed a statute authorizing the Hawaii Housing Authority to condemn residential tracts of more than five acres and to allow the existing lessees to purchase the condemned fees. The statute has many complexities, but in sum it ensures that existing landowners will receive full compensation. The key legal issue, therefore, was whether the legislation was for a "public use," and the Supreme Court concluded that it was. "The Hawaii Legislature enacted its Land Reform Act not to benefit a particular class of identifiable individuals but to attack certain perceived evils of concentrated property ownership in Hawaii – a legitimate public purpose."[39]

Epstein is a prominent critic of the *Midkiff* decision. He makes two main points. First, *pace* the Court,[40] there was no oligopolistic control of land prices. "No antitrust expert thinks 'oligopoly' because there are 'only' seventy or twenty-two or eighteen landowners in a given market."[41] A better villain is state land use regulation. Second, the Hawaii land already involved a "surplus," and the statute effectively allowed the lessees to get the surplus. Thus the legislature actually promoted a private use. "Takings for private use are therefore forbidden because the takers get to keep the full surplus, even if just compensation is paid."[42]

38 Hawaii Land Reform Act of 1967, Hawaii Rev. Stat. ch. 516 (1985).
39 467 U.S. at 245.
40 See 467 U.S. at 241–42.
41 Epstein, *Takings*, p. 181.
42 Ibid., p. 164.

If one thinks through the case along the lines suggested in this book, an answer to Epstein emerges. Both the principle of utility and efficiency (§ 8.6) and the principle of justice and equality (§§ 9.4 and 9.5) allow redistribution under some circumstances. Specifically, § 14.4 recognizes that property arrangements in the United States do not fully conform to the basic theory. Various means, including redistributive taxation, exist to bring these arrangements more nearly into line with the basic theory. If a specific current arrangement is one of partial conformity, government action affecting property is one such means. Hence such action may have a corrective aim; § 14.4 illustrated this possibility, for the principle of desert based on labor, with a hypothetical history of heavy manufacturing.

The *Midkiff* case does not call upon that principle, but plainly the Hawaii legislation has a corrective purpose. To some extent, one can subsume the correction under the principle of utility and efficiency. The legislature professed concern not only over a shortage of fee simple residential land and artificially high prices[43] but also over the pressing public necessity for a secure, strong, and stable economy.[44] But one can also argue that the principle of justice and equality is in play. For the legislature suggested that the existing system and high land prices could lead to "a large population of persons deprived of decent and healthful standards of life."[45] It is not suggested here that the legislature did, or would, endorse the basic theory, but rather that this reading is a plausible understanding of what, in effect, it did.

This interpretation of the legislature's aims, if correct, shows only that the moral and political theory of takings supports its action, not that the constitutional theory of § 15.3 does so. For that one needs some additional but plausible assumptions. One assumption is that the received constitutional doctrine does not view the "public use" language

---

43 Hawaii Rev. Stat. § 516–83(a)(2) (1985).
44 Ibid., § 516–83(a)(9) and (11).
45 Ibid., § 516–83(a)(7).

of the takings clause as imposing a severe restriction. Adequate case support exists for this assumption.[46] Thus, the Court seems correct in seeing the legislative purpose as public rather than private. *Midkiff* does work a change in constitutional norms, however, because earlier cases had not read "public use" so broadly as to encompass a redistributive land program. Another assumption is that the case either involves a "fundamental commitment on principle" or at least does not involve "indirect incompatibility" (§ 15.3). This assumption is well grounded, too. The corrective purpose of the legislation fundamentally implicates the basic theory of property. And there is no evidence that the *Midkiff* outcome is incompatible, directly or indirectly, with prior cases. A final assumption is that the Court properly deferred to the legislature's fact finding and statement of its purpose. This assumption is also defensible, for in general courts do not second-guess legislatures on such matters.

One would need to articulate this argument in detail to convert it from a schematic application of constitutional theory to a legal brief. In particular, one would need to tie the analytical elements of the argument carefully to the facts of the *Midkiff* case. Yet even this schematic application reveals the inadequacy of Epstein's criticisms. First, one need not rely on the description of "oligopoly" as economists or antitrust specialists might understand it. For sake of argument, let it be granted that the facts do not establish the existence of an oligopoly under any of the usual tests of market power and hence that Epstein exposes a technical flaw in the Court's use of economic terminology. Nevertheless, the Court has correctly identified that something is amiss. If less than seventy-five landowners own nearly half

46 See, for example, Berman v. Parker, 348 U.S. 26 (1954); Poletown Neighborhood Council v. City of Detroit, 410 Mich. 616, 304 N.W.2d 455 (1981); Courtesy Sandwich Shop, Inc. v. Port of New York Auth., 12 N.Y.2d 379, 190 N.E.2d 402, 240 N.Y.S.2d 1, *appeal dismissed*, 375 U.S. 78 (1963). However, state courts interpret the "public use" requirement less deferentially than federal courts. See Thomas W. Merrill, "The Economics of Public Use," *Cornell Law Review*, 72 (1986): 61–116, at 65, 93–109.

the land in Hawaii, then that might have been enough, despite the absence of an oligopoly, to skew the market for fee simple ownership. In fact, the evidence shows that skewing did occur, for very little residential land was available for purchase in fee simple – a situation duplicated nowhere else in the United States. Only long-term leases were generally available in Hawaii. Thus, the Hawaii legislature relied on relevant evidence in enacting the land reform scheme. It may be that extensive state and federal holdings should be sold in some more comprehensive scheme, but that possibility is not a sufficient basis on which to invalidate the Hawaii land reform statute.

Second, the "surplus" argument is muddled. Under existing case law, "just compensation" requires payment of fair market value.[47] Hence, if surplus is understood in any straightforward way, it will be part of fair market value and so will be fully compensated. In fact, the basic theory sometimes justifies corrective redistributions, including those using takings and land reform mechanisms, that fail to offer full compensation (§ 14.4). But since the legislation in *Midkiff* did not take this route, one need not address that possibility here.[48]

So much for the correctly decided case. Incorrectly decided was the case of *Nollan v. California Coastal Commission*.[49] In a five-to-four decision, the Supreme Court held that the Coastal Commission could not require the Nollans to grant a

47 See cases cited in note 2 above.
48 On *Midkiff*, see also Gia L. Cincone, "Land Reform and Corporate Redistribution: The Republican Legacy," *Stanford Law Review*, 39 (1987): 1229–57, at 1242–46. Though both *Midkiff* and Poletown Neighborhood Council v. City of Detroit, 410 Mich. 616, 304 N.W.2d 455 (1981) (upholding eminent domain in clearing a large neighborhood for a new General Motors plant), correctly reject a stringent reading of the public-use doctrine, the *Midkiff* reading may still be too broad. In fact, *Midkiff* and *Poletown* are distinguishable, and so it is possible to preserve the *Midkiff* result while rejecting the disquieting outcome in *Poletown*, as is ably argued in Note, "The Supreme Court, 1983 Term: Leading Cases of the 1983 Term," *Harvard Law Review*, 98 (1984): 87–314, at 232–36.
49 107 S. Ct. 3141 (1987).

lateral easement across their beachfront property as a condition of obtaining a building permit. The background of the case involves the California policy of ensuring beach access to the general public. In pursuit of that policy, the Commission had generally sought to condition building permits on provision of access. That is exactly what it did when the Nollans wanted to substitute a larger building for an existing bungalow. The easement would have allowed persons to traverse the beach area of the Nollans' property – which was separated from the rest of their property by a seawall – in order to go to and from public beaches on either side. Justice Scalia, writing for the majority, did not regard the Commission's decision as "substantially" related to "legitimate state interests,"[50] and asserted that if the Commission "wants an easement across the Nollans' property, it must pay for it."[51]

If one accepts the theory advanced in this book, one should approach the *Nollan* case as follows. Under the basic theory of property, both the principle of utility and efficiency and the principle of justice and equality justify some public property (§§ 8.6, 9.4, and 9.5). Since beach areas are limited, as population increases it becomes more important to ensure that members of the general public – that is, all who do not own beachfront property – have beach access. The state can secure this aim both by purchasing property in fee simple for public beaches and by acquiring easements for access to public beaches. Of course, since much beachfront property was already under private ownership before the population of California increased enormously, the moral and political theory of takings comes into play. At this point, that theory would not justify the state's taking title without paying for it, and it would not prevent the state's acquiring an easement by paying for it. The issue here is narrower: Should the state have to pay for a lateral easement across a private beach between two public beaches? It should not. The state,

50   Ibid., at 3148.
51   Ibid., at 3150.

through the Coastal Commission, is engaging in corrective action in a situation of partial conformity (§ 14.4). It is attempting to make known the existence of and to ensure full access to public beaches in circumstances where increased private building blocks the view of public beaches below.[52]

Though the moral and political theory of takings supports the Commission's action, it is a closer question whether the constitutional theory of § 15.3 does so. Three points come to the fore. One relates to the legal context of the Commission's action. Had the Nollans not sought to redevelop their property, the Commission would have been powerless to obtain an easement without paying for it. In this respect, the received constitutional doctrine constrains the moral and political theory (§ 15.3). But this is not the actual case. Rather, the Commission sought the easement only after the Nollans applied for a building permit. The application made relevant the standards for so-called subdivision exaction or mandatory dedication cases.[53] Justice Scalia imposed a "substantially related" standard. But the prevailing case law requires only a "reasonable relationship" between the condition and the building project.[54] The constitutional theory of this chapter would prefer the "reasonable relationship" standard, for it fits better with the moral and political theory of takings. Here the constitutional theory sides with Justice Brennan's dissent in *Nollan*.[55]

A second point is an argument in terms of expectations. The principle of utility and efficiency attaches special importance to expectations that are "rational" and "institutionally legitimate" (§ 8.7). So does the moral and political theory of takings that is based, in part, on that principle (§ 14.3). This point is relevant to the legal position of the Nollans. What matters most is not their actual expectations

---

52 Ibid., at 3143–44.
53 See note 5 above.
54 The main California case is Associated Home Builders, Inc. v. City of Walnut Creek, 4 Cal. 3d 633, 484 P.2d 606, 94 Cal Rptr. 630, *appeal dismissed*, 404 U.S. 878 (1971).
55 107 S. Ct. at 3150–62 (Brennan, J., dissenting).

but which expectations they could rationally and legitimately have had under federal and state law. Plainly the United States Constitution reigns supreme over California law. But if the federal constitution does not address the Nollans' situation specifically, California law becomes especially pertinent. A section of the California Constitution provides in part: "No individual . . . claiming or possessing the frontage or tidal lands of a harbor, bay, inlet, estuary, or other navigable water in this State, shall be permitted to exclude the right of way to any such water whenever it is required for any public purpose, . . . and the Legislature shall enact such laws as will give the most liberal construction to this provision, so that access to the navigable waters of this State shall always be attainable for the people thereof."[56]

As Justice Brennan's dissent points out, this provision was adopted in 1879 – long before private development on the coast.[57] Hence, from the late nineteenth century the California Constitution circumscribed the rational and legitimate expectations of owners of beachfront property. Subsequently, the California legislature created the Coastal Commission, and the Commission embarked on its policy of securing an easement of lateral access in return for granting a building permit. Thus, when the Nollans originally purchased the property in 1982, it was doubtful that they could have had rational and institutionally legitimate expectations, within the framework of California law, of building a larger structure without granting an easement. Furthermore, while their case was making its way through the courts, the California Court of Appeal ruled in another case that, in a situation essentially parallel to that of the Nollans, it was constitutional to condition a building permit on the granting of an easement.[58] Although arguments in terms of expectations

---

56 Cal. Const. art. X, § 4.
57 107 S. Ct. at 3153 (Brennan, J., dissenting).
58 Grupe v. California Coastal Comm'n, 166 Cal. App. 3d 148, 212 Cal. Rptr. 578 (1985). See also Remmenga v. California Coastal Comm'n, 163 Cal. App. 3d 623, 628, 209 Cal. Rptr. 628, 631, *appeal dismissed*, 474 U.S. 915 (1985).

are not decisive, the argument just sketched supports the view that, under California law, the Nollans had no expectations worthy of federal constitutional protection.

A final point is factual. What burden would the easement have inflicted and what benefits would it have secured? The evidence suggests that the burden on the Nollans would have been light. The easement was only ten feet wide, and it crossed a beach area that was separated by a seawall from the rest of the Nollans' property. The benefits, on the other hand, would probably have been more substantial than the majority allowed. Justice Scalia understood the easement to be concerned solely with lateral passage, and deemed it unconnected with visual blockage or any "psychological barrier" to public beach use.[59] Here Justice Brennan's dissent is subtler. He thought that the easement would have promoted public access by making beach use more visible from the road in circumstances where high private buildings along the shore suggest that the public may not use any of the beaches below.[60] If this reading is correct, it would support the Commission's action even if one used Justice Scalia's more stringent substantial-relationship standard.[61]

It therefore appears that the theory of takings advanced here would have led to a different decision in *Nollan*. Obviously, this schematic analysis requires more case support and closer attention to the factual record to convert it into a legal brief. Still, it confirms that the theory of property that this book offers has practical implications for actual legal cases.

15.5 REPRISE

This study has sought to advance understanding of both theoretical and practical issues. It has tried to explain the idea of property, and to show why some, but not all, rights

---

59 Nollan v. California Coastal Comm'n, 107 S. Ct. at 3149–50.
60 Ibid., at 3154–55 (Brennan, J., dissenting).
61 See ibid., at 3154 (Brennan, J., dissenting).

in the human body can be seen as property rights. More important, it has made a case for a "pluralist" theory of property – a theory that preserves independent and irreducible roles for utility, justice, and desert based on labor as justifications for both public and private property. The resulting trio of principles applies to both capitalist and socialist economies, and supports moderate egalitarianism concerning the distribution of private property.

A salient feature of this book is its refusal to theorize about property in a vacuum. On the one hand, the three principles rest on a background theory that pays attention to human beings as individuals and as members of particular societies. The background account of social context addresses the connections between property and control, privacy, and individuality, investigates the bearing of property on moral character, and explores the relations of property to alienation, exploitation, and power. On the other hand, the justificatory principles illuminate practical problems. They favor workers' rights within business corporations. They support substantial taxes on large gifts and bequests. And they justify a good deal of government regulation of private property. The principles, then, serve as a reminder that a satisfactory examination of property must weave together the theoretical and the concrete, and help to solve real-world problems. A theory of property should not be an intellectual plaything but an instrument for reforming institutions of property.

Table of cases

A. Magnano Co. v. Hamilton 421
Alaska Fish Salting & By-Products Co. v. Smith 421
Alco Parking Corp. v. City of Pittsburgh 449
Almota Farmers Elevator & Warehouse Co. v. United States 443
Arnett v. Kennedy 55
Associated Home Builders, Inc. v. City of Walnut Creek 444, 466
Ayres v. City Council of Los Angeles 444

Berman v. Parker 463
Bishop v. Wood 55
Board of Regents v. Roth 54–55
Board of Supervisors of Cerro Gordo County v. Miller 222
Boyd v. United States 46
Broadway Nat'l Bank v. Adams 49

City of Pittsburgh v. Alco Parking Corp. 421, 449
City of Plainfield v. Borough of Middlesex 444
City of Temple Terrace v. Hillsborough Ass'n for
   Retarded Citizens, Inc. 422
Cleveland Bd. of Educ. v. Loudermill 55
Courtesy Sandwich Shop, Inc. v. Port of New York Auth. 463
Crownhill Homes, Inc. v. City of San Antonio 444

Edwards v. Habib 187

Fertilizing Co. v. Hyde Park 443
Flemming v. Nestor 115

Garrison v. Louisiana 51
Goldblatt v. Town of Hempstead 447
Grupe v. California Coastal Comm'n 467

Hadacheck v. Sebastian 443, 449
Haelan Laboratories, Inc. v. Topps Chewing Gum, Inc. 52
Hawaii Housing Authority v. Midkiff 460–64

Johnson v. M'Intosh 76
Just v. Marinette County 445

Kaiser Aetna v. United States 447
Katz v. United States 46
Keystone Bituminous Coal Ass'n v. DeBenedictis 446
Kohl v. United States 442

TABLE OF CASES

L'Hote v. New Orleans   443

Local 1330, United Steel Workers of America v. United States
   Steel Corp.   359

Lochner v. New York   442

Loretto v. Teleprompter Manhattan CATV Corp.   444

Miller v. Schoene   445

Mugler v. Kansas   443

Nollan v. California Coastal Commission   464–68

Paul v. Davis   46

Penn Central Transp. Co. v. New York City   445, 447

Pennsylvania Coal Co. v. Mahon   445

Pierson v. Post   77

Poletown Neighborhood Council v. City of Detroit   463, 464

PruneYard Shopping Center v. Robins   187

Pumpelly v. Green Bay Co.   443

Quinn v. Leathem   20–21

Remmenga v. California Coastal Comm'n   467

Rogers v. United States   51

Snepp v. United States   50

State v. Shack   187

Swimming Turtle v. Bd. of County Comm'rs of Miami County   421

Tee-Hit-Ton Indians v. United States   76

United States Civil Serv. Comm'n v. Nat'l Ass'n of Letter Carriers   51

United States v. Caltex (Philippines), Inc.   444

United States v. Carmack   442

United States v. Causby   443

United States v. Commodities Trading Corp.   443

United States v. Fuller   443

United States v. 564.54 Acres of Land   443

Vaughn v. Vermillion Corp.   447

Village of Euclid v. Ambler Realty Co.   431, 445

Vitek v. Jones   55

Wyman v. James   114

Yara Engineering Corp. v. City of Newark   444

Index of names

Abel, Richard L., 317n
Aberg, Dawn, 191n
Ackerman, Bruce A., 445n, 454–55
Alchian, Armen A., 348
Alexander, *see* Hales, Alexander of
Alexander, Larry, 361n
Allport, Gordon W., 84
Anderson, Lyle V., 301n
Anderson, Richard, 61n
Andrews, William D., 407n
Appleby, Joyce, 141n
Aquinas, Saint Thomas, 122, 124, 130n, 146, 300n
Aristotle, 120, 122, 124–25, 127–29, 130n, 132, 135, 144n, 146
Arnold, N. Scott, 170n
Arrow, Kenneth J., 204–05, 295n
Atkinson, A. B., 384, 387n, 405n, 407n
Auerbach, Alan J., 409n
Avineri, Shlomo, 110n, 149n, 154n, 155, 159n, 370n, 372n
Ayer, A. J., 42n

Barlow, Robin, 390n
Barrack, Martin, 317n, 326n
Battin, Margaret Pabst, 54n
Baumol, William J., 322n, 330n
Beaglehole, Ernest, 84, 85n, 86n
Becker, Lawrence C., 120n, 129n,

145n, 191n, 195n, 196n, 257n, 264n, 266n, 293, 302n
Beitz, Charles R., 8n, 262n
Bellas, Carl J., 340n
Benn, Stanley I., 93n
Ben-Ner, Avner, 340n
Bennett, John G., 251n
Bentham, Jeremy
   and interest theories of rights, 48n
   on expectations, 29–30, 80, 194–95, 219, 401
   on gratuitous transfers, 401
   on property, 7, 29–30, 80, 193n, 194–95
   on utility, 7, 194–95, 401
Bergin, Thomas F., 90n
Berle, Adolf A., Jr., 320–32, 334n, 344, 355
Berman, Katrina V., 339n
Bernheim, B. Douglas, 402n
Blasi, Joseph Raphael, 338–39n
Blum, Walter J., 213n, 214n, 400n
Blume, Lawrence, 434n
Bork, Robert H., 252n
Boskin, Michael J., 389n, 415n
Bossy, John, 111n
Bothwell, James L., 330n
Boudreaux, Kenneth J., 331n
Brandeis, Louis D., 93n
Brandt, Anthony, 97n

473

Braudel, Fernand, 94n, 108n
Braybrooke, David, 64n, 241–42n, 273n
Brazer, Harvey E., 390n
Brennan, Justice William J., Jr., 46n, 466–68
Brittain, John A., 387n, 388n, 390n, 393–94
Brudney, Victor, 323n, 335n
Brumberg, Richard, 387n
Buchanan, Allen E., 170n, 236n, 238n, 239n
Buchanan, James M., 205n, 239n
Buck, Pearl S., 97
Budziszewski, J., 124n
Burnham, Sophy, 97n
Butler, Joseph, 107, 109

Calabresi, Guido, 27n
Campsey, B. J., 328n
Chamberlain, Wilt, 180–81
Chirelstein, Marvin, 335n
Chiu, John S., 331n
Christman, John, 64n
Cincone, Gia L., 422n, 440n, 464n
Clark, Robert Charles, 370–72
Coase, R. H., 220n, 348
Cobb, Jonathan, 249n
Coffee, John C., Jr., 334
Cohen, G. A., 56–57, 180–81, 191, 271n, 272n, 288–89
Cohen, Morris R., 92n, 179
Coleman, Jules L., 27n, 200n, 205n
Conn, Robert L., 330n
Conte, Michael, 340n
Cooley, David E., 331n
Cooter, Robert, 196n
Copp, David, 308n

Daniels, Norman, 142n, 238n, 252n, 308n, 309n
Davy, Samuel J., 340n
DeAngelo, Harry, 335n
DeAngelo, Linda, 335n

de la Rocha, Raquelle, 317n
DeMong, R. F., 328n
Demsetz, Harold, 211–12, 323–24, 334, 348
DePaul, Michael R., 308n
Diggins, John Patrick, 139n, 140n
Dodge, Joseph M., 409n
Doernberg, Richard L., 338n
Dolinko, David, 53n
Donagan, Alan, 286n, 300n, 306n
Dukeminier, Jesse, 317n
Dworkin, Ronald, 224n, 232, 250–51n, 457

Easterbrook, Frank H., 332n
Ellerman, David P., 290n, 337n, 338n
Ellickson, Robert C., 432n
Elster, Jon, 164–65n, 170n
Ely, John Hart, 55n
Engels, Friedrich, 320n
Epstein, Richard A., 288n, 317n, 333n, 445n, 457n, 461–63

Fama, Eugene F., 322, 323, 343n
Feinberg, Joel, 167n, 259, 262n
Feist, Jess, 83n
Feldman, Allan, 201n, 208n
Ferejohn, John, 205n
Feuerbach, Ludwig, 156n
Fischel, William A., 434n
Fischer, John Martin, 191n
Foot, Philippa, 122, 146–47, 307n
Forgus, Ronald, 83n
Fortescue, Sir John, 130n
Frankfurt, Harry, 251n
Franklin, Stephen D., 387n
French, J. Lawrence, 341n
Fressola, Anthony, 257n
Fried, Charles, 93n
Fusfeld, Daniel R., 340n

Galbraith, John Kenneth, 360n
Gauthier, David, 269, 272–73, 285
Gavison, Ruth, 92n

Gerety, Tom, 92n
Gerstein, Robert S., 46n, 53n
Gibbard, Allan, 275n
Glassman, Cynthia A., 329n
Goldmann, Lucien, 132n
Gordon, David M., 387n
Graetz, Michael J., 408n
Graham, Kenneth W., Jr., 317n
Gratian, 130n
Gregor, Mary, 131n
Grey, Thomas C., 15n, 31–35
Grice, H. P., 78n
Griffin, James, 197n, 198n
Griffin, Joseph P., 435n
Groves, Harold M., 213n, 214n
Grunebaum, James O., 25n, 382n
Gueron, Judith M., 116n
Gunn, Christopher Eaton, 338n
Gunzler, Mitch, 191n
Guttenplan, Samuel, 307n

Halbach, Edward C., Jr., 407n,
    415n
Hale, Robert L., 179
Hales, Alexander of, 130n
Hallowell, A. Irving, 26n
Hampton, Jean, 273n
Harbury, C. D., 383, 384, 392–94
Hare, R. M., 10–11, 163n, 193n,
    197n, 198n, 199n, 224n, 253n,
    306n
Harrington, James, 138, 139n
Harrison, A. J., 384
Hart, H. L. A., 18n, 48n, 238n
Haskell, Paul G., 90n
Haslett, D. W., 382n, 387n, 390n,
    407n, 409–15
Hasse, Lizbeth L., 242n
Hayek, F. A., 107n, 184
Hegel, G. W. F.
    Philosophy of Right, 67–70, 73,
        76n, 110n, 130n, 149–55,
        157
    and Marx, 149, 155–57, 160,
        163–74

and the projection theory, 62,
    67–70, 73, 79
on agency, 78–80
on civil society, 150–55
on personality, 68–69, 81–82,
    87, 152, 154
on poverty, 87, 154–55, 160
on property, 67–70, 73, 79–82,
    110n, 149–55
on the landed gentry, 152–53,
    155–57
on the philosophy of history,
    156–57
on the state, 150–55
on taxation, 150, 152
on welfare, 110n, 150n, 154
Heim, Peggy, 330n
Held, Virginia, 61n
Hicks, J. R., 200n
Hill, Charles W. L., 331n, 334n
Hill, Thomas E., Jr., 167n
Hindley, Brian, 331n
Hirschman, Albert O., 106n,
    133n, 137n, 139n
Hitchens, D. M. W. H., 383, 384,
    392–94
Hobbes, Thomas, 41n, 257n
Hobsbawm, E. J., 161n
Hoebel, E. Adamson, 26–27
Hohfeld, Wesley Newcomb, 17–
    27, 29, 31, 34, 40, 48, 76, 178,
    202, 260, 263
Holl, Peter, 328n, 330n
Hollander, Cynthia, 97n
Holmes, Justice Oliver Wendell,
    442, 445n
Honoré, A. M., 22, 23, 25, 27n,
    31, 57, 76, 178, 202
Hont, Istvan, 134n, 140n
Horne, Thomas A., 141n
Hudson, Stephen D., 21n
Hughes, Gwenn, 330–31n
Hume, David
    *Enquiry Concerning the Principles
        of Morals*, 107n

Treatise of Human Nature, 80n, 194n, 217n, 325n
and human motivation, 107, 109
and the utilitarian tradition, 80, 194
and transactional powers, 217
Hume's Law, 325–26
on conventions, 194, 221–22
on expectations and stability, 29, 194, 221–22
on property rules, 194, 221–22
on utility, 194, 217
Husak, Douglas N., 21n

Ignatieff, Michael, 134n, 140n
Ihara, Craig, 61n
Ioannides, Yannis M., 389n
Israel, Joachim, 171n

Jackall, Robert, 337n
Jensen, Michael C., 322, 343n, 376–77
John Paul II, Pope, 185n
Jones, Derek C., 339n

Kahneman, Daniel, 223n
Kaldor, Nicholas, 200n
Kalven, Harry, Jr., 213n, 214n, 400n
Kant, Immanuel
Critique of Practical Reason, 227n
Groundwork of the Metaphysic of Morals, 227n
Philosophy of Law, 47n, 68n, 130n, 131n
and character, 132–33
and the social contract, 130–31
"Kantian" interpretation of equal moral worth, 192, 227, 229, 230, 248
on autonomy, 80n
on occupancy, 130
on personhood, 68, 87
on property, 80n, 125, 130–33

on welfare, 131n
Kaplow, Louis, 411n, 434n
Karst, Kenneth L., 93n, 115n, 251–52
Kennedy, Duncan, 212n
Kim, Jaegwon, 163n, 164n
Klein, Katherine J., 339n, 340n
Klein, William A., 213n, 214n, 218n, 317, 323, 334, 344
Kluge, Eike-Henner W., 54n
Knowles, Dudley, 79n
Koch, Andreas, 61n
Kotlikoff, Laurence J., 388–89, 409n
Koven, Vance R., 435n
Kraus, Jody, 27n
Krause, David S., 330n
Krausz, Michael, 8n
Kronman, Anthony T., 262n
Kupfer, Joseph, 93n

Lamoureux, James, 191n, 295n
Lawriwsky, Michael L., 328n
Lehn, Kenneth, 334n
Lemmon, E. J., 305n
Levi, Isaac, 296n
Levin, Henry M., 337n
Levy, Leonard W., 93n
Lewis, David, 172n
Lewis, Ronald L., 364n
Liao, Shu S., 329n
Liebeler, Wesley J., 46n
Lindblom, Charles E., 249n
Lindgren, J. Ralph, 134n
Lindley, Lord, 21n
Littleton, Christine A., 317n
Locke, John
First Treatise of Government, 267n
Second Treatise of Government, 38n, 41n, 66n, 67n, 74n, 75n, 256–57n, 268n, 269n, 278n
and body rights, 41n, 64, 66n
on labor, 7, 38, 58, 67, 75n, 256–57n, 268n, 395

on property rights, 67, 131, 256–57n, 268n, 395
Lomasky, Loren E., 289n
Long, Douglas C., 42n
Long, Richard J., 341n
Lyons, David, 48n, 224n

Macey, Jonathan R., 338n
Machiavelli, Niccolò, 138, 139n
Mackie, J. L., 306n
Macpherson, C. B., 41n, 257n
Madden, Gerald P., 330n
Madison, James, 138
Mahoney, Dennis J., 93n
Malkiel, Burton G., 330n
Manne, Henry G., 360n
Marcus, Ruth Barcan, 301n, 305n
Marcuse, Herbert, 132n
Marris, Robin, 322n
Martin, Donald L., 360n
Marx, Karl
    Capital, 33, 157n, 161n, 178, 179n, 320n, 370n, 372n
    Communist Manifesto, 159
    Critique of Hegel's "Philosophy of Right," 97n, 155n
    Critique of the Gotha Programme, 168, 373n
    Economic and Philosophic Manuscripts of 1844, 33, 108n, 157–58, 159n, 160–61n, 163n, 371n
    German Ideology, 161n, 168
    Grundrisse, 161, 163
    Pre-Capitalist Economic Formations, 161n
    and Engels, 159n
    and exploitation, 173–74
    and Hegel, 97n, 149, 155–57, 160, 163, 164
    and justice, 173–74
    and separation of ownership and control, 320n, 370
    on alienation, 6–7, 87, 157–69, 369–73

on capitalism, 32–34, 157–69, 173, 369–73
on communism, 159, 160, 168–69, 373
on cooperatives, 370, 373
on division of labor, 168
on false consciousness, 166–68, 172n
on historical periodization, 161–62n
on labor, 157–62, 163n, 164, 166, 168, 173
on production, 158–61, 162n, 164–66, 369–70
on property, 32–34, 87, 148–49, 159–65, 169, 178–79, 319
on socialism, 168–69, 369–71, 373
on "species-being," 158–59, 166–70
on stock companies, 370, 372n
on utopianism, 168
Mautner, Thomas, 74–75n
McCloskey, H. J., 54n
McConnell, Terrance C., 296n, 301n
McEachern, William A., 328n
McFetridge, Donald G., 330n
Meade, J. E., 407n
Means, Gardiner C., 320–32, 334n, 344, 355
Meckling, William H., 376–77
Meiland, Jack W., 8n
Melamed, A. Douglas, 27n
Merrill, Thomas W., 423, 426n, 463n
Metzger, Suzanne K., 191n
Michelman, Frank I., 139n, 142n, 196n, 211–12, 252n, 425–27, 445n, 446–48, 455
Mill, John Stuart, 184, 196n, 264n, 278n, 319, 361, 405
Miller, David, 172n
Modigliani, Franco, 387n, 389n
Monaghan, Henry Paul, 46–47n

Monsen, R. Joseph, 331n
Moore, G. E., 165n
Morawetz, Thomas, 317n
Morgan, James N., 390n
Morris, Christopher W., 317n, 440n
Moynihan, Cornelius J., 90n
Munzer, Stephen R., 3n, 11n, 28n, 62n, 81n, 193n, 221n, 231n, 236n, 253n, 257n, 275n, 293n, 295n, 298n, 302n, 305n, 307n, 310n, 425n, 450n, 455n, 456n, 457n

Nagel, Thomas, 3n
Nelson, Grant S., 90n
Nickel, James W., 20n, 191n, 242n, 282n, 311, 450n, 456, 457n
Nielsen, Kai, 173n
Nove, Alec, 373–77
Nozick, Robert, 38, 58, 64, 75, 153, 180–81, 192n, 260n, 269–72, 285–89, 302n, 395
Nutting, Kurt, 61n

Ollman, Bertell, 164–65
O'Malley, Joseph, 97n, 155n
Osborne, George E., 90n
Oulton, Nicholas, 387n, 389n
Overton, Richard, 41n

Panichas, George E., 80–81n
Parent, W. A., 92n
Park, Ann I., 191n
Paul, Ellen Frankel, 288n
Paul, Jeffrey, 287n
Paul, Saint, 41n
Pears, David, 172n
Perry, Thomas D., 21n
Peter, Karl, 83n
Phillipson, Nicholas, 134
Plato, 120, 125–29, 132, 135, 152
Pocock, J. G. A., 139n
Polinsky, David, 61n

Posner, Richard A., 212n, 218n
Postema, Gerald J., 194n
Presley, Elvis, 52
Prosser, William L., 93n
Proudhon, Pierre-Joseph, 264, 319

Quandt, Richard E., 330n
Quarrey, Michael, 339n
Quigley, Eileen V., 345n
Quine, Willard Van Orman, 78n
Quinn, Warren, 61n

Rachels, James, 93n
Radice, H. K., 331n
Radin, Margaret Jane, 82n, 288n, 317n
Ramirez, Gregory J., 317n
Rappaport, Peter, 196n
Rawls, John, 7, 10n, 89n, 103, 142n, 143, 184, 227n, 233–49, 252n, 261n, 272n, 303n, 308n, 310n, 311, 405n
Raz, Joseph, 48n, 191n, 302n
Reeve, Andrew, 22n, 382n
Regan, Donald, 224n
Reich, Charles, 116n
Rhoades, Stephen A., 329n
Rice, Edward M., 335n
Riker, William H., 205n
Rocha, see de la Rocha, Raquelle
Rodes, Robert E., Jr., 252
Roemer, John E., 170n, 173n, 251n
Rose, Carol M., 317n
Rosen, Corey M., 339n, 340n
Rosenstein, Joseph, 341n
Ross, W. D., 304n
Rubinfeld, Daniel L., 434n
Rubinstein, W. D., 385, 386, 395n
Rudmin, Floyd, 84n
Rufinus, 130n
Ryan, Alan, 132n, 133n, 195–96n

Sachs, David, 116n, 228n
Sade, Marquis de, 231

Sandford, C. T., 407n
Sartorius, Rolf, 269n
Sato, Ryuzo, 389n
Sax, Joseph L., 444n, 445–46, 448–55
Scalia, Justice Antonin, 465–68
Schill, Michael H., 422n, 434n
Schlatter, Richard, 25n, 129n, 130n
Schopenhauer, Arthur, 54n
Schulman, Bernard H., 83n
Schwartz, Adina, 185n
Schwartz, Thomas, 204n
Scitovsky, T. de, 201
Seidman, Louis M., 142n
Sen, Amartya, 182n, 196n, 241n
Seneca, 130n
Sennett, Richard, 249n
Shapiro, Daniel M., 330–31n
Shapiro, Perry, 434n
Sher, George, 259n, 261n, 287n
Shiffrin, Steven, 15n, 61n
Shleifer, Andrei, 402n
Shue, Henry, 8n, 241n
Sibley, Frank, 163n
Sicade, Lynn, 191n
Sidgwick, Henry, 401–02
Simon, William E., 345n
Simon, William H., 116n
Sims, William A., 330–31n
Sing, Bill, 345n
Singer, Joseph William, 20n, 23n, 347
Slote, Michael A., 259n, 296n
Smart, J. J. C., 427n
Smith, Adam
    Theory of Moral Sentiments, 106n, 133, 134n
    Wealth of Nations, 106n, 133, 320n
    and character, 133–36
    and classical liberalism, 184
    and economic enterprise, 319, 321
    and separation of ownership and control, 320n
    on empathy and sympathy, 133–34
    on labor, 133–35
    on virtue versus propriety, 134–35
Smith, E. Daniel, 329–30n
Smith, James D., 387n
Smith, Jane S., 52n
Smith, M. B. E., 139n, 309n
Snell, Scott A., 331n, 334n
Socher, Abe, 61n
Solow, Robert M., 360n
Spencer, Herbert, 442
Steinberg, David, 61n
Stephen, Frank H., 339n
Sterba, James P., 262n
Stone, Geoffrey R., 142n
Strasnick, Steven, 239n
Strawson, P. F., 42n, 78n
Stutchbury, O., 407n
Summers, Lawrence H., 388–89, 402n
Sunstein, Cass R., 139n, 142n
Svejnar, Jan, 339n
Swanton, Christine, 310n

Tannenbaum, Arnold S., 340n
Teichgraeber, Richard, 110n, 154–55n
Ten, Katrina P., 61n
Teresa, Mother, 231
Terrell, Timothy P., 52n
Tettemer, John, 85n
Thomas, Saint, *see* Aquinas, Saint Thomas
Thompson, E. P., 108n, 413
Thompson, Judith J., 93n
Thompson, Victor A., 358–59
Tullock, Gordon, 205n
Tully, James, 257n
Tushnet, Mark V., 142n
Tversky, Amos, 223n

Urmson, J. O., 3n, 310n

Van Alstyne, William, 47n
van Fraassen, Bas C., 306n
Varat, Jonathan D., 15n
Varian, Hal R., 272n

Waldron, Jeremy, 269n
Wallace, James D., 125
Walzer, Michael, 186, 259n, 262n
Ware, Robert F., 329n, 330n
Warren, Samuel D., 93n
Wedgwood, Josiah, 196n, 392–93, 400, 416n
Weiler, Paul, 291n
Weiss, Leonard W., 355n
Wellman, Carl, 19n, 20n, 48n, 113n
Wheeler, Samuel C., III, 61n, 64–67
Whitaker, Ian, 83n

White, Betsy Buttrill, 389n
Whitman, Dale A., 90n
Whittington, G., 330n
Wiley, John Shepard, Jr., 317n
Williams, Bernard, 133n, 144, 199n, 241–42n, 305–06n, 427n
Williams, Howard, 131n, 132n
Williams, Stephen F., 116n
Williamson, Oliver E., 322n, 343n
Wilson, William Julius, 115n
Wines, Michael, 387n
Wolff, Robert Paul, 239n
Wood, Allen W., 170n
Wright, Judge J. Skelly, 187n
Wycliffe, John, 130n

Young, Karen M., 339n, 340n

Zacarias, Ruth, 191n
Zaitchik, Alan, 261n
Zimmerman, David, 308n
Zola, Émile, 108n

Index of subjects

Acquisition, original
  Hegel on, 67–70
  incorporation theory of, 61–67
  post-acquisition changes, 274–79
  process of, 269–74
  projection theory of, 61, 67–75,
    79, 255–56
  "right" of, 263–64
  roles of intention and conven-
    tion in, 75–78
  wrongful, 278–79
Agency
  economic understanding of,
    319, 323n
  philosophical sense, 79–80
Alienation
  and capitalism, 157–58, 160–69,
    178n
  and communism, 159–60, 168–
    69, 171
  and differences in economic
    power, 178–79
  and division of labor, 174–76
  and exploitation, 169, 171–74
  and private property, 160–65
  and separation of ownership
    and control, 369–73
  and work, 158–59, 160–62
  definitions of, 157 (Marxian),
    170 (revised)
  end of, 168–69

in relation to corporate owner-
    ship, 369–73
  Marx on, 6–7, 87, 157–69, 369–
    73
Allocation, 89n
American Law Institute
  Principles of Corporate Gov-
    ernance, 362–65
  Restatement of the Law of Prop-
    erty, 20n, 90n
Autonomy
  definition of, 39
  Kant's conception of, 80n

Background theory, see Theory,
    background theory of prop-
    erty institutions
Basic theory, see Theory, basic
    theory of property
Bequests, see Gratuitous transfers
Body rights, 37–58, 63–64, 420

Capabilities, basic, 228, 241–43
Capitalism
  and concept of property, 31–
    35
  and motivation, 105–09
  and personality, 86n
  laissez-faire
    and moral character, 142–43
    definition of, 98

481

shortcomings of, 98–99, 106–
10, 117–18
Marx's understanding of, 32–34,
157–69, 173, 369–73
stages of, 370–73
see also Economy, private-
property; System, private-
property
Cardinality, 203–04
Claim-right, 18–19, 21–22
see also Conceptions, fundamental legal; Hohfeld,
Wesley Newcomb
Character
in relation to economic systems,
142–45, 378–79
in relation to property, 125–38,
145–47
nature of, 121–25
republican view of, 138–42
see also Moral character; Vices;
Virtues
Charity, 110–12, 116–17
see also Gratuitous transfers
Commensurateness, see Fittingness and commensurateness
Common property, see Ownership, varieties of
Communal ownership, see
Ownership, varieties of
Communism, 159–60, 168–69, 171,
172, 373
see also Marx, Karl; Socialism,
"feasible" (Nove)
Compensation, 424–31, 433, 436–
41, 442–43
Conceptions
contrasted with concepts, 457
fundamental legal, 17–22
see also Dworkin, Ronald;
Hohfeld, Wesley Newcomb
Conflicts
among principles, 295
and logical consistency, 304–06
and moral character, 378–79

and moral realism, 306–08
and pluralism, 292–97
and prima facie obligations,
304–05
and theory acceptance, 308–10
between principles, 295
definition of, 295
frequency of, 297–98
genesis of, 300–02
irresolvable, 304–10
potential, involving corporations, 355–57
priority rules for resolving, 302–
04, 355–57
resolvable, 302–04
varieties of, 298–300
within a principle, 296–97
Conformity to the basic theory,
full versus partial, 435–39
Constitution, see United States
Constitution
Contracts, and corporations, 318–
19, 323–24, 348–49
Control
as personal good, 90–93, 96–98
definition of, 91
relation to problems of distribution, 98–105, 109–10
see also Goods, personal; Separation of ownership and
control
Copyrights, 16, 33
Corporations
actual firms versus idealized
firms, 333–34
American Law Institute proposal regarding, 362–68
and interests of all, 350–57
and labor-desert principle, 346–
50, 352, 354–57, 359, 366–67
and principle of justice and
equality, 346, 349–50, 352–
54, 367
and profit maximization, 361
and the public interest, 361–62

and transaction costs, 336
applying a pluralist theory to, 310–12
contrasted with persons, 359–60, 367–68
cooperatives, 337–41, 370, 373, 374–77
employee-oriented firms, 319, 336–43
employee stock ownership plans (ESOPs), 336–41
level of corporate enterprise as a whole, 352–57
level of each corporation, 351–52
leveraged buyouts of, 335–36, 344–45
manager-controlled (MC) firms, 319, 325–33
"mythical ideal" of owner-managed firm, 334–35
nexus-of-contracts model of, 323–24, 348
owner-controlled (OC firms), 319, 325–33
performance of, tests for, 324–25, 328–32
standards of corporate behavior, 317–19, 357–68, 377–78
under socialism, 369, 373–78
see also Separation of ownership and control
Costs
compensation, 427–31, 433
"demoralization" (Michelman), 425–29
incentive effect, 428–29, 431, 433
moral hazard, 428–29, 433–34
noncompensation, 429–33
of agency, 312, 323n
revenue, 428–33

"settlement" (Michelman), 425–28
transaction, 336, 423–24

Defamation, 51
Desert
absolute versus relative, 260–61
and justice, 254
and persons, 5, 255–56
and projection theory, 255–56
and wages, 280, 282–84
as a general moral principle, 284
basis for, 259–63, 266
definition of, 257
see also Labor-desert principle; Merit, moral; Worth, moral
Distribution
bearing of utility and efficiency on, 212–14
contrasted with allocation, 89n
definition of, 89n
equity in, 192
fixed and unfixed, 420–21
problems of, 98–110, 176–78, 184
see also Floor Thesis; Gap Thesis; Production, problems of; Redistribution
Due process, 54–55
Duty, 18–19
see also Conceptions, fundamental legal; Hohfeld, Wesley Newcomb; Obligations, prima facie and all things considered

Easement
across private beach, 464–68
as example of limited property, 23
Economic Recovery Tax Act of 1981, 408n

Economy
  "capitalism," Marx's understanding of, 32–34, 157–58, 164–68
  laissez-faire capitalist, 98–99, 106–10, 117–18, 142–43
  private-property
    definition of, 89
    relation to alienation and exploitation, 182–83
    relation to character, 143–44
    relation to division of labor, 176
    relation to private-property system, 89, 118–19
  relation to moral ideals, 145–47
  see also Communism; Socialism, "feasible" (Nove)
Efficiency
  and rights, 224–26
  as normative criterion of corporate performance, 325–26
  contrasted with utility, 4, 195–96, 202–05
  criteria of, 199–202, 324–25
  "efficiency gains" (Michelman), 425–28
  efficiency-wealth maximization, 212n
  general sense of, 324–25, 343, 344
  utility/efficiency gains, 428–29
  see also Kaldor-Hicks efficiency; Pareto optimality and superiority; Utility; Utility and efficiency, principle of
Egalitarianism
  moderate, 212–14
  Rawlsian conception of equal property, 233–41, 248
  strict, 230–33, 251n
  see also Distribution; Floor Thesis; Gap Thesis
Eminent domain, 423–24, 442n
  see also Takings

Employee Retirement Income Security Act of 1974 (ERISA), 337n
Entitlement
  broad sense of, 260n
  contrasted with desert, 5, 192
  Nozick's sense of, 192n
  see also Merit, moral; Worth, moral
Entitlements, 27n
Entrepreneurial success, as explanation of inequality of wealth, 390–93
Equality
  nature of, 5, 227
  of resources and welfare, 250–51n
  see also Egalitarianism; Inequality; Justice and equality, principle of
Equilibrium, reflective, 10, 308–09, 366
Excludability, 89–90
Expectations
  and gratuitous transfers, 401–02
  and preferences, 221–24
  and takings, 429–32, 466–68
  definition of, 28–31
  institutionally legitimate, 223–24, 429–32, 466–67
  rational, 223–24, 429–32, 466–67
  stability of, 29, 79–80
  see also Property, and expectations
Exploitation, 169, 171–74, 178–79
Expropriation, see Takings

First possession, see Acquisition, original; Possession, first
Fittingness and commensurateness, as factors in desert, 259, 262–63, 281, 290–91
Floor Thesis
  applied, 245–47
  elaborated, 241–45

in relation to problems of distribution, 110
stated, 229, 241
Foundations, moral, 9–12, 294–
95
see also Equilibrium, reflective;
Intuition; Pluralism

Gap Thesis
applied, 249–53
elaborated, 247–49
in relation to problems of distribution, 110
stated, 229, 247
Gifts, *see* Gratuitous transfers
Goods, personal
and charity, 111–12
and economic arrangements,
117–19
and problems of distribution,
98–110
and welfare, 112–17
examples, 90–91
Government regulation and taking of property, *see* Takings
Gratuitous transfers
abolition of, rejected, 382n,
409–11
and consumption, 415–16
and expectations, 401–02
and labor-desert principle, 395–
96, 403, 409
and principle of justice and
equality, 397–400, 403, 407,
411, 416
and principle of utility and efficiency, 215–16, 396–97, 403,
407, 411, 416
applying a pluralist theory to,
311–12
as a cause of inequality of
wealth, 381, 387, 392–95
definition of, 380
economic effect of taxing, 414–
16

enforceability of taxes on, 416–
17
generation-skipping, 417
limitations on, 403–06
social impact of taxing, 411–14
taxation of, 381–82, 396, 400–18

Hawaii Land Reform Act of 1967,
461–62

Ideal theory, contrasted with
nonideal theory, 300–01
Illusion, fiscal, 430
see also Self-deception
Immunity, 18–20
see also Conceptions, fundamental legal; Hohfeld,
Wesley Newcomb
Incidents, of property and ownership, 22–24, 43–44
see also Honoré, A. M.; Excludability; Transferability
Income, 97–98, 292–93, 311, 312
see also Wealth
Incorporation theory, 61, 63–67
Individuality
as personal good, 90, 95–98
definition of, 95
relation to problems of distribution, 98–105, 110
see also Goods, personal
Inequality
of income, 99n, 383
of personal goods, 99–105, 110
of wealth (property)
causes of, 383–95
consequences of, 99–105, 109–
10
extent of, 383–87
reduction of, 395–411
social impact of reducing,
411–14
tables summarizing, 383–85
Inheritance, *see* Gratuitous transfers

Insurance, and takings, 433–35
Interpretation, constitutional, 456–60
Intestacy, *see* Succession, intestate
Intuition
  as guide to action, 11
  intuitionism, 9–12, 309–10, 366
  intuitions, 9–12, 366
  see also Equilibrium, reflective; Judgments, considered

Joint ownership, *see* Ownership, varieties of
Judgments, considered, 9, 12, 308–09, 366
Justice
  as character trait, 143–44
  nature of, 5, 181–82, 227
  see also Justice and equality, principle of; Rawls, John
Justice and equality, principle of
  applied, 245–47, 249–53, 346, 349–50, 353–54, 367, 397–99, 403, 407, 411, 416, 435–37, 462, 465
  elaborated, 227–30, 241–45, 247–49
  specific to property, 229
  stated, 5, 227
  see also Floor Thesis; Gap Thesis
Justification, 6–7, 58, 191–93, 255

Kaldor-Hicks efficiency, 200–02, 344–45, 424, 433

Labor
  definitions of, 256–57, 281
  division of, 168, 174–76
  see also Work
Labor theory of property
  and wrongful acquisition, 278–79
  initial, 256–66, 285–86

mixing, metaphor of, 67, 75, 256n
  no-loss requirement, 262–63, 264, 271–72
  revised, 266–91
  transferability of property rights under, 276–79, 395–96
  see also Labor-desert principle; Cohen, G. A.; Gauthier, David; Locke, John; Nozick, Robert
Labor theory of value, 173
Labor-desert principle
  applied, 346–49, 352, 354, 367, 395–96, 403, 409, 424, 435, 437, 439–40
  elaborated, 284–85
  explained, 285–89
  significance assessed, 289–91
  specific to property, 284
  stated, 5, 283–84
Land reform, 314, 422, 461–64
Liability, Hohfeldian sense of, 18–19
Libertarianism, 287–89, 361, 420
Liberty
  and gratuitous transfers, 381, 411–12, 414
  as Hohfeldian privilege, 18–19
  derivative in the basic theory of property, 217, 246, 287–88
Life-cycle hypothesis, 387–90

Massachusetts Employee Cooperative Corporations Act, 337n
Merit, moral, 5, 191–93, 255, 284
Method, transformative, 156n
Moral character
  and entrepreneurial risk-taking, 391
  and inequality of wealth, 397–98, 402
  in relation to economic systems, 142–45

in relation to property, 125–38,
145–47
nature of, 123
see also Vices; Virtues
Motivation
for plan to tax gratuitous transfers, 417–18
in relation to problems of distribution, 105–10
of gratuitous transferors, 402,
410, 411
of managers and shareholders,
327

Needs, basic, 228, 241–43

Obligations, prima facie and all
things considered, 304–05
Occupancy, *see* Possession
Oligopoly, 461, 463–64
Ordinality, 203–05
Original acquisition, *see* Acquisition, original
Ownership
contrasted with limited property rights, 22–23n
Honoré on, 22–23
self-ownership, 38, 41, 56–57,
181
varieties of, 22–27 *passim*, 218–
19, 321–22
see also Property; Property
rights

Pareto optimality and superiority,
200–02, 344
Patents, 16, 33, 303
Personal rights
contrasted with property rights
in the body, 48–49
definition of, 48–49
examples of, 50–51
Personality
as personal good, 90
conceptions of
Hegelian, 67, 81–82, 154

philosophical, 82–83
psychological, 84–87
development of, 85
retention of, 85
Persons
contrasted with corporations,
359–60, 367–68
conceptions of, 307–08
nature of, 42–43
property as an attribute of, 149–
57
separateness of, 228
Pluralism
interest-group, 138
moral, 9, 11–12, 147, 292–95,
304–14
see also Equilibrium, reflective;
Intuition
Possession
first, 288n
Hegel on, 69
see also Acquisition, original;
Property; Ownership
Poverty, 99n, 154–55
Power
economic, 178–81
Hohfeldian sense of, 18–19
Preferences and preference-
satisfaction
and expectations, 221–24
assumptions concerning, 206–
14, 217–18, 219–20, 398
contrasted with basic needs and
basic capabilities, 228, 243
definition of, 196–97
moral assessment of, 231
rational alteration of, 219–21,
430–32, 433
Principles, *see* Justice and equality, principle of; Labor-desert
principle; Utility and efficiency, principle of
Privacy
as personal good, 90, 92–95,
96–98

definition of, 92
relation to problems of distribution, 98–105, 110
see also Goods, personal
Privilege, 18–19, 21
Production, problems of, 174–78, 184–85
Projection theory, 61–62, 67–78, 86–87, 255–56
Property
  and expectations, 28, 29–31, 79–80
  and historical periodization, 161–62n
  as an attribute of persons and societies, 149–57
  "disintegration" of (Grey), 17, 31–36
  evaluation of, 2–3
  idea of, 22–27 *passim*
  imperial view of, 45–47
  incidents of, 22–23
  individual private, 25
  institutions, design and reform of, 7–8, 214–18, 219–21
  intangible, 16, 33, 72–73, 78
  justification of, 2
  limited, 23–24
  no-property world, 15–16
  ordinary conception of (as things), 16–17, 32–35
  private, 25, 209–12, 245–47, 252–53, 255–56
  public, 25, 206–09, 245, 252–53, 255–56
  sophisticated conception of (as relations), 16–17, 23–24, 26–27, 33–34, 35–36
  transcendental features of, 61–62, 71–74
  see also Economy, private-property; Ownership; Property rights; System, private-property

Property rights
  and claim-rights, 24–25
  and utility and efficiency, 224–26
  as involving only advantageous incidents, 24
  contrasted with personal rights, 48–49
  contrasted with property interests, 224–25, 432–33
  full, *see* Ownership
  in corporations, 321
  in the body, 48–49
  limited, 24, 41–44, 347
  natural, 77
  private, 25
  public, 25
  weak versus strong, 49, 52
Proviso, as restriction on labor theory of property, 269–72
  see also Labor-desert principle; Cohen, G. A.; Gauthier, David; Locke, John; Nozick, Robert
Publicity, right of, 52–53

Redistribution, 313–14, 381–82, 399–400, 421–22, 437, 486
Regulation, of property by government, *see* Takings
Relativism, 8–9
Republicanism, 138–42, 143–44, 144–45
Retroactivity, 275
Right-holders, 25
Rights
  and utility and efficiency, 224–26
  broad sense of, 20, 24–25
  combined will and interest theory of, 228
  content of, 27n
  form of, 27n
  interest theory of, 20n, 47–48
  waivability of, 50–52

will theory of, 20n, 47–48
see also Body rights; Entitlements; Personal rights; Property rights; Rightholders
Roman law, 69, 76, 130, 195

Scarcity, 274–76, 278, 279–80
Selection, adverse, 434–35
Self-deception, 166–67, 170–72
Self-esteem
    contrasted with self-respect, 116–17
    definition of, 116
    misassessment of, 250
Self-ownership, 37–38, 41n, 56–57, 181
Self-respect
    contrasted with self-esteem, 116–17
    definition of, 116
    misassessment of, 250
Separation of ownership and control
    and alienation, 369–73
    and levels of significance, 318, 319, 324–26, 331–32, 334–35, 342, 343
    and managerialism, 322
    Berle and Means on, 320–22, 326, 327, 332n
    contrasted with unity of ownership and control, 326, 327
    economic response to, 322–24
    definition of, 320
    empirical evidence concerning, 326–33, 336–43
    in different economic systems, 318, 319, 369, 374–77
    Marx's identification of, 320n, 369–70
Skepticism, moral, 363, 365–67
Slavery, 56, 364–65
Socialism, "feasible" (Nove), 373–77

Spoilage, 268
Stability, 79–80
Succession, intestate, 404
Suicide, 53, 54n
System, private-property
    definition of, 89
    relation to alienation and exploitation, 182–83
    relation to character, 143, 144–45
    relation to laissez-faire capitalism, 118
    relation to private-property economy, 118–19

Tables
    conceptions, Hohfeld's fundamental legal, 19
    distribution of wealth, 383, 384, 385
    principles, conflicting combinations of, 299
    transfers, taxonomy of, 277
Takings
    academic theories of, 448–56
    and constitutional interpretation, 456–60
    and insurance, 433–35
    and labor-desert principle, 424, 435, 437, 439–40
    and land reform, 460–64
    and lateral easement, 464–68
    and principle of justice and equality, 424, 435, 436–37
    and principle of utility and efficiency, 216–17, 423–25, 429–39
    clause, 419, 442
    compensation for, 424–32, 437–41
    contrasted with taxings, 420–22
    doctrine, received constitutional, 458

judicial tests for
  diminution of value, 445–46,
    447
  noxious use, 443–45, 446–47
  physical invasion, 443, 444,
    446
  principle, fundamental commit-
    ment on, 459
  "public use" requirement, 442n,
    461–63
Tax Reform Act of 1986, 408
Taxation
  and redistribution, 381–82, 399–
    400, 421–22, 437, 439
  and transfer, 313–14
  contrasted with takings, 420–22
  of gratuitous transfers, 381–82,
    396, 399–400, 403, 404–05,
    411–17
  of income, 399–400, 409
  of wealth, 405n
Theory
  background theory of property
    institutions, 7, 58, 86–87,
    148–49, 181, 191, 317, 469
  basic theory of property
    definition of, 317
    full versus partial conformity
      to, 436–39
  interest theory of rights, 20n,
    47–48
  nature of theorizing about
    property, 183–87
  of takings, moral and political,
    419, 422–23
  will theory of rights, 20n, 47–48
  see also Incorporation theory;
    Projection theory
Transferability, 47–50, 276–79
Transfers, taxonomy of, 277
  see also Gratuitous transfers;
    Succession, intestate

Uniform Anatomical Gift Act, 52
Uniform Probate Code, 404n

United States Constitution
  amend. I, 24–25, 50
  amend. IV, 46n
  amend. V, 46n, 54n, 419n, 442n
  amend. XIV, 54n
  due process clause, 54–55n
  interpretation of, 456–60
  takings clause, 419n, 442n
Use, rights of, contrasted with
  ownership, 270
Utilitarianism, 194–96, 427–28,
  432–33
Utilitarians, 194–96
Utility
  and rights, 224–26
  contrasted with efficiency, 3–4,
    195–96, 202–03
  definitions of, 193, 196
  diminishing marginal, 213,
    396
  interpersonal comparisons of,
    195–96, 198–202, 203–05,
    426, 428
  utility/efficiency gains, 428–29
  see also Cardinality; Efficiency;
    Ordinality; Utility and effi-
    ciency, principle of
Utility and efficiency, principle of
  applied, 221–38, 319, 343–46,
    351–52, 352–53, 356–57,
    396–97, 398–99, 403–04, 407,
    411, 416, 423–25, 429–39
  elaborated, 203–06
  specific to property, 205–06
  stated, 4, 202

Value, see Labor theory of value
Vices
  and character, 122–23
  and inequality of wealth, 397–
    98, 402
  classification of, 124
  definition of, 122
  in relation to economic systems,
    142–46

in relation to property, 125–29, 133–38, 145–47
republican conceptions of, 138–42, 144–45
varieties of, 122
see also Virtues
Virtues
and character, 122–23
and entrepreneurial risk-taking, 390–92
and labor, 255–56
classification of, 123–25
definition of, 121
in relation to economic systems, 142–46, 378–79
in relation to property, 125–29, 133–38, 145–47
republican conceptions of, 138–42, 145
varieties of, 121–23
see also Vices; Aquinas, Saint Thomas; Aristotle; Kant, Immanuel; Plato; Smith, Adam

Waste, 268
Wealth
and income, 97–98, 99n
human, 381, 414
material, 381
see also Income; Property
Welfare, 110, 112–17, 131n, 142, 150n
Work
and alienation, 157–59, 160–62
and division of labor, 174–76
as a social activity, 280–83
meaningful, 185
synonymous with labor, 257
see also Labor
Workfare, 116n
Worth, equal moral
and equal treatment, 231–32, 248
as equal counting of preferences, 3–4, 192, 197
as right-based, 4, 192, 227–28
Kantian interpretation of, 227

Zoning, 429–32